# DATA PROTECTION AND PRIVACY

This book offers conceptual analyses, highlights issues, proposes solutions, and discusses practices regarding privacy and data protection in transitional times. It is one of the results of the 15th annual International Conference on Computers, Privacy and Data Protection (CPDP), which was held in Brussels in May 2022.

We are in a time of transition. Artificial Intelligence is making significant breakthroughs in how humans use data and information, and is changing our lives in virtually all aspects. The pandemic has pushed society to adopt changes in how, when, why, and the media through which, we interact. A new generation of European digital regulations – such as the AI Act, Digital Services Act, Digital Markets Act, Data Governance Act, and Data Act – is on the horizon. This raises difficult questions as to which rights we should have, the degree to which these rights should be balanced against other poignant social interests, and how these rights should be enforced in light of the fluidity and uncertainty of circumstances.

The book covers a range of topics, including: data protection risks in European retail banks; data protection, privacy legislation and litigation in China; synthetic data generation as a privacy-preserving technique for the training of machine learning models; effectiveness of privacy consent dialogues; legal analysis of the role of individuals in data protection law; and the role of data subject rights in the platform economy.

This interdisciplinary book has been written at a time when the scale and impact of data processing on society – on individuals as well as on social systems – is becoming ever more important. It discusses open issues as well as daring and prospective approaches and is an insightful resource for readers with an interest in computers, privacy and data protection.

**Computers, Privacy and Data Protection**

Previous volumes in this series (published by Springer)

2009
*Reinventing Data Protection?*
Editors: Serge Gutwirth, Yves Poullet, Paul De Hert, Cécile de Terwangne, Sjaak Nouwt
ISBN 978-1-4020-9497-2 (Print) ISBN 978-1-4020-9498-9 (Online)

2010
*Data Protection in A Profiled World?*
Editors: Serge Gutwirth, Yves Poullet, Paul De Hert
ISBN 978-90-481-8864-2 (Print) ISBN: 978-90-481-8865-9 (Online)

2011
*Computers, Privacy and Data Protection: An Element of Choice*
Editors: Serge Gutwirth, Yves Poullet, Paul De Hert, Ronald Leenes
ISBN: 978-94-007-0640-8 (Print) 978-94-007-0641-5 (Online)

2012
*European Data Protection: In Good Health?*
Editors: Serge Gutwirth, Ronald Leenes, Paul De Hert, Yves Poullet
ISBN: 978-94-007-2902-5 (Print) 978-94-007-2903-2 (Online)

2013
*European Data Protection: Coming of Age*
Editors: Serge Gutwirth, Ronald Leenes, Paul De Hert, Yves Poullet
ISBN: 978-94-007-5184-2 (Print) 978-94-007-5170-5 (Online)

2014
*Reloading Data Protection*
*Multidisciplinary Insights and Contemporary Challenges*
Editors: Serge Gutwirth, Ronald Leenes, Paul De Hert
ISBN: 978-94-007-7539-8 (Print) 978-94-007-7540-4 (Online)

2015
*Reforming European Data Protection Law*
Editors: Serge Gutwirth, Ronald Leenes, Paul De Hert
ISBN: 978-94-017-9384-1 (Print) 978-94-017-9385-8 (Online)

2016
*Data Protection on the Move*
Current Developments in ICT and Privacy/Data Protection
Editors: Serge Gutwirth, Ronald Leenes, Paul De Hert
ISBN: 978-94-017-7375-1 (Print) 978-94-017-7376-8 (Online)

2017
*Data Protection and Privacy: (In)visibilities and Infrastructures*
Editors: Ronald Leenes, Rosamunde van Brakel, Serge Gutwirth, Paul De Hert
ISBN: 978-3-319-56177-6 (Print) 978-3-319-50796-5 (Online)

Previous titles in this series (published by Hart Publishing)

2018
*Data Protection and Privacy: The Age of Intelligent Machines*
Editors: Ronald Leenes, Rosamunde van Brakel, Serge Gutwirth, Paul De Hert
ISBN: 978-1-509-91934-5 (Print) 978-1-509-91935-2 (EPDF) 978-1-509-91936-9 (EPUB)

2019
*Data Protection and Privacy: The Internet of Bodies*
Editors: Ronald Leenes, Rosamunde van Brakel, Serge Gutwirth, Paul De Hert
ISBN: 978-1-509-92620-6 (Print) 978-1-509-92621-3 (EPDF) 978-1-509-9622-0 (EPUB)

2020
*Data Protection and Privacy: Data Protection and Democracy*
Editors: Ronald Leenes, Dara Hallinan, Serge Gutwirth, Paul De Hert
ISBN: 978-1-509-93274-0 (Print) 978-1-509-93275-7 (EPDF) 978-1-509-93276-4 (EPUB)

2021
*Data Protection and Privacy: Data Protection and Artificial Intelligence*
Editors: Dara Hallinan, Ronald Leenes, Paul De Hert
ISBN: 978-1-509-94175-9 (Print) 978-1-509-94176-6 (EPDF) 978-1-509-94177-3 (EPUB)

2022
*Data Protection and Privacy: Enforcing Rights in a Changing World*
Editors: Dara Hallinan, Ronald Leenes, Paul De Hert
ISBN: 978-1-509-95451-3 (Print) 978-1-509-95453-7 (EPDF) 978-1-509-95452-0 (EPUB)

2023
*Data Protection and Privacy: In Transitional Times*
Editors: Hideyuki Matsumi, Dara Hallinan, Diana Dimitrova, Eleni Kosta and Paul De Hert
ISBN: 978-1-509-96590-8 (Print) 978-1-509-96592-2 (EPDF) 978-1-509-95691-5 (EPUB)

# Data Protection and Privacy

*In Transitional Times*

Edited by
Hideyuki Matsumi
Dara Hallinan
Diana Dimitrova
Eleni Kosta
and
Paul De Hert

·HART·
OXFORD · LONDON · NEW YORK · NEW DELHI · SYDNEY

HART PUBLISHING

Bloomsbury Publishing Plc

Kemp House, Chawley Park, Cumnor Hill, Oxford, OX2 9PH, UK

1385 Broadway, New York, NY 10018, USA

29 Earlsfort Terrace, Dublin 2, Ireland

HART PUBLISHING, the Hart/Stag logo, BLOOMSBURY and the Diana logo are trademarks of Bloomsbury Publishing Plc

First published in Great Britain 2023

Copyright © The editors and contributors severally 2023

The editors and contributors have asserted their right under the Copyright, Designs and Patents Act 1988 to be identified as Authors of this work.

All rights reserved. No part of this publication may be reproduced or transmitted in any form or by any means, electronic or mechanical, including photocopying, recording, or any information storage or retrieval system, without prior permission in writing from the publishers.

While every care has been taken to ensure the accuracy of this work, no responsibility for loss or damage occasioned to any person acting or refraining from action as a result of any statement in it can be accepted by the authors, editors or publishers.

All UK Government legislation and other public sector information used in the work is Crown Copyright ©. All House of Lords and House of Commons information used in the work is Parliamentary Copyright ©. This information is reused under the terms of the Open Government Licence v3.0 (http://www.nationalarchives.gov.uk/doc/open-government-licence/version/3) except where otherwise stated.

All Eur-lex material used in the work is © European Union, http://eur-lex.europa.eu/, 1998–2023.

A catalogue record for this book is available from the British Library.

A catalogue record for this book is available from the Library of Congress.

| ISBN: | HB: | 978-1-50996-590-8 |
|---|---|---|
| | ePDF: | 978-1-50996-592-2 |
| | ePub: | 978-1-50996-591-5 |

Typeset by Compuscript Ltd, Shannon

To find out more about our authors and books visit www.hartpublishing.co.uk. Here you will find extracts, author information, details of forthcoming events and the option to sign up for our newsletters.

# PREFACE

It is now March 2023 as we write this preface for the CPDP 2022 Conference Book. It was during the Computers, Privacy and Data Protection Conference 2017 that we adopted 'Artificial Intelligence' (AI) as the overarching theme to pave the way for a discussion on a broad range of ethical, legal and policy issues. In 2022 'generative AI' was one of the most hotly discussed topics, and it is likely to remain so during 2023. The advent and advancement of AI technologies which encourage us to use cliched phrases such as 'AI coupled with Big Data is (still) changing everything, including how we work, study and learn, communicate, socialise, govern ourselves, etc.,' raised fundamental questions over the course of last year, such as: if what we once regarded as intelligence can be virtually mimicked by 'generative AI' or statistical predictions, what distinguishes humans from machines? How do such technologies change and challenge the foundations and institutions of our society? How should we treat these technologies?

Over the past five years, problems surrounding AI became even more complex, multitiered, and fundamental, however so too did the legal landscape. The GDPR was the main keyword in our Preface for the CPDP 2018 book which was written shortly after 25 May 2018 – the date the GDPR came into force. Today, in addition to the GDPR there are other forms of legislation such as the Digital Services Act, Digital Market Act and Data Governance Act along with proposals for an AI Act, a Data Act and a European Health Data Space, which together will shape EU digital policy. Yet some challenging and novel questions remain unanswered: where is the line between legitimate and illegitimate use of such new technologies? How should and can these technologies be regulated? To what extent should approaches and perspectives on new technologies converge, and can they diverge, internationally?

Under these circumstances, the international privacy and data protection crowd gathered for the fifteenth time to participate in the Computers, Privacy and Data Protection Conference, or CPDP. We had 92 panel sessions and over 450 international speakers from academia, public and private sectors and civil society groups. In addition to the general programme, the conference also offered several workshops, meet-ups, lectures, exhibitions and a bookstore. Over 1,400 attendees from 40 countries had the chance to discuss a variety of contemporary topics and issues during the panels, breaks, side events and at ad-hoc dinners and pub crawls.

We also decided to change the date of the conference. It usually takes place during the last week of January, but in 2022 we postponed it to 23–25 May, mainly due to the COVID-19 pandemic. In the wake of this decision, we were able to gather in person again at Les Halles and Area 42 in Brussels. We refer the interested reader to the conference website: www.cpdpconferences.org. Additionally, we filmed most of the sessions with the explicit permission of the panellists; these are available at: www.youtube.com/user/CPDPConferences.

The conference was a hive of activity and discussion and we are delighted to be able to deliver a tangible spin-off every year: the CPDP book. Papers in the book are cited frequently and the series has a broad readership. Customarily, the book cycle starts with a call for papers, submissions are peer reviewed, and authors whose papers are accepted present their work to the various academic panels at the conference. Speakers are then invited to submit papers based on panel discussions after the conference. This year we made a slight deviation, partly due to the change of conference dates. We made the call for papers public, inviting not only speakers at the conference to contribute, but also a wide range of external authors. Finally, all papers submitted are double-blind peer reviewed. While the current volume is extensive, it offers a fraction of what was available across the whole conference. Nevertheless, the editors consider this volume consists of an important set of papers addressing both contemporary and prospective privacy and data protection issues.

For each chapter, at least two reviewers with expertise and interest in the relevant subject matter peer reviewed and commented on the contents. Since their work is crucial for maintaining the scientific quality of the book, we would like to take this opportunity to thank all the CPDP book reviewers for their commitment and efforts: Alessandra Calvi, Andrés Chomczyk Penedo, Ana Hriscu, Barbara da Rosa Lazarotto, Bianca-Ioana Marcu, Cristina Cocito, Ian Brown, Kristina Irion, Onntje Hinrichs, René Mahieu and Simone Casiraghi.

As is now customary, the conference concluded with some closing remarks from the European Data Protection Supervisor, Wojciech Wiewiórowski. We are honoured that he is willing to continue this tradition, and we look forward to more of his closing speeches in the future.

Hideyuki Matsumi, Dara Hallinan, Diana Dimitrova,
Eleni Kosta, and Paul de Hert
*16 March 2023*

# CONTENTS

*Preface* .................................................................................................... *vii*
*Contributors* ........................................................................................... *xi*

1. *Data Protection Risks in Transitional Times: The Case of European Retail Banks* ...................................................................................... *1*
   **Ine Van Zeeland and Jo Pierson**

2. *Synthetic Data Generation in Service of Privacy-Preserving Deep Learning: Three Practical Case Studies* ................................... *27*
   **Jerome R Bellegarda**

3. *Chinese Data Protection in Transition: A Look at Enforceability of Rights and the Role of Courts* ....................................................... *43*
   **Hunter Dorwart**

4. *Conflicting Privacy Preference Signals in the Wild* ........................... *75*
   **Maximilian Hils, Daniel W. Woods and Rainer Böhme**

5. *The Multi-faceted Role of the Individual in EU Data Protection Law* ...... *89*
   **Katherine Nolan**

6. *Data Subject Rights as a Tool for Platform Worker Resistance: Lessons from the* Uber/Ola *Judgments* .......................................... *119*
   **Wenlong Li and Jill Toh**

7. *From the Fight against Money Laundering and Financing of Terrorism Towards the Fight for Fundamental Rights: The Role of Data Protection* ........................................................................................ *157*
   **Magdalena Brewczyńska and Eleni Kosta**

8. *Cybercrime Convention-based Access to Personal Data Held by Big Tech: Decades of Council of Europe's Greenlighting Codified in a New Protocol* ............................................................................ *185*
   **Paul De Hert and Angela Aguinaldo**

9. *'Privacy in the Resilient State of the Human Condition': Closing Remarks at the Computers, Privacy and Data Protection Conference* ........... *215*
   **Wojciech Wiewiórowski**

*Index* ..................................................................................................... *219*

# CONTRIBUTORS

**Angela Aguinaldo** is a Philippine lawyer currently based in Germany.

**Jerome R Bellegarda** was Apple Distinguished Scientist in Intelligent System Experience at Apple Inc, Cupertino, California, where the work described in this book was performed. He is now Etsy Distinguished Scientist at Etsy Inc, Brooklyn, New York.

**Rainer Boehme** is a professor for Security and Privacy, Department of Computer Science, University of Innsbruck, Austria.

**Magdalena Brewczyńska** is a PhD researcher at the Tilburg Institute for Law, Technology, and Society (TILT) at Tilburg University, the Netherlands.

**Paul de Hert** is Professor of Law at Vrije Universiteit Brussel, Belgium. He is also Associate Professor of Law and Technology at the Tilburg Institute for Law, Technology and Society (TILT) at Tilburg University.

**Hunter Dorwart** is a Policy Counsel for the Future of Privacy Forum's Global Privacy team.

**Maximilian Hils** is a PhD student at the University of Innsbruck, Austria.

**Eleni Kosta** is Professor of Technology Law and Human Rights at the Tilburg Institute for Law, Technology and Society (TILT) at Tilburg University, the Netherlands.

**Katherine Nolan** is a PhD Candidate at the London School of Economics and Political Science, and a Teaching Fellow at University College Dublin.

**Wenlong Li** is a postdoctoral Research Fellow in Law, Ethics and Computers at the University of Birmingham, LEADS Lab.

**Jo Pierson** is full professor of responsible digitalisation and head of the School of Social Sciences at Hasselt University, Belgium.

**Jill Toh** is a PhD researcher at the University of Amsterdam Institute for Information Law (IViR).

**Wojciech Wiewiórowski** is the European Data Protection Supervisor (EDPS) and an adjunct professor in the Faculty of Law and Administration, University of Gdańsk.

**Daniel Woods** is a Lecturer in Cyber Security at the University of Edinburgh, jointly appointed by the British University in Dubai.

**Ine van Zeeland** is a PhD researcher within the research centre Studies in Media, Innovation and Technology (SMIT), at imec and Vrije Universiteit Brussel.

# 1
# Data Protection Risks in Transitional Times: The Case of European Retail Banks

INE VAN ZEELAND[*] AND JO PIERSON[≠]

## Abstract

The banking sector has a highly developed procedural approach to risk. Faced with legal requirements to protect personal data using a risk-based approach, it may seem natural for banks to 'translate' existing risk management procedures to these new types of risks. We present findings of an empirical study into practices of personal data protection in European retail banks, with a focus on their conceptualisation of data protection risks. The study was mostly carried out during 2020, the first year of the COVID-19 pandemic. This offered the additional opportunity to study banks' practices in managing data protection risks in transitional times, under conditions of accelerated digitalisation. Based on our findings, we argue that banks did not fully anticipate and mitigate risks that negatively affect data subjects' interests. The reconciliation of the GDPR's risk-based approach and banks' procedural approach is likely to leave gaps in the latter's management of data protection risks. We suggest including data subjects in risk assessment procedures as a potential remedy.

## Keywords

Retail banks, GDPR, privacy, risk

---

[*] imec-SMIT, Vrije Universiteit Brussel.
[≠] School of Social Sciences, Hasselt University and imec-SMIT, Vrije Universiteit Brussel.

## I. Introduction

In the early 1990s, the sociologist Ulrich Beck described the 'risk society', at the heart of which lie public perceptions of new technologies. Beck characterised a risk society as a society dealing in a systematic way with the hazards and insecurities introduced by modernisation.[1] Today, when we consider the risks of new digital technologies, few topics strike closer to that heart than public perceptions of information privacy and the use of personal data. It may therefore come as no surprise that practical approaches to privacy and data protection often aim to deal with risks in a systematic way.

The General Data Protection Regulation[2] (GDPR) is the prime piece of legislation in the European Union (EU) regulating the protection of personal data, and it was introduced as taking a 'risk-based approach'.[3] It requires organisations that process people's personal data in novel ways or on a large scale to conduct a Data Protection Impact Assessment (DPIA). The risks that are to be assessed in a DPIA are risks 'to the rights and freedoms' of the people whose personal data are processed (the 'data subjects').[4] Examples of such risks may be chilling effects on public speech or (indirect) discrimination – risks that are notoriously difficult to quantify.[5] While the GDPR details several requirements for DPIAs, it gives wide discretion to organisations that process personal data to create their own risk assessment methods. They may, for instance, operationalise DPIA requirements in their organisational context by following ISO standards[6] or adapt existing risk assessments previously used for information security purposes.

The history of the organisational risk approach is described by Power, who traces the managerial concept of risk to its origins. The emergence of the idea of 'operational risk'[7] in the 1990s, specifically in the banking sector, introduced a new object of managerial attention and a new management role, the Chief Risk Officer (CRO). Newly minted CROs needed to rapidly substantiate their field of expertise. As 'operational risk also represents a programme to develop formalised risk knowledge in areas which are traditionally resistant to calculability',[8] risks that

---

[1] Ulrich Beck, *Risk Society: Towards a New Modernity* (London: Sage Publications, 1992).

[2] Regulation (EU) 2016/679 of the European Parliament and of the Council of 27 April 2016 on the protection of natural persons with regard to the processing of personal data and on the free movement of such data, and repealing Directive 95/46/EC, OJ L 119/1.

[3] Article 29 Data Protection Working Party, *Statement on the role of a risk-based approach in data protection legal frameworks* (2014).

[4] GDPR Art 35.

[5] Athena Christofi et al., 'Erosion by Standardisation: Is ISO/IEC 29134: 2017 on Privacy Impact Assessment Up to (GDPR) Standard?,' in *Personal Data Protection and Legal Developments in the European Union*, ed. Maria Tzanou (Pennsylvania: IGI Global, 2020), 140–167.

[6] Specifically, the standard ISO/IEC 29134:2017 'Information technology – Security techniques – Guidelines for privacy impact assessment'.

[7] Operational risk is defined by the Basel Committee of Banking Supervision as 'the risk of loss resulting from inadequate or failed internal processes, people, and systems or from external events,' see www.bis.org/basel_framework/chapter/OPE/10.htm?tldate=20221231.

[8] Michael Power, *Organized uncertainty: Designing a world of risk management* (Oxford: Oxford University Press, 2007), 104.

were previously deemed incalculable, such as the reputational consequences of employee fraud, were constructed in quantitative assessments appraising their likelihood (eg, on five-point scales) and severity (eg, expressed in monetary damages). Over time, such approaches to constructing operational risks and mitigating them became institutionalised. Black contends that calculative practices, such as probability calculations, are cognitive and communicative frameworks that create a discourse and a set of practices that aim to reflect the world in a certain way which may only be understandable for people in the same epistemic community.[9]

However, this quantification logic of organisational risk management is difficult to align with the GDPR's focus on risks to human rights.[10] One reason is that risks to human rights are often intangible and therefore difficult to quantify or represent on a scale.[11] Another reason is a difference in perspectives: traditional organisational risk assessments take the perspective of the organisation processing the data, while the GDPR takes the perspective of the data subject whose risks are to be assessed. The GDPR does not necessarily require organisations to consult data subjects,[12] though it promotes doing so 'where appropriate'.[13] While risk management tools do often incorporate public risk perceptions (as organisations fear scandals and public condemnation), this turns public perception itself into a risk to be managed, ie a reputational risk or a risk to liability claims.

Recital 75 of the GDPR describes a number of risk categories for data controllers to take into account during a risk assessment:

> the processing may give rise to discrimination, identity theft or fraud, financial loss, damage to the reputation, loss of confidentiality of personal data protected by professional secrecy, unauthorised reversal of pseudonymisation, or any other significant economic or social disadvantage.

The same recital also describes in more general terms other instances in which risks need to be assessed and mitigated or prevented:

- where data subjects might be deprived of their rights and freedoms or prevented from exercising control over their personal data;
- where personal data are processed which reveal racial or ethnic origin, political opinions, religion or philosophical beliefs or trade union membership;
- the processing of genetic data, data concerning health or data concerning sex life or criminal convictions and offences or related security measures;
- where personal aspects are evaluated, in particular aspects concerning performance at work, economic situation, health, personal preferences or interests,

---

[9] Julia Black, 'Reconceiving Financial Markets – From the Economic to the Social,' *Journal of Corporate Law Studies* 13.2 (2013): 401–442.
[10] Niels Van Dijk, Raphaël Gellert and Kjetil Rommetveit, 'A risk to a right? Beyond data protection risk assessments,' *Computer Law & Security Review* 32.2 (2016): 286–306. See also Christofi et al. (n. 5).
[11] See Christofi et al. (n. 5).
[12] Raphaël Gellert, 'Understanding the notion of risk in the General Data Protection Regulation,' *Computer Law & Security Review* 34.2 (2018): 279–288.
[13] GDPR Art 35(9).

- reliability or behaviour, location or movements, in order to create or use personal profiles;
- where personal data of vulnerable natural persons, particularly children, are processed;
- where processing involves a large amount of personal data and affects a large number of data subjects.

These descriptions of risk categories are broad enough to provoke deeper consideration and discussion about interpretations. An advantage of such broad descriptions is that there is enough flexibility for considerations of risks in all the different sectors of society to which the GDPR applies. However, for controllers with a strict tick-the-box compliance mindset, whose main aim is to reduce risks of fines and public condemnation, these descriptions may appear too vague to quantify or respond to in a calculated manner.

Moreover, data protection risks are moving targets, highly contingent on circumstances and changing social and technological realities. A prominent example is the risk of 'unauthorised reversal of pseudonimisation', as data subjects in an 'anonymised' data set may be reidentified when that data set is combined with additional information, or with new data sets.[14] This may happen when previously unforeseen ('disruptive') technologies are introduced into society or when digital technologies are suddenly adopted at an accelerated pace, dramatically increasing the amount of personal data available. Given the extensive discretion provided to controllers and the fast-moving pace of the digital economy, a question with real-life consequences is how controllers interpret and understand risks in their daily practices, and how these understandings are translated into risk assessments.

This chapter describes real-world understandings of data protection risks under fast-changing circumstances. As an example, we have chosen the case of the banking sector, with its highly developed procedural approach to risks. Specifically, we look at retail banking, as this is the segment of banking in which most personal data of individuals are handled, unlike for example investment banking or corporate banking. To tease out the element of fast-changing circumstances, we have studied whether the COVID-19 pandemic has affected understandings of data protection risks in retail banks. While the pandemic has in some respects been a catalyst for change in retail banking (eg, widespread teleworking for bank staff[15]), it has mostly accelerated existing digitalisation strategies, such as the platformisation and 'appification' of banking. The main question we aim to answer is: How do European retail banks conceive of data protection risks, and how were these conceptions of data protection risks affected by pandemic measures?

---

[14] Yves-Alexandre De Montjoye et al., 'Unique in the Crowd: The privacy bounds of human mobility,' *Scientific Reports* 3 (2013): 1376.

[15] National Bank of Belgium, *Financial Market Infrastructures and Payment Services Report 2022*, National Bank of Belgium (2022): 61. See www.nbb.be/nl/artikels/financial-market-infrastructures-and-payment-services-report-2022.

The next section (section II) introduces the framework we have used in analysing this question. The subsequent section (section III) describes our methodological approach to gathering empirical information in answer to our research question. Our findings are presented in section IV, which is divided into three themes: (a) how large European retail banks organise personal data protection in practice, (b) how banks view and handle risks to the protection of personal data, and (c) the effects of COVID-19 pandemic measures on the protection of personal data in banks. Our findings are discussed in relation to our analytical framework in section V, after which we offer our conclusions in section VI.

## II. Analytical Framework

Banks have extensive procedures for the mitigation of risks because they face a heavy regulatory burden. More than a few regulations have been introduced precisely because of banks' risky behaviour. Power relates how banking industry mythology associates the emergence of the operational risk discourse with the collapse of Barings Bank in 1995, which was ascribed to both a dramatic failure in Barings' risk management systems and failures in supervision by regulators.[16] Similarly, the 2008 financial crisis prompted revisions of supervision and regulatory oversight.[17] In her analysis of the 2008 financial crisis, Black concludes that governments, regulators and market actors had relied too much on neoclassical economics to support compliance by banks, overlooking the importance of power differences and organisational behaviour.[18] After the crisis, both oversight and supervision became stricter and more rule-based.

The heavy regulatory burden for banks comes with a multitude of supervisory authorities in this sector, from central banks to competition and consumer authorities, and – relevant to our research question – privacy and data protection authorities. In addition, Black emphasises that supervisory authorities are not the only actors creating binding rules for the banking sector. Other rule-making actors are credit rating agencies, auditors and standard setters like the International Organization for Standardization (ISO), among others. These rule-makers have differential power and will therefore use different means to influence organisational behaviour. Doing so, they may compete with other rule-makers,[19]

---

[16] See Power (n. 8).
[17] Basel Committee on Banking Supervision, *Principles for effective risk data aggregation and risk reporting* (Basel: BIS, 2013), www.bis.org/publ/bcbs239.pdf.
[18] See Black (n. 9).
[19] In earlier work, Black contends that when principles like 'fairness' or 'accountability' are applied in a substantive manner (ie, not necessarily laid down in rulebooks, but applied in practice), there will be extensive debates between regulator, regulatees and others about the application of those principles (a 'battle for interpretive control'). These debates will centre around the interpretation that is right for some final arbiter, for instance the courts, regulators, an ombudsman and the interpretation of choice will have real consequences in terms of enforcement. See Julia Black, 'The Rise, Fall and Fate

collaborate,[20] or simply co-exist. In other words, risks in the banking sector are managed by a variety of approaches from multiple sources of power.

For a comprehensive analysis of this 'poly-centric' regulatory regime, Black proposes an interdisciplinary framework that combines approaches from economic, legal and other social sciences.[21] The framework is further elaborated by Black and Murray, who argue that the goal of regulatory systems for new technologies should indeed be to manage risks.[22] Crucial to the success of regulation in managing risks are the knowledge and understandings that different actors, including the regulated, have of the risks. Apart from knowledge and understandings, other elements that should be analysed are:

- goals and values;
- trust and legitimacy;
- regulatory tools and techniques;
- behaviours of individuals; and
- behaviours of organisations.

We will therefore concentrate on 'knowledge and understandings' of data protection risks and analyse these in coherence with the other elements. While the framework is indeed rather comprehensive, we believe an important component is missing for our case, which throws a spotlight on a period of accelerated digitalisation: a material component we will call 'infrastructure and platformisation'. In the last few years before the COVID-19 pandemic, retail bank services had been developing towards 'Open Banking'. In broad terms, Open Banking is to do with sharing banking data more widely, to spur innovation and offer a wider range of services to consumers. The EU's revised Payment Services Directive (PSD2)[23] aims to regulate and promote Open Banking. Within the PSD2 framework, bank clients can consent to sharing payment data from their bank with a so-called third-party provider (TPP), which can, for instance, be an online shop or a budgeting app, to allow for easier payments or personalised services.[24] TPPs can also be other banks,

---

of Principles Based Regulation,' *LSE Law, Society and Economy Working Papers*, LSE Law, Society and Economy Working Papers 17 (2010): 26.

[20] For example, in its oversight of the Belgium-based Society for Worldwide Interbank Financial Telecommunication (SWIFT), which offers essential messaging infrastructure (and software) in support of international payments, the National Bank of Belgium collaborates with authorities in the G20 jurisdictions to assess compliance with international standards for payment systems. Such standards include guidance on incident response and on cyber threat analysis, among other Cyber Resilience Oversight Expectations (CROE).

[21] See Black (n. 9).

[22] Julia Black and Andrew Murray, 'Regulating AI and Machine Learning: Setting the Regulatory Agenda,' *European Journal of Law and Technology* 10.3 (2019): 21.

[23] Directive 2015/2366/EU of the European Parliament and of the Council of 25 November 2015 on payment services in the internal market, amending Directives 2002/65/EC, 2009/110/EC and 2013/36/EU and Regulation (EU) No 1093/2010, and repealing Directive 2007/64/EC.

[24] Christian M. Stiefmueller, 'Open Banking and PSD 2: The Promise of Transforming Banking by "Empowering Customers"', in *Advances in the Human Side of Service Engineering*, ed. Jim Spohrer

or large technology platforms that offer payment services.[25] However, sharing payment data may also expose sensitive information to the TPP. Certain payment data (eg, donations or membership fees) may betray for example religious affiliation, union membership or sexual preferences, to name a few situations that can pose heightened risks to the rights and freedoms of data subjects described in the GDPR.

As risks to personal data are particularly prominent when data are exchanged between organisations, we see a need for an additional element to the analytical framework. How different partners handle risks in a data-sharing environment is mostly a material question: technological infrastructures allow or do not allow certain behaviour, conferring power to some actors and not to others.[26] For example, after recognising that banks were reluctant to facilitate smooth data-sharing with financial technology (FinTech) newcomers, the Competition and Markets Authority (CMA) in the UK imposed a standard for open Application Programming Interfaces (APIs).[27] The idea was that standardised open APIs would improve competition by making it easier for innovative services to use client data from various banks. The resulting infrastructure, however, poses risks to the protection of personal data: lowering thresholds to sharing data means additional protective measures are needed to prevent misuse or data ending up in the wrong hands.

The material element of the analysis should not be reduced to purely the physical connections of cables and technological networks, but also encompass software and different actors working within the infrastructure – for example including the developers who create the APIs and the bank clients who use FinTech services. This material element should be analysed in coherence with the other elements in the framework proposed by Black and Murray. For instance, in the example of the CMA's open API standard, it was the *behaviour* of banks that prompted the introduction of the regulatory *tool* (the open API standard) that changed the *infrastructure*.

To analyse infrastructure, we can learn from the field of infrastructure studies. Infrastructure studies teach us that key features of infrastructures are ubiquity, reliability, invisibility and their functioning as gateways.[28] Applied to retail banking,

---

and Christine Leitner, *Advances in Intelligent Systems and Computing* (Cham: Springer International Publishing, 2020), 299–305.

[25] Think of, eg, Google Pay, Amazon Pay and Apple Pay. Apple recently announced the introduction of Apple Tap to Pay, a digital wallet that allows for contactless payments between iPhones, see www.apple.com/newsroom/2022/02/apple-unveils-contactless-payments-via-tap-to-pay-on-iphone/.

[26] Marieke De Goede, 'Finance/security infrastructures,' *Review of International Political Economy* 28.2 (2021): 351–368. De Goede specifically refers to how sanctions are enforced through the SWIFT infrastructure (see n. 20), which was exemplified by the disconnection from the SWIFT network of seven Russian and three Belarussian financial institutions in March 2022 in response to the Russian invasion of Ukraine, as directed by the EU, the UK, Canada and the USA.

[27] Adriano Basso et al., 'Recent Developments at the CMA: 2017–2018,' *Review of Industrial Organization* 53.4 (2018): 615–635.

[28] Jean-Christophe Plantin et al., 'Infrastructure studies meet platform studies in the age of Google and Facebook,' *New Media & Society* 20.1 (2016): 293–310.

we see that the ubiquity, reliability and durability of the banking infrastructure has led consumers and wider society to depend on it, as habits and practices have developed around it. For instance, in western societies, employees often need to have a bank account to receive their salaries or obtain credit. The banking infrastructure thus creates interdependencies between banks, their clients, employers, retail, authorities and the services industry.[29]

When infrastructural systems need to incorporate more actors, a redesign of technologies, networks, standards and routines is also needed, and people on all sides of the system will need to change their habits. Open Banking is part of and contributes to the platformisation of banking,[30] a redesign of banking infrastructure. Banks have been setting up digital platforms to reduce costs,[31] capitalise on their data collections,[32] meet clients' evolving needs for online service,[33] and comply with Open Banking legislation.[34] The users of banking platforms are clients, TPPs and other platforms from large technology companies. The heterogeneity of platform users is a key characteristic studied in platform studies, alongside platforms' programmability, affordances and constraints.[35] Key points of interest are also the accessibility of data through platforms and the logic imposed by APIs. Digital platforms position themselves: (a) between users, and (b) as the 'space' in which users' activities occur, which gives them privileged access to those activities, as well as the power to set rules.[36] We include learnings from both infrastructure studies and platform studies in our analysis as part of the material element of the framework.

An example of the added value of analysing this material element is provided by Dieter and Tkacz, who describe how the banking experience has become 'appified' in recent years.[37] They define 'appification' as 'the re-composing of an everyday activity into a "grammar of action" that fits a smartphone app'.[38]

---

[29] Paul Edwards et al., 'Understanding infrastructure: dynamics, tensions, and design,' *Report of a Workshop on 'History & Theory of Infrastructure: Lessons for New Scientific Cyberinfrastructures'* (2007).

[30] For an in-depth examination of platformisation, see José Van Dijck, Thomas Poëll and Martijn De Waal, *The Platform Society: Public Values in a Connective World* (Oxford: Oxford University Press, 2018). For a more specific discussion of platformisation in banking, see Reijer Hendrikse, David Bassens and Michiel Van Meeteren, 'The Appleization of finance: Charting incumbent finance's embrace of FinTech,' *Finance and Society* 4.2 (2018): 159–180.

[31] Nick Srnicek, *Platform capitalism* (Cambridge: Polity Press, 2017).

[32] See Hendrikse et al. (n. 30).

[33] Magdalena Swacha-Lech, 'The main challenges facing the retail banking industry in the era of digitalization,' *Financial Markets* 26.4 (2017): 94–116.

[34] Giuseppe Colangelo and Mariateresa Maggiolino, 'From fragile to smart consumers: Shifting paradigm for the digital era,' *Computer Law & Security Review* 35.2 (2017): 173–181.

[35] See Plantin et al. (n. 28).

[36] See Srnicek (n. 31).

[37] Michael Dieter and Nathaniel Tkacz, 'The Patterning of Finance/Security: A Designerly Walkthrough of Challenger Banking Apps,' *Computational Culture* 7 (2020), computationalculture.net/the-patterning-of-finance-security/.

[38] The concept of 'grammars of action' refers to the ways in which technological systems structure human activities. See: Philip Agre, 'Surveillance and capture: Two models of privacy,' *The Information Society* 10.2 (1994): 101–127.

Appification promotes a new banking routine as something that people always have with them instead of the old routine of banking as somewhere a client goes.[39] People thus adapt their routines to rely on appified banking. At the same time, banking apps adapt their designs to users' behavioural patterns. Society changes as a result of both adaptations: shops and restaurants increasingly provide (traceable) smartphone payment options while (anonymous) cash payments are phased out. The consequence of this mutual shaping of routines and designs may be that eventually there is no return to offline banking. People's banking practices become inextricably entangled with new technologies.[40]

**Figure 1** Framework to analyse conceptions of data protection risks in banks (adaptation based on Black & Murray (2019))

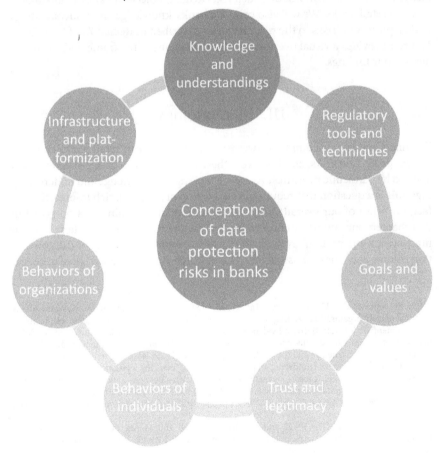

---

[39] See Dieter and Tkacz (n. 37).
[40] Wanda Orlikowski and Susan Scott, '10 Sociomateriality: Challenging the Separation of Technology, Work and Organization,' *The Academy of Management Annals* 2.1 (2008): 433–474.

Platformised banking associates even small-scale transactions with individuals, and seamlessly connects payment data with other personal data. As for the consequences for personal data protection, the risk categories enumerated in Article 75 of the GDPR come to mind. Especially 'significant economic and social disadvantages' may arise when data obtained from a payment-processing app are used in authorities' investigations of political dissent (giving rise to chilling effects in donations to civil society organisations).[41] Moreover, in the Open Banking paradigm, bank clients are responsibilised to verify the authenticity of payment requests themselves, while the digital environment exposes them far more than in-person payments to so-called 'confidence crimes' like (identity) fraud, phishing and other scams.[42] Indeed, confidence crimes soared during the pandemic.[43] Our analysis concentrates on whether such risks to data subjects are known and understood in retail banks. We will also compare banks' knowledge and understandings of data protection risks to the risk categories described in Recital 75 of the GDPR. Figure 1 provides a visual overview of all the elements of the framework we use to analyse our findings.

## III. Methodology

The main question we aim to answer is: How do European retail banks conceive of data protection risks, and how were these conceptions of data protection risks affected by pandemic measures? As we are looking for knowledge and understandings, this is a question that requires the collection of nuanced, rich information. In fact, the remit of our overall study was broader than the main question posed in this chapter: our aim was to find contextual factors that influence data protection practices 'on the ground' in the banking sector, with conceptions of data protection risks as only one of those factors. Our research strategy was designed to collect

---

[41] In the summer of 2022, authorities in India used data from a payment app to investigate donations to a civil society organisation, leading to a marked decrease in civil society donations, see: 'In India, Your Payment Data Could Become Evidence of Dissent' (*Rest of World*, 2022) restofworld.org/2022/newsletter-south-asia-india-data-evidence-of-dissent/. Valeria Ferrari points out that the digitalisation of the payment infrastructure and the gradual disappearance of cash is leading to a situation of perfect enforcement of anti-money laundering and counter-terrorist financing legislation, see Valeria Ferrari, 'Crosshatching Privacy: Financial Intermediaries' Data Practices Between Law Enforcement and Data Economy,' *European Data Protection Law Review* 6.4 (2020): 522–535. It should be noted, however, that these risk categories in Article 75 of the GDPR are primarily addressed to actions by the data controller, in this case the bank.
[42] I. Lammerts et al., 'The PSD2 and the Risks of Fraud and Money Laundering' (*Anti-Money Laundering Centre*, 2017) www.amlc.eu/wp-content/uploads/2019/04/The-PSD2-and-the-Risks-of-Fraud-and-Money-Laundering.pdf.
[43] See eg Phil Muncaster, '#COVID19 Fears Drive Phishing Emails Up 667% in Under a Month' (*Infosecurity Magazine*, 26 March 2020) www.infosecurity-magazine.com/news/covid19-drive-phishing-emails-667/. As another example, see the 2020 annual report of the Belgian Ombudsman for the banking sector (in Dutch): Ombudsman van de bancaire sector, 'Jaarverslag 2020' (2021) www.ombudsfin.be/sites/default/files/JV-Ombudsfin%202020_0.pdf.

so-called 'thick' descriptions, focusing on expert practitioners' views, priorities and practices to identify what they regard as crucial factors in data protection. The study design therefore involved a variety of research methods: expert discussions and interviews, observational field research and document analysis.

Our first step was an exploratory round table discussion with 13 experts representing different stakeholder groups in the financial sector, in September 2019. This discussion yielded a list of focal points for the subsequent data collection, including bank clients' low awareness of risks related to the sharing of financial data. The next step was a panel discussion at the Computers, Privacy and Data Protection Conference (CPDP 2020) about 'Practical consequences of PSD2 for personal data protection' between representatives of different stakeholders in the banking sector (a payments processor, a European consortium of consumer associations, a major bank and a European data protection authority).

Subsequently, the study consisted of fieldwork at the hub of a global systemically important bank (G-SIB) from March to December 2020. Due to pandemic measures requiring social distancing and work-from-home, we followed the field online using a 'digital ethnography' approach. Digital ethnography acknowledges that many fields are entangled with digital 'technologies, content, presence and communication', while 'the digital has become part of the material, sensory and social worlds we inhabit'.[44] The pandemic measures meant that the field of banking became decidedly digital: not only was in-person contact between researcher and respondents hardly possible, but the respondents themselves were also mostly meeting colleagues and clients online. 'Co-location' in work was replaced with 'co-presence' in a digital environment. 'Being there' effectively meant 'being online', interacting via videoconferencing tools, email, chat, digital newsletters, blogs, social media, online conferences and telephone conversations.

Additionally, we conducted 25 expert interviews (three in-person, two over the telephone and 20 via videoconferencing tools). The interviews were semi-structured, based on the focal points listed in the exploratory discussion, and all lasted approximately 60 minutes. As people became habituated to online conversation, experts who were physically located in different countries (Belgium, France, South Africa) could be interviewed without the need for travel or additional technical support. This allowed us to co-organise three online panel discussions in late 2020 and early 2021, between experts from around the world ('Banking on Personal Data'), the European Union ('Peer-to-peer: Open Banking, Comparing Notes on the EDPB Consultation') and Belgium ('Open Banking and Smart Cities'). The experts who took part in our panels and interviews were (G-SIB) bank executives and board members, data protection officers, innovation specialists, auditors, legal specialists, data governance specialists, client-facing bank staff, consumer association representatives, representatives of regulatory authorities, government authorities and consultants.

---

[44] Sarah Pink et al., *Digital Ethnography: Principles and Practice* (London: SAGE, 2016), 2, 7.

The information thus collected consisted of interview and panel transcripts, digital documents and thousands of fieldnotes. These were systematically analysed using qualitative data analysis software (MaxQDA) to find patterns, themes and concepts.[45] The information was triangulated with secondary materials, consisting of internal and public documentation, including industry reports, audit reviews, planning documents, newspaper articles and opinion pieces, as well as presentations to the board of the G-SIB. Our findings were validated in presentations and feedback sessions with banking professionals, including some of our respondents.

## IV. Findings

### A. Data Protection and Governance in Large European Retail Banks

In the wake of the 2008 financial crisis, legislators and regulators realised national regulation would not suffice to manage risks in global banking, and so they introduced stricter cross-border regulation. For lack of a global regulator, oversight was aligned between supervisory authorities via the Basel Committee on Banking Supervision (BCBS).[46] The BCBS covers 28 jurisdictions and sets global standards. It does not have supranational authority but relies on its members to implement its decisions. Among the new standards the BCBS introduced was standard 239 ('BCBS 239'), entitled: 'Principles for effective risk data aggregation and risk reporting'.[47] BCBS 239 applies to Global Systemically Important Banks (G-SIBs). It emphasises accountability: 'roles and responsibilities should be established as they relate to the ownership and quality of risk data and information'.[48] This aligns well with the GDPR, which also emphasises organisations' accountability for data processing activities.[49]

Risk governance, and specifically the governance of data about risks to banks (imposed by supervisory authorities), clearly influenced data protection practices in European banks, according to our respondents. Several interviewees emphasised that BCBS 239 profoundly impacted data governance in banks, restructuring internal processes and infrastructure, responsibilities and controls. The G-SIB where we conducted our study implemented a special programme 'to turn a regulatory constraint into a concrete and meaningful project for the bank' that ran over several years and comprised over 700 sub-projects. Part of the project deliverables were the creation of the position of Chief Data Officer (CDO) for all subsidiaries, the establishment of a Data Office within the G-SIB and the introduction of a data

---

[45] Sarah Daynes and Terry Williams, *On Etnography* (Cambridge: Polity Press, 2018).
[46] For more information about the BCBS, see www.bis.org/bcbs/.
[47] See Basel Committee on Banking Supervision (n. 17).
[48] ibid.
[49] GDPR Art 5(2).

governance framework. This BCBS 239 project was still running when the GDPR was to take effect, and the programme managers strategically chose to include GDPR compliance in it to obtain support for GDPR compliance from the G-SIB's executive committee.

The bank's executive committee may not have needed much convincing, as the importance of improving and standardising (risk) data governance was broadly supported by financial institutions.[50] An executive in our study recounted how the Chief Information Officer and an adviser to the Chief Executive Officer readily took the opportunity to modernise data governance. The new data governance framework had broader goals than risk data reporting; the newly introduced data department also included an 'AI and analytics' team and a data strategy team. One manager of the BCBS 239 project said: 'We leveraged a lot on the BCBS 239. There was some risk aspect, there are also some finance aspects of that.'

Not only risk *data* governance, but risk governance in general influence how personal data are protected in banks. For risk governance, banks adhere to the 'three lines of defence' model. Client-facing and operational departments (the 'first line') are guided, advised, coordinated and monitored by specialists in the 'second line', and both lines are audited by the 'third line'. The second line of defence mostly consists of a risk department, legal and compliance teams and the (GDPR-mandated) Data Protection Officer (DPO).[51] When it comes to personal data protection, the first line implements practical measures; the second line sets out policies, gives advice and monitors practices; and the third line audits implementation of data protection policies and measures throughout the bank.

In the G-SIB where we conducted our study, the data department in the first line hosted a privacy and data protection team. This team provided tools for the exercise of data subject rights, implemented controls and conducted DPIAs, among other tasks. The data department also maintained a Register of Processing Activities.[52] This may appear to overlap with BCBS 239 requirements for a data governance infrastructure, but according to the manager of the data department the goals are quite different: 'The goal of this Register of Processing Activities is to be able to explain, in simple words, to somebody who is not in your company, what you are doing with the [personal] data.' A data governance infrastructure for internal use would be much more granular and too complex to explain to outsiders.

The Register of Processing Activities contained around 350 activities at the time of our study. It needed to be filled manually, by all bank managers in charge of operations involving personal data. In a retail bank, this means virtually all

---

[50] Institute for International Finance, *Risk IT and Operations: Strengthening Capabilities* (2011), www.mckinsey.com/~/media/mckinsey/dotcom/client_service/risk/pdfs/iif_mck_report_on_risk_it_and_operations.pdf.
[51] GDPR Art 37. In large, hierarchically structured organisations, data protection specialists are often added to risk management departments, embedding them in practices that are centred around corporate cost-benefit analyses, see Ari Ezra Waldman, *Industry Unbound* (Cambridge: Cambridge University Press, 2021).
[52] GDPR Art 30.

processes. As the GDPR is not specific on the delimitation of a 'processing activity', in the sense that it does not specify the scope or size of 'activity', the bank was left to create its own outline of the term's application. Instead of the 350 processing activities included in the register, there could have been tens of thousands, or only a few dozen, depending on definition choices. A delimitation problem was presented by the fact that processes consist of multiple micro processes. The data governance tools manager explained:

> The activity of 'providing a credit card' can be counted as one processing activity or as a handful of them: 'taking down a client's information', 'verifying the client's creditworthiness', 'sending out the credit card by mail', and so on. In addition, the size of this bank means that there are many processes in different parts of the bank that include providing a credit card.

The privacy and data protection team within the data department decided to only include so-called 'macro processes' in the register, such as 'providing credit', 'managing account' or 'processing payments'. Their data governance IT system then linked different data flows to these activities. The data flow descriptions included flows of data to external providers, for example payment processors. This system also allowed for rapid data breach reporting, as the data department manager explained:

> Imagine one day we hear: Visa has had a massive data breach. There have been stolen so many data. What we can do at that moment, is to look back into our RPA, look where Visa is active in our different processes and then come back to: Visa is active there and there and there and there, so basically, potentially all those clients can be impacted.

The privacy and data protection team (first line of defence) was also in charge of a standardised procedure for DPIAs under the guidance of the DPO (second line of defence, in the Operational Risk department). The DPIA procedure consisted of several stages. In the first stage, a personal data protection questionnaire is filled in by the person(s) introducing a new processing activity involving personal data. The questionnaire serves as a registration of the new activity and it serves to determine whether an extensive DPIA will be necessary. If so, a second stage starts with a longer questionnaire that requires ratings for several questions about risks. In this second stage, the privacy and data protection team fills in the questionnaire. In the third stage, the DPO reviews the assessment and discusses risk mitigation measures with the privacy and data protection team. The latter team communicates these measures to the person(s) in charge of the new data processing activity and follows up on implementation.

The DPO expressed reservations about the veracity of answers in the first stage of the procedure, when a new activity is reported by an operational manager, due to the fact that these employees may reason too much from their own perspectives. He remarked:

> One of the questions that need to be answered in the first questionnaire by a business manager or a data scientist is: Do you feel comfortable explaining this to the data subject? And of course they will always reply with 'yes'.

It is in the second stage of the DPIA procedure that potential risks are assessed, which will be discussed in the next section.

There were two additional risk assessments for new activities: a thorough review by the 'New Activities Committee' (also discussed in the next section) and the 'newspaper test' introduced by the CDO. The newspaper test consists of an exercise in which the press officer writes up a hypothetical newspaper article highlighting the worst imaginable consequences of the new activity, presented in the most critical light. If the activity turns out to be very sensitive in this presentation, the executive board of the bank will be consulted. The DPO said:

> It is not the GDPR, but more of a reputational risk perspective. To me, this is related: if you can defend your point of view to the press, you will feel comfortable explaining the activity to a data subject.

Reputational risk may indeed be one of the most important drivers for the protection of personal data in banks. For example, while many of our respondents mentioned that data governance should 'create value' for the bank, selling client data to third parties was assumed to be too big a reputational risk: 'If we make money over the backs of customers, it could backfire'. However, providing access to or selling aggregated client data to third parties against a fee ('data insights services'), or other data monetisation strategies, including advertising within bank services, were actively considered. With respect to the GDPR, such considerations lead to the exploration of 'consent strategies', since additional consent from bank clients would be needed to use their personal data beyond the originally stated purposes.[53]

The improved data governance introduced by BCBS 239 thus improved accountability but also created an infrastructure that allowed for more extensive use of personal data in banks, beyond original purposes (if clients consent). Notably, consent requirements are another impetus for banks to accord special attention to their reputation of trustworthiness.

## B. Banks and Data Protection Risks

In the DPIA procedure outlined in the previous section, data protection risks are appraised by the privacy and data protection team, which consists of legal, technical and operational staff who have been selected for their 'risk mindset'. The team uses software that automates risks assessments, integrating different risk management domains, including personal data protection. The software follows classical assessment procedures for all risk management domains, based on security risk assessments. Risks are reported on 'risk cards' that describe the risk's source, its

---

[53] Manipulative discourses on privacy-as-consent for corporate benefit are an important recurring theme in Ari Waldman's research into US technology companies' privacy practices, see eg Waldman (n. 51).

category, its 'owner' and the number of data subjects involved. Risk categories may be assigned automatically. For example, when a minimum threshold for the number of data subjects is reached, the risk will automatically be labelled a 'data disclosure' risk ('data disclosure risks' are classified as 'non-financial risks related to ICT'). This threshold is linked to the total number of bank account owners in the country. This reflects knowledge and/or understanding of the last element of the description of risk categories in Article 75 of the GDPR: 'Where processing involves a large amount of personal data and affects a large number of data subjects.'

Part of the procedure is the acceptance of a risk by a designated risk owner in the bank. There may be discussion about who 'owns' a risk, which in practical terms means taking responsibility for mitigating it. According to the privacy and data protection team, negotiations were sometimes needed. The CDO even complained that other departments regularly refused to accept ownership for data disclosure risks, by arguing that these had to do with data and therefore should be mitigated by the data department. However, from the perspective of the data department, data disclosure risks could very simply be resolved by ending the risky activity, which would not please affected business departments. The CDO therefore often insisted on 'co-ownership': the data department and the department that needed the personal data would take joint responsibility for mitigating associated risks.

After an owner accepts the risk, both the risk itself and its mitigation by the owner are evaluated. As in traditional risk assessments, likelihood and severity (or impact) are the main axes for this evaluation. The risk assessment software maintains four levels of likelihood: very likely, likely, occasional and rare. An example of a very likely data disclosure risk provided is 'an external human source getting access to stolen unprotected file storage device', whereas it would be deemed rare for this human source to get access if the device is encrypted and has password protection. This understanding of the risk likelihood reflects a traditional IT security perspective on data disclosure (that of course serves the protection of human rights equally well). Risk severity is also divided into four levels: extreme, serious, moderate and low. Low severity is described as 'a few inconveniences' to the data subject, while extreme severity is described as 'significant, or even irreversible consequences'. An example of the latter is 'Disclosure of personal data that can lead to the identification of more than 100.000 data subjects', again reflective of the last element of Recital 75 of the GDPR.

Apart from the general DPIA procedure described here, specific DPIA procedures had been created for processes that posed particular risks to personal data, for example 'analytics & artificial intelligence' and 'robotics'. DPIAs for running activities also differ from DPIAs for new activities in granularity, as the latter are more thoroughly vetted. DPOs within the G-SIB banking consortium are advised to be actively involved in the continuous updating of these procedures.

In the second line of defence, the DPO monitored the procedures of the privacy and data protection team. The bank consortium's guidance to the DPO describes data protection risks as follows:

> Risks exist from the mishandling of data subjects' personal data, these include financial penalties from regulators, enforcement action and reputational damage.
>
> Impacts to *data subjects* when personal data is compromised or processed in a well-meant but non-complaint [sic] manner can include financial loss, loss of confidentiality, discrimination, reputational damage, identity theft, fraud and/or other economic or social disadvantage.
>
> Impacts to [*the bank*][54] is financial loss, but perhaps more importantly the reputational damage stemming from a failure to treat personal data fairly and responsibly.

With the exception of 'unauthorised reversal of pseudonymisation', the second paragraph mirrors the first description of risk categories in Recital 75 of the GDPR. Notably, that paragraph is proceeded and succeeded by paragraphs that emphasise two risks to the bank itself: fines and reputational damage. The guidance proceeds by listing several examples. For example, a risk can be that 'personal data is not obtained by lawful and fair means resulting in reputational damage and fines'. All of these examples end with the warning that they will lead to fines, and almost all mention that they will lead to reputational damage.

The risk management framework presented in the guidance consisted of four risk categories (for a total of 15 risks):

1. data governance
   (risks within this category included 'The basic principles for processing, including conditions for consent are not considered' and 'Data processing activities do not enable the rights of data subjects');
2. data security
   (risks within this category included 'Unauthorized persons (ie, "malicious insider") having access to personal data' and 'Analytics activities are impacting the rights of the data subject');
3. regulatory oversight
   (eg 'Non-compliance with Supervisory Authority investigation or orders'); and
4. insufficient training
   (eg 'Employees are not aware of the relevant policies and procedures in relation to personal data').

These risk categories to some extent reflect the descriptions in Recital 75 of the GDPR, specifically the element of impeding the exercise of data subject rights.

---

[54] For reasons of confidentiality, the name of the bank is redacted here.

The category of regulatory oversight yet again reverts attention to risks to the bank itself. This may be for reasons of internal strategy, to convince executives of the importance of GDPR compliance. Translating the GDPR requirements in terms of financial risks resulting from supervisory enforcement, or in terms of risks to reputation, proved a useful way to impress the importance of protecting personal data to the bank's upper management. The CDO noted: 'The fact that I come to the executive committee with a story about risk exposure related to the GDPR due to insufficient data minimalisation [...] that sentence no longer needs an explanation there.'

The DPO is not the only function in the second line monitoring risks. Newly developed activities in the bank need to pass by the New Activity Committee. The committee brings together different specialists: the DPO, legal experts, compliance specialists, operational risk experts, tax experts, security experts and financial specialists. The point is to combine perspectives from all relevant disciplines to envision different risk scenarios. The committee starts from a dossier on the new activity compiled by those proposing the activity. The dossier extensively discusses all risks that the initiators foresee. As the committee's review is an intense process that generally takes several months, a team of operational risk staff conducts a preliminary screening to ascertain whether the new activity does indeed introduce new risks. The team does not consist of specialists. To judge whether an activity is risky, team members compare the activity to previously reviewed activities and to scandals in the news. In case of uncertainty, specific experts are consulted.

In recent years, the committee reviewed several new activities that involved data monetisation. To the committee these activities at first appeared foreign, unlike what the bank had traditionally been doing. Previously, such proposals would have had little chance of being accepted due to perceived high risks. If a risk cannot be prevented and would need to be accepted, (a member of) the executive board will have to sign off on it. Before 2020, there had been one instance of a new activity aimed at data monetisation, but it had failed in the bank's executive committee, which at the time had little appetite for such risks to the bank's reputation.

If a new activity is accepted, the committee provides a framework and timeline for controls on its risks. The committee's evaluation guidelines have had to catch up with new data-driven activities by including guidance on data storage and the protection of data assets.

## C. COVID-19 Effects on Data Protection Risk Perceptions in Banks

This section describes the rapid acceleration in both provision and adoption of digital banking services during the COVID-19 pandemic, with special attention paid to the situation in Belgium, where part of the study was conducted.

The digitalisation of banking services had started well before the COVID-19 pandemic but received an enormous boost when distance measures were introduced in March 2020. These measures had an instantaneous impact on the use of digital banking services by consumers: average weekly hours spent on finance apps instantly rose around the world.[55] By the end of 2020, the industry association FinTech Belgium reported that investments in financial technologies had increased six-fold in the past year. According to the president of FinTech Belgium, consumers had made 'a 5-year leap in terms of adopting new technologies' in 2020. He pointed to an 'explosion of online retailers', increased contactless payments in the physical world and new legislation as the main drivers of the FinTech investment boom.[56]

During full lockdowns, consumers could only shop online, and bank offices were closed. During partial lockdowns, consumers switched from cash to contactless payment, despite reassurances from the European Central Bank that banknotes did not represent a significant risk of infection.[57] In Belgium in particular, contactless payment rose to 123 per cent over a year. A survey held by Belgium's largest electronic payment processor showed trust in contactless payment had risen from 37 per cent in 2019 to 59 per cent in 2020. 62 per cent of respondents intended to continue using contactless payment after the pandemic.[58]

The spectacular growth of online and contactless payments vastly increased the amount of digital payment data, advancing further digitalisation of banking. A global survey among 250 senior staff at banks and financial institutions found that the pandemic changed their prioritisations. Most notably, the majority of banks and financial institutions (83 per cent) discerned a need to build data-sharing ecosystems with external partners.[59] Two major Belgian banks made announcements in 2020 that evidenced this reorientation in priorities. The first one announced the introduction of a digital assistant that could transfer money or file an insurance claim for clients by voice command. The bank's CEO specifically referred to the pandemic-induced acceleration of digital banking for this move.[60] The other bank announced a partnership with a telecom provider to facilitate cashless payments in the telecom provider's online services.[61]

---

[55] App Annie, *The Impact of Coronavirus on the Mobile Economy* (17 March 2020), www.appannie.com/en/insights/market-data/coronavirus-impact-mobile-economy/.

[56] FinTech Belgium, *Belgian fintech fever: a 600% increase in capital raised amidst Covid crisis!* (18 November 2020), fintechbelgium.be/news/2020/11/17/press-release-belgian-fintech-fever.

[57] Fabio Panetta, 'Beyond Monetary Policy – Protecting the Continuity and Safety of Payments during the Coronavirus Crisis' (*European Central Bank*, 28 April 2020), www.ecb.europa.eu/press/blog/date/2020/html/ecb.blog200428~328d7ca065.en.html.

[58] Bancontact Payconiq Company, *Contactloos leven én betalen is het nieuwe codewoord. Vertrouwen in contactloze betalingen groeit spectaculair* (20 September 2021), assets-us-01.kc-usercontent.com/0d76cd9b-cf9d-007c-62ee-e50e20111691/d62ed46e-dcec-4f2e-89ed-ccd09f5a1826/PRNL.pdf.

[59] See www.finextra.com/finextra-downloads/research/documents/160/payments-transformation-immediate-intelligent-and-inclusive.pdf.

[60] Patrick Claerhout, 'KBC lanceert digitale assistente Kate' (*Knack Trends*, 19 June 2020), trends.knack.be/economie/bedrijven/kbc-lanceert-digitale-assistente-kate/article-analyse-1612181.html.

[61] Belfius (2020), *Belfius en Proximus tekenen een uniek strategisch partnership* (12 June 2020), www.belfius.be/about-us/nl/nieuws/belfius-proximus.

Such partnerships introduced new potential risks to the reputation of banks. An operational risk staff member of the bank where we conducted our study mentioned:

> The client looks at us to evaluate whether those partners are trustworthy. [...] To a judge, the bank, as the most powerful party, will always be guilty. We know very well what it will cost us if we do not comply.

There are different aspects to reputational risk in platformisation. For instance, a partner in the data-sharing ecosystem may use personal data provided by a bank in an inappropriate manner, making newspaper headlines that implicate the bank. Even if the partner's use of the data is not inappropriate, consumers may feel uncomfortable with it. 'The reputation of an ecosystem is as strong as its weakest link,' remarked a banking data monetisation expert in one of our panels. Another panelist remarked: 'Reputational risk is difficult to quantify but we need to be careful with it. It takes years to build a reputation and seconds for it to be destroyed.' While the panel discussed that the purposes of Open Banking partnerships should be beneficial to citizens, risks to data subjects were mostly discussed in terms of potential damage to trust in banks. Specific risks to data subjects were not mentioned in this discussion.

Along with the accelerated adoption of digital payments, digital financial fraud and phishing soared to unprecedented heights. While authorities called on banks to become more proactive in educating and protecting their clients,[62] and banks issued warnings about fraudulent tactics, bank staff we interviewed felt unable to help clients who had already fallen into a phishing trap, which became more and more common. Basically, the banks' view was that clients were themselves largely responsible for the mitigation of risks that came with the pandemic-induced shift to appified banking.

## V. Discussion

Our analysis aims to answer the question: How do European retail banks conceive of data protection risks, and how were these conceptions of data protection risks affected by pandemic measures? We have presented our findings on the approach to personal data protection risks in banks, how data protection risks are perceived in banks, and how the 'transitional period' of the COVID-19 pandemic has affected risk perceptions.

---

[62] See eg Ombudsman van de bancaire sector, 'Jaarverslag 2020' (2021), www.ombudsfin.be/sites/default/files/JV-Ombudsfin%202020_0.pdf.

Table 1 Retail banks' perspectives on risks to data subjects

| Elements of analysis | Before COVID-19 pandemic | During COVID-19 pandemic |
| --- | --- | --- |
| Knowledge and understandings | Risks interpreted in terms of known approaches to operational risk governance, which do not include consulting data subjects. | No change. |
| Goals and values | Avoiding reputational risk and financial risk to the organisation are the main goals for retail banks. | No change. |
| Trust and legitimacy | Platformised banking is seen as a potential risk to trust in banks due to third-party risks of data sharing. | As bank clients become habituated to platformised banking, further steps in digitalisation are seen as legitimate. |
| Regulatory tools and techniques | Data protection is connected to regulatory tools from strong banking authorities to improve chances of compliance. | No change. |
| Behaviours of individuals | Bank clients are hesitant to adopt platformised banking; the prevalence of cash payment reduces personal data processing. | As bank clients en masse switch to digital payments and appified banking, the amount of personal data processing, as well as confidence crimes, increase dramatically. |
| Behaviours of organisations | Avoiding reputational risks, banks are hesitant to move forward in platformised banking. | Mass adoption of digital payments and appified banking give new impetus to digitalisation strategies. |

The focal point in our analysis was the element of 'knowledge and understandings'. Bank staff struggle with the practical realisation of unspecific data protection requirements like creating a register of data processing activities or assessing risks for new data-driven activities, and fill in knowledge gaps by referring to common understandings within banks or scandals in the news. Financial loss (in the shape of fines) and reputation risk are known threats to banks that help explain what is at stake throughout the bank, up until executive level.

The analysis showed that existing risk governance frameworks influenced how data protection risks were understood by banks. In addition, risk (data) governance standards and models clarified roles and responsibilities towards personal data; this refers to the element of behaviour of organisations in our analytical framework. As for the element of regulatory tools and techniques, we found that the regulatory tool of BCBS standard 239, and its interaction with the GDPR, positively influenced the protection of personal data and certainly emphasised the importance of risk data governance, but may have done little to shift the perspective of bankers to take the view of data subjects. Goals and values between the GDPR and banks' risk assessments were misaligned in the sense that the GDPR aims to protect data subjects' rights and banks aim to protect their own interests. Platformisation of banking was an important theme in our findings, but yet again, the risks associated with it in bankers' views were related to reputation and fines, not to clients' challenges in facing new types of digital fraud.

Compared to the risk descriptions of Recital 75 of the GDPR, there was considerable overlap in conceptualisations of risks, but several elements appeared to be lacking, mostly related to sensitive data or vulnerable data subjects. This is not to say that these elements were completely absent in risk assessments, but they seemed to be open to individual interpretations. It should be noted that ongoing (re)evaluation of procedures within banks may mean that these elements have become more prominent in assessments over time – after all, our methodology provided but a snapshot of the state of affairs.

However, assessments of risks to vulnerable data subjects are best conducted by taking a large diversity of perspectives into account. According to Lupton (2006), social and cultural norms, concepts and habits play a major role in the identification of risk.[63] As a consequence, risk knowledges are contingent and dynamic, dependent on time and space. Different stakeholders may therefore perceive different risks; for instance, lay people may see different risks than experts, while both risk knowledges are 'the products of the pre-established beliefs and assumptions that individuals bring with them in making their judgements on risk'.[64] As a consequence, bank specialists may too easily dismiss data subjects' risk estimations, leading to gaps in risk perceptions.

A potential risk that is specifically mentioned in Recital 75 and yet conspicuously absent in the guidance of the bank where we conducted our study, is 'unauthorised reversal of pseudonimisation'. This risk is particularly heightened in times of accelerated digitalisation such as the first year of the COVID-19 pandemic, because of the rapid increase in amounts and types of personal data available. However, we found no evidence of increased attention for this risk in retail banks. Again, including data subjects in risk assessments may draw more attention to sensitivities to the risks related to re-identification, particularly among vulnerable groups.

---

[63] Deborah Lupton, 'Sociology and Risk,' in *Beyond the Risk Society: Critical Reflections on Risk and Human Security*, eds. Gabe Mythen and Sandra Walklate (Maidenhead: Open University Press, 2006), 11–24.
[64] ibid.

Our findings make two points clear about knowledge and understandings:
1. Banks base their understanding of data protection risks on classical risk assessment methodologies, which view data protection in terms of IT security.
2. Banks are highly sensitive to reputational risks and translate risks to the rights and freedoms of data subjects into enforcement risks or risks to their reputation.

Regarding the first point, this was evidenced by the way the risk assessment software that was used by the privacy and data protection team classified data protection risks, but also by how business departments of the bank regarded data protection risks as issues for the data governance department to solve. From an information security perspective, risks are mostly regarded in terms of data breaches and unauthorised access, while the GDPR focuses on (often unquantifiable) risks to human rights, eg chilling effects on speech, anxiety or indirect discrimination.

As for the second point, this was evidenced by the guidance and examples given to the bank's DPO, the newspaper test, the pre-screening approach to new activities and the way data protection risks are presented to the bank's top executives. Increasing public awareness of privacy issues has made bankers more sensitive to reputational risk associated with personal data protection. Efforts at data monetisation, accelerated by the rapid digitalisation resulting from pandemic measures, are approached with caution due to fears about public responses (relating to the element of trust and legitimacy in our analytical framework).

Pandemic measures meant that digital, especially 'appified', banking made a giant leap forward. The entanglement of banking with digital technologies approached a point of no return, as bank offices not only closed during lockdowns but often remained closed after distancing measures had been lifted. While the pandemic situation raised acceptance of digital payment methods and online services, bank clients had to become habituated to new 'grammars of action' with insufficient support in recognising fraudulent requests and phishing attempts. New or increased risks to the protection of people's personal data caused by digital banking, such as increased identity fraud risks, are apportioned to bank clients. This suggests that perceptions of data protection risks in banks appear not to have been much affected in the transitional times of the pandemic; banks hold on to their traditional organisation-focused perspective.

## VI. Conclusions

Our analysis shows that banks do not take the perspective of their clients (or other affected data subjects) in risk assessments. This is in line with conclusions of previous studies showing that banking managers have not developed a genuinely customer-focused mindset.[65] The analysis also shows that banks are sensitive to two risks: fines and reputational damage. Hence, to meet the goals of a regulatory regime focused on personal data protection, regulators might wield tools and techniques that connect with these two risks that banks understand. Moreover, industry-specific data protection guidance, in a collaboration between data protection authorities and banking authorities, could help expand knowledge and understandings, for instance guidance on the interpretation of 'processing activities' and on risk classifications.

Additionally, the data subjects – bank clients – themselves can be tapped for knowledge and understandings of data protection risks from their perspectives. Data subjects could, or perhaps should, be included in the DPIA procedure, as suggested by the GDPR in Article 35(9). In the DPIA procedure described in this chapter, data subjects could for instance add their views in the preliminary stage of a DPIA when a first questionnaire is used to determine whether a full DPIA will be necessary. Data subjects could also be invited to give their views on the likelihood and severity of risks, with the added benefit of allowing banks to gauge potential impact of a data processing activity on their reputations. Lastly, participation of data subjects in DPIAs may lead, for instance, to collaboratively coordinated approaches to combating identity fraud, phishing and other forms of confidence crimes. Further (empirical) research will be needed to investigate the specifics and modalities of including data subjects in DPIA procedures.

# References

Agre, Philip E. 'Surveillance and Capture: Two Models of Privacy.' *The Information Society* 10, no. 2 (1994): 101–127. doi.org/10.1080/01972243.1994.9960162.
App Annie. 'The Impact of Coronavirus on the Mobile Economy.' 17 March 2020. www.appannie.com/en/insights/market-data/coronavirus-impact-mobile-economy/.
Article 29 Data Protection Working Party. 'Statement on the role of a risk-based approach in data protection legal frameworks.' 30 May 2014. ec.europa.eu/justice/article-29/documentation/opinion-recommendation/files/2014/wp218_en.pdf.
Bancontact Payconiq Company. 'Contactloos leven én betalen is het nieuwe codewoord. Vertrouwen in contactloze betalingen groeit spectaculair.' 16 November 2020. assets-us-01.kc-usercontent.com/0d76cd9b-cf9d-007c-62ee-e50e20111691/d62ed46e-dcec-4f2e-89ed-ccd09f5a1826/PRNL.pdf.
Basel Committee on Banking Supervision. *Principles for effective risk data aggregation and risk reporting*. Basel: Bank for International Settlements, 2013. www.bis.org/publ/bcbs239.pdf.

---

[65] See eg Hannele Haapio, Heikki Karjaluoto and Joel Mero, 'Antecedents of Market Orientation in The Banking Sector During Its Digital Transformation,' in *32nd Bled eConference : Humanizing Technology for a Sustainable Society*, eds. A. Puciharet al. (Maribor: University of Maribor, 2019), 289–305.

Basso, Adriano, Julie Bon, Bethany Tasker, Natalie Timan, Mike Walker and Chris Whitcombe. 'Recent Developments at the CMA: 2017-2018.' *Review of Industrial Organization* 53, no. 4 (2018): 615-635. doi.org/10.1007/s11151-018-9668-2.
Beck, Ulrich. *Risk Society: Towards a New Modernity*. Translated by Mark Ritter. London: Sage Publications, 1992.
Black, Julia. 'The Rise, Fall and Fate of Principles Based Regulation.' *LSE Law, Society and Economy Working Papers* 17 (2010).
──, 'Reconceiving Financial Markets – From the Economic to the Social.' *Journal of Corporate Law Studies* 13, no. 2 (2013): 401-442. doi.org/10.5235/14735970.13.2.401.
Black, Julia and Andrew Murray. 'Regulating AI and Machine Learning: Setting the Regulatory Agenda.' *European Journal of Law and Technology* 10, no. 3 (2019): 21.
Christofi, Athena, Pierre Dewitte, Charlotte Ducuing and Peggy Valcke. (2020). 'Erosion by Standardisation: Is ISO/IEC 29134: 2017 on Privacy Impact Assessment Up to (GDPR) Standard?' In *Personal Data Protection and Legal Developments in the European Union*, edited by Maria Tzanou, 140-167. Pennsylvania: IGI Global, 2020.
Claerhout, Patrick. 'KBC lanceert digitale assistente Kate.' *Knack Trends*, 19 June 2020. trends.knack.be/economie/bedrijven/kbc-lanceert-digitale-assistente-kate/article-analyse-1612181.html.
Colangelo, Giuseppe and Mariateresa Maggiolino. 'From fragile to smart consumers: Shifting paradigm for the digital era.' *Computer Law & Security Review* 35 no. 2 (2019): 173-181. doi.org/10.1016/j.clsr.2018.12.004.
Daynes, Sarah and Terry Williams. *On Ethnography*. New Jersey: John Wiley & Sons, 2018.
De Goede, Marieke. 'Finance/security infrastructures.' *Review of International Political Economy* 28 no. 2 (2021): 351-368. www.tandfonline.com/doi/full/10.1080/09692290. 2020.1830832.
De Montjoye, Yves-Alexandre, César A. Hidalgo, Michel Verleysen and Vincent D. Blondel. 'Unique in the Crowd: The privacy bounds of human mobility.' *Scientific Reports* 3 no. 1376 (2013). doi.org/10.1038/srep01376.
Dieter, Michael and Nathaniel Tkacz. 'The Patterning of Finance/Security: A Designerly Walkthrough of Challenger Banking Apps.' *Computational Culture* 7 (2020).
Edwards, Paul N., Steven J. Jackson, Geoffrey C. Bowker and Cory P. Knobel. *Understanding infrastructure: dynamics, tensions, and design* (2007). deepblue.lib.umich.edu/handle/2027.42/49353.
Ferrari, Valeria. 'Crosshatching Privacy: Financial Intermediaries' Data Practices Between Law Enforcement and Data Economy.' *European Data Protection Law Review* 6 no. 4 (2020): 522-535. doi.org/10.21552/edpl/2020/4/8.
FinTech Belgium. 'Belgian fintech fever: a 600% increase in capital raised amidst Covid crisis!.' 18 November 2020. fintechbelgium.be/news/2020/11/17/press-release-belgian-fintech-fever.
Gellert, Raphaël. 'Understanding the notion of risk in the General Data Protection Regulation.' *Computer Law & Security Review* 34 no. 2 (2018): 279-288.
Haapio, Hannele, Heikki Karjaluoto and Joel Mero. 'Antecedents of Market Orientation in The Banking Sector During Its Digital Transformation.' *32nd Bled eConference : Humanizing Technology for a Sustainable Society* (2019). doi.org/10.18690/978-961-286-280-0.16.
Hendrikse, Reijer, David Bassens and Michiel van Meeteren. 'The Appleization of finance: Charting incumbent finance's embrace of FinTech.' *Finance and Society* 4 no. 2 (2018): 159-180. doi.org/10.2218/finsoc.v4i2.2870.

Institute for International Finance. 'Risk IT and Operations: Strengthening Capabilities.' 17 June 2011. www.mckinsey.com/~/media/mckinsey/dotcom/client_service/risk/pdfs/iif_mck_report_on_risk_it_and_operations.pdf.

Lammerts, I., D. Ma, N. Ploeger, B.A. Deutekom, S.J. van Eerten, N. Vink, T.N. Wagemakers, K.I.M. Sanders, C.L.S. Visser and R.B. Schaap. 'The PSD2 and the Risks of Fraud and Money Laundering.' Anti-Money Laundering Centre, 2017. www.amlc.eu/wp-content/uploads/2019/04/The-PSD2-and-the-Risks-of-Fraud-and-Money-Laundering.pdf.

Lupton, Deborah. 'Sociology and Risk.' In *Beyond the Risk Society: Critical Reflections on Risk and Human Security*, edited by Gabe Mythen and Sandra Walklate, 11–24. Maidenhead: Open University Press, 2006.

Muncaster, Phil. '#COVID19 Fears Drive Phishing Emails Up 667% in Under a Month.' *Infosecurity Magazine*, 26 March 2020. www.infosecurity-magazine.com/news/covid19-drive-phishing-emails-667/.

National Bank of Belgium. 'Financial Market Infrastructures and Payment Services Report 2022.' National Bank of Belgium. www.nbb.be/nl/artikels/financial-market-infrastructures-and-payment-services-report-2022.

Ombudsman van de bancaire sector. 'Jaarverslag 2020.' 2021. www.ombudsfin.be/sites/default/files/JV-Ombudsfin%202020_0.pdf.

Orlikowski, Wanda and Susan Scott. '10 Sociomateriality: Challenging the Separation of Technology, Work and Organisation.' *The Academy of Management Annals* 2 no. 1 (2008): 433–474. doi.org/10.1080/19416520802211644.

Panetta, F. *Beyond monetary policy – protecting the continuity and safety of payments during the coronavirus crisis*. European Central Bank, 28 April 2020. www.ecb.europa.eu/press/blog/date/2020/html/ecb.blog200428~328d7ca065.en.html.

Pink, Sarah, Heather Horst, John Postill, Larissa Hjorth, Tania Lewis, and Jo Tacchi. (2016). *Digital Ethnography: Principles and Practice*. London: SAGE, 2016.

Plantin, Jean-Christophe, Carl Lagoze, Paul Edwards and Christian Sandvig. 'Infrastructure studies meet platform studies in the age of Google and Facebook.' *New Media & Society* 20 no. 1 (2019): 293–310. doi.org/10.1177/1461444816661553.

Power, Michael. *Organized uncertainty: Designing a world of risk management*. Oxford University Press on Demand, 2007.

Srnicek, Nick. *Platform Capitalism*. Cambridge: Polity Press, 2017.

Stiefmueller, Christian M. 'Open Banking and PSD 2: The Promise of Transforming Banking by "Empowering Customers".' In *Advances in the Human Side of Service Engineering*, edited by Jim Spohrer and Christine Leitner, 299–305. Advances in Intelligent Systems and Computing. Cham: Springer International Publishing, 2020. doi.org/10.1007/978-3-030-51057-2_41.

Swacha-Lech, Magdalena. 'The main challenges facing the retail banking industry in the era of digitalisation.' *Financial Markets* 26 no. 4 (2017): 94–116.

Van Dijck, José, Thomas Poell and Martijn De Waal. *The platform society: Public values in a connective world*. Oxford: Oxford University Press, 2018.

Van Dijk, Niels, Raphaël Gellert and Kjetil Rommetveit. 'A risk to a right? Beyond data protection risk assessments.' *Computer Law & Security Review* 32 no. 2 (2016): 286–306.

Waldman, Ari Ezra. *Industry Unbound*. Cambridge: Cambridge University Press, 2021.

# 2

# Synthetic Data Generation in Service of Privacy-Preserving Deep Learning: Three Practical Case Studies

JEROME R BELLEGARDA*

## Abstract

Artificial Intelligence (AI) technologies, fast becoming pervasive across a growing variety of application domains, typically involve deep machine learning (ML) models that must be trained on very large volumes of data. As training corpora scale up to unprecedented sizes, it is increasingly unrealistic to assume that they can be thoroughly curated. This state of affairs raises serious privacy concerns because of the risk of leakage of private, secure or otherwise sensitive information. Training ML models with synthetic data naturally promotes data privacy and protection, by virtue of reducing the amount of real data to collect. But synthetic data generation has additional benefits as well, in terms of both training diversity and model deployment. This chapter illustrates such benefits through the analysis of three practical use cases associated with common day-to-day features affecting millions of users. These three case studies illuminate key messages associated with synthetic data generation, including inherent limitations and possible mitigation measures.

## Keywords

Large-scale deep learning, model robustness, data augmentation, style transfer, generative modelling, training diversity, responsible AI

* Etsy Inc, Brooklyn, NY 11201, USA.

# I. Introduction

## A. Recent AI Advances

Over the past decade, the confluence of sophisticated algorithms and tools, computational infrastructure and data science has fuelled a machine learning revolution in multiple technical fields, including speech and handwriting recognition, natural language processing, computer vision, social network filtering and machine translation, among many others.[1] Ensuing advances are powering pervasive AI features that are changing the way we interact with technology in our daily lives, with a profound impact across a growing variety of application domains, ranging from healthcare to vehicular networks to intelligent manufacturing.[2] To reach adequate performance, however, deep learning models must be trained on very large volumes of data. As illustrated in Figure 1, on a log-log plot the generalisation error rate tends to decrease more or less linearly with the size of the training data: it thus behooves the model designer to move the operating point as far down the learning curve as possible. In other words, the more data the better.[3] The problem is that some of that data may be gathered from highly sensitive sources such as, for example, healthcare providers, financial institutions, Internet-of-Things device vendors and other third-party data processors that handle confidential information for analysis, storage or transfer.

Because of the danger of leakage of private, secure or otherwise sensitive information, the collection and processing of such data and its subsequent encapsulation within deep learning models raise serious privacy concerns. Leakage risk is inherent in any large-scale collection and use of personal data. As demonstrated with past data breaches, it is an ongoing challenge to guarantee resilience to cyber-attacks.[4] In addition, adversarial exploits have alerted us to the possibility of recovering private information from a model via membership inference attacks,[5] model inversion attacks,[6] property inference attacks,[7] and privacy leakage from exchanged gradients in distributed ML architectures.[8] (In a representative example

---

[1] Yann LeCun et al., 'Deep Learning,' *Nature* 521.7553 (2015).

[2] Iyad Rahwan et al., 'Machine Behaviour,' *Nature* 568.7753 (2019).

[3] Joel Hestness et al., 'Predicting Deep Learning Scaling,' U.S. Patent App. Pub. No. US 2020/0175374, June 2020.

[4] Pierangelo Rosati et al., 'Social Media and Stock Price Reaction to Data Breach Announcements: Evidence from US Listed Companies,' *Research in International Business and Finance* 47 (2019).

[5] Reza Shokri et al., 'Membership Inference Attacks Against Machine Learning Models,' *Symp. Security & Privacy* (2017).

[6] Zecheng He et al., 'Model Inversion Attacks Against Collaborative Inference,' in *Proc. 35th Ann. Computer Security Applications Conf.* (2019).

[7] Mathias PM Parisot et al., 'Property Inference Attacks on Convolutional Neural Networks: Influence and Implications of Target Model's Complexity' in *Proc 18th Int Conf Security and Cryptography (SECRYPT)* July 2021.

[8] Aidmar Wainakh et al., 'User-Level Label Leakage from Gradients in Federated Learning,' in *Proc. Privacy Enhancing Technologies* (2022).

**Figure 1** Visualisation of a characteristic learning curve: log-log plot showing error rate against training dataset size – the particular application domain will be further discussed in section V

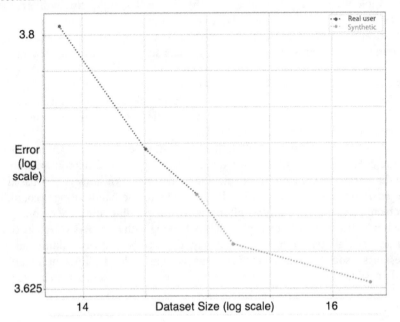

of membership inference attacks, an attacker can gain the ability to infer whether or not data related to a particular patient has been included in the training of an HIV-related ML model.) It is worth noting that resilience to such attacks normally decreases as the associated collections scale up in size, because thorough human curation to verify proper anonymisation, debiasing, coverage, etc rapidly becomes too impractical to perform.

As privacy and data protection concerns gradually gained prominence, a variety of regulations emerged around the world, such as the US Health Insurance Portability and Accountability Act (HIPPA), the European General Data Protection Regulation (GDPR), the Cybersecurity Law of China, the California Consumer Privacy Act (CCPA) etc. Such regulations are increasingly restricting the availability and use of privacy-sensitive data. As a result, they have been changing the way in which deep learning models are trained for real-world applications. With privacy preservation becoming a core requirement, two main compliance directions have emerged: (i) design ML pipelines to be fully private to begin with, and (ii) minimise the scope of data collection by generating artificial data acting as proxy for real data. The present chapter is focused on the latter approach, examining ways synthetic data generation can advantageously serve privacy-preserving deep learning.

## B. Organisation

To sample the typical usage spectrum, the chapter highlights three different use cases associated with common day-to-day features affecting millions of users: statistical language modelling (deployed as part of, eg, speech-to-text recognition in voice assistants like Siri or Alexa), unconstrained handwriting recognition (frequent for data entry on an electronic tablet like Surface or iPad), and swiping keyboard input (a popular option for entering text on a smartphone like iPhone or Galaxy). Each of these application domains faces unique issues requiring a different kind of artificial data, so these three case studies rely on different strategies for practical data generation in the real world.

The chapter is organised as follows. In the next section, we begin by looking at the generic idea of using synthetic data as proxy for real data. In section III, we discuss statistical language modelling, and review synthesis efforts based on targeted augmentation. In section IV, we move to the handwriting recognition problem, and review synthesis efforts based on priming and generation. Next, section V discusses swiping keyboard input, along with a synthesis strategy based on adversarial style transfer. Collectively, these three use cases illuminate key messages associated with synthetic data generation, including inherent limitations and possible mitigation measures. Finally, the chapter concludes with section VI, which summmarises the discussion and offers perspectives for future work.

# II. Privacy and Data Protection

## A. Privacy by Design

An attractive proposition to address the privacy and data protection concerns mentioned in the previous section is to architect ML pipelines to be fully private by design. Toward that goal, two main courses of action have emerged: (i) integrate established encryption mechanisms directly into ML pipelines, or (ii) ensure anonymisation by introducing privacy-preserving methods into ML training and inference. A prominent example of the latter is the introduction of differential privacy techniques into federated learning.[9] Unfortunately, the injection of differential privacy noise into ML training is often deleterious to the accuracy of the resulting model, leading to an inherent trade-off between utility and privacy.

To this day, no unified privacy-preserving solution has yet been found that does not involve sacrificing some utility. To illustrate this, the use of secure multi-party computation approaches incurs either high communication overhead (because of a large volume of intermediate data such as garbled tables of circuitgates that

---

[9] Xuefei Yin et al., 'A Comprehensive Survey of Privacy-Preserving Federated Learning: A Taxonomy, Review, and Future Directions,' *ACM Computing Surveys (CSUR)* 54.6 (2021).

need to be transmitted during the execution of the protocols) or high computation overhead (due to the adopted ciphertext-computational cryptosystems).[10]

## B. Data Synthesis

An alternative proposition is to rely more systematically on synthetic data. Since it is normally sufficient to inform the generation of such data with only a limited amount of real data, data synthesis entails no incremental impact on privacy loss. In addition, this loss becomes much easier to manage given the smaller size of the real dataset. And finally, the artificial nature of the generated data makes it more conducive to detailed error analysis and introspection.

Traditionally, data augmentation has been used as a way to increase the volume of a dataset by adding certain variations to the original dataset to generate 'slightly modified and multiplied' data. This strategy alleviates the problem of limited dataset size and limited data variation, and is therefore useful to enhance model robustness. Based on the type of dataset, different types of synthetic data can be used: there are many data augmentation techniques available for the image/video, audio and text data.[11] But synthetic data can also alleviate a variety of class imbalance problems. Imbalanced datasets are harmful because they bias models toward majority class predictions; they can also make accuracy a deceitful performance metric.[12] Hence both data volume and data diversity considerations can drive synthetic data generation efforts.

Viewing data augmentation through the prism of diversity coverage is particularly interesting given the many variability factors that underlie data diversity. Such factors range from the personal style of the user to the particular task being addressed, to the semantics of the domain, to the level of formality expected by the target audience, to the ambient noise conditions, to the circumstances of the interaction and many other aspects depending on the application domain. Those factors considerably increase the combinatorics of what would need to be represented in the training data for the model to be robust enough to handle all proverbial 'corner cases'. In addition, as training corpora scale up to cover rare combinations of factors, so do opportunities to track down individual users who might be associated with such rare events. Plausible data artificially generated from such rare combinations thus circumvent a potentially severe privacy loss for some users.

In practice, synthetic data generation is therefore necessary to achieve sufficient diversity coverage and model robustness, and thus emerges as an indispensable

---

[10] Runhua Xu et al., 'Privacy-Preserving Machine Learning: Methods, Challenges and Directions,' arxiv.org/abs/2108.04417 (2021).

[11] Connor Shorten and Taghi M. Khoshgoftaar. 'A Survey on Image Data Augmentation for Deep Learning,' *J. Big Data* 6 (2019).

[12] Mateusz Buda et al., 'A Systematic Study of the Class Imbalance Problem in Convolutional Neural Networks,' *Neural Networks* 106 (2018).

complement to conventional data collection efforts. As is well known, failure to properly address the variability factors mentioned above can contribute to well-documented flaws in the resulting machine learning model, such as brittleness, bias, overconfidence and lack of explainability.[13] The question is to what extent it is possible, within a given application domain, to mitigate such flaws via data synthesis. In the following, we focus on three particular case studies to gain insights into the matter.

**Figure 2** Encoder – decoder paradigm for neural statistical language modelling – the role of the encoder is to capture the relevant characteristics of the word history, and the role of the decoder is to predict a word sequence congruent with that general fabric of discourse

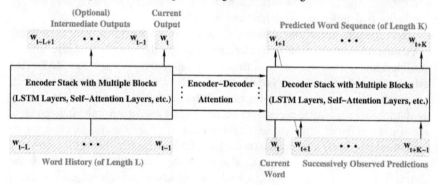

## III. Case Study #1: Statistical Language Modelling

### A. Application Domain

Statistical language modelling plays a central role in many prediction and recognition problems, such as speech/handwriting recognition and keyboard input prediction. An effective language model (LM) is critical to constrain the underlying pattern analysis, guide the search through various (partial) text hypotheses, and/or contribute to the determination of the final outcome. For example, an $n$-gram language model conveys the probability of occurrence in the language of all observed strings of $n$ words, as extracted from a large text database of representative documents.[14] More recently, neural language models have become the de facto standard for estimating the probability distribution of a given text corpus. Many different architectures have been explored, mainly based on recurrent or self-attentive neural networks. Fundamentally, they can all be cast as various

---

[13] Atul Rawal et al., 'Recent Advances in Trustworthy Explainable Artificial Intelligence: Status, Challenges and Perspectives,' *IEEE Transactions on Artificial Intelligence* (November 2021).

[14] Jerome Bellegarda, 'Exploiting Latent Semantic Information in Statistical Language Modeling,' *Proc. IEEE* 88.8 (2000).

instances of sequence-to-sequence learning using the encoder-decoder paradigm[15] illustrated in Figure 2.

As state-of-the-art implementations have grown to comprise an unprecedented number of parameters (175 billion in the case of GPT-3[16] and up to 540 billion in the case of PaLM[17]), training such LMs requires access to massive text corpora for reliable estimation. PaLM, for example, was trained on close to a trillion tokens drawn from a wide variety of domains. Yet, due to the inherent sparsity of natural language, it is impossible for any training corpus to cover all potential words and sentences that can ever be formed in a given language, let alone across multiple languages. It is therefore unlikely that the training data would ever achieve any prescribed level of coverage with minimal redundancy.

An immediate corollary is that the resulting models routinely reflect a variety of deleterious biases naturally occurring in the training data. Bias, fairness and inclusion metrics, disaggregated by different unitary and intersectional population groups, have exposed unintended bias in applications as varied as the detection of smiling faces in images and the detection of toxic comments in text.[18] Such bias can usually be traced to the training data not being sufficiently aligned with previously unforeseen evaluation factors. This misalignment behaviour is even more salient when (private) federated learning is involved, as it becomes impossible to review data contributions from individual sources.

Unfortunately, any finite text corpus is intrinsically imperfect in that regard. Given any large collection of English text, for example, the word 'cat' tends to be more frequent than 'cats' – underscoring a bias toward singular rather than plural forms. It is also much more likely that the word 'surgeon' be associated with masculine than feminine pronouns, whereas for 'nurse' the opposite is true: historically, there has been a systematic gender bias in most professional occupations. By further reinforcing stereotypes like male surgeon/female nurse, such a state of affairs runs counter to the principle of gender equity expected from a 'fair' prediction model.

## B. Synthesis Strategy: Targeted Augmentation

The latter observation has sparked interest into various ways to identify and reduce gender bias in text.[19] One possibility is to alleviate gender imbalance via synthetic

---

[15] Ashish Vaswani et al., 'Attention Is All You Need,' in *Advances in Neural Information Processing Systems* (2018).
[16] Tom B. Brown et al., 'Language Models are Few-Shot Learners,' in *Proc. 34th Int. Conf. Neural Information Processing Systems* (December 2020).
[17] Aakanksha Chowdhery et al., 'PaLM: Scaling Language Modeling with Pathways,' arxiv.org/abs/2204.02311 (October 2022).
[18] Margaret Mitchell et al., 'Model Cards for Model Reporting,' in *ACM Conf. on Fairness, Accountability, and Transparency* (2019).
[19] Emily Dinan et al., 'Multi-Dimensional Gender Bias Classification,' in *Proc. Conf. Empirical Methods in Natural Language Processing (EMNLP)* (November 2020).

data augmentation: for every training sentence referring to a 'surgeon' as a 'he', the training corpus can be augmented with the same sentence referring to the 'surgeon' as a 'she'. The role of such augmentation is to restore gender balance in the corpus by generating artificial sentences modelled after the original sentences but with their pronouns flipped. Similarly, to restore number balance in applications where it matters, data augmentation would generate 'plural' versions of 'singular' sentences, and vice versa, so the model no longer singles out number as a relevant factor.

Note that the success of such targeted augmentation strategy heavily depends on a detailed specification of imbalance targets relevant to a specific application. An illustration of this aspect is provided in Figure 3. The first two sentence pairs correspond to the simple gender bias case evoked earlier, and the next two sentence pairs similarly address straightforward number bias. The last sentence pair involves a more complex take on gender bias, which underscores how arbitrarily tedious the targeted augmentation process can become.

In practice, of course, it is not always obvious what factors are germane to what situation. As a result, this type of rule-based data augmentation strategy comes across as an incomplete solution, which in turn motivates the more sophisticated approaches developed below. Still, in a given application domain, there may not exist any alternative synthesis technique to completely remedy the above shortcomings. For example, we discuss below different techniques targeting other use cases, which cannot be immediately applied to the present case study. Hence targeted augmentation has its place in a well-balanced portfolio of data synthesis recipes, and in particular can often be useful to pre-empt potential information leakage associated with a known type of bias (such as gender bias).

**Figure 3** Examples of targeted data augmentation for language modelling, in case of simple gender bias (first two sentence pairs), simple number bias (next two sentence pairs), and a more complex case of gender bias (last sentence pair)

| Original Sentences | Added Sentences |
| --- | --- |
| The surgeon must scrub his hands | The surgeon must scrub her hands |
| The nurse must scrub her hands | The nurse must scrub his hands |
| The cat is a small carnivorous mammal | Cats are small carnivorous mammals |
| Cats can have kittens from spring to late autumn | A cat can have kittens from spring to late autumn |
| Such scraggly beard makes you look like a Viking | Such long hair makes you look like a Mermaid |

## IV. Case Study #2: Unconstrained Handwriting Recognition

### A. Application Domain

Given the increasing popularity of mobile hardware platforms such as electronic tablets and associated styli, and the related spread of handwriting-friendly software features, handwriting is fast on track to reach the level of prominence of other familiar input modalities like typing and speech. Indeed, it is now easier than ever before for users to generate, archive and retrieve handwritten documents. This in turn has sparked interest in making handwriting recognition ever more robust across many different styles of handwriting, with varying degrees of legibility. (As a speedy input tends to drive toward cursive styles, it tends to increase ambiguity.) To illustrate, Figure 4 shows a number of different idiosyncratic user styles, arranged from pure printed (top) to pure cursive (bottom) handwriting.

Given such a wide range of existing user styles, a data collection effort aimed at sampling words from a large enough vocabulary in every possible writing style at every possible speed is unrealistic. The best that can be hoped for is to collect a limited amount of material from a limited number of distinct writers in a limited number of geographical locations. The outcome is typically not sufficient to train a sufficiently robust handwriting recognition model.[20] At a minimum, there is therefore a need to generate synthetic data to flesh out every style represented in this limited amount of material, for example across many more words than available in the collection.

### B. Synthesis Strategy: Priming and Generation

This problem can be viewed as an instance of priming, where the goal is to synthesize a different semantic content while biasing the synthesis to a given style of expression. Handwriting is generated by converting text into handwriting strokes, and in order to specify which style to generate, the network is primed with a sample from a particular writer. The generated sample ends up copying style elements it has just seen in the priming sample.

This method is quite effective at generating a variety of realistic handwriting styles. To illustrate, Figure 5 shows some examples of priming samples on the left, and the resulting synthesized samples on the right.

---

[20] Salma Shofia Rosyda and Tito Waluyo Purboyo. 'A Review of Various Handwriting Recognition Methods,' *Int. J. of Applied Engineering Research* 13.2 (2018).

**Figure 4** Examples of idiosyncratic handwriting user styles, arranged from printed to cursive (leading to many more strokes in samples at the top than in samples at the bottom) – each stroke is rendered in a different colour for better visualisation

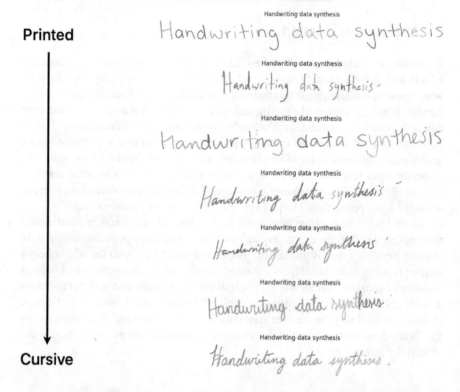

All synthetic samples are reasonably convincing, with two observations particularly worth pointing out. First, in the first sample pair, while the careful printing style is faithfully adopted, upper case is not reproduced in the generated material. Second, in the sample pair with the slanted horizontal baseline, the synthetized sample faithfully reproduces the slant, even though the presence of slant here may only be incidental, as opposed to a strong marker of the underlying style.

As these examples show, which style elements get reproduced is hard to predict with priming, as it is not possible to isolate certain specific aspects of style to be primed. This lack of control may have deleterious consequences for data augmentation, to the extent that it negatively impacts the level of effective coverage that can be achieved. Still, in many common situations, data generation via priming can considerably reduce the need to collect real data, and is therefore useful to alleviate data protection concerns. In other situations where finer control is necessary, the more advanced generative models described in the next section can provide a suitable remedy. Note that this time the more advanced models are also applicable to the present case study since the two setups are close.

## V. Case Study #3: Swiping Keyboard Input

### A. Application Domain

Entering text on a mobile device with a software keyboard can be done via either: (i) tapping virtual keys on the keyboard one after the other, or (ii) sliding the finger on the glass surface in a single continuous motion across successive keys until the intended word is complete. The latter option is referred to as continuous path, or swiping keyboard, input mode. After users gain proficiency with this alternative modality, they often find entering words easier and faster.[21] As in standard tapping, recognition relies on statistical pattern matching enhanced with linguistic knowledge in order to predict the intended word.

**Figure 5** Examples of priming material (left) and corresponding generated handwriting samples (right)

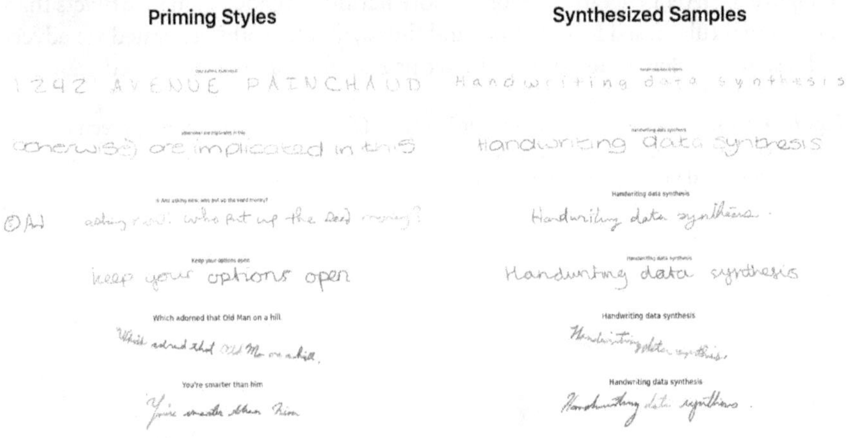

Continuous path keyboard input has higher inherent ambiguity than tapping, because the path trace may exhibit not just local overshoots/undershoots but also, depending on the user, substantial mid-path excursions. Deploying a robust solution requires a large amount of high-quality training data, which is difficult/expensive to collect and annotate. This situation has sparked interest into synthetic paths that could be used as proxies for real user-generated paths.

For example, it is possible to programmatically generate paths by connecting the characters within a word using an algorithm that minimises jerk.[22] The

---

[21] Shyam Reyal et al., 'Performance and User Experience of Touchscreen and Gesture Keyboards in a Lab Setting and in the Wild,' in *Proc. 33rd Ann. ACM Conf. on Human Factors in Computing Systems* (2015).
[22] Ouais Alsharif et al., 'Long Short Term Memory Neural Network for Keyboard Gesture Decoding,' in *Proc. Int. Conf. Acoustics, Speech, Signal Processing* (2015).

parameters of such synthesis algorithms are tuned manually until generated paths look 'similar enough' to real user paths (based on human judgements of a small number of paths). While credible, the ensuing paths are inherently restricted in their expressiveness and, as a result, do not fully capture the variability of user paths. To illustrate, Figure 6 shows a typical user path (top) and synthetic path (bottom left) for the word 'anybody'.

## B. Synthesis Strategy: Adversarial Style Transfer

More recently, generative adversarial networks (GANs) have been used to synthetize more user-realistic training data.[23] In that approach, the problem is cast as an instance of style transfer, where an initial synthetic path produced with simple cubic splines is transformed to conform to user idiosyncrasies observed across a set of real user paths. The kind of path that results is illustrated at the bottom right of Figure 6. GAN generation tends to more faithfully render human artifacts than the original rule-based formulation, and thus synthetic paths generated via adversarial style transfer come across as better proxies for real user-generated paths.

**Figure 6** Path visualisation for input word '**anybody**' – colour changes from green to yellow with time. Typical user path (top), programmatically generated synthetic path (bottom left) and GAN-generated synthetic path (bottom right)

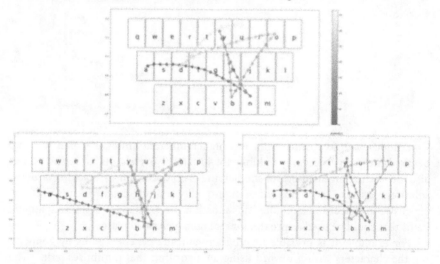

Adversarial style transfer can involve either implicit or explicit style encoding. In the first case, human artifacts are abstracted out from a reference corpus of user paths, which are collectively representative of a range of observed user

---

[23] Akash Mehra et al., 'Leveraging GANs to Improve Continuous Path Keyboard Input Models,' in *Proc. Int. Conf. Acoustics, Speech, Signal Processing* (2020).

idiosyncrasies and/or styles: the notion of style remains diffuse across the entire reference corpus. In contrast, explicit style transfer seeks to disentangle the various factors influencing style by encoding the notion of style at the individual user level. The two approaches have been shown to be complementary in the kind of user-realistic artifacts they generate.[24]

Similar to the previous case study, synthetic data generation in this application helps cope with both high path heterogeneity and unorthodox individual renderings. In particular, it is instrumental to achieving broad coverage in terms of the number of words supported and their associated paths, not just in English but across different languages and layouts. Such behaviour is reflected in the learning curve shown in section I (Figure 1). Since the 'steepness' of that learning curve conveys how quickly a model can learn from adding more training samples, for a given model architecture it also implicitly reflects the quality of the added samples. As the green (GAN) slope is roughly comparable to the blue (user) slope, adding GAN-generated data appears to be almost as effective as adding real user data.

That said, GAN-generated data does not quite capture *all* of the desired user characteristics, as evidenced by the fact that the green slope is slightly less than the blue slope. In principle, explicit adversarial style transfer is capable of bridging the gap since it offers fine control over the various factors influencing style. It nonetheless remains difficult to ascertain with precision to which degree specific factors contribute to a given style. Still, the learning curve of Figure 1 bodes well for reducing data collection costs when extending to other languages and scripts. As a result, adversarial style transfer can advantageously replace the costly collection of potentially privacy-infringing user data.

## VI. Conclusion

### A. Summary

Training ML models with synthetic data naturally promotes data privacy and protection, by virtue of reducing the volume of real data to collect. But beyond being 'just' a means to increase data volume, data synthesis can also have additional benefits. This chapter approached synthetic data generation through the specific prism of expanding training data diversity and speeding up model deployment. Through the analysis of three practical use cases, we have underscored the role of synthetic data in the large-scale deployment of common day-to-day features affecting millions of users.

In statistical language modelling, data synthesis helps address the typical bias we observe in training corpora, such as gender bias in professional occupations.

---

[24] Akash Mehra et al., 'Implicit vs. Explicit Style Transfer? A Comparison of GAN Architectures for Continuous Path Keyboard Input Modeling,' in *Proc. Int. Conf. Acoustics, Speech, Signal Processing* (2021).

In handwriting recognition, it helps make the model more robust to the large variety of idiosyncratic user styles. And in swiping keyboard input, it helps reduce expansion costs by minimising data collection across multiple languages, physical devices and keyboard layouts.

## B. Perspectives

Such case studies suggest that synthetic data generation has a useful role to play in alleviating well documented AI concerns like bias, brittleness and overconfidence. By scaling up training corpora to cover rare combinations of the many variability factors that underlie data diversity, it can contribute to enhancing model robustness without resorting to additional (and potentially privacy-infringing) data collection.

Given the inherent combinatorics of diversity factors, it is highly likely that the ability to synthesize plausible data pertinent to all inevitable 'corner cases' will become ever more critical in the future. In that regard, we believe that synthetic data generation will ultimately prove indispensable to the responsible large-scale deployment of AI technologies.

# VII. Acknowledgments

The author would like to thank the organisers of the CPDP-2022 panel 'Synthetic data meet the GDPR: Opportunities and challenges for scientific research and AI technologies' – this panel served as a fertile catalyst for many profitable discussions on synthetic data generation. He is also grateful to the anonymous reviewers for their constructive remarks on the initial version of the manuscript.

# References

Alsharif, Ouais, Tom Ouyang, Françoise Beaufays, Shumin Zhai, Thomas Breuel and Johan Schalkwyk. 'Long Short Term Memory Neural Network for Keyboard Gesture Decoding.' In *Proc. Int. Conf. Acoustics, Speech, Signal Processing (ICASSP)* (2015).

Bellegarda, Jerome. 'Exploiting Latent Semantic Information in Statistical Language Modeling.' *Proc. IEEE* 88 no. 8 (2000): 1279–1296.

Brown, Tom B., Benjamin Mann, Nick Ryder, Melanie Subbiah, Jared Kaplan, Prafulla Dhariwal, Arvind Neelakantan, Pranav Shyam, Girish Sastry, Amanda Askell, Sandhini Agarwal, Ariel Herbert-Voss, Gretchen Krueger, Tom Henighan, Rewon Child, Aditya Ramesh, Daniel M. Ziegler, Jeffrey Wu, Clemens Winter, Christopher Hesse, Mark Chen, Eric Sigler, Mateusz Litwin, Scott Gray, Benjamin Chess, Jack Clark, Christopher Berner, Sam McCandlish, Alec Radford, Ilya Sutskever and Dario Amodei. 'Language Models are Few-Shot Learners.' In *Proc. 34th Int. Conf. Neural Information Processing Systems (NeurIPS)* (2020): 1877–1901.

Buda, Mateusz, Atsuto Maki and Maciej A. Mazurowski. 'A Systematic Study of the Class Imbalance Problem in Convolutional Neural Networks.' *Neural Networks* 106 (2018): 249-259.

Chowdhery, Aakanksha, Sharan Narang, Jacob Devlin, Maarten Bosma, Gaurav Mishra, Adam Roberts, Paul Barham, Hyung Won Chung, Charles Sutton, Sebastian Gehrmann, Parker Schuh, Kensen Shi, Sasha Tsvyashchenko, Joshua Maynez, Abhishek Rao, Parker Barnes, Yi Tay, Noam Shazeer, Vinodkumar Prabhakaran, Emily Reif, Nan Du, Ben Hutchinson, Reiner Pope, James Bradbury, Jacob Austin, Michael Isard, Guy Gur-Ari, Pengcheng Yin, Toju Duke, Anselm Levskaya, Sanjay Ghemawat, Sunipa Dev, Henryk Michalewski, Xavier Garcia, Vedant Misra, Kevin Robinson, Liam Fedus, Denny Zhou, Daphne Ippolito, David Luan, Hyeontaek Lim, Barret Zoph, Alexander Spiridonov, Ryan Sepassi, David Dohan, Shivani Agrawal, Mark Omernick, Andrew M. Dai, Thanumalayan Sankaranarayana Pillai, Marie Pellat, Aitor Lewkowycz, Erica Moreira, Rewon Child, Oleksandr Polozov, Katherine Lee, Zongwei Zhou, Xuezhi Wang, Brennan Saeta, Mark Diaz, Orhan Firat, Michele Catasta, Jason Wei, Kathy MeierHellstern, Douglas Eck, Jeff Dean, Slav Petrov and Noah Fiedel. 'PaLM: Scaling Language Modeling with Pathways' (2022). arxiv.org/abs/2204.02311.

Dinan, Emily, Angela Fan, Ledell Wu, Jason Weston, Douwe Kiela and Adina Williams. 'MultiDimensional Gender Bias Classification.' In *Proc. Conf. Empirical Methods in Natural Language Processing (EMNLP)* (2020): 314-331.

He, Zecheng, Tianwei Zhang and Ruby B. Lee. 'Model Inversion Attacks Against Collaborative Inference.' In *Proc. 35th Ann. Computer Security Applications Conference (ACSAC)* (2019): 148-162.

Hestness, Joel, Gregory Diamos, Heewoo Jun, Sharan Narang, Newsha Ardalani, Md. Mostofa Ali Patwary and Yanqi Zhou. 'Predicting Deep Learning Scaling.' U.S. Patent Application Publication No. US 2020/0175374 (2020).

LeCun, Yann, Yoshua Bengio and Geoffrey Hinton. 'Deep Learning.' *Nature* 521 no. 7553 (2015): 436-444.

Mehra, Akash, Jerome R. Bellegarda, Ojas Bapat, Hema Koppula, Rick Chang, Ashish Shrivastava and Oncel Tuzel. 'Implicit vs. Explicit Style Transfer? A Comparison of GAN Architectures for Continuous Path Keyboard Input Modeling.' In *Proc. Int. Conf. Acoustics, Speech, Signal Processing (ICASSP)* (2021).

Mehra, Akash, Jerome R. Bellegarda, Ojas Bapat, Partha Lal and Xin Wang. 'Leveraging GANs to Improve Continuous Path Keyboard Input Models.' In *Proc. Int. Conf. Acoustics, Speech, Signal Processing (ICASSP)* (2020).

Mitchell, Margaret, Simone Wu, Andrew Zaldivar, Parker Barnes, Lucy Vasserman, Ben Hutchinson, Elena Spitzer, Inioluwa Deborah Raji and Timnit Gebru. 'Model Cards for Model Reporting.' In *ACM Conf. on Fairness, Accountability, and Transparency (FAT)* (2019): 220-229.

Parisot, Mathias P.M., Balazs Pejo and Dayana Spagnuelo. 'Property Inference Attacks on Convolutional Neural Networks: Influence and Implications of Target Model's Complexity.' In *Proc. 18th Int. Conf. Security & Cryptography (SECRYPT)* (2021).

Rahwan, Iyad, Manuel Cebrian, Nick Obradovich, Josh Bongard, Jean-François Bonnefon, Cynthia Breazeal, Jacob W. Crandall, Nicholas A. Christakis, Iain D. Couzin, Matthew O. Jackson, Nicholas R. Jennings, Ece Kamar, Isabel M. Kloumann, Hugo Larochelle, David Lazer, Richard McElreath, Alan Mislove, David C. Parkes, Alex 'Sandy' Pentland, Margaret E. Roberts, Azim Shariff, Joshua B. Tenenbaum and Michael Wellman. 'Machine Behaviour.' *Nature* 568 no. 7753 (2019): 477-486.

Rawal, Atul, James Mccoy, Danda B. Rawat, Brian M. Sadler and Robert St. Amant, 'Recent Advances in Trustworthy Explainable Artificial Intelligence: Status, Challenges and Perspectives.' *IEEE Transactions on Artificial Intelligence* (2021).

Reyal, Shyam, Shumin Zhai and Per Ola Kristensson. 'Performance and User Experience of Touchscreen and Gesture Keyboards in a Lab Setting and in the Wild.' In *Proc. 33rd Ann. ACM Conf. on Human Factors in Computing Systems* (2015): 679–688.

Rosati, Pierangelo, Peter Deeney, Mark Cummins, Lisa Van der Werff and Theo Lynn. 'Social Media and Stock Price Reaction to Data Breach Announcements: Evidence from US Listed Companies.' *Research in International Business and Finance* 47 (2019): 458–469.

Rosyda, Salma Shofia and Tito Waluyo Purboyo. 'A Review of Various Handwriting Recognition Methods.' *Int. J. of Applied Engineering Research* 13 no. 2 (2018): 1155–1164.

Shokri, Reza, Marco Stronati, Congzheng Song and Vitaly Shmatikov. 'Membership Inference Attacks Against Machine Learning Models.' *IEEE Symposium on Security and Privacy (SP)* (2017): 3–18.

Shorten, Connor and Taghi M. Khoshgoftaar. 'A Survey on Image Data Augmentation for Deep Learning.' *J. Big Data* 6 no. 1 (2019): 1:48.

Vaswani, Ashish, Noam Shazeer, Niki Parmar, Jakob Uszkoreit, Llion Jones, Aidan N. Gomez, Lukasz Kaiser and Illia Polosukhin. 'Attention Is All You Need.' In *Advances in Neural Information Processing Systems* (2018): 1–11.

Wainakh, Aidmar, Fabrizio G. Ventola, Till Mu¨ßig, Jens Keim, Carlos Garcia Cordero, Ephraim Zimmer, Tim Grube, Kristian Kersting and M. Mu¨hlh¨auser, 'User-Level Label Leakage from Gradients in Federated Learning.' In *Proc. Privacy Enhancing Technologies* (2022): 227–244.

Xu, Runhua, Nathalie Baracaldo and James Joshi. 'Privacy-Preserving Machine Learning: Methods, Challenges and Directions' (2021). arxiv.org/abs/2108.04417.

Yin, Xuefei, Yanming Zhu and Jiankun Hu. 'A Comprehensive Survey of Privacy-Preserving Federated Learning: A Taxonomy, Review, and Future Directions.' *ACM Computing Surveys (CSUR)* 54 no. 6 (2021): 1–36.

# 3

# Chinese Data Protection in Transition: A Look at Enforceability of Rights and the Role of Courts

HUNTER DORWART*

## Abstract

In recent years, the Chinese government has solidified its data protection framework through a series of laws and regulations to address the social, economic and political challenges posed by the digital age. Many of these policy instruments explicitly recognise data subject rights and set forth numerous obligations for entities processing personal information – a trend seen in other regulatory approaches around the world. While much of the academic community has focused on the implementation of this larger framework through China's top-down, centrally administered institutions, little discussion has focused on the role of courts in enforcing these rights at the local level. This chapter attempts to address that gap by examining recent privacy litigation in China and situating it within China's larger governance structure. While privacy litigation is increasing, such litigation will likely play a secondary and complementary role to efforts undertaken by other central institutions. Nonetheless, courts in China will likely help resolve smaller-scale disputes on the local level where enforcement from the top proves challenging. Unravelling this role puts the international data protection community one step ahead in understanding the complexities of data privacy enforcement in China.

## Keywords

Chinese data protection, global privacy, Chinese law, Chinese courts, data subject rights

* The Future of Policy Forum, USA.

## I. Introduction

In recent years, data protection and governance has become an important topic for policymakers in China.[1] While debates around Internet governance have circulated in the country for quite some time, an elevated sense of urgency now permeates much of the discourse. Indeed many stakeholders in government, industry and academia agree that the widespread collection and use of data now operates as a central prism through which the government can realise its societal and economic goals.[2] Communication networks enable individuals to connect with one another at an unprecedented scale, streamlining operational processes and generating new sources of value for individuals and companies.[3] Advances in cloud computing and fifth-generation (5G) low latency networks promise to enable a range of cybernetic industrial activities, revolutionise global logistics and introduce applications related to connected vehicles and smart cities.[4] Key to this is transforming China into the next technological and scientific world leader – a priority outlined extensively in the country's 14th Five Year Plan (FYP).[5]

Yet the realisation of China's goals has not come without obstacles. On the one hand, the rapid transition to the online world has also resulted in a multitude of harms to individuals and consumers in the country. Government authorities have struggled to combat deceptive data practices including unfair algorithmic decision-making, unauthorised disclosures and profiling through online tracking.[6] The rapid growth of large-scale platforms through network effects and data aggregation has given rise to anti-monopoly concerns that have led to a series of recent enforcement targeting nearly every aspect of the digital economy.[7] This has generated a growing public backlash against the widespread collection, use and disclosure of personal information by the largest tech firms in China.[8]

On the other hand, such technologies have also redefined the contours of power on a global stage. Chinese leaders increasingly view technology through the

---

[1] For a general overview see eg, Chuanman You, 'Law and Policy of Platform Economy in China,' *Computer Law & Security Review* 39 (2020); William Chou, Iris Li and Lingxiao Zhang, 'New Governance of the Platform Economy' (Deloitte, 2020), 75–85.

[2] 'Outline of the People's Republic of China 14th Five-Year Plan for National Economic and Social Development and Long-Range Objectives for 2035' (*Xinhua News Agency*, 12 March 2021) cset.georgetown.edu/wp-content/uploads/t0284_14th_Five_Year_Plan_EN.pdf.

[3] See Gerald C. Kane et al., 'Aligning the Organization for its Digital Future' (MIT Sloan Management Review, 2016).

[4] S. Aslam and H. Sami Ullah, 'A Comprehensive Review of Smart Cities Components, Applications, and Technologies Based on Internet of Thing' (*Arxiv*, 2020) arxiv.org/abs/2002.01716; Leonardo Guevara and Fernando Auat Cheein, 'The Role of 5G Technologies: Challenges in Smart Cities and Intelligent Transportation Systems' Sustainability (2020): 6469–6492, www.mdpi.com/2071-1050/12/16/6469.

[5] See n. 2.

[6] Wei Han, 'Baidu Sued Over Claim It Illegally Obtained Users' Data' (*Caixin*, 2018); Jianhuang Qin, Tong Qian and Wei Han, 'Cover Story: The Fight Over China's Law to Protect Personal Data' (*Caixin*, 2020).

[7] See eg Hunter Dorwart and Gabriela Zanfir-Fortuna, 'Spotlight on the Emerging Chinese Data Protection Framework: Lessons Learned From the Unprecedented Investigation of Didi Chuxing' (Future of Privacy Forum, 2021).

[8] Qin, Qian and Han (n. 6).

lens of national security and related interests.[9] As a result, policymakers in China have formulated government strategies to minimise dependency on international supply chains, build self-reliance on domestic capabilities and develop resiliency in sourcing critical technological inputs.[10] From semiconductors and software to critical infrastructure, powerful interest groups within the country now perceive technological interdependence as undermining national interest and generating exploitable vulnerabilities in information technology (IT) networks.[11]

In partial response to these obstacles, the Chinese government adopted a series of laws and regulations to better solidify the country's legal framework for data governance. Like other jurisdictions around the globe, data protection and privacy form a crucial pillar in this larger legal framework.[12] China promulgated the Cybersecurity Law in 2017, which mandates that network operators comply with a series of security requirements including those related to personal information processing, compiled a Civil Code in 2020 containing a chapter on personality rights involving privacy and data protection, and adopted both the Data Security Law and the Personal Information Protection Law (PIPL) in 2021. Additionally, multiple ministries within China's vast bureaucracy have formulated their own regulations and industry standards, which deal primarily with sector-specific issues and clarify key aspects of the laws mentioned above.

Both the Civil Code and the PIPL create enforceable data subject rights modelled explicitly off the EU's General Data Protection Regulation (GDPR) and impose obligations on data controllers to give effect to these rights when requested.[13] Moreover, under Chinese law, public bodies must also comply with these requirements and follow the principles of transparency, fairness and accountability – a process well-aligned with internationally recognised norms.[14] While the laws serve other interests besides protecting individuals, the emergence of this legal architecture underscores the government's desire to empower such individuals to enforce their data subject rights and promote a healthier data ecosystem in the future.[15]

Like other aspects of governance in China, privacy and security regulation has largely been realised through centralised, top-down institutions. Analysts focus heavily on the formulation of laws, regulations and industry standards for signals of market risk while emphasising enforcement actions to explain changes in corporate behaviour. They do so for good reason – China's legal system places a great deal of importance on the central bureaucracy to accomplish its regulatory

---

[9] Ambak Kak and Samm Sacks, 'Shifting Narratives and Emergent Trends in Data-Governance Policy: Developments in China, India, and the EU' (Policy Memo, 2021), 6.
[10] Ryan Fedasiuk, Emily Weinstein and Anna Puglisi, 'China's Foreign Technology Wish List' (Center for Security and Emerging Technology, 2021) 3.
[11] See section II below.
[12] Emmanuel Pernot-Leplay, 'China's Approach on Data Privacy Law: A Third Way Between the U.S. and the EU?' *Penn State Journal of Law & International Affairs* 8 (2020): 49–117.
[13] See section II(B) below.
[14] ibid.
[15] See section II(B) below.

goals and often relies on informal relationships between government regulators and industry leaders to effectuate larger policies. However, ignored in this focus is the role of courts in China and how they will guide the enforceability of data protection rights on a national level. Given the country's unique political and legal system, many questions remain as to the specifics of enforceability. How will individuals in China meaningfully enforce their rights when faced with a complex set of institutional and political barriers? To what extent will the legal system play a role in this process and what is the best way to characterise this role? Are individuals in China exercising their rights through courts or other forms of judicial adjudication? Do courts have the authority and the ability within China to significantly change the data processing behaviours of local governments or corporate entities? Does Chinese data protection law meaningfully constrain the power of public bodies?[16]

This chapter seeks to address these issues by offering an analysis of privacy and data protection litigation in China. Specifically it attempts to address the role of courts in China for data protection and in particular the exercise of data protection rights. First, it examines the relevant provisions in both the PIPL and the recently compiled (编纂) Civil Code (2020) that sets forth data protection rights and obligations for entities processing personal information. Second, it analyses recent privacy case law in Chinese courts and attempts to identify notable trends in the enforceability of data subject rights on the grassroots level. Last, it contextualises these trends within the overall structure of China's governmental system by addressing the structural limitations of litigation in the country as a mechanism for broad policy implementation as well as the complexities behind enforcing rights in the civil context.

While data privacy litigation is increasing in both scale and frequency, it will most likely play a backseat role in China's overall regulatory system. China's unique governance system creates the impression that when courts act, they do so largely with the approval of the central government or within an accepted governance framework. In other words, legal compliance culture revolves around understanding what the central authorities want, who often formulate regulatory guidelines before the passage of any law or the announcement of any enforcement action.[17] Indeed, this system demands that lawyers and analysts trained in other models of legal organisation such as those in the US or European Union reevaluate their preconceptions about the appropriate legal structure of government and the role of the judiciary in that structure. Instead, properly contextualising China's legal system within the overall regulatory structure of the government requires approaching China on its own terms.[18]

Nonetheless, while the central government in China will take the lead in targeting large-scale market participants for their data privacy and protection abuses,

---

[16] See section IV below.

[17] Paul Triolo et al., 'China's Cybersecurity Law One Year On: An Evolving and Interlocking Framework' (*New America*, 2019), 3.

[18] Jingjing Liu, 'Overview of the Chinese Legal System,' *Environmental Law Institute* 1 (2013): 1–12.

courts will still play a role in resolving smaller-scale disputes, offer private litigants the ability to hold certain entities accountable and even bring cases against larger actors through the civil public interest litigation vehicle. They may also help fill in the details of certain regulations or industry standards issued from ministries by providing guidance on ambiguous terms or the requirements for compliance.

This chapter does not attempt to provide an exhaustive overview of privacy litigation in China, nor does it offer a comprehensive model through which to view developments in Chinese law regarding data protection. Rather it aims to present a useful framework within which to address these concerns and explore ways in which recent litigation data fits within the larger trends related to data governance. Due to this more tailored goal, this chapter does not address some of the notable issues that characterise the problems of legal reform in China such as the execution of civil judgments, the lack of consistency or uniformity in the structure of the bureaucracy or the subordination of courts to other institutions. Nor does it focus on other notable laws in Chinese data governance that deal primarily with security and data classification issues.

Section II presents an overview of how data protection and privacy has evolved in China with a particular focus on the provisions of the PIPL and the Civil Code that touch upon data subject rights. Section III, in turn, delves into the case law regarding these provisions and highlights some notable takeaways from the data. Section IV offers a synthesized account of the roles of courts for data protection in China and addresses some of the key questions facing their efficacy in relation to other governance institutions. Section V provides concluding remarks.

## II. Overview of Personal Data Protection in China

The development of data privacy in China presents a long and complicated history.[19] Mirroring the profound socio-technological developments in China at the end of the twentieth century, conceptions of privacy in the 1980s began to expand to accommodate the new demands of the transition to a market-based mixed economy.[20] While not always directly visible, Chinese scholars at the time took great care to document the changes on the local level and often framed their analyses through psychological terms and sociological concepts.[21] Such studies highlighted a variety of changing social expectations that led to the emergence of a 'self-consciousness' right of privacy such as declining an interlocutor's questions about a sensitive topic, conceptualising privacy beyond its limited definition in

---

[19] Yehan Huang and Mingli Shi, 'Top Scholar Zhou Hanhua Illuminates 15+ Years of History Behind China's Personal Information Protection Law' (*DigiChina*, 2021).
[20] Yao Huai Lu, 'Privacy and Data Privacy Issues in Contemporary China,' *Ethics and Information Technology* 7 (2005): 7–15.
[21] See eg D.L. Liu, 'On Privacy and Right to Privacy,' *Social Science* 8 (2003); R.F. Li and Y. Na, 'A Philosophical Reflection on the Loss of Privacy,' *Science, Technology and Dialectics* 5 (2003): 38–41.

the common word *yinsi* (阴私) (ie, a shameful secret) and expecting privacy in new circumstances around the family and one's education.[22] Legal scholars similarly noted important changes within the law that reinforced privacy protection in certain circumstances.[23]

With the popularisation of the Internet in the 1990s, privacy problems around data began to emerge, both as a matter of domestic regulation and foreign engagement.[24] The rapid spread of e-commerce introduced new risks for consumer protection and facilitated a market for all types of personal and confidential information.[25] In addition, communication networks provided a new infrastructure for the dissemination of information that greatly increased the possibility of connectivity and information sharing.[26] Chinese leaders quickly saw the immense potential of Internet technologies not only for the digitalisation of the market economy but also for China's capacity to lead innovation and secure the promise of building a robust middle class of consumers.[27] Over time, these goals became more explicitly tied to the Chinese government's larger developmental and global engagement objectives, especially in the post-2008 period.[28]

However, these leaders also recognised that if unregulated, global communication technologies could undermine the structures of social, economic and political stability.[29] In fact, the Chinese government was one of the first in the world to place special attention on *the role of the state* in regulating the ICT industry.[30] In the late 1990s, it developed comprehensive censorship protocols early on, initiated a nationwide network-security and traffic management system through the Golden Shield Project (金盾工程), and operationalised both offensive and defensive cyber capabilities.[31] It also laid the foundation for state regulation of Internet

---

[22] See eg Hansheng Zheng, '21st Century Chinese: Time, Competition, and Privacy,' (二十一世纪的中国人—时间，竞争，隐私). *China Soft Science* 2 (1994): 47–49.《中国软科学》(1994 年第 2 期第 47–49 页).

[23] C.M. Zhou and C.W. Qu, 'Right to Data Privacy and Legal Protection of It,' *Lawyers World* (2001): 30.

[24] X.B. Zhang, 'The Development of IT and the Protection of Right to Privacy,' *Law and Social Development* (1996): 16–25.

[25] See Huang and Shi (n. 19).

[26] See Haiping Zheng, 'Regulating the Internet: China's Law and Practice,' *Beijing Law Review* 4 (2013).

[27] While these developmental goals have changed in nature and context over time, there is a striking continuity between the early rationalisations of what the Internet could provide, and more recent policy iterations outlined in the 14th Five Year Plan (2020–2025). Severine Arsene, 'China, Internet Governance and the Global Public Interest,' *A New Responsible Power China* (2018): 72–83.

[28] Shulin Gu and Bengt-Ake Lundvall, 'China's Innovation System and the Move Towards Harmonious Growth and Endogenous Innovation,' *Innovation: Organization and Management* 8 (2006): 1–26.

[29] Chuanying Lu (鲁传颖), 'Evolution of the Concept of Sovereignty in the Challenges of the Interne Age,' (主权概念的演进及其在网络时代的挑战). *International Relations Studies* 1 (2014): 75–77. 《国际关系研究》.

[30] Rongjun Yang (杨嵘均), 'On Problems and Strategies of International Cooperation in Cyberspace Governance,' (伦王国空间治理国际合作面临的及其应对策略). *Normal University Journal of Social Studies* 79 (2014) (廣西師範大學學报): 79.

[31] Sonali Chandel et al., 'The Golden Shield Project of China: A Decade Later,' (Institute of Electrical and Electronics Engineers (IEEE), 2019).

companies through strengthening the country's licensing and certification mechanisms.[32] The Chinese government accomplished this through a combination of laws, regulations and technical standards with the State Council playing a leading role in the coordination of lower-level operational departments.[33]

To be sure, China was not the only country to prioritise regulation over the Internet and communication technologies. Indeed, building institutional and technical capacity in this space was a challenge faced by nearly all countries that had access to the technologies, even if such access was uneven due to historical and developmental conditions.[34] Yet what made China's approach unique was its emphasis on the priority of *national* competence over the Internet space and the clear demarcation of Chinese sovereignty from a transnational system of interconnected networks largely overseen by non-governmental entities.[35]

China recognised early on the importance of data protection in this ecosystem of technologies. While debates around privacy began to change in the late 1990s, personal information protection issues took on an independent direction from privacy and often intertwined with larger Internet governance issues like network traffic monitoring, cyber incident reporting, critical infrastructure management and information security.[36] In 2001, China initiated a legislative process to regulate data protection through the National Informatization Leading Group and the Informatization Office and Export Advisory Committee under the State Council.[37] While these offices formulated many regulations and standards and even proposed a draft Personal Information Protection law in 2005, the Chinese government chose not to promulgate a comprehensive law but rather improved and passed a series of sectoral laws, regulations and industrial standards to address the issue.[38]

However, in recent years, the Chinese government has recognised the necessity of developing a nationally coordinated framework for data protection and security to strengthen compliance and provide for a more consistent governance and enforcement system.[39] It adopted a comprehensive Cybersecurity Law in 2017,

---

[32] Lu Wei et al., 'Internet Development in China', *Journal of Information Science* 28 (2002).
[33] ibid.
[34] See Milton L. Mueller, *Networks and States: The Global Politics of Internet Governance* (Boston: MIT Press, 2010).
[35] To be clear, China's engagement in the international Internet governance debate is far from straightforward. Government leaders have at many times both supported and distanced themselves from international organisations like ICANN and multistakeholder standard-setting bodies like the W3C or the IETF. This dual strategy should come as no surprise as Chinese leaders have emphasised that while needing reform, the current architecture of the Internet serves a useful purpose. See Zhixiong Huang (黄志雄), 'International Law in Cyberspace: China's Status, Position, and Strategy,' (网络空间国际法制：中国的立场主张和对策). *Yunnan Minzu University Press* 32 (2015): 137 (云南民族大学学报).
[36] See Huang and Shi (n. 19).
[37] ibid.
[38] For instance, the Law on the Protection of Consumers (2013) applied nascent data protection expectations on companies while various regulations governed network security and trafficking.
[39] See eg Peixi Xu, 'A Chinese Perspective on the Future of Cyberspace' (Cyberstability Paper Series, 2021); Rogier Creemers, 'The Pivot in Chinese Cybergovernance: Integrating Internet Control in Xi Jinping's China' (China Perspectives, 2015), 5–13.

promulgated new rules on data security, classification and exchange through the Data Security Law and recently formulated the Personal Information Protection Law in 2021, as well as an innumerable number of regulations and technical standards on the ministerial level.[40] Additionally, immediately prior to this, the State Council pursued government reform measures that reorganised the competences of the central bureaucracy, refurbished departments within key agencies, and created new supra-ministerial bodies such as the Cyberspace Administration of China (CAC) and the Central Cyberspace Affairs Commission. The goals of these regulatory activities are strikingly similar to those outlined in a 2003 State Informatization Leading Group report (ZBF. No. [2003]27): to develop a comprehensive network and information system that protects critical technologies through industrial competitiveness, cyber awareness and talent management and data protection standards.[41]

Part of this larger strategy involves granting individuals data subject rights and imposing obligations on data controllers to respect these rights in their processing activities. This section seeks to provide more details on how this legal mechanism will work by offering an analysis of two legal instruments – the PIPL and the Civil Code. First, it provides a brief overview of the PIPL with a particular emphasis on the provisions concerning data subject rights and processing obligations. Second, it outlines relevant provisions in China's recently compiled (编纂) Civil Code, which sets out a new chapter covering data protection rights and significantly improves an older chapter dealing with privacy. This section does not provide an exhaustive analysis of the laws but rather highlights their key takeaways and situates them within the broader context of how data subjects in China enforce rights vis-à-vis data controllers and processors, particularly in the context of legal adjudication via courts and other court-sanctioned methods.

## A. The Personal Information Protection Law (PIPL)

On 20 August 2021, the National People's Congress (NPC) adopted China's first comprehensive data protection law – the Personal Information Protection Law (PIPL) – concluding a legislative process that began a year earlier. The PIPL represents one pillar of China's emerging data protection architecture that includes a myriad of other laws, industry-specific regulations, and standards.[42] Additionally,

---

[40] DigiChina, Stanford Cyber Policy Center. digichina.stanford.edu/.
[41] 'Opinions Concerning Strengthening Information Security Protection Work' (State Informatization Leading Group, ZBF No. [2003]27), chinacopyrightandmedia.wordpress.com/2003/09/07/opinions-concerning-strengthening-information-security-protection-work.
[42] For instance, the recently enacted Data Security Law (DSL) sets forth a comprehensive list of requirements regarding the security and transferability of other types of data. It also establishes a 'marketplace for data' to enable data exchange and digitalisation.

the PIPL explicitly references China's Constitution to provide a firmer legal basis for the law's implementation, particularly around the compilation and enactment of the Civil Code (see below). As such, the PIPL should not be viewed in isolation but rather examined in relation to these other regulatory tools that serve complimentary, albeit different purposes.

Throughout the legislative process, privacy professionals within China played a key role in formulating not only the normative goals of the law but also the principles through which it will be operationalised. These experts drew heavily on the lessons learned from the implementation of the GDPR, which served both as a reference for the PIPL and previous data protection regulations such as the Personal Information Specification of 2018.[43] Indeed, like the GDPR, the PIPL sets forth a range of obligations, administrative guidelines and enforcement mechanisms with respect to the processing of personal information. For instance, it applies to very broadly defined 'personal information' (which carries an element of identifiability), includes lawful grounds for processing after the GDPR model, and applies to the 'handling' (处理) of personal information, including the collection of data itself.[44] Notably, the PIPL does not contain a legitimate interest exception and, although other lawful grounds exist, it relies heavily on consent for most processing activities.[45]

Additionally, the PIPL has rules for joint handling with respect to processing on behalf of an original handler, including agreements that must be put in place before subsequent processing like Articles 26 and 28 in the GDPR. The law applies both to the 'private' and 'public' sectors but contains provisions that exempt compliance when other laws or regulations take priority, including when processing must be done in coordination with state secrecy and confidentiality requirements.[46] For instance, state organs, critical information infrastructure operators and other handlers reaching a specific volume of processed personal

---

[43] As discussed below more thoroughly, Chinese legal scholars have drawn heavily from texts and codes from European continental law traditions and often look to other models of regulation for guidance and inspiration when contemplating their own drafting. See section II(B) below.

[44] Note the PIPL nor the Civil Code use the concept of 'processing' but rather prefer the term 'handling'. In terms of definition, there is no big difference between handling as understood in Chinese law and processing as understood by the GDPR.

[45] These include where necessary to conclude a contract or for human resource management, where necessary to fulfill statutory duties; where necessary to respond to sudden public health incidents, where done in a reasonable manner for the purpose of news reporting, where the data processed has been publicly disclosed by the data subject, or other circumstances provided in laws or regulations.

[46] As discussed below more thoroughly, the distinction between private and public bodies does not readily apply to China's unique political economy, which complicates using the dichotomy to understand Chinese law.

Nevertheless, it is important to highlight that the PIPL will restrict the processing activities of certain public bodies, particularly those on the local level. Indeed, one point of this chapter is to highlight that the Chinese data protection law does in fact empower Chinese nationals to enforce their rights vis-à-vis public bodies. See section III below.

information must meet a broad range of data localisation requirements. Specifically, these handlers must comply with certain obligations before transferring data abroad, such as undergoing a security assessment by relevant authorities or complying with a standard contractual clause (SCC).[47] Like the GDPR, the law mandates risk assessments in the form of a personal information impact assessment for specific processing including automated decision-making and handling that could have 'a major influence on individuals'. Data handlers must also appoint Data Protection Officers (DPOs) in specific situations, which vary depending on the volume of PI processed, and conduct regular compliance training.

This broad convergence with the GDPR indicates that Chinese data protection leaders envision the regulation of data in the country in a manner not too dissimilar from well-established principles in the EU and around the world. Perhaps the most notable convergence of the EU tradition with the Chinese framework comes through the provisions of the PIPL dealing with the rights of the data subject. Under the law, personal information handlers must establish mechanisms to accept and process applications from individuals to exercise their rights. If the information handlers reject the request, they must explain the reason for doing so. The draft law recognises the following rights:

- Right to *know, decide, refuse, and limit* the handling of their personal information by others. Note it is unclear if this processing needs to be based on consent or if the individual must provide the information prior to the processing.
- Right to *access and copy* their personal information in a *timely manner*.
- Right to *correct or complete* inaccurate personal information in a *timely manner*.
- Right to *deletion* if: (i) the agreed retention period has expired, or the handling purpose has been achieved; (ii) personal information handlers cease the provision of services; (iii) the individual rescinds consent; (iv) the information is handled in violation of laws, regulations, or agreements.
- Right to request handlers *explain* their handling rules, including when an individual believes an algorithm has made a decision that affects their interests.
- Right to *data portability* to be defined by subsequent regulations.

As discussed below, the Civil Code also promulgates these rights but goes further in establishing legal requirements specific to privacy and outlines key instances in which a handler can violate a data subject's privacy rights.

However, in contrast to the GDPR, which serves the fundamental right to protection of personal data and aims to ensure the free flow of personal data between Member States, the PIPL serves several other objectives. For example, it aims to promote and protect China's national security and affirms China's

---

[47] The CAC released a draft version of the SCCs in mid-2022.

intention to defend its digital sovereignty as articulated through the concept of cyber-sovereignty.[48] Under the law, overseas entities which infringe the rights of Chinese citizens or jeopardise the national security or public interests of China will be placed on a blacklist and any transfers of personal information of Chinese citizens to these entities will be restricted or even barred. China will also reciprocate against countries or regions that take discriminatory, prohibitive or restrictive measures against China with respect to the protection of personal information.[49] These provisions, in part, also reinforce China's ambition to take full part in international protection discussions and actively contribute to setting global standards for technology regulation generally.

**Table 1** Comparisons of PIPL to GDPR

|  | PIPL | GDPR |
| --- | --- | --- |
| Right to access data | ✓ | ✓ |
| Right to correct data | ✓ | ✓ |
| Right to delete data | ✓ | ✓ |
| Right to data portability | ✓ | ✓ |
| Right to decline processing | ✓ | ✓ |
| Subject to automated decision* | ✗ | ✓ |
| Right to explanation | ✓ | ✓ |
| Purpose limitation | ✓ | ✓ |

* There is some debate as to what the automated decision-making provisions in the PIPL mean in context and practice, especially as they relate to the GDPR's own provisions on the subject matter.

## B. Compiled Privacy and Data Protection Provisions in the Chinese Civil Code

A year before the adoption of the PIPL, Chinese regulators took one step forward in operationalising China's data protection architecture by concluding the compilation process of the country's generally applicable Civil Code. On 28 May 2020, the National People's Congress (NPC) approved the Civil Code of the People's Republic of China[50] (中华人民共和国民法) (the Code) after a relatively lengthy compilation process.[51] The Code, which came into effect in 2021, explicitly recognises

---

[48] This refers to the idea that the Internet and the technological networks that make global communication possible should not override the ability of the state to determine its own rules over cyberspace.
[49] Article 43.
[50] Civil Code of the People's Republic of China (2020) (Civil Code).
[51] ibid.

the 'right to privacy' as one of the personality rights stipulated under Part 4 and includes a chapter on 'Privacy and Personal Information Protection'.[52] Other categories of rights of personality include life, body and health rights, portrait rights (ie, right to one's own image) and rights of reputation and honor.[53] As a generally applicable code of civil laws, the provisions concerning privacy and data protection will apply across industries and in all civil and commercial matters. The rights laid out likewise belong to individuals as natural persons, regardless of whether they are consumers, employees, taxpayers or minors and can be enforced against a person or entity that infringes them unless special laws take precedence.

The codification of the Civil Code in China has followed a long historical path that predates the formal creation of the People's Republic of China (PRC) in 1949.[54] While the process of formulating a civil law system faced many political obstacles during the early years of the PRC, there were multiple attempts to develop preliminary draft materials throughout the 1950s and 1960s, modelled on the Soviet Union Civil Code of 1922.[55] After 1978, Chinese leaders recognised the necessity of reforming the legal system to better accommodate civil and commercial matters for China's transition to a semi-market economy but were hesitant in finalising the civil code due to uncertainties as to how it would relate to the competences of the larger administrative structure.[56] In 1986, the NPC promulgated the General Principles of Civil Law as a temporary solution, which set forth a foundation for the development of private law in China, including laws that governed property relations between individuals as private economic actors.[57]

In the transition to a 'socialist market economy' in 1993, the NPC initiated another round of codification and by 2002 had introduced a Draft Code.[58] The legislative process faced numerous hurdles at this time as the Draft Code contained a patchwork of existing laws that generated much controversy between members

---

[52] ibid Arts 1032–1039.

[53] ibid.

[54] China has long belonged to the 'civil law' tradition, with codification of legal rules dating back to its early dynastic history. Before the 'modern' period, China's laws were largely punitive in nature, resulting in the development of criminal legal processes but relatively few laws directly concerning private or civil matters. Towards the end of the Qing dynasty, China's rulers introduced some basic legal concepts eventually codified in a Draft Civil Law and Commercial Law modelled largely from the German and Japanese experience. In the 1930s, the Nationalist Government promulgated a Civil Code modelled directly from the German Civil Code and adopted a series of laws to complement the larger legal architectural design. See Xianchu Zhang, 'The New Round of Civil Law Codification in China,' *University of Bologna Law Review* 1 (2016): 106–137.

[55] ibid 6–7.

[56] Hui Xing Liang, 'Revisited Certain Issues in Civil Law Codification With Response to De-Codification' Aisixiang (2015).

[57] A series of other private laws have been promulgated in this framework including those relating to marriage, tort liability, contract, corporate structure, partnerships, banking, securities, maritime issues, trusts, commercial paper and intellectual property. See Zhang (n. 54).

[58] Chen Lei and C.H. van Rhee, 'Towards A Chinese Civil Code: Comparative and Historical Perspectives,' *Historical Journal of Film Radio and Television* (2012): 1–18.

of the drafting group.[59] Indeed, the variety and extent of the various sectoral laws became too unwieldy and presented too many discrete problems for one codification process to solve. At this time, many working groups engaged in broad debates about the appropriate formulation of civil laws and their relationship not only to the practical administration of China's centralised system but also to the country's larger social and economic goals.[60] Many issues lurking in previous rounds of codification resurfaced, such as the extent to which the judicial system should recognise private law and enforce the personality rights enumerated in Draft Code.[61]

With new leadership in 2013, the CCP adopted its Decision on Major Issues Concerning Comprehensively Deepening Reforms to initiate another compilation round for the Civil Code.[62] In 2014 the CCP explicitly linked the civil law codification process to its larger objectives of better protecting individual rights and safeguarding market development.[63] As a consequence, the Standing Committee of the NPC included civil law codification into its five-year legislative plan for 2013–2018, triggering a momentous push to solidify civil law principles, including those related to privacy and data protection.[64] While the first steps of the compilation process were completed in 2018, it took two additional years before the working committees within the drafting process could agree on the relative scope and reach of the provisions.

The Code divides privacy and data protection into separate provisions, with the rights and obligations differing depending on the context. As such, they reflect a hybrid regime like the European model in the sense that some of the definitions and the overreliance on consent demonstrate a focus on confidentiality and one's private life, while other definitions and processing obligations relate to fair information practice principles and exist independent of the right to privacy. In so doing, the Code converges nicely with other data protection regulations in China (including the PIPL), which relate to personal information processing, while also serving as a legal vehicle that uniquely emphasises privacy in the normative sense.

---

[59] Zhang (n. 54).
[60] Xiaolin Sun, 'The Debates between Civil and Commercial Law Circles on Adoption of General Principles of Commercial Law Comes Back,' Sina (2009).
[61] See eg Huixing Liang, 'Three Thinking Paths on Civil Codification,.' *Lawyer's World* 4 (2003): 4–5; Jing Wei Liu, 'Two Basic Problems Need to Be Settled in Civil Law Codification,' *Approaching to China to Cross Straight Private Law in the 21st Century* (2004): 125–146; Ping Jiang, 'Adopting An Open Civil Code,' *No. 2 Tribune of Political Science and Law* 2 (2003): 115–116; Ping Jiang, 'Civil Law: Retrospective and Prospective,' *No. 2. Journal of Comparative Law* 2 (2006): 1–12.
[62] Decision of the CCCPC on Some Major Issues Concerning Comprehensively Deepening the Reform, The Supreme People's Court of the People's Republic of China (2013), china.usc.edu/decision-central-committee-communist-party-china-some-major-issues-concerning-comprehensively.
[63] CCP Decision 2014, www.chinalawtranslate.com/en/fourth-plenum-decision/.
[64] 'China Includes Civil Law Codification in Legislation Plan' (*Global Times*, 2015) www.globaltimes.cn/content/935674.shtml.

While previous iterations of the Code contained provisions creating enforceable privacy rights, the newest compilation significantly expands those rights and creates a set of new obligations around personal data processing. Chapter Six defines privacy as a 'natural person's peace of life and the private space, private activities and private information which she is unwilling to let others know' (Article 1032) and lists activities that require consent from data subjects. Such activities include:

- Disturbing people's private lives through the telephone, text message, instant messaging tools, email and leaflets (Article 1033).
- Entering, peeping into, or recording other people's private spaces such as houses and hotel rooms (Article 1033).
- Eavesdropping on and publicising other people's private activities (Article 1033).
- Processing other people's private information (Article 1033).

While violations of the right to privacy may result in civil liability, these provisions say little about data processing in the context of the digital economy. As we will see, this may be one reason why privacy litigation in China will likely not have that large an impact on the regulation of large internet firms. Notwithstanding this, the Code outlines explicit provisions related to other data processing activities that share many similarities with other international data protection models.

For instance, the Code defines personal information (个人敏感信息) broadly as 'all types of information recorded electronically or in other ways that can identify a specific natural person alone or in combination with other information' (Article 1034).[65] A similar definition has been operationalised by other regulations around the world, including in the EU, Brazil, South Korea and Singapore. Furthermore, personal information handlers (个人信息的处理者) must obtain consent from the data subject when collecting, storing, using, transmitting, providing or publicising personal data, unless another law or regulation provides otherwise.[66] They must also publicise the rules of processing, and express the purpose, method and scope of processing when obtaining consent.

Additionally, the Code notably sets forth data subject rights that align with the PIPL including the right to inquire about, copy, correct and delete information held by an information handler. Broad exemptions exist for handlers that obtain

---

[65] The same definition is offered in the PIPL.
[66] Indeed, although heavily reliant on consent, the PIPL lists other lawful grounds for when data processing is appropriate. See Hunter Dorwart, Gabriela Zanfir-Fortuna and Clarisse Girot, 'China's New Comprehensive Data Protection Law: Context, Stated Objectives, Key Provisions' (Future of Privacy Forum, 2021).

consent, process information that is already public unless the data subject explicitly rejects the processing of the information or doing so would infringe upon her significant interests, and when reasonable to maintain a public interest such as public security or health.[67] Finally, the Code imposes information security obligations on information handlers. It specifically requires handlers to take technical and other necessary measures to ensure the security of the personal information it processes.[68] While the Code does not explicitly reference any other law or regulation, these technical measures converge completely with notable provisions in China's emerging data security infrastructure.[69]

The broad convergence of the Civil Code and the PIPL with other data protection frameworks indicates that the central government envisions a role for courts to adjudicate individual claims on a smaller-scale basis. Indeed, as discussed below, cases based on the Code are increasing in both scale and frequency, and in certain circumstances have generated significant attention from regulators. However, the recent compilation of the Code should not be divorced from the larger issues and debates that have centred around the complicated development of private law in China. Legal reforms in this space have consistently faced institutional pressure stemming from the country's unique political and administrative structure, its embedded interests and its practical constraints.[70] Leading up to the compilation process, many scholars disagreed about the path of codification, the degree to which the Code should represent a unified and holistic set of legal rights and obligations and the relationship of the Code to other areas of commercial law.[71] It is important therefore not to overinflate the law's relevance as some watershed moment for judicial representation but still acknowledge that its current iteration represents an important step in solidifying the legal process in the country.[72]

Where data governance ultimately goes is the subject of much debate.[73] There is real pressure on the Chinese government to respond to the growing social harms

---

[67] One notable example of this is the processing of personal data in response to the COVID-19 pandemic.

[68] Civil Code Art 1038.

[69] Both the Cybersecurity Law and the Data Security Law outline relevant security protocols to follow with respect to the processing of both personal and non-personal data. In addition, a proliferation of data security standards.

[70] See Zhang (n. 54).

[71] See Sun (n. 60).

[72] Although the codification process was completed, leaders in China will certainly revisit some of the larger outstanding issues in the civil law process. Indeed, the recent 'Plan on Building the Rule of Law in China (2020–2025)' to better develop China's 'socialist rule of law with Chinese characteristics' suggests that the conversation around civil law codification in the country will enter a new 'implementation' and 'evaluation' phase shortly.

[73] Moritz Rudolf, 'Xi Jinping Thought on the Rule of Law' (SWP, 2021) www.swp-berlin.org/10.18449/2021C28/.

of the digital economy and develop a functional civil legal system that suits China's particular needs and unique political structure.[74] Yet there are also real barriers facing legal reform generally (see below) and it is unclear to what extent individuals will use the judicial process, if at all, to enforce civil data privacy and protection expectations in the market economy and whether the exercise matters in the first place given the primacy of the larger centrally-coordinated bureaucracy in making regulatory decisions.

All of this exists in the context of how Chinese regulators generally enforce law. The PIPL creates enforceable rights and overlaps broadly with the Civil Code in terms of substance and the types of entities included in the scope of law. But the law's enforcement will largely be the responsibility of Chinese administrative institutions such as the Cyberspace Administration of China (CAC) and the Ministry of Industry and Information Technologies (MIIT). Courts can and do draw from general laws like the PIPL in their decisions, but cases rarely come from these sources of law because their implementation primarily belongs to regulators who operate within the State Council. Thus, while the PIPL will play a role in protection of individual rights, litigants will likely draw from the Civil Code when seeking redress through judicial institutions, as case evidence indicates.

## III. Privacy Litigation in China – Trends and Data[75]

Privacy litigation in China is increasing both in scale and frequency. While the Civil Code is not the only legal basis through which individuals bring these claims, its recent compilation has witnessed an uptick in cases in many provinces throughout China. As a generally applicable law across jurisdictions, the Civil Code applies broadly and creates enforceable rights and obligations on several natural and legal persons. Many cases recently litigated were initiated prior to the adoption of the Civil Code in 2020 and cite previous articles of law as causes of action. More recently, litigants have brought claims under the new provisions of the Code that deal specifically with personal information protection. Some of these cases have generated considerable media attention both within and outside of Chinese sources, including a now famous case in Hangzhou concerning the use of facial recognition technologies.[76] Nearly all the cases involve the prevalence of surveillance technologies or large databases of information. Finally, the introduction of a new system of prosecution, the civil public interest litigation system, may serve as one vehicle through which courts enforce privacy and data protection laws.

---

[74] Huang and Shi (n. 19).
[75] All of these cases were researched using China Judgments Online (中国裁判文书网) wenshu.court.gov.cn/.
[76] Yuan Ye, 'A Professor, a Zoo, and the Future of Facial Recognition in China' (*Sixth Tone*, 2021) www.sixthtone.com/news/1007300/a-professor%2C-a-zoo%2C-and-the-future-of-facial-recognition-in-china.

As discussed in the next section, an analysis of case law in China must recognise that while cases evidence a growing trend of data governance from the bottom up, they also mask that a huge majority of disputes are resolved through other mechanisms such as mediation or settlement.[77] Therefore, while the data suggests definitive and concrete trends, it inherently paints an incomplete picture. This will become critical for also contextualising the role courts play in China vis-à-vis the central administrative system, a task necessary for any holistic approach to data regulation. While privacy litigation is increasing, its significance in China's overall regulatory system may remain relatively underwhelming and stagnant, not the least because of the larger barriers in China's civil law system and its underlying legal culture.

This chapter selected cases through a comprehensive search in China Judgments Online, utilising three methodological considerations. First, cases were sought where plaintiffs explicitly based their claims on the Civil Code's provisions concerning privacy (Articles 1032–1033) and data protection (Articles 1034–1039). Second, this chapter employed general privacy terms and language taken from key regulatory instruments including the Civil Code, the newly adopted PIPL and the Chinese Consumer Protection law in a generic search to filter cases not explicitly based on the Civil Code but that nonetheless implicate privacy. Third, this chapter selected civil public interest litigation cases (最高人民法院关于审理消费民事公益诉讼案件适用法律若干问题的解释), by cross-referencing notable privacy terms and large companies in China. For each of these considerations, no priority was given to geographical location or timeframe, although about half of the cases found were initiated prior to the adoption of the Civil Code in 2021. Finally, while not exhaustive, the cases examined below represent a substantial portion of the suits located online during the time of writing. After filtering cases that contained key words, cases were chosen depending on the variation of their outcome and the types of provisions of the Civil Code in question.

## A. Cases Brought under the Civil Code and Other Civil Laws

Most of the noteworthy cases brought under the Civil Code involve smaller scale disputes between private citizens such as neighbours or family members and not conglomerated entities that collect and process large swathes of personal information. They have primarily occurred in more developed jurisdictions in China and in circumstances where other avenues of conciliation were unsuccessful. While some litigants expressly reference Articles 1032–1039 of the Civil Code as the primary cause of action, many others centre their claim around other theories such as breach of contract, tort or violation of statutory law (eg, consumer protection)

---

[77] Sida Liu, 'The Shape of Chinese Law', *Peking University Law Journal* 1 (2014): 415–444.

and cite the Civil Code as evidence of the violation. As discussed above, there is a clear separation of privacy claims under the Civil Code (Article 1032) from those related to data protection (Articles 1034–1039). Recent cases do not suggest a pattern of outcome, as those identified demonstrate no asymmetrical favourability for either plaintiffs or defendants. However, plaintiffs have generally won more cases in two circumstances: (1) when they sue under the privacy provisions rather than those related to data protection; and (2) when they sue natural persons rather than corporate bodies or government offices. Courts have varied in their judgments and as a result, fact-specific particularities outweigh any general pattern in the data. In other words, while courts side with plaintiffs in certain circumstances over others, the *reasons* for doing so vary with the facts and do not justify any empirical generalisation.

In judgments held for the plaintiff, defendants either obtained or disclosed personal information covered by the law without the plaintiff's clear consent. For instance, one early case in Guangdong province held that setting up a surveillance camera pointed at a neighbour's door was a clear violation of Article 1032's protection against unwanted intrusion, while another in Sichuan found that disclosing a customer's address, contact number and WeChat name on a social media forum violated Article 1034's relevant data protection provision, including the need for the controller to have a lawful ground for processing.[78] Both cases involve a private dispute between two *individual natural persons* and are straightforward insofar as the circumstances fall nicely within the statutory text of the Civil Code.[79] Other cases examined exhibited a similar tendency in their outcomes. Indeed, the author could find no cases where the defendant won as a private individual, unassociated with a company or other business entity.

By contrast, plaintiffs were more likely to lose when suing a private company or public office – something not too dissimilar from the US experience. Under Article 1032 privacy provisions, courts in China have dismissed cases when the information gathered was previously made public to a third-party. For instance, in Shandong province, a man unsuccessfully sued his boss for obtaining his home address through the man's job application and subsequently acting upon that information by visiting him at home.[80] Another case in Guangdong found that a mobile app did not violate the plaintiff's privacy rights when it disclosed a maintenance record of used cars because the company legally collected the information.[81]

With respect to claims brought under the data protection provisions, a similar trend is noticeable. In the same case in Guangdong, the court also dismissed claims

---

[78] 丁伟洪雅县云洁干洗店一审民事判决书(2021)川 1423 民初 38 号; 谭永森与谭锦林隐私权纠纷一案民事一审判决书（2020）粤 0605 民初 29988 号.

[79] Setting up a camera is a textual violation of the law, while disclosing private information gained during a business transaction falls nicely within the personal information processing obligations.

[80] 张磊与谢强隐私权纠纷二审(2021)鲁 01 民终 579 号民事判决书 （2021）鲁 01 民终 579 号.

[81] 余某与北京酷车易美网络科技有限公司隐私权纠纷一审民事判决书.

under Article 1034 because the company properly de-identified the data prior to disclosure.[82] In Chongqing, a plaintiff tried to bring a case against a credit lending platform after the platform disclosed the plaintiff's information to a government credit reporting entity when he defaulted on the loan.[83] The plaintiff argued that the credit reports harmed him by making it more difficult to get a mortgage in violation of Article 1036 of the Civil Code. The court dismissed the case, reasoning that the platform took reasonable steps to verify the information, ensured that it was not disclosed to other people, and therefore did not harm the plaintiff sufficient to violate the law.

Additionally, courts have been even more reluctant to side with plaintiffs against public bodies. In one case, an individual requested information about another from a local civil affairs bureau, arguing that the law gave him the right to request information 'related to government affairs'.[84] The court disagreed and cited Article 1039 of the Civil Code to justify its claim that the law required government offices to protect personal information if disclosure of such information would have harmful effects on the data subject. Here, the information concerned a recent divorcee – any disclosure of that information would have negative repercussions in the community as understood in the Chinese cultural context. In another notable case, a man requested information from the Beijing Yanqing District Jingzhuang Town Government and then sued the municipal body when it published a statement in its disclosure that the plaintiff specifically requested the disclosure.[85] The court held for the defendant and reasoned that releasing the name of the person who requested the information promotes transparency of government and therefore is pertinent to public welfare (an exception under the Civil Code).

Nonetheless, plaintiffs have won cases brought against larger corporate bodies or public organisations. In one case, an employer terminated an employee's contract for missing work without providing proof of medical conditions as per the company's policy.[86] The plaintiff employee had in fact sent relevant materials to the employer, but not to the level of specificity the company demanded. The court ruled in favour of the plaintiff, finding that Article 1034's processing obligations protected the details of a medical condition when the company only required proof of the medical condition itself.

Perhaps the most famous privacy case so far in China, an attorney in Hangzhou brought a case against a zoo after they required him to agree to their use of facial recognition technology to monitor people accessing the zoo through an annual pass that previously required obtaining customers' fingerprints.[87] Notably, the plaintiff

---

[82] ibid.
[83] 潘洪霞与北京捷越联合金融信息服务有限公司中国人民银行征信中心侵权责任纠纷一审民事判决书 （2021）渝 0104 民初 778 号.
[84] 徐宏强与玉环市民政局、玉环市人民政府行政监察(监察)一审行政判决书 （2021）浙 1021 行初 10 号.
[85] 枢琦与北京市延庆区人民政府等其他二审行政判决书 （2021）京 01 行终 44 号.
[86] 达科信息科技（北京）有限公司与谢涛劳动争议二审民事判决书 （2021）京 03 民终 106 号.
[87] 兵与杭州野生动物世界有限公司服务合同纠纷一审民事判决书 (2019) 浙 0111 民初 6971 号.

brought claims under multiple sources of law, including the Consumer Protection Law and breach of contract. The court dismissed his claim under the Consumer Protection Law, reasoning that the zoo was transparent about its requirements for purchasing the annual pass but sided with the plaintiff under a theory of breach of contract. Specifically, the court held that by unilaterally modifying its terms of contract to include new provisions on collecting facial recognition information, it violated the law. The plaintiff did not agree with nor negotiate against the additional terms and the new requirements, and the zoo, while not restricting the ability of the plaintiff to use the pass, nevertheless increased his burden under the new requirements. The attorney in this case not only collected a total refund of the annual pass but also persuaded the court to require the zoo to delete his biometric information.

He did not, however, stop the zoo or other similar entities from using facial recognition altogether. This has now become his public goal and he is currently appealing his case to a higher judicial body.[88] The case generated noticeable attention both inside and outside of China because it not only demonstrated public backlash against facial recognition technology generally but also the successful use of the court system in China to combat its use.[89] While awaiting appeal, the SPC released regulations clarifying its interpretation of the law with respect to facial recognition.[90] These regulations notably reference other laws in China's emerging ecosystem such as the PIPL and the Civil Code and may have a direct impact on the future proceeding of this case and others.

## B. Civil Public Interest Litigation

One unique form of judicial enforcement of privacy and data protection provisions concerns the civil public interest litigation system, a relatively new process where prosecutors bring civil cases against larger defendants on behalf of the public interest.[91] Cases of this nature usually involve very sensitive activities of private actors that risk harm to a great number of individuals. For instance, prosecutors have brought cases under the civil public interest mechanism to enforce environmental and consumer rights laws.[92] As discussed below more thoroughly, this enforcement system should be seen as complementary to the larger top-down central administrative process and used in circumstances to

---

[88] See Ye (n. 76).
[89] Xinmei Shen, 'China's First Facial-Recognition Lawsuit Comes to an End with New Ruling and New Questions About the Fate of Individuals' Data' (South China Morning Post, 2021).
[90] Supreme People's Court Guidelines on the Use of Facial Recognition Technology. www.court.gov.cn/fabu- xiangqing-315851.html.
[91] 最高人民法院关于审理消费民事公益诉讼案件适用法律若干问题的解释.
[92] 'Public Interest Litigation in China' (Yale Law School: Paul Tsai China Center, 2021) law.yale.edu/china- center/resources/public-interest-litigation-china.

enforce the laws against companies evading enforcement action from ministerial bodies.

The civil public interest litigation system may soon focus more on data protection and privacy generally. In June 2020, the China's Supreme People's Procuratorate stated it would expand the scope of these lawsuits to digital rights, including the rights of minors online.[93] Since then, prosecutors across China have brought cases that directly implicate privacy and personal information protection. Up until 2021, these cases mostly involved intervening against actors that take advantage of a firm's cybersecurity vulnerabilities and not against the companies themselves. For instance, in Shanghai, prosecutors brought a case against an employee of Zhongtong (one of the biggest delivery companies in China) who gathered and sold personal information of shipping orders by abusing his position within the company.[94] In addition, another litigation witnessed a group of individuals in Jiangsu face liability for abusing Baidu's password recovery process to gain unauthorised access into users' accounts and then sell that information on a black market.[95]

However, recent data suggests that civil public interest lawsuits may soon target larger firms for violating privacy and data protection regulations. In August 2021, prosecutors in Beijing initiated a lawsuit against WeChat on the grounds that the company was violating China's child protection laws with its service.[96] Likewise, Kuaishou recently settled a public interest lawsuit in Hangzhou specifically over its violation of child protection laws when it collected information on minors without notifying their parents or guardians.[97] Both companies have offered specialised services and product offerings to minors for years and often in ways that raised eyebrows in Beijing's larger regulatory circles.[98] The introduction of the civil public interest litigation system in this context could increase regulatory pressures on firms and may serve as one vehicle through which courts directly enforce privacy and data protection laws.

---

[93] 'Work Report of the Supreme People's Procuratorate' (*Xinhua*, 2020) www.spp.gov.cn/spp/gzbg/202006/t20200601_463798.shtml.

[94] 暨原审附带民事公益诉讼被告人王耀杰侵犯公民个人信息二审刑事裁定书（2021）沪 02 刑终 245 号.

[95] 刘某侵犯公民个人信息二审刑事裁定书（2020）苏 02 刑终 333 号.

[96] 'Announcement of the People's Procuratorate of Haidian District of Beijing on the Initiation of a Civil Public Interest Lawsuit Against Shenzhen Tencent Computer System Co., Ltd.' (*Justice Net*, 2021), www.scmp.com/tech/big-tech/article/3144180/tencent-targeted-public-interest-litigation-beijing-procuratorate.

[97] Iris Deng, 'Beijing's Prosecutor's Public Interest Lawsuit Against Tencent Raises New Concerns for China's Big Tech Sector' (*South China Morning Post*, 2021) www.scmp.com/tech/big-tech/article/3144426/beijing- prosecutors-public-interest-lawsuit-against-tencent-raises.

[98] 'Report of the Constitution and Law Committee of the National People's Congress on the Deliberation Results of the Personal Information Protection Law of the People's Republic of China (Draft)' (*National People's Congress*, 2021) www.npc.gov.cn/npc/c30834/202108/a528d76d41c44f33980eaffe0e329ffe.shtml.

**Table 2** Outline of Recent Data Privacy Cases in China

| Name | Source of Law | Major Issue | Date |
|---|---|---|---|
| Tan Yongsen v Tan Jinlin, Privacy Dispute Case, First Civil Judgment (Guangdong 0605 No. 29988) 谭永森与谭锦林隐私权纠纷一案民事一审判决书 (粤 0605 民初 29988 号) | Civil Code (Article 1032) 中华人民共和国民法典第一千零三十二条 | Setting up a surveillance camera towards a neighbour's door | 2020 |
| Jueqi v People's Government of Yanqing District, Second Administrative Judgment (Beijing 01 No. 44) 桀琦与北京市延庆区人民政府等其他二审行政判决书 (京 01 行终 44 号) | Civil Code (Article 1032) 中华人民共和国民法典第一千零三十二条 | Disclosure of a DSAR against a town government | 2021 |
| Zhang Lei v Xie Qiang, Privacy Dispute Case, Second Civil Judgment (Shandong 01 No. 579) 张磊与谢强隐私权纠纷二审 (鲁 01 民终 579 号民事判决书) | Civil Code (Article 1032) 中华人民共和国民法典第一千零三十二条 | Unauthorised disclosure of employment data from employer | 2021 |
| Dingwei Hongya County v Yunjie Dry Cleaner, First Civil Judgment (Sichuan 1423 No. 38) 丁伟洪雅县云洁干洗店一审民事判决书 (川 1423 民初 38 号) | Civil Code (Articles 1032–1034) 中华人民共和国民法典第一千零三十二条 | Business disclosed customers' private information online | 2021 |
| Yu Mou v Beijing Kuche Yimei Network Technology Co., Privacy Dispute Case, First Civil Judgment (Guangdong 0192 No. 928) 余某与北京酷车易美网络科技有限公司隐私权纠纷一审民事判决书 (粤 0192 民初 928) | Civil Code (Articles 1032–1034) 中华人民共和国民法典第一千零三十二条 | App provided personal information connected to the sale of used cars | 2021 |
| Bing v Hangzhou Wildlife World Co., Contract Dispute, First Civil Judgment (Zhejiang 0111 No. 6971) 兵与杭州野生动物世界有限公司服务合同纠纷一审民事判决书 (浙 0111 民初 6971 号) | Consumer Protection Law 中华人民共和国消费者权益保护法 | Zoo in Hangzhou suddenly required patrons to register facial information | 2019 |

Chinese Data Protection in Transition 65

| | | | |
|---|---|---|---|
| Dake Information Technology Co. v Xie Tao, Labor Dispute, Second Civil Judgment (Beijing 03 No. 106) 达科信息科技有限公司与谢涛劳动争议二审民事判决书(京 03 民终 106 号) | Civil Code (Articles 1032–1034) 中华人民共和国民法典第一千零三十四条 | Employer demanded employee disclose sensitive medical data | 2021 |
| Pan Hongxia v Beijing Jie Yue United Financial Information Service Co., Tort Liability Dispute (Chongqing 0104 No. 778) 潘洪霞与北京捷越联合金融信息服务有限公司中国人民银行征信中心侵权责任纠纷一审民事判决书(渝 0104 民初 778 号) | Civil Code (Article 1036) 中华人民共和国民法典第一千零三十六条 | Loan service platform disclosed the customer's default on loan to government credit offices | 2021 |
| Xu Hongqing v Yuhuan Municipal People's Government, First Administrative Judgment (Zhejiang 1021 No. 10). 徐宏强与玉环市民政局，玉环市人民政府行政监察(监察)一审行政判决（浙 1021 行初 10 号） | Civil Code (Article 1036) 中华人民共和国民法典第一千零三十九条 | Plaintiff sues government office for not disclosing information of a recent divorcee | 2021 |
| Yu, Second Criminal Ruling for Illegally Obtaining Citizen's Personal Information (No. 995) 余*非法获取公民个人信息罪二审刑事裁定书(二中刑终字第 995 号) | Criminal Code (Article 253) 《刑法》第二百五十三条 | Illegal purchasing of PI over the Internet | 2014 |
| Zhang Yajun & Zhou Zhigang, Second Criminal Ruling (Zhejiang 07 No. 1183) 张亚军、周志刚出售、非法提供公民个人信息罪二审刑事裁定书(浙 07 刑终 1183 号) | Criminal Code (Article 253) 《刑法》第二百五十三条 | Illegal selling of PI (phone numbers and names) online | 2018 |
| Li Kaiquan, First Criminal Judgment (Guangxi 0405 No. 206) 郑槠泉侵犯公民个人信息罪一审刑事判决书(桂 0405 刑初 206 号) | Criminal Code (Article 253) 《刑法》第二百五十三条 | Illegal selling of WeChat and QQ accounts for profit | 2019 |

(continued)

Table 2 (Continued)

| Name | Source of Law | Major Issue | Date |
|---|---|---|---|
| Deng Changjiu & Zhang Guofang, Second Criminal Ruling (Hainan 97 No. 297) 邓长久、张国芳等出售、非法提供公民个人信息罪二审刑事裁定书（琼 97 刑终 297 号） | Criminal Code (Article 253) 《刑法》第二百五十三条 | Spam calling regarding changes to airline tickets | 2018 |
| Li Junjie & Huang Mou, Second Criminal Ruling (Zhejiang 311) 李骏杰犯破坏计算机信息系统罪胡某犯出售、非法提供公民个人信息罪董某、黄某等犯非法获取公民个人信息罪二审刑事裁定书（浙杭刑终字第 311 号） | Criminal Code (Article 253) 《刑法》第二百五十三条 | Hacking and sabotaging computer systems and public records | 2015 |
| Wang Yaojie, Civil Public Interest Lawsuit (Shanghai 02 No. 245) 暨原审附带民事公益诉讼被告人王耀杰侵犯公民个人信息罪二审刑事裁定书（沪 02 刑终 245 号） | Civil Public Interest Litigation | An employee of a large delivery company collected and sold personal information of customers | 2021 |
| Liu, Second Criminal Ruling (Jiangsu 02 No. 333) 刘某侵犯公民个人信息二审刑事裁定书（苏 02 刑终 333 号） | Civil Public Interest Litigation | Defendant abused Baidu password recovery system to gain unauthorised access to accounts | 2020 |

## IV. The Role of Courts – Complementary or Insignificant

While these recent cases suggest that the court system could play a role in regulating the digital economy, it is important to contextualise this role with the larger administrative and regulatory system to avoid drawing improper conclusions. Because of China's unique administrative system, privacy and data protection litigation should be seen as a secondary yet complementary mechanism of data governance. In other words, courts will likely intervene against big dominant firms and other tech companies as a *stop-gap* measure in cases where regulation from the ministerial and super-ministerial levels falls short. They will not be the source of an independent lever of governance power in the digital economy nor will they drastically alter the internal compliance analysis of the biggest tech companies.[99] Despite this, courts will likely play a smaller role in resolving disputes that fall outside of the ambit of the central regulators and may even complement the larger regulatory system with civil public interest lawsuits.

Although all regulatory agencies in China are subordinated under the State Council, their competences often overlap in ways that produce regulatory ambiguity. Such ambiguity has proven an effective cornerstone of developing compliance culture in China's private sector as any company may be subject to oversight from multiple regulatory authorities under the same law or regulation. For instance, many of the key regulations in China's emerging data protection ecosystem were drafted in coordination with multiple agencies including the State Administration for Market Regulation (SAMR), the Ministry of Industry and Information Technology (MIIT), the Ministry for Public Security (MPS), the Ministry for State Security (MSS), and the Ministry of Transport (MOT).

The CAC, which serves as the primary Internet regulator, has been a key player in the enforcement of data protection law in China. It operates as a super-ministerial coordination and consultation body, and has its own prerogatives for developing regulations and technical standards, many of which have often predated formal law and operate as the de facto standard for compliance. The CAC has in recent years increased its enforcement of the PIPL and related laws. It engages in monitoring of the market, including special investigations or 'campaigns' to identify violations of particular focus areas or provisions of law. Most of its enforcement activities happen behind closed doors, with companies receiving notices that they are in violation of the law with a deadline for rectification. In some instances, the CAC has publicly announced a more serious investigation, which has led to more severe enforcement decisions where clear aspects of the law come into question. This has happened, however, only on a few occasions, leaving much of the day-to-day enforcement activities of the authority unknown. Its authority to take cases is largely undefined and has been expanded by the ministry actively asserting itself into regulatory matters handled by other bodies.

---

[99] See eg Randall Peerenboom, *China's Long March Toward Rule of Law* (Cambridge: Cambridge University Press, 2002); Kenneth Lieberthal, *Governing China* (New York: W.W. Norton, 1995).

Due to the complexity of this system, Chinese authorities will administer cyber regulation largely from the top-down and not the bottom-up. This complements the country's deep- rooted historical practice, summarised in the phrase 'three positions, one unity' (三位一体), that places great emphasis on the differentiation of legal compliance between multiple administrative institutions.[100] The prevalence of this large coordination and enforcement system in regulating the digital economy also reinforces the expectation that the political structure will continue to predominantly guide the development of commercial and private affairs in China. While this does not mean there is no role for courts and individuals in this system, these institutional mechanisms primarily operate as a warning for other market participants to comply with the expectations of the central authorities – a process of 'killing the chicken to scare the monkey' (杀鸡儆猴).

The relationship of the courts to the larger administration system also complements longstanding debates about the codification of civil law and the penetration of the Chinese legal system into commercial and private affairs. Indeed, while Chinese courts have witnessed an uptick in cases brought under the updated personality rights and data protection provisions in the recently compiled Code, such data ignores the widespread institutional presence of other forms of dispute resolution such as mediation through People's Mediation Committees or other forms of extra-judicial settlement.[101]

This complicates a strict analysis of data protection through China's court system for many reasons. First, because civil law has always been relatively underdeveloped in China, especially when compared to criminal law, the transition to a 'socialist market economy' in the 1980s brought with it many challenges to facilitate commercial and private matters.[102] The completion of the Civil Code may evidence resolution of some of those challenges but leaves others unaddressed. For instance, although the updated personality rights give individuals an ability to enforce privacy and data protection standards vis-à-vis other 'private' actors, they do little to differentiate between private natural persons and private legal persons in the form of companies or other related legal constructions. This leaves much room for the central administration to continue to exercise great influence in the overall direction of regulation in the country.

Second, the use of legal categories commonly found in the EU and the US such as 'private/public' and 'citizen/government' does not readily apply in the Chinese context and any attempts to reduce them to explain developments in Chinese law should not ignore the issue.[103] Indeed, the Chinese legal system must be understood through analytical frameworks attached to its own historical practice – including the use of conventional terms and conceptual schema to describe the functioning of government and the differential power-sharing

---

[100] See Liu (n. 77).
[101] ibid.
[102] See Zhang (n. 54).
[103] Donald C. Clarke, 'Methodologies for Research in Chinese Law,' *University of British Columbia Law Review* (1996): 201–209.

relationships within it.[104] Historical experience suggests that law serves as an instrument to effectuate other social and moral goals and operates underneath the purview of the state administrative complex. This does not mean that the operationalisation of law in China has been stagnant or consistent over time. On the contrary, China's legal system has reflected the country's recent history – it has evolved to accommodate the country's rapid growth in the past four decades but has in other respects retained its unique Chinese characteristics. China's legal system, like many other aspects of the country, is likewise undergoing a new phase of transformation and demands a reevaluation of the conceptual schema used to describe it.

Third and relatedly, despite these conceptual issues, data protection case law in China has so far focused solely on the 'private-to-private' or 'private-to-government' relationship and not the 'private-to-company' relationship that many within China highlight as the primary source of corporate-related harms. Trends do not indicate that individuals will pursue claims against private companies in the same way they would in other legal systems such as the US. Nor does the structure and function of China's legal system suggest that the law should be operationalised to do so. However, recent suits brought under the civil public interest litigation system may indicate a trend towards a more active court system in China, albeit one that directly aligns with the overall regulatory objectives of the central level.

Fourth, in some circumstances, the Chinese government struggles to implement national laws evenly and effectively on the local levels. The same may be true of China's data protection arsenal – including the PIPL. Indeed, many commentators have highlighted how the party cadre appointment process coupled with relative decentralised power-sharing arrangements creates incentives for local government officials to selectively implement the laws, which has led to problems of effective governance management from the top.[105] Courts are uniquely situated to ensure that laws passed in Beijing are enforced on the ground, but for a variety of reasons struggle to execute their orders.[106] Like other civil matters, with

---

[104] Donald C. Clarke, 'Regulation and Its Discontents: Understanding Economic Law in China,' *Stanford Journal of International Law* 28 (1992): 283–322.

[105] See eg Rogier Creemers and Susan Trevaskes, 'Ideology and Organization in Chinese Law: Towards A New Paradigm for Legality,' *Law and the Party in China* (2021): 1–28. Neysun Mahboubi, 'The Future of China's Legal System' Chinafile (2016); Benjamin Van Rooji et al., 'Pollution Enforcement in China: Understanding National and Regional Variation,' in *Routledge Handbook of Environmental Policy in China*, ed. Eva Sternfeld (London: Taylor & Francis, 2017); Yanrong Zhao, 'The Courts' Active Role in the Striving for Judicial Independence in China,' *Frontiers Law China* (2017): 278–309.

[106] Local governments in some instances have more power than courts, which creates effective legal governance problems when a defendant is associated with the head of the local government or someone influential in the local party committee. Courts may issue orders declaring that an individual or corporation violated the law but without stronger authority cannot force that individual or corporation to comply with the judgment. While over time this problem has been addressed at the central level, notably with the 14th Plenum's Decision Concerning Some Major Questions in Comprehensively Moving Governing the Country According to the Law Forward, the incentive structures have not changed much. See Donald C. Clarke, 'Power and Politics in the Chinese Court System: The Enforcement of Civil Judgments,' *Columbia Journal of Asian Law* 10 (1996): 1–125.

respect to data protection, courts may provide one mechanism for the centre to ensure that obligations and rights contained in the law are followed on the ground. Without meaningful enforcement on the local level, the data protection provisions concerning data subject rights may fall short of their goals and become ineffective mechanisms for addressing social harm in the online world. This ability to funnel power from the top may see the role of courts enhanced in the future, especially if regulators in Beijing find it difficult to target data processing practices outside of the major industrial and urban centres.

## V. Conclusion

In China, the recent adoption of the PIPL and the Civil Code has introduced a new set of data subject rights directly related to data protection. While many of the provisions dealing with privacy predate the most recent iteration of the Code, the latter's completion significantly inscribes these civil principles into China's larger legal system and gives individuals the ability to bring forth claims against other private actors. Such rights are reinforced by the PIPL, China's first comprehensive and nationally applicable data protection law, which sets forth similar terminology, processing obligations and legal frameworks seen in the GDPR.

Individuals in the country have and continue to bring more privacy and security claims against individuals and companies under various laws, including the newly compiled Civil Code. Such litigation is increasing both in frequency and scope in China, although litigants mostly pursue claims against smaller-scale actors and not major companies or large-scale public bodies. This is in conformity with expectations of how China's legal system operates, as judicial institutions have historically not been the source of social change in the country. However, the relatively new civil public interest litigation system may witness more cases brought against larger organisations that directly alter corporate behaviour in line with actions taken on the ministerial level.

The nature of the Chinese judicial system makes such litigation less important in the overall regulatory scheme. Rather, the central government will continue to drive regulatory decision-making with respect to the activities of large online companies. Nonetheless, privacy litigation may help individuals and organisations address harms caused by smaller and less visible businesses and even shed further light on how companies should comply with the myriad sectoral regulations passed by various competent authorities. Litigation in China thus complements the vast apparatus of ministries centralised under the State Council and their goals regarding the digital economy but in a secondary and limited way. Further legal developments in China could complicate this image and resonate broadly with debates regarding the penetration of Chinese law into civil and private matters.

# References

'Announcement of the People's Procuratorate of Haidian District of Beijing on the Initiation of a Civil Public Interest Lawsuit Against Shenzhen Tencent Computer System Co., Ltd.' *Justice Net* (2021).

Arsene, Severine. 'China, Internet Governance and the Global Public Interest.' *A New Responsible Power China* (2018).

Aslam, S. and H. Sami Ullah, 'A Comprehensive Review of Smart Cities Components, Applications, and Technologies Based on Internet of Things.' *Arxiv* (2020).

Chandel, Sonali et al. 'The Golden Shield Project of China: A Decade Later.' *Institute of Electrical and Electronics Engineers (IEEE)* (2019).

Chen, Lei and C.H. van Rhee, 'Towards A Chinese Civil Code: Comparative and Historical Perspectives.' *Historical Journal of Film Radio and Television* (2012).

'China Includes Civil Law Codification in Legislation Plan.' *Global Times* (2015).

Chou, William, Iris Li and Lingxiao Zhang, 'New Governance of the Platform Economy' *Deloitte* (2020).

Clarke, Donald C. 'Power and Politics in the Chinese Court System: The Enforcement of Civil Judgments' Columbia Journal of Asian Law 10 (1996).

———, 'Regulation and Its Discontents: Understanding Economic Law in China.' *Stanford Journal of International Law* 28 (1992).

———, 'Methodologies for Research in Chinese Law' *University of British Columbia Law Review* (1996).

Creemers, Rogier. 'The Pivot in Chinese Cybergovernance: Integrating Internet Control in Xi Jinping's China.' *China Perspectives* (2015).

Creemers, Rogier and Susan Trevaskes. 'Ideology and Organization in Chinese Law: Towards a New Paradigm for Legality' In *Law and the Party in China*, edited by Rogier Creemers and Susan Trevaskes. Cambridge: Cambridge University Press, 2021.

Decision of the CCCPC on Some Major Issues Concerning Comprehensively Deepening the Reform, The Supreme People's Court of the People's Republic of China (2013).

Deng, Iris. 'Beijing's Prosecutor's Public Interest Lawsuit Against Tencent Raises New Concerns for China's Big Tech Sector.' *South China Morning Post* (2021).

Dorwart, Hunter and Gabriela Zanfir-Fortuna. 'Spotlight on the Emerging Chinese Data Protection Framework: Lessons Learned From the Unprecedented Investigation of Didi Chuxing.' *Future of Privacy Forum* (2021).

Dorwart, Hunter, Gabriela Zanfir-Fortuna and Clarisse Girot, 'China's New Comprehensive Data Protection Law: Context, Stated Objectives, Key Provisions.' *Future of Privacy Forum* (2021).

Fedasiuk, Ryan and Emily Weinstein and Anna Puglisi, 'China's Foreign Technology Wish List.' *Center for Security and Emerging Technology* (2021).

Guevara, Leonardo and Fernando Auat Cheein, 'The Role of 5G Technologies: Challenges in Smart Cities and Intelligent Transportation Systems.' *Sustainability* (2020).

Gu, Shulin and Bengt-Ake Lundvall, 'China's Innovation System and the Move Towards Harmonious Growth and Endogenous Innovation.' *Innovation: Organization and Management* 8 (2006).

Han, Jianhuang Tong Qian and Wei Han, 'Cover Story: The Fight Over China's Law to Protect Personal Data.' *Caixin* (2020).

Han, Wei. 'Baidu Sued Over Claim It Illegally Obtained Users' Data.' *Caixin* (2018).

Huang, Yehan and Mingli Shi. 'Top Scholar Zhou Hanhua Illuminates 15+ Years of History Behind China's Personal Information Protection Law.' *DigiChina* (2021).
Huang, Zhixiong. (黄志雄), 'International Law in Cyberspace: China's Status, Position, and Strategy.' (网络空间国际法制：中国的立场主张和对策) *Yunnan Minzu University Press* 32 (2015): 137 (云南民族大学学报).
Jiang, Min. 'Cybersecurity Policies in China.' In *CyberBRICS: Cybersecurity Regulation in the BRICS Countries*, edited by Luca Belli. New York: Springer Nature, 2021.
Jiang, Ping. 'Adopting An Open Civil Code.' *Tribune of Political Science and Law* 2 (2003).
——, 'Civil Law: Retrospective and Prospective.' *Journal of Comparative Law* 2 (2006).
Kak, Ambak and Samm Sacks, 'Shifting Narratives and Emergent Trends in Data-Governance Policy: Developments in China, India, and the EU.' *Policy Memo* (2021).
Kane, Gerald C. et al., 'Aligning the Organization for its Digital Future.' *MIT Sloan Management Review* (2016).
Li, R.F. and Y. Na. 'A Philosophical Reflection on the Loss of Privacy.' *Science, Technology and Dialectics* 5 (2003).
Liang, Huixing. 'Three Thinking Paths on Civil Codification.' *Lawyer's World* 4 (2003).
——, 'Revisited Certain Issues in Civil Law Codification With Response to De-Codification.' *Aisixiang* (2015).
Lieberthal, Kenneth. *Governing China*. New York: W.W. Norton, 1995.
Liu, D.L. 'On Privacy and Right to Privacy.' *Social Science* 8 (2003).
Liu, Jing Wei. 'Two Basic Problems Need to Be Settled in Civil Law Codification.' *Approaching to China to Cross Straight Private Law in the 21st Century* (2004).
Liu, Jingjing. 'Overview of the Chinese Legal System.' *Environmental Law Institute* 1 (2013).
Liu, Sida. 'The Shape of Chinese Law.' *Peking University Law Journal* 1 (2014).
Lu, Chuanying. (鲁传颖) 'Evolution of the Concept of Sovereignty in the Challenges of the Internet Age.' (主权概念的演进及其在网络时代的挑战) *International Relations Studies* 1 (2014): 75–77 《国际关系研究》.
Lu Wei et al., 'Internet Development in China.' *Journal of Information Science* 28 (2002).
Mahboubi, Neysun. 'The Future of China's Legal System.' *Chinafile* (2016).
Mueller, Milton. *Networks and States: The Global Politics of Internet Governance*. Boston: MIT Press, 2010.
National Science Foundation Science & Engineering Indicators, 2018.
Opinions Concerning Strengthening Information Security Protection Work, State Informatization Leading Group, ZBF No. [2003]27.
'Outline of the People's Republic of China 14th Five-Year Plan for National Economic and Social Development and Long-Range Objectives for 2035.' *Xinhua News Agency* (12 March 2021).
Pernot-Leplay, Emmanuel. 'China's Approach on Data Privacy Law: A Third Way Between the U.S. and the EU?' *Penn State Journal of Law & International Affairs* 8 (2020).
Peerenboom, Randall. *China's Long March Toward Rule of Law*. Cambridge: Cambridge University Press, 2002.
Pongratz, Stefan. 'Key Takeaways – The Telecom Equipment Market 1H20.' *Dell'Oro Group* (2020).
Public Interest Litigation in China, Yale Law School: Paul Tsai China Center (2021).
Report of the Constitution and Law Committee of the National People's Congress on the Deliberation Results of the 'Personal Information Protection Law of the People's Republic of China (Draft).' *National People's Congress* (2021).

*Rising Innovation in China: China Innovation Ecosystem Development Report 2019.* Deloitte China 7–8 (2019).

Rooji, Benjamin van et al. 'Pollution Enforcement in China: Understanding National and Regional Variation.' In *Routledge Handbook of Environmental Policy in China*, edited by Eva Sternfeld. London: Taylor and Francis, 2017.

Ross, Sean. '5 Biggest Chinese Software Companies.' *Investopedia* (25 February 2020).

Rudolf, Moritz. 'Xi Jinping Thought on the Rule of Law.' *SWP* (2021).

Shen, Xinmei. 'China's First Facial-Recognition Lawsuit Comes to an End with New Ruling and New Questions About the Fate of Individuals' Data.' *South China Morning Post* (2021).

Stapleton, Katherine. 'China Now Produces Twice as Many Graduates a Year as the US.' *World Economic Forum* (2017).

Supreme People's Court Guidelines on the Use of Facial Recognition Technology.

Sun, Xiaolin. 'The Debates between Civil and Commercial Law Circles on Adoption of General Principles of Commercial Law Comes Back.' *Sina* (2009).

Triolo, Paul et al. 'China's Cybersecurity Law One Year On: An Evolving and Interlocking Framework.' *New America* (2019).

Work Report of the Supreme People's Procuratorate, Xinhua (2020).

Xu, Peixi. 'A Chinese Perspective on the Future of Cyberspace.' *Cyberstability Paper Series* (2021).

Yang, Rongjun. (杨嵘均) 'On Problems and Strategies of International Cooperation in Cyberspace Governance.' (伦王国空间治理国际合作面临的及其应对策略) *Normal University Journal of Social Studies* 79 (2014), (廣西師範大學学报).

Yao, Huai Lu. 'Privacy and Data Privacy Issues in Contemporary China.' *Ethics and Information Technology* 7 (2005).

You, Chuanman. 'Law and Policy of Platform Economy in China.' *Computer Law & Security Review* 39 (2020).

Ye, Yuan. 'A Professor, a Zoo, and the Future of Facial Recognition in China.' *Sixth Tone* (2021).

Zhang, Longmei and Sally Chen. 'China's Digital Economy: Opportunities and Risks.' *Working Paper 19/16, International Monetary Fund* 5 (2019).

Zhang, Xianchu. 'The New Round of Civil Law Codification in China.' *University of Bologna Law Review* 1 (2016).

Zhang, X.B. 'The Development of IT and the Protection of Right to Privacy.' *Law and Social Development* (1996).

Zheng, Haiping. 'Regulation the Internet: China's Law and Practice.' *Beijing Law Review* 4 (2013).

Zheng, Hansheng. '21st Century Chinese: Time, Competition, and Privacy.'" (二十一世纪的中国人 – 时间，竞争，隐私) *China Soft Science* 2 (1994): 47–49. 《中国软科学》(1994 年第 2 期第 47–49 页).

Zhao, Yanrong. 'The Courts' Active Role in the Striving for Judicial Independence in China.' *Frontiers Law China* (2017).

Zhou, C.M. and C.W. Qu. 'Right to Data Privacy and Legal Protection of It.' *Lawyers World* (2001).

# 4

## Conflicting Privacy Preference Signals in the Wild

MAXIMILIAN HILS[*], DANIEL W. WOODS[≠]
AND RAINER BÖHME[≈]

**Figure 1** Which privacy preference signal takes precedence?

```
GET / HTTP/1.1
Cookie: euconsent-v2=<...>
Sec-GPC: 1
```

## Abstract

Privacy preference signals allow users to express preferences over how their personal data is processed. These signals become important in determining privacy outcomes when they reference an enforceable legal basis, as is the case with recent signals such as the Global Privacy Control and the Transparency & Consent Framework. However, the coexistence of multiple privacy preference signals creates ambiguity as users may transmit more than one signal. This chapter collects evidence about ambiguity flowing from the aforementioned two signals and the historic Do Not Track signal. We provide the first empirical evidence that ambiguous signals are sent by web users in the wild. We also show that preferences stored in the browser are reliable predictors of privacy preferences expressed in web dialogs. Finally, we provide the first evidence that popular cookie dialogs are blocked by the majority of users who adopted the Do Not Track and Global Privacy Control standards. These empirical results inform forthcoming legal debates about how to interpret privacy preference signals.

[*] University of Innsbruck, Austria.
[≠] University of Innsbruck, Austria.
[≈] University of Innsbruck, Austria.

## Keywords

Consent, cookies, GDPR, TCF, GPC, ADPC, DNT

## I. Introduction

Privacy laws like General Data Protection Regulation (GDPR)[1] and the California Consumer Privacy Act (CCPA)[2] empower users, at least in theory, to control how their personal data is processed. To do so, individuals must be able to communicate their privacy preferences with data controllers. A web standard for communicating privacy preference signals would make this convenient and easy. However, the literature suggests coordinating senders and recipients to adopt one standard has failed multiple times due to the competing interests of stakeholders.[3] The same competing interests lead stakeholders to propose different signals, leading to the coexistence of multiple signals. Users may transmit more than one signal and thereby express conflicting or ambiguous preferences, which creates uncertainty over which legal rules apply.

Multiple signals can be sent when signals are collected at different technical layers. In this chapter, we focus on the two dominant ways for users to express privacy preferences: on individual websites and globally in their browser. The first approach is chosen by the Transparency & Consent Framework (TCF), a standard developed by the Interactive Advertising Bureau and adopted by hundreds of ad-tech vendors and thousands of websites.[4] The second approach was chosen by the Do Not Track (DNT) mechanism[5] and also the Global Privacy Control (GPC), which now boasts over 40 million users.[6]

The possibility of users sending multiple signals raises questions about legal interpretation under both the CCPA and the GDPR. Such questions can only be

---

[1] European Union, 'Regulation (EU) 2016/679 of the European Parliament and of the Council of 27 April 2016 on the protection of natural persons with regard to the processing of personal data and on the free movement of such data, and repealing Directive 95/46/EC (General Data Protection Regulation),' *Official Journal L110* 59 (2016): 1–88.

[2] California Civil Code § 1798, 'California Consumer Privacy Act of 2018.'

[3] Maximilian Hils, Daniel W. Woods, and Rainer Böhme, 'Privacy Preference Signals: Past, Present and Future,' *Proceedings on Privacy Enhancing Technologies* 4 (2021). petsymposium.org/2021/files/papers/issue4/popets-2021-0069.pdf.

[4] Célestin Matte, Nataliia Bielova, and Cristiana Santos, 'Do Cookie Banners Respect my Choice? Measuring Legal Compliance of Banners from IAB Europe's Transparency and Consent Framework,' in *IEEE Symposium on Security and Privacy* (New York: IEEE, 2020), 791–809. doi.org/10.1109/SP40000.2020.00076.

[5] Jonathan Mayer, Arvind Narayanan, and Sid Stamm, 'Do Not Track: A Universal Third-Party Web Tracking Opt Out' (*Center for Internet and Society*, 2011), datatracker.ietf.org/doc/html/draft-mayer-do-not-track-00.

[6] Global Privacy Control, *GPC Privacy Browser Signal Now Used by Millions and Honored By Major Publishers* (Global Privacy Control, 2021) globalprivacycontrol. org/press-release/20210128.

answered by legal analysis. Such scholarship would be supported by first establishing which signals users send in the wild, the problem addressed by this chapter. We observe 16k impressions on websites that embed TCF dialogs and simultaneously detect the presence of a DNT and/or GPC signal.

Our results uncover a number of sources of ambiguity not previously identified in the literature. First, an industry standard dialog for collecting TCF signals is blocked by 27 per cent of users, and this percentage rises to 50 per cent/73 per cent of users with DNT/GPC turned on. Second, users who send a GPC signal are two times more likely to withhold consent than other users, which suggests the signal captures genuine privacy preferences. Finally, even though they are more likely to not give consent, 73 per cent of users with GPC turned on still consent to being tracked by clicking 'I Accept' in a TCF consent dialog. This shows that conflicting signals are a reality.

Section II provides background on relevant laws and signals. Section III describes our research design. Section IV presents the results. Section V discusses the results and suggests directions for future work. Section VI concludes the chapter.

## II. Background

We split the background into laws and privacy preference signals.

### A. Privacy Laws

The two laws most relevant to privacy preference signals are the General Data Protection Regulation (GDPR) and the California Consumer Privacy Act (CCPA). Article 6 of the GDPR[7] establishes a number of legal bases for processing personal data, of which (opt-in) consent is the most common legal basis claimed in a sample of hundreds of AdTech vendors.[8] Article 4 of the GDPR defines consent as any freely given, specific, informed and unambiguous indication of the data subject's wishes.

Taking a different approach to opt-in consent, the CCPA establishes 'the right to direct a business to not sell consumers' personal information'.[9] For the

---

[7] European Union, 'Regulation (EU) 2016/679 of the European Parliament and of the Council of 27 April 2016 on the protection of natural persons with regard to the processing of personal data and on the free movement of such data, and repealing Directive 95/46/EC (General Data Protection Regulation)'.

[8] Célestin Matte, Cristiana Santos and Nataliia Bielova, 'Purposes in IAB Europe's TCF: which legal basis and how are they used by advertisers?', in *Annual Privacy Forum* (2020), Figure 2.

[9] Sebastian Zimmeck and Kuba Alicki, 'Standardizing and Implementing Do Not Sell', in *Proceedings of the 19th Workshop on Privacy in the Electronic Society*, WPES'20 (Virtual Event, USA: Association for Computing Machinery, 2020), 15. doi.org/10.1145/3411497.3420224.

purposes of this chapter, it is important to note that both laws link the legality of data processing to the privacy preferences of users, creating a need for signals that communicate preferences. However, neither law anticipates the ambiguity resulting from one user sending multiple signals with differing semantics. This is made possible by the decentralised Web ecosystem in which multiple actors and institutions design and propose privacy preference signals, which is described in the following section.

## B. Privacy Preference Signals

Hils, Daniel W. Woods, and Böhme[10] identify five signals that have been adopted at various points in the last 20 years. We ignore P3P because it was deprecated in 2017 and ignore NAI opt-outs as they remain an unpopular and narrow signal.[11] We focus on the remaining three signals. DNT and GPC have a similar technical design in that they extend HTTP headers by a single bit signal, but they differ in semantics. The law does not require recipients to respect DNT, and many ad-tech companies in fact decided to ignore the signal.[12] Nonetheless, it can still be turned on in Chrome's and Firefox's settings dialog. In contrast, the Global Privacy Control is designed to trigger the 'Do Not Sell' clause (the aforementioned legal right[13]) under the CCPA. It also provides a possible interpretation under the GDPR in its specification. However, major browsers have not yet adopted GPC outside of browser extensions.

The third signal, the TCF, is collected via dialogs embedded in the webpage. TCF signals can only be collected by registered intermediaries, of which QuantCast and OneTrust are the most popular.[14] The semantics of this signal are much more complex[15] but revolve around opting-in to various data processing purposes where consent is required. We discuss the nature of the ambiguity resulting from sending DNT/GPC opt-outs and TCF opt-ins in section V.

Finally, it is worth noting that niche and emerging signals exist that we did not consider. Do Not Sell signals can also be collected via webpages and stored as cookies, which use the standardised *US Privacy String* format.[16] These

---

[10] Hils, Woods and Böhme (n. 3).

[11] Pam Dixon, *The Network Advertising Initiative: Failing at Consumer Protection and at Self-Regulation*, www.worldprivacyforum. org/wp-content/uploads/2007/11/WPF_NAI_report_Nov2_2007fs.pdf (*World Privacy Forum*, 2007).

[12] Zimmeck and Alicki (n. 9) 15.

[13] ibid.

[14] Hils, Woods and Böhme (n. 3).

[15] Matte, Santos and Bielova (n. 8); Cristiana Santos, Nataliia Bielova, and Célestin Matte, 'Are cookie banners indeed compliant with the law? Deciphering EU legal requirements on consent and technical means to verify compliance of cookie banners,' *Technology and Regulation* (2020): 91–135.

[16] Interactive Advertising Bureau, 'IAB CCPA Compliance Framework For Publishers & Technology Companies' (2020) iabtechlab.com/standards/ccpa/.

cookies were successfully reset using the OptMeowt add-on for 17 of 30 websites in a recent study.[17] A technical specification for the Advanced Data Protection Control[18] was proposed that could automatically send privacy preference signals including TCF and Do Not Sell, but does not define any new signals in terms of semantics.

## III. Method

To examine the interplay between privacy preference signals, we embedded Quantcast's cookie consent dialog on the landing page of three websites for a short period of time and also logged visitors' DNT/GPC headers. In contrast to previous research,[19] we not only measure a user's decision when they are presented with a TCF consent dialog, but also if they are shown a consent dialog at all. This is important as our findings indicate that a non-negligible number of users employ techniques that block popular consent dialogs entirely.

### A. Study Participants

We sampled a very technical audience on all three websites. The majority of our measurements were made on mitmproxy.org, the website of an open-source program primarily used by software developers (72 per cent of all impressions).[20] Additionally, our research group's website and the website of a security competition we hosted contributed 14 per cent of observations each. Note that all numbers in this chapter are reported as impressions of the landing page. We do not perform any additional grouping to not overrepresent users who employ additional privacy measures (such as clearing cookies). In total, we observe 16,761 impressions by 8,033 IPv4 addresses from 7,432 /24 subnets.

In terms of browsers used, 53 per cent of visitors used Chrome/Chromium, 23 per cent Firefox, 9 per cent mobile browsers, 8 per cent Safari and 4 per cent Edge. For comparison, Wikimedia reports 55 per cent Chrome, 13 per cent Firefox, 10 per cent Safari and 8 per cent Edge on their desktop sites (June 2021).

---

[17] Zimmeck and Alicki (n. 9).
[18] Soheil Human et al., 'Advanced Data Protection Control (ADPC)' (2021) www.dataprotectioncontrol.org/adpc-spec/.
[19] Maximilian Hils, Daniel W. Woods, and Rainer Böhme, 'Measuring the Emergence of Consent Management on the Web,' in *Proceedings of the Internet Measurement Conference 2020*, IMC '20 (ACM, 2020).
[20] Aldo Cortesi et al., *mitmproxy: A free and open source interactive HTTPS proxy* (2010) mitmproxy.org/.

**Figure 2** Our Consent Dialog Measurement Pipeline

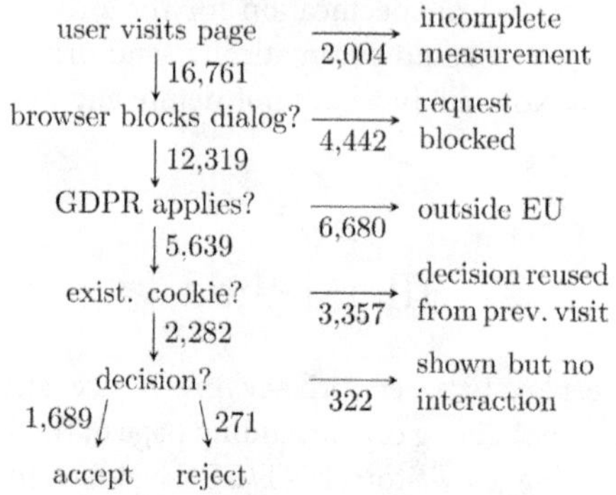

```
           user visits page      ────→   incomplete
                 │ 16,761       2,004     measurement
                 ↓
          browser blocks dialog? ────→   request
                 │ 12,319       4,442     blocked
                 ↓
           GDPR applies?         ────→   outside EU
                 │ 5,639         6,680
                 ↓
           exist. cookie?        ────→   decision reused
                 │ 2,282         3,357    from prev. visit
                 ↓
             decision?           ────→   shown but no
          1,689 /     \ 271       322     interaction
          accept      reject
```

## B. Data Collection

During our study period we embedded a logging script on all three websites and recorded the following data (see Figure 2):

(1) the user's browser and whether they sent a GPC/DNT header;
(2) state transitions from the browser's page visibility API;
(3) whether Quantcast's dialog could be loaded.

If loading the dialog was successful, we additionally recorded:

(1) Quantcast's assessment of whether GDPR applies to the current user;
(2) existing consent decisions from previous visits;
(3) the user's (new) consent decision when a dialog is shown.

To determine whether Quantcast's dialog can be loaded, we manually inject its main script tag and add load and error event listeners. We cannot detect what prevents this resource from loading, but we suspect that the majority is via ad-blocking browser extensions and DNS-level content blockers.

If Quantcast's JavaScript code could be loaded successfully, we interact with their implementation of the TCF API to determine if GDPR applies to the current user. We only show dialogs to users in the EU, which is Quantcast's default setting.

If we find that GDPR applies, we present the user with a dialog (see Figure 4) unless a decision has already been made. We track prior decisions via a cookie set by the dialog. This means the individuals behind the decisions are unique to the extent these cookies are preserved. In total, a consent dialog is only shown for 14 per cent of impressions.

To get a more accurate picture of the user's interaction with the web page, we observe the browser's page visibility API, which emits visibility change events when the page becomes visible, hidden, or closed. We use the Beacon API (navigator.sendBeacon) to record all events as this interface still works when the page is closed. As of 2021, both APIs are available in all major browsers. We discard all measurements for which we did not receive a complete set of events. This also reduces the impact of general network problems, which otherwise may be misattributed as blocking.

**Figure 3** The majority of users who have GPC turned on (bottom pair of bars) outright block consent dialogs. Those who do not block are relatively more likely to reject tracking when presented with a dialog offering equal choice. Still, the majority of GPC users click 'Accept' and thus send an ambiguous signal. The top pair of bars show the baseline without a browser-based privacy signal. The deprecated DNT signal (middle) was more prevalent than GPC, exhibited less extreme blocking and had a similar behavioural response

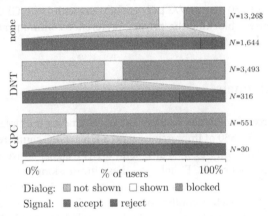

## C. Research Ethics

Our research design requires ethical consideration as each dialog takes user time. Given thousands of websites already impose these dialogs on users,[21] we judge that the time cost is outweighed by the value of information derived from our study in shaping the design and adoption of these dialogs. Previous research has shown that Quantcast's dialogs are completed in 3.2s on average.[22] While our institution does not require IRB review for minimal risk studies, we ensured that we did not deceive or harm website visitors and their privacy. All displayed consent notices functioned as described and respected the visitor's choice.

Explaining the research purpose before/after the experiment would lead to a much longer interruption than the initial dialog.

---

[21] Matte, Bielova and Santos (n. 4).
[22] Hils, Woods and Böhme (n. 19).

## IV. Results

We split our results into two aspects of ambiguity, namely blocked dialogs and multiple signals, and then consider robustness.

### A. Blocked Dialogs

The top bars in Figure 3 show that collecting a TCF signal via a dialog is non-trivial. The default version of the market-leading dialog does not load for 27 per cent of users, which rises to 50 per cent/73 per cent of users with DNT/GPC enabled. This technical response – blocking the privacy preference communication channel – was not previously considered in the literature.

### B. Multiple Signals

The second source of ambiguity results from users sending multiple signals simultaneously. First, 3.5k/550 of impressions send a DNT/GPC signal respectively. All but three of the GPC impressions also send a DNT signal so we do not further differentiate. Displaying a TCF dialog to these impressions creates the potential for a conflict, namely when users send an accept TCF signal while also sending a DNT/GPC signal. Such a conflict occurred for 5 per cent of all impressions, or 77/73 per cent when looking at DNT/GPC-enabled users only. We discuss the nature of the ambiguity later in the chapter.

The co-existence of these signals does not only increase ambiguity as the DNT/GPC signals have explanatory power over privacy preferences expressed via the TCF signal. Users with DNT/GPC enabled were 1.9/2.0 times more likely to click 'I do not accept' on the TCF dialog than those without. These results are significant at the $< 0.01$ level for DNT and $< 0.05$ for GPC. Note we cannot reject the null hypothesis that DNT/GPC are drawn from the same distribution ($\chi^2 (1, N = 346) = 0.07, p = 0.80$).

### C. Robustness

We run a number of checks to reduce the risk of spurious findings. It could be that GPC adoption was driven by browsers and browser extensions turning it on by default, as it was done by Brave browser.[23] In our sample, Firefox users are most likely to send a GPC signal (8.9 per cent), followed by Chromium (2.3 per cent)

---

[23] Peter Snyder and Anton Lazarev, 'Global Privacy Control, a new Privacy Standard Proposal, now Available in Brave's Desktop and Android Testing Versions' (2020) brave.com/global-privacy-control/.

and Edge (1.6 per cent). The share of GPC signals from other user agents is statistically zero. Note that Chromium includes Chrome, the most popular browser on the web, as well as Brave, a niche browser catering pro-privacy and cryptocoin-savy users, which identifies as Chrome in the user-agent string. To our knowledge, at the time of our study Brave was the only browser that sent GPC signals by default without asking the user. While we suspect that a number of the Chromium cases with GPC turned on do originate from Brave, the fact that other browsers emit more GPC signals, in both relative and absolute numbers, reassures us that the results are not purely driven by a single browser's default setting. The finding that users who emit DNT or GPC signals tend to choose more privacy-minded TCF options corroborates the behavioural interpretation.

## V. Discussion

We discuss how to collect preferences, the nature of the ambiguity, and the validity of our results.

### A. Collecting Preferences

Research into GDPR cookie consent dialogs consistently shows that dialogs contain dark patterns that erode user autonomy.[24] Our findings could be interpreted as further evidence that industry standard dialogs lead users to express untrue preferences. For example, 77 per cent of DNT-enabled users accept data processing in a TCF dialog despite sending a global 'Do Not Track' signal.

On the other hand, one could argue that the browser-controlled signals do not capture the true preferences of users. For example, Brave browser turns the

---

[24] Rainer Böhme and Stefan Köpsell, 'Trained to Accept? A Field Experiment on Consent Dialogs,' in *Proceedings of the SIGCHI Conference on Human Factors in Computing Systems*, CHI '10 (ACM, 2010), 2403–2406, doi.org/10.1145/1753326.1753689; Idris Adjerid et al., 'Sleights of Privacy: Framing, Disclosures, and the Limits of Transparency,' in *Proceedings of the Ninth Symposium on Usable Privacy and Security*, SOUPS'13 (ACM, 2013), doi.org/10.1145/2501604.2501613; Christine Utz et al., '(Un)informed Consent: Studying GDPR Consent Notices in the Field,' in *Proceedings of the 2019 ACM SIGSAC Conference on Computer and Communications Security*, CCS '19 (ACM, 2019), 973–990, doi.org/10.1145/3319535.3354212; Arunesh Mathur et al., 'Dark patterns at scale: Findings from a crawl of 11K shopping websites,' *Proceedings of the ACM on Human-Computer Interaction* 3 (2019): 1–32; Dominique Machuletz and Rainer Böhme, 'Multiple Purposes, Multiple Problems: A User Study of Consent Dialogs after GDPR,' *Proceedings on Privacy Enhancing Technologies* 2 (2020): 481–498, doi.org/10.2478/popets-2020-0037; Midas Nouwens et al., 'Dark Patterns after the GDPR: Scraping Consent Pop-Ups and Demonstrating Their Influence,' in *Proceedings of the 2020 CHI Conference on Human Factors in Computing Systems*, CHI '20 (ACM, 2020), doi.org/10.1145/3313831.3376321; Sean O'Connor, Ryan Nurwono and Eleanor Birrell, *(Un)clear and (In)conspicuous: The right to opt-out of sale under CCPA*, 2020 (arXiv: 2009.07884 [cs.CR]); Hana Habib et al., '"It's a Scavenger Hunt": Usability of Websites' Opt-Out and Data Deletion Choices,' in *Proceedings of the 2020 CHI Conference on Human Factors in Computing Systems*, CHI '20 (Honolulu, HI, USA: ACM, 2020), doi.org/10.1145/3313831.3376511.

signal on by default and does not provide an off-toggle.[25] The lack of an off-toggle goes even further than Microsoft's decision to turn DNT on by default in 2012, which led an AdTech industry group to withdraw from the DNT initiative.[26] This argument is undermined by new counter-arguments found in the CCPA, which establishes that 'affirmatively choosing products or services with privacy-protective features ... is considered a sufficiently clear manifestation of opting out'.[27]

This argument may not apply in jurisdictions outside of California. Consider that general purpose technologies like browsers contain multiple features. Users may adopt such technologies for any combination of these features, and so the browser may not have been chosen for the privacy features. For example, in addition to Brave containing 'privacy-protective features', it also contains features beyond privacy protection (eg, cryptotokens) that change the distribution of advertising revenues. Products and services with a narrow range of privacy relevant features, such as browser add-ons like Privacy Badger, may be more reliable indicators of a user's underlying privacy preferences.

Regardless of how the GPC signal is set, we have shown it explains a significant portion of the variance in expressed privacy preferences, which motivates further research into permanently storing privacy preferences in the browser. In particular, browsers could think about collecting more than 1 bit from users (0 bits in the case of Brave) given that their preferences must apply across a range of jurisdictions. Taking Colorado's new privacy law as an example, the 1 bit GPC signal has to cover not only the 'Do Not Sell' clause but also opt-in consent for storing sensitive data. While arguments can be made for how to interpret GPC's single bit under each law, the ambiguity could be used by AdTech firms to interpret the signal in their own interest or even request additional signals to 'clarify' the situation, which imposes yet more decision burden on users.

Our findings suggest an alternative way forward to protect user privacy, at least for opt-in consent. Unlike opt-out signals which default to tracking, opt-in requirements force data processors to collect a privacy preference signal before processing personal data. If browsers block the interface collecting preferences, such as dialogs embedded in web-pages, then firms have no legal basis under an opt-in requirement. This is particularly relevant given a back-of-the-envelope calculation reveals that users have already wasted at least 2,500 years[28] sending TCF signals. This will likely invoke counter-measures from websites leading to an arms race.[29]

---

[25] Snyder and Lazarev (n. 23).
[26] Interactive Advertising Bureau, 'Do Not Track' set to 'On' by Default in Internet Explorer 10 – IAB Response (2012) www.iab.com/news/do-not-track-set-to-on-by-default-in-internet-explorer-10iab-response/.
[27] Zimmeck and Alicki (n. 9).
[28] Hils, Woods and Böhme (n. 3).
[29] Rishab Nithyanand et al., 'Adblocking and Counter Blocking: A Slice of the Arms Race,' in 6th USENIX Workshop on Free and Open Communications on the Internet (FOCI 2016) (Austin, TX: USENIX Association, August 2016) www.usenix.org/conference/foci16/workshop-program/presentation/nithyanand.

## B. Ambiguous Signals

Two sources of ambiguity we identified, namely blocking dialogs and multiple signals, are particularly relevant for the GDPR where many data processors[30] rely on an 'unambiguous' (Article 4)[31] opt-in consent as a legal basis. Blocked dialogs should be resolved in favour of the user not having provided consent. Multiple signals are less easily resolved and may require focusing on the semantics of each signal. For example, the DNT signal 'represents a superset of what is covered by Do Not Sell'[32] and so is a less ambiguous objection to some of the TCF's data processing purposes.

While many resolution approaches are conceivable (eg, most/least privacy-minded, temporal or normative order, user intervention), we defer this question to legal analysis with the Blogosphere providing preliminary arguments.[33] The same sources of ambiguity will likely be resolved differently in non-EU jurisdictions. This creates a technical problem for firms processing data from users across multiple jurisdictions – firms must infer each user's jurisdiction. Could privacy aware users masquerade as residents of the jurisdiction with the strongest privacy rights?

Going beyond ambiguity, users can send two conflicting signals expressed under the same standard when both the webpage and the browser collect preferences. For example, this could occur with the proposed ADPC signal[34] if a user clicked 'I accept' in the TCF consent dialog while sending a 'No consent under TCF' ADPC header.

## C. Validity

We argue that our study has high ecological validity in that we chose the most popular dialog on the Web[35] and displayed it to users browsing a real website. Unfortunately, we could only present this design to the users of three websites, all of which likely over-sample privacy aware and technically literate users. The majority of our participants visited the website of an open-source program targeting developers, and the remaining from our research group's webpages. Future work could embed the same study in a broader range of websites. In fact, our 'experiment' could be carried out passively by any website collecting TCF signals.

---

[30] Hils, Woods and Böhme (n. 19).
[31] European Union, 'Regulation (EU) 2016/679 of the European Parliament and of the Council of 27 April 2016 on the protection of natural persons with regard to the processing of personal data and on the free movement of such data, and repealing Directive 95/46/EC (General Data Protection Regulation).'
[32] Zimmeck and Alicki (n. 9) 15.
[33] Robin Berjon, 'GPC under the GDPR,' (2021), berjon.com/gpc-under-the-gdpr/; Harshvardhan J. Pandit, 'GPC + GDPR: will it work?,' (2021), harshp.com/research/blog/gpc-gdpr-can-it-work.
[34] Human et al. (n. 18).
[35] Hils, Woods and Böhme (n. 3).

## VI. Conclusion

We first present evidence that websites do receive ambiguous privacy preference signals, namely opt-in TCF signals sent alongside a GPC opt-out signal. Moreover, the share of ambiguous privacy signals due to blocked TCF dialogs is significant. Both phenomena have been overlooked in the empirical literature. Finally, our study suggests that user adoption of the GPC helps to explain privacy preferences, and is associated with a greater propensity to reject consent.

## References

Adjerid, Idris, Alessandro Acquisti, Laura Brandimarte and George Loewenstein. 'Sleights of Privacy: Framing, Disclosures, and the Limits of Transparency.' In *Proceedings of the Ninth Symposium on Usable Privacy and Security*. SOUPS '13. ACM, 2013. doi. org/10.1145/2501604.2501613.

Berjon, Robin. 'GPC under the GDPR' (2021). berjon.com/gpc-under-the-gdpr/.

Böhme, Rainer and Stefan Köpsell. 'Trained to Accept? A Field Experiment on Consent Dialogs.' In *Proceedings of the SIGCHI Conference on Human Factors in Computing Systems*, 2403–2406. CHI '10. ACM, 2010. doi.org/10.1145/1753326.1753689.

California Civil Code § 1798. 'California Consumer Privacy Act of 2018.'

Cortesi, Aldo, Maximilian Hils, Thomas Kriechbaumer and contributors. *mitmproxy: A free and open source interactive HTTPS proxy* (2010–).mitmproxy.org/.

Dixon, Pam. *The Network Advertising Initiative: Failing at Consumer Protection and at Self-Regulation* (World Privacy Forum, 2007). www.worldprivacyforum.org/wp-content/uploads/2007/11/WPF_NAI_report_Nov2_2007fs.pdf.

European Union. 'Regulation (EU) 2016/679 of the European Parliament and of the Council of 27 April 2016 on the protection of natural persons with regard to the processing of personal data and on the free movement of such data, and repealing Directive 95/46/EC (General Data Protection Regulation).' *Official Journal L110* 59 (2016): 1–88.

Global Privacy Control. *GPC Privacy Browser Signal Now Used by Millions and Honored By Major Publishers.* (2021). globalprivacycontrol.org/press-release/20210128.

Habib, Hana, Sarah Pearman, Jiamin Wang, Yixin Zou, Alessandro Acquisti, Lorrie Faith Cranor, Norman Sadeh and Florian Schaub. '"It's a Scavenger Hunt": Usability of Websites' Opt-Out and Data Deletion Choices.' In *Proceedings of the 2020 CHI Conference on Human Factors in Computing Systems*. CHI '20. Honolulu, HI, USA: ACM, 2020. doi.org/10.1145/3313831.3376511.

Hils, Maximilian, Daniel W Woods, and Rainer Böhme. 'Measuring the Emergence of Consent Management on the Web.' In *Proceedings of the Internet Measurement Conference 2020*. IMC '20. ACM, 2020.

———, 'Privacy Preference Signals: Past, Present and Future.' *Proceedings on Privacy Enhancing Technologies* no. 4 (2021). petsymposium.org/2021/files/papers/issue4/popets-2021-0069.pdf.

Human, Soheil, Max Schrems, Alan Toner, Gerben and Ben Wagner. 'Advanced Data Protection Control (ADPC)' (2021) www.dataprotectioncontrol.org/adpc-spec/.

Interactive Advertising Bureau. 'Do Not Track' set to 'On' by Default in Internet Explorer 10 – IAB Response. (2012) www.iab.com/news/do-not-track-set-to-on-by-default-in-internet-explorer-10iab-response/, 2012.

———, 'IAB CCPA Compliance Framework For Publishers & Technology Companies' (2020) iabtechlab.com/standards/ccpa/.

Machuletz, Dominique and Rainer Böhme. 'Multiple Purposes, Multiple Problems: A User Study of Consent Dialogs after GDPR.' *Proceedings on Privacy Enhancing Technologies* no. 2 (2020): 481–498. doi.org/10.2478/popets-2020-0037.

Mathur, Arunesh, Gunes Acar, Michael J Friedman, Elena Lucherini, Jonathan Mayer, Marshini Chetty and Arvind Narayanan. 'Dark patterns at scale: Findings from a crawl of 11K shopping websites.' *Proceedings of the ACM on Human-Computer Interaction* 3 no. CSCW (2019): 1–32.

Matte, Célestin, Nataliia Bielova and Cristiana Santos. 'Do Cookie Banners Respect my Choice? Measuring Legal Compliance of Banners from IAB Europe's Transparency and Consent Framework.' In *IEEE Symposium on Security and Privacy*, 791–809. New York: IEEE, 2020. doi.org/10.1109/SP40000.2020.00076.

Matte, Célestin, Cristiana Santos and Nataliia Bielova. 'Purposes in IAB Europe's TCF: which legal basis and how are they used by advertisers?' In *Annual Privacy Forum* (2020).

Mayer, Jonathan, Arvind Narayanan and Sid Stamm. 'Do Not Track: A Universal Third-Party Web Tracking Opt Out.' *Center for Internet and Society* (2011). datatracker.ietf.org/doc/html/draft-mayer-do-not-track-00.

Nithyanand, Rishab, Sheharbano Khattak, Mobin Javed, Narseo Vallina-Rodriguez, Marjan Falahrastegar, Julia E. Powles, Emiliano De Cristofaro, Hamed Haddadi and Steven J. Murdoch. 'Adblocking and Counter Blocking: A Slice of the Arms Race.' In *6th USENIX Workshop on Free and Open Communications on the Internet (FOCI 16)*. Austin, TX: USENIX Association, August 2016. www.usenix.org/conference/foci16/workshop-program/presentation/nithyanand.

Nouwens, Midas, Ilaria Liccardi, Michael Veale, David Karger and Lalana Kagal. 'Dark Patterns after the GDPR: Scraping Consent Pop-Ups and Demonstrating Their Influence.' In *Proceedings of the 2020 CHI Conference on Human Factors in Computing Systems*. CHI '20. ACM, 2020. doi.org/10.1145/3313831.3376321.

O'Connor, Sean, Ryan Nurwono and Eleanor Birrell. *(Un)clear and (In)conspicuous: The right to opt-out of sale under CCPA*, 2020. arXiv: 2009.07884 [cs.CR].

Pandit, Harshvardhan J. 'GPC + GDPR: will it work?,' (2021). harshp.com/research/blog/gpc-gdpr-can-it- work.

Santos, Cristiana, Nataliia Bielova and Célestin Matte. 'Are cookie banners indeed compliant with the law? Deciphering EU legal requirements on consent and technical means to verify compliance of cookie banners.' *Technology and Regulation* (2020) 91–135.

Snyder, Peter and Anton Lazarev. 'Global Privacy Control, a new Privacy Standard Proposal, now Available in Brave's Desktop and Android Testing Versions,' (2020) brave.com/global-privacy-control/.

Utz, Christine, Martin Degeling, Sascha Fahl, Florian Schaub and Thorsten Holz. '(Un)informed Consent: Studying GDPR Consent Notices in the Field.' In *Proceedings of the 2019 ACM SIGSAC Conference on Computer and Communications Security*, pp. 973–990. CCS '19. ACM, 2019. doi.org/10.1145/3319535.3354212.

Zimmeck, Sebastian and Kuba Alicki. 'Standardizing and Implementing Do Not Sell.' In *Proceedings of the 19th Workshop on Privacy in the Electronic Society*, 15–20. WPES'20. Virtual Event, USA: Association for Computing Machinery, 2020. doi.org/10.1145/3411497.3420224.

## A. Appendix

**Figure 4** Quantcast's TCF cookie dialog used in this study. Note that we used Quantcast's default configuration, which renders the 'I accept' button more prominently and thus does not provide an equal choice

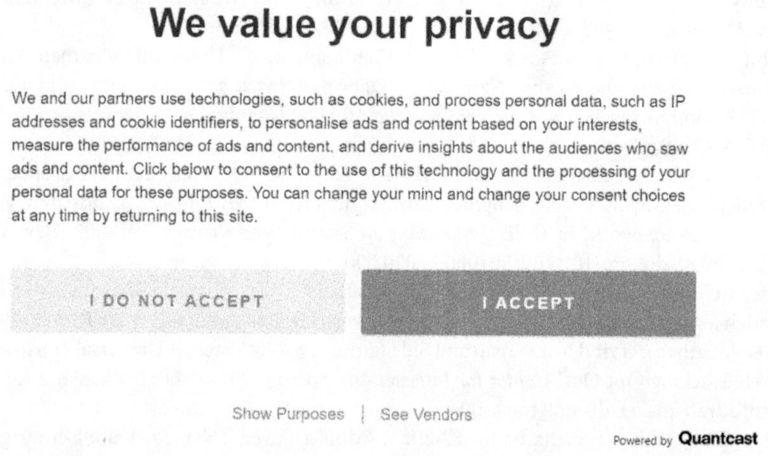

### We value your privacy

We and our partners use technologies, such as cookies, and process personal data, such as IP addresses and cookie identifiers, to personalise ads and content based on your interests, measure the performance of ads and content, and derive insights about the audiences who saw ads and content. Click below to consent to the use of this technology and the processing of your personal data for these purposes. You can change your mind and change your consent choices at any time by returning to this site.

I DO NOT ACCEPT        I ACCEPT

Show Purposes | See Vendors

Powered by **Quantcast**

# 5

# The Multi-faceted Role of the Individual in EU Data Protection Law

KATHERINE NOLAN[*]

## Abstract

In an environment of mass digitalisation and datafication, myriad concerns arise about the effectiveness of information privacy and data protection laws. But a significant line of that criticism calls into the question the role of an individual. Is it correct to categorise EU data protection law as individualistic? Understanding the place of the individual within EU data protection law is an important precursor to debates about whether we should frame our legislative regime around the individual protection. In order to engage with this issue, one must first examine the role of the individual in data protection law.

Through an examination of the Data Protection Directive, General Data Protection Regulation, Article 8 of the Charter of Fundamental Rights in the European Union and associated case law of the Court of Justice of the European Union, this chapter offers an account of the role of the individual in EU data protection law, with two aims.

First, this chapter demonstrates the centrality of the individual to EU data protection law, arguing that while EU data protection is not entirely individualistic, the individual is central to the regime through its important position throughout key elements of the regime.

Second, recognising that the individual plays a number of roles within EU data protection, it is useful to develop a framework for understanding those roles. This chapter offers a conceptual framework to understand the role of the individual in the regime. It argues that the individual serves multiple, if overlapping, functions in EU data protection law: as the object and subject of EU data protection law. The individual serves as the normative foundation underpinning the regime, the primary protected subject of data protection law and is central to the enforcement

---

[*] PhD Candidate, London School of Economics and Political Science.

of data protection law, empowered to act in their self-defence through decision-making and individual rights.

## Keywords

Personal data, GDPR, the data subject, enforcement, the right to protection of personal data

## I. Introduction

The individual is central to the EU data protection framework. This centrality has drawn scholarly attention that criticises the place of the individual in these fields,[1] or individualist aspects of data protection and privacy regimes, such as consent or individual decision making.[2] Others have called for alternative perspectives to individual privacy or data protection, calling for social,[3] group[4] or democratic perspectives.[5] However, understanding the place of the individual within EU data

---

[1] Priscilla M. Regan, *Legislating Privacy: Technology, Social Values, and Public Policy* (United States of America: The University of North Carolina Press, 1995); Brendan Van Alsenoy, 'The Evolving Role of the Individual under EU Data Protection Law.' *CiTiP Working Paper Series* 23 (2015): 36; Bart van der Sloot, *Privacy as Virtue: Moving beyond the Individual in the Age of Big Data*, School of Human Rights Research Series; Volume 81 (Cambridge, United States: Intersentia, 2017); Helen Nissenbaum, *Privacy in Context: Technology, Policy and the Integrity of Social Life* (California: Stanford University Press, 2010); Julie E. Cohen, 'Turning Privacy Inside Out,' *Theoretical Inquiries in Law* 20 (2019): 1–32; Orla Lynskey, 'Delivering Data Protection: The Next Chapter,' *German Law Journal* 21.1 (2020): 80–84, doi.org/10.1017/glj.2019.100; Susanna Lindroos-Hovinheimo, *Private Selves: Legal Personhood in European Privacy Protection*, Cambridge Studies in European Law and Policy (Cambridge: Cambridge University Press, 2021); Nathalie A. Smuha, 'Beyond the Individual: Governing AI's Societal Harm,' *Internet Policy Review* 10.3 (2021), doi.org/10.14763/2021.3.1574; Felix Bieker, *The Right to Data Protection: Individual and Structural Dimensions of Data Protection in EU Law*, vol. 34, Information Technology and Law Series (The Hague: T.M.C. Asser Press, 2022), doi.org/10.1007/978-94-6265-503-4.

[2] For example, Woodrow Hartzog, 'Opinions – The Case Against Idealising Control,' *European Data Protection Law Review* 4.4 (2018): 423–432; Bert-Jaap Koops, 'The Trouble with European Data Protection Law,' *International Data Privacy Law* 4.4 (2014): 252; Orla Lynskey, *The Foundations of EU Data Protection Law* (Oxford: Oxford University Press, 2015), 249; Daniel J. Solove, 'Privacy Self-Management and the Consent Dilemma,' *Harvard Law Review* 126.7 (2013): 1880–1903.

[3] Regan (n. 1); Nissenbaum (n. 1).

[4] Alessandro Mantelero, 'Personal Data for Decisional Purposes in the Age of Analytics: From an Individual to a Collective Dimension of Data Protection,' *Computer Law & Security Review* 32.2 (2016): 238–255, doi.org/10.1016/j.clsr.2016.01.014; Linnet Taylor, Luciano Floridi and Bart van der Sloot (eds.), *Group Privacy: New Challenges of Data Technologies* (Cham: Springer International Publishing, 2017), doi.org/10.1007/978-3-319-46608-8; Ugo Pagallo, 'The Group, the Private, and the Individual: A New Level of Data Protection?,' in Taylor, Floridi and van der Sloot (ibid), 159–73; Luciano Floridi, 'Group Privacy: A Defence and an Interpretation,' in Taylor, Floridi and van der Sloot (ibid), 83–100.

[5] Paul M. Schwartz, 'Privacy and Democracy in Cyberspace,' *Vanderbilt Law Review; Nashville* 52.6 (1999): 1609–1702; Yves Poullet, 'Data Protection Legislation: What Is at Stake for Our Society and Democracy?' *Computer Law & Security Review* 25.3 (2009): 211–226; Salomé Viljoen, 'A Relational Theory of Data Governance,' *The Yale Law Journal* (2021): 82.

protection law is an important precursor to such debates. Before we conceive of alternatives, one must first examine the present regime, and the role of the individual in data protection law.

In the context of EU data protection law, however, there has been no comprehensive elucidation of the role of the individual,[6] against which we can evaluate the claims that an individually oriented data protection law is failing. This chapter seeks to offer such a contribution. While the data protection regime cannot be said to be entirely individualistic, I argue that the individual is central to the regime. The role of the individual is multi-dimensional, and the individual serves as both object and subject within EU data protection law.

## A. The Role of the Individual: Object and Subject

The individual plays a central but multi-faceted role in EU data protection law. Through an examination of the framework of the General Data Protection Regulation (GDPR),[7] its predecessor, the Data Protection Directive,[8] Article 8 of the Charter and the associated case law of the Court of Justice of the European Union (CJEU), it can be said that the individual serves as both object and subject of EU data protection law.

The Data Protection Directive in its very title set out to achieve 'the protection of *individuals* with regard to the processing of personal data',[9] which in the GDPR has been replaced with references to the protection of 'natural persons'. The concept of the 'individual' offers us a particular way in which to think about the natural person, a construct of an autonomous, individuated person endowed with dignity and agency,[10] ideas which find representation in the EU data protection regime.

---

[6] Lindroos-Hovinheimo contributes a wonderful work on the philosophy of the person underpinning EU data protection law, but does not engage in a doctrinal categorisation such as is offered herein. Lindroos-Hovinheimo, *Private Selves: Legal Personhood in European Privacy Protection*.

[7] REGULATION (EU) 2016/679 OF THE EUROPEAN PARLIAMENT AND OF THE COUNCIL of 27 April 2016 on the protection of natural persons with regard to the processing of personal data and on the free movement of such data, and repealing Directive 95/46/EC (General Data Protection Regulation) (OJ L 119, 4/5/2016, 1–88).

[8] DIRECTIVE 95/46/EC OF THE EUROPEAN PARLIAMENT AND OF THE COUNCIL of 24 October 1995 on the protection of individuals with regard to the processing of personal data and on the free movement of such data (OJ L 281, 23/11/1995, 31–50).

[9] Data Protection Directive. Emphasis added.

[10] Often associated with a liberal theory of law or human rights, though with precursors in earlier religious and humanist traditions. See Costas Douzinas, *The End of Human Rights: Critical Thought at the Turn of the Century* (London: Bloomsbury Publishing Plc, 2000); Alexander Somek, *Individualism: An Essay on the Authority of the European Union* (Oxford: Oxford University Press, 2008); Larry Siedentop, *Inventing the Individual: The Origins of Western Liberalism* (Milton Keynes: Penguin Books, 2014); Catherine Dupré, *The Age of Dignity: Human Rights and Constitutionalism in Europe* (London: Bloomsbury Publishing Plc, 2015); Sarah Jane Trotter, 'On Coming to Terms: How European Human Rights Law Imagines the Human Condition' (Doctor of Philosophy, London, The London School of Economics and Political Science, 2018), etheses.lse.ac.uk/3946/1/Trotter__On-coming-terms-European-human-rights.pdf.

Rather than offering a normative position on the role for the individual, this conceptual model for understanding the individual is built upon a doctrinal analysis of the current, multi-partite role the idea of the individual is playing within the regime. The conceptual model was developed through an inductive reading of the relevant legislation (the Data Protection Directive, GDPR) and case law relating to those legal instruments and Article 8 of the Charter. The method of review was doctrinal, informed by the qualitative method of thematic analysis,[11] in order to be systematic in the review of the materials and to be cognisant of the process of assigning analytical labels to themes in the case law and legislation.[12] The legislation and decisions were coded, identifying aspects of the legislation or decisions which related to the individual. Once coded, the codes were then grouped into thematic classifications, in order to allow analysis according to those themes. This was an iterative process, in which cases and thematic classifications were revisited in light of parallel reading in academic literature and overall themes (that of the individual as object and subject) were identified.

The thematic categorisation which emerges is that of the individual as both object and subject. This categorisation of the roles of the individual is inspired by works of Weiler,[13] Marx,[14] Azoulai et al.[15] and Cohen[16] in parallel scholarship. The individual, as object, is observed by the legislature and the courts, who adopt approaches which are said to be in their interest, and that interest comes to be identified with the normative underpinnings of EU data protection law. The individual, as subject, is engaged directly through data protection law as an actor. They are subjectified, as a participant in a new order of relationships, a rights-holder and a protected data subject in relation to the regulated data controller, as well as deputised as an agent in the enforcement of data protection law itself. I will explain each of these roles in a little further detail.

---

[11] On the process of thematic analysis, see Virginia Braun and Victoria Clarke, 'Using Thematic Analysis in Psychology,' *Qualitative Research in Psychology* 3.2 (2006): 77–101, doi.org/10.1191/1478088706qp063oa; Jennifer Fereday and Eimear Muir-Cochrane, 'Demonstrating Rigor Using Thematic Analysis: A Hybrid Approach of Inductive and Deductive Coding and Theme Development,' *International Journal of Qualitative Methods* 5.1 (2006): 80–92, doi.org/10.1177/160940690600500107.

[12] For similar adoption of an inductive qualitative approach for the review of case law, see eg Saïla Ouald Chaib, 'Procedural Fairness as a Vehicle for Inclusion in the Freedom of Religion Jurisprudence of the Strasbourg Court,' *Human Rights Law Review* 16.3 (2016): 483–510, doi.org/10.1093/hrlr/ngw020.

[13] Weiler has observed that through direct effect, EU law can reach the individual as an object and subject of its laws, bypassing the Member States. J.H.H. Weiler, 'Van Gend En Loos: The Individual as Subject and Object and the Dilemma of European Legitimacy,' *International Journal of Constitutional Law* 12.1 (2014): 98, doi.org/10.1093/icon/mou011.

[14] Marx, contrasting surveillance and privacy, considers that surveillance emphasises the agent who accesses data, whereas privacy emphasises the subject who restricts access. Gary T. Marx, *Windows into the Soul: Surveillance and Society in an Age of High Technology* (Chicago: University of Chicago Press, 2016), 23.

[15] Loïc Azoulai, Etienne Pataut and Ségolène Barbou des Places, 'Being a Person in the European Union,' in *Constructing the Person in EU Law: Rights, Roles, Identities*, ed. Loïc Azoulai, Etienne Pataut and Ségolène Barbou des Places (Oxford: Hart Publishing, 2016), 9.

[16] Julie E. Cohen, 'Examined Lives: Informational Privacy and the Subject as Object,' *Stanford Law Review* 52. 5 (2000): 1373, doi.org/10.2307/1229517.

The individual is the object of EU data protection law in the sense that the courts and legislature take the individual and their interest as their object in the design, implementation and enforcement of EU data protection law. This objectification of the individual is seen in two main manners. First, the protection of the individual and their fundamental rights provide the normative basis and primary law competence justifying the regime – the object of the legislature. Second, this explicit role has driven a purposive approach to the interpretation of data protection law – the object of the judiciary.

The individual is also a subject of data protection law, not merely acted upon by the legislature and judiciary. The individual's subjectivity is also multi-dimensional. As a protected actor, the central legal actor of the EU data protection law – the 'data subject', the individual comes to be central to the logic of the regime, particularly to the scope of data protection law, as well as the assessment of legality under the GDPR. Moreover, the individual may also be a regulated subject of data protection law. While less explicitly discussed, and beyond the scope of this chapter, the individual may also be a data controller, the responsible entity in data protection law.[17] Finally, the individual is also a participant in the enforcement of data protection law, which I name 'an agent' of data protection law. Through the protection of individual decision-making and the grant of procedural rights to the individual, the individual is one of the actors in the regime through which the protection of personal data is enacted. This multi-faceted role of the individual is depicted below.

**Figure 1** The multi-faceted role of the individual

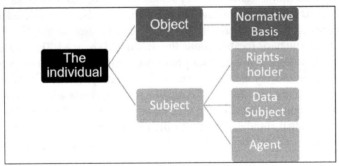

---

[17] Such a classification has become broader due to the narrowing of the household and personal processing exemption and the broadening of the joint controllership concept. On this, see further Lilian Edwards et al., 'Data Subjects as Data Controllers: A Fashion(Able) Concept?,' *Internet Policy Review*, policyreview.info/articles/news/data-subjects-data-controllers-fashionable-concept/1400; Van Alsenoy, 'The Evolving Role of the Individual under EU Data Protection Law'; Jiahong Chen et al., 'Who Is Responsible for Data Processing in Smart Homes? Reconsidering Joint Controllership and the Household Exemption,' *International Data Privacy Law* 10.4 (2020): 279–293; Michèle Finck, 'Cobwebs of Control: The Two Imaginations of the Data Controller in EU Law,' *International Data Privacy Law* 11.4 (2021): 333–347, doi.org/10.1093/idpl/ipab017. While this is certainly an interesting

## II. The Individual as the Object of Data Protection Law

As the object of the adopters and enforcers of EU data protection law, the individual and the protection of their rights and interest serve as the normative foundation for the regime. This normative status has legal significance in three important ways to be explored: first, the primary law competence to adopt EU data protection legislation under the Treaties is linked to the individual, second, the purposive interpretation adopted by the CJEU is driven by the individual interest and third, the individual right to personal data protection transports the right to personal data protection into other areas of EU law.

### A. The Normative Basis for EU Data Protection Law

The normative foundation for EU data protection law has undergone some transition over time, but from the outset has been linked to the protection of the individual.

The Data Protection Directive had two express aims; the free flow of personal data throughout the EU and the protection of the rights and freedoms of individuals.[18] The right to privacy was conceived as the particular basis for protection of individuals. Alongside this desire to protect individual interests, the Data Protection Directive was also adopted as a measure of market harmonisation. In order to facilitate the completion of the single market and associated cross-border flows of data, harmonisation of privacy standards was seen to be necessary.[19] Thus, at its outset, EU data protection law had two primary goals, with the need to reconcile the needs of the individual with the market harmonisation aim.[20]

Over time, the basis for data protection in the EU changed. The Lisbon Treaty introduced new legal status to data protection, with an explicit competence for data protection and recognition of the right to data protection.[21] Additionally, and importantly, the EU Charter of Fundamental Rights was adopted and became part of the EU constitutional order, with equal status to the Treaties. The Charter contains an explicit standalone right to the protection of personal data,[22] alongside the right to respect for private life.[23] The Charter has played an increasingly

---

phenomenon, it has arguably arisen due to interpretation rather than design, and often conflicts with the intended operation of the data protection regime. For this reason I have excluded this parallel development from this chapter.

[18] Data Protection Directive Art 1.
[19] Data Protection Directive Recitals 5, 8.
[20] Of course, these objectives are not framed in absolutist terms and in the implementation of these objectives through legislation, other rights and interests come to be balanced with such objectives, but as we shall see, the express objectives have important legal significance. See section II(B) below.
[21] TFEU Art 16.
[22] Charter Art 8.
[23] Charter Art 7.

prominent role in the CJEU's decision making,[24] as predicted by Lynskey, who notes that EU data protection has transitioned from a measure of market harmonisation with high protection of fundamental rights and freedoms to a regime with a fundamental rights orientation.[25]

The GDPR, adopted in 2016 and replacing the Data Protection Directive, still acknowledges the desire to achieve free movement of personal data throughout the EU,[26] but is more firmly grounded as a fundamental rights instrument. The substance of the rules of the GDPR is to protect individuals, grounded in the right to data protection.[27]

In its focus on the protection of data protection as a fundamental right, the normative legitimacy of the GDPR is grounded in the protection of the individual. The fundamental right to data protection may have emerged after data protection legislation,[28] but it has consolidated existing emphasis on the individual in predecessor legislation. In this shifting emphasis, the GDPR reflects the emergence of the EU fundamental rights project.[29] The GDPR imposes compliance obligations upon controllers, which necessarily interferes with the freedoms and interests of others, including the freedom to conduct a business,[30] and the freedom to engage in work and provide services.[31] These interferences are said to be necessary or justified because of the need to safeguard affected individuals. Despite being a Regulation in name, there is substantial room for Member States to derogate, thus limiting its capacity to ensure free movement of data throughout the Union,[32] and explicitly sets out to assure the protection of the fundamental right to data

---

[24] See discussion in section II(B) below.

[25] Orla Lynskey, 'From Market-Making Tool to Fundamental Right: The Role of the Court of Justice in Data Protection's Identity Crisis,' in *European Data Protection: Coming of Age*, ed. Serge Gutwirth et al. (The Netherlands: Springer Netherlands, 2013), 59–84.

[26] Article 1(1) of the GDPR provides: 'This Regulation lays down rules relating to the protection of natural persons with regard to the processing of personal data and rules relating to the free movement of personal data.' Article 1(3) provides that 'The free movement of personal data within the Union shall be neither restricted nor prohibited for reasons connected with the protection of natural persons with regard to the processing of personal data.'

[27] See discussion in section III(B) below.

[28] See eg Gloria González Fuster, *The Emergence of Personal Data Protection as a Fundamental Right of the EU* Vol. 16. Law, Governance and Technology Series (Cham: Springer International Publishing, 2014); David Erdos, *European Data Protection Regulation, Journalism, and Traditional Publishers: Balancing on a Tightrope?* (Oxford: Oxford University Press, 2019).

[29] See González Fuster (n. 28) ch 5.

[30] Charter Art 16.

[31] Charter Art 15.

[32] The GDPR allows Member States to introduce national variations on a wide number of GDPR provisions, including; the age of children's consent (GDPR Art 8(1)), additional conditions as to the processing of genetic data, biometric data or data concerning health (GDPR Art 9(4)), restrictions necessary to safeguard national security, defence, public security, criminal investigations and prosecutions and a series of other public interests (GDPR Art 23), restrictions necessary to protect the right to freedom of expression and information (GDPR Art 85(1)), rules relating to public access to official documents (GDPR Art 86), conditions for the processing of national identification numbers (GDPR Art 87), conditions for the protection of employee data (GDPR Art 88), derogations for scientific or historical research purposes or statistical purposes (GDPR Art 89) or obligations of official secrecy (GDPR Art 90).

protection. The free market objectives of the Regulation may thus be said to have been subsumed by the need to protect individuals. On its own terms, therefore, the success of the GDPR can be judged in accordance with its ability to effectively protect individuals.

## B. The Legal Significance of the Object of Individual Protection

### i. Primary Law Basis for EU Data Protection Law

Under the principle of conferral, the EU may only act where it has been conferred with an express competence under the Treaties.[33] After the Lisbon Treaty, along with the adoption of Article 8 of the Charter, there was a change in competence for the adoption of EU data protection law. The Data Protection Directive was adopted as a measure of market harmonisation.[34] As such, it was not tied expressly to a rights-orientation or any substantive approach to data protection. However, over time, a shift in the primary law basis for EU data protection law has occurred, in line with broader constitutional and institutional shifts in the EU. Now, the legislature must take as their object the individual and their right to data protection.

After Lisbon, Article 16 TFEU was introduced as the basis for the adoption of EU data protection measures, founded on the right to protection of personal data, formulated as follows:

1. Everyone has the right to the protection of personal data concerning them.
2. The European Parliament and the Council, acting in accordance with the ordinary legislative procedure, shall lay down the rules relating to the protection of individuals with regard to the processing of personal data by Union institutions, bodies, offices and agencies, and by the Member States when carrying out activities which fall within the scope of Union law, and the rules relating to the free movement of such data. Compliance with these rules shall be subject to the control of independent authorities.

The rules adopted on the basis of this Article shall be without prejudice to the specific rules laid down in Article 39 of the Treaty on European Union.

In this way, the legislative basis for data protection initiatives is now explicitly linked to the protection of individuals and their fundamental right to data protection.[35]

---

[33] TEU Art 5.
[34] Grounded on the precursor to TFEU Art 114, which allows the EU to adopt measures for the approximation of laws in the interest of the establishment and functioning of the internal market.
[35] As with Gellert, I prefer a non-absolutist vision of rights-based regulation. R. Gellert, 'Data Protection: A Risk Regulation? Between the Risk Management of Everything and the Precautionary Alternative,' *International Data Privacy Law* 5.1 (2015): 3–19.

Article 8 of the Charter provides further details for the nature of the right to data protection, in particular indicating some of the core aspects to the manner in which that right is to be safeguarded:

1. Everyone has the right to the protection of personal data concerning him or her.
2. Such data must be processed fairly for specified purposes and on the basis of the consent of the person concerned or some other legitimate basis laid down by law. Everyone has the right of access to data which has been collected concerning him or her, and the right to have it rectified.
3. Compliance with these rules shall be subject to control by an independent authority.

Thus, data protection now has its roots in EU primary law, and in its formulation, is expressly tied to a particular type of regime, founded on the protection of individuals with a rights orientation.[36]

How the rights orientation must inform the legislative implementation of Article 16(2) TFEU, such as the GDPR is still a matter of contention. For example, the question of whether a rights-based approach to data protection is necessarily absolutist or in opposition to a risk-based approach has emerged.[37] While this full debate is beyond the scope of this chapter, nevertheless we can see that the rights-based competence does seem to shape the permissible boundaries of data protection legislation. Hustinx questioned 'how much flexibility Article 16 TFEU allows and where the impact of the Charter might pose certain limits.'[38] As he notes, this is not simply theoretical.[39] During the development of the GDPR, the Council's Legal Service questioned the compatibility of the one-stop-shop mechanism with the right to an effective remedy.[40] More concretely, the CJEU has repeatedly confirmed that independent supervision is an essential component of data protection.[41] Similarly, the appropriate competence of the Canadian/EU PNR Agreement was the subject of judicial scrutiny, as the CJEU considered

---

[36] This transformation has been named the constitutionalisation of data protection law. Serge Gutwirth and Paul De Hert, 'Data Protection in the Case Law of Strasbourg and Luxemburg: Constitutionalisation in Action,' in *Reinventing Data Protection?*, ed. Serge Gutwirth et al. (Cham: Springer, 2009), 3–44. See also Federico Fabbrini, 'The EU Charter of Fundamental Rights and the Rights to Data Privacy: The EU Court of Justice as a Human Rights Court,' in *The EU Charter of Fundamental Rights as a Binding Instrument: Five Years On*, ed. Sybe A. De Vries, Ulf Bernitz, and Stephen Weatherill, vol. 20, Studies of the Oxford Institute of European and Comparative Law (Oxford: Hart Publishing, 2015), 266; Jeff Ausloos, *The Right to Erasure in EU Data Protection Law: From Individual Rights to Effective Protection*, Oxford Data Protection and Privacy Law (Oxford: Oxford University Press, 2020), 69.

[37] See on this question Gellert (n. 35); Raphaël Gellert, *The Risk-Based Approach to Data Protection* 1st edn (Oxford: Oxford University Press, 2020).

[38] Peter Hustinx, 'EU Data Protection Law: The Review of Directive 95/46/EC and the General Data Protection Regulation,' in *New Technologies and EU Law*, ed. Marise Cremona (Oxford: Oxford University Press, 2017), 166.

[39] ibid 166.
[40] ibid 161.
[41] ibid 166–167.

that an agreement to facilitate the sharing of passenger name data with Canada should have joint data protection and police cooperation.[42]

Thus, the individual as an object of the data protection regime is cemented in EU primary law, the legislature must look to the individual's right in the adoption of data protection law and this may serve to constrain reorientation or reimagination of the regime, should the criticisms of its individualistic tendencies be accepted.

### ii. The Purposive Interpretation of Data Protection Legislation

The object of individual protection repeatedly appears in the case law of the CJEU through its use of purposive interpretation. Thus, as the legislature orient its activities to the individual and their rights and interests, the Court has adopted the individual interest in its interpretive approach. Many of the terms of the Data Protection Directive and GDPR are drafted at a high level of abstraction, and by interpreting these provisions in light of the aims of the legislation, the CJEU has had considerable influence on the shape of data protection law.

The desire to ensure free movement of data had some impact in the interpretation of the Data Protection Directive. It informed a judicial determination that data protection authorities should ensure a fair balance between the right to private life and free movement of personal data in the exercise of their duties.[43] It also led to a finding that the Data Protection Directive amounted to generally complete harmonisation, and therefore precluded more onerous national implementation of its terms.[44] In YS, the CJEU emphasised that the concept of 'personal data' must be interpreted in light of the dual aims of the Data Protection Directive: the protection of fundamental rights and free movement of personal data.[45]

However, the need to protect individuals has received much more frequent and significant attention by the CJEU, resulting in a transformative effect on EU data protection. Reflecting a broader trend of the CJEU's greater role as a fundamental rights adjudicator,[46] consideration of the free market aims have been largely ignored by more recent CJEU cases. Rather, we see frequent statements that the objective of the Data Protection Directive is 'to guarantee a high level of protection of personal data throughout the European Union', without having any regard at all to the explicit dual aims of the Data Protection Directive.[47]

---

[42] TFEU Arts 16 and 87(2)(a); Opinion 1/15 *Passenger Name Record Agreement*, ECLI:EU:C:2016:656, para 118.

[43] Case C-518/07 *Commission v Germany* ECLI:EU:C:2010:125, para 24; Case C-362/14 *Schrems v Data Protection Commissioner* ECLI:EU:C:2015:650, para 42.

[44] Joined Cases C-468/10 and C-469/10 *ASNEF* ECLI:EU:C:2011:777, paras 29–39.

[45] Joined Cases C-141/12 and C-372/12 *YS and Others* ECLI:EU:C:2014:2081, para 41.

[46] Gráinne de Búrca, 'After the EU Charter of Fundamental Rights: The Court of Justice as a Human Rights Adjudicator?,' *Maastricht Journal of European and Comparative Law* 20.2 (2013): 168–184, doi.org/10.1177/1023263X1302000202.

[47] See eg Case C-131/12 *Google Spain and Google* ECLI:EU:2014:317, para 53; Case C-507/17 *Google v CNIL* ECLI:EU:C:2019:772, para 54.

One way in which we can see this transformative effect is in the interpretation of key threshold concepts on the territorial and material application of data protection law. Confronted with cross-border data processing, the CJEU has expanded the territorial reach of EU data protection law, and the powers of data protection authorities. While the GDPR has explicit extra-territorial provisions,[48] the same was not the case under the Data Protection Directive, which was contingent on a controller engaged in processing 'in the context of the activities of an establishment of the controller on the territory of the Member State'. This requirement was interpreted expansively across a series of cases. The 'establishment' criterion was to be interpreted in order to ensure protection of fundamental rights and freedoms,[49] which led in *Google Spain* to the finding that Google Inc., the ultimate US parent company of the Google group of companies, was deemed to be subject to the Data Protection Directive.[50] The reasoning of this case informed the determination of intra-EU powers in a series of cases about the capacity of national DPAs to exercise their authority across national borders. In *Weltimmo*, the Hungarian data protection authority was deemed to be competent over a Slovakian company,[51] the CJEU again emphasising that 'establishment' should be understood broadly in light of the objective of protecting fundamental rights and freedoms of natural persons.[52] This reasoning has been extended to allow the application of multiple national data protection laws to the activities of a single data controller.[53] In this way, the interpretation of a measure intended to have both free movement and fundamental rights aims in light of only the second aim has arguably frustrated the first. The CJEU's purported intention to ensure 'effective and complete protection' of individuals has justified the application of multiple national versions of the Data Protection Directive, which was intended to act as a measure of harmonisation.

To some extent, more recently, the Court has had to try and contain its expansionism, when faced with the practical implications of that expansion. In *Google France v CNIL*, the CJEU once again considers the objective of the Data Protection Directive and GDPR and the importance of ensuring a high level of protection of personal data.[54] But the CJEU draws a limit to that objective, considering the global

---

[48] GDPR Art 3(2).
[49] Case C-131/12 *Google Spain and Google* ECLI:EU:2014:317, para 53.
[50] ibid paras 55–60.
[51] Case C-230/14 *Weltimmo* ECLI:EU:C:2015:639.
[52] Therefore, the concept of establishment extended 'to any real and effective activity – even a minimal one – exercised through stable arrangements'. ibid para 31.
[53] See Case C-191/15 *Verein für Konsumenteninformation* (ECLI:EU:C:2016:612) wherein the CJEU accepted that Amazon EU might have establishments in both Luxembourg and Germany and would therefore be subject to both Luxembourg and Germany's national data protection laws. In Case C-210/16 *Wirtschaftsakademie Schleswig-Holstein* ECLI:EU:C:2018:388 the CJEU confirmed that Facebook Inc. might be subject to the application of both Irish and German data protection laws, on the basis that it had an establishment in each jurisdiction over whom the relevant data protection authorities might exercise their competence, paras 45–64.
[54] Case C-507/17 *Google v CNIL* ECLI:EU:C:2019:772, para 54.

nature of the internet[55] and the impact on access to the information, and need to balance these interests,[56] determining that the de-referencing to be conducted in response to the right to be forgotten need only extend to the territory of the EU.[57] Thus, even where central to the assessment, the aim of individual protection is not absolute.

This expansive tendency seen in the territorial cases has also been seen in a series of cases on the material application of EU data protection law, including a broad interpretation of the concept of the data controller[58] and a narrow understanding of the exemptions from data protection law,[59] and a broad understanding of the types of data are captured by the regime as 'personal data' is seen.[60] In each instance, the CJEU expressly links the need to adopt a broad interpretation of the relevant terms with the desire to ensure protection of individuals' data protection rights.

Thus, the Court's focus upon the object of the individual and their protection has shaped the expansion in scope of EU data protection law. It has also impacted the application of the regime, as other central concepts have also been interpreted in light of the objective of the protection of individuals.[61]

In this way, the CJEU's heavy reliance on purposive interpretation of the legal regime in light of the goal of protecting individuals illustrates both the status and impact of the individual as the object of EU data protection law.

## III. The Individual as Subject of Data Protection Law

Beyond serving as the object of the legislature and judiciary, the individual is also a central subject of data protection law, as they are invested with legal status, rights and powers. In this sense, as the primary subject of data protection law, data protection law is ordered around the protection of the individual; first as a rights-holder, second, as the 'data subject', under the Data Protection Directive and GDPR,[62] and third, as an agent, endowed with the powers to defend their own interest and enforce data protection law.

---

[55] ibid para 56.
[56] ibid paras 57–67.
[57] ibid para 73.
[58] Case C-131/12 *Google Spain and Google* ECLI:EU:2014:317; Case C-210/16 *Wirtschaftsakademie Schleswig-Holstein* ECLI:EU:C:2018:388; Case C-25/17 *Jehovan todistajat* ECLI:EU:C:2018:551; Case C-40/17 *Fashion ID* ECLI:EU:C:2019:629.
[59] In a line of cases: Case C-101/01 *Bodil Lindqvist* ECLI:EU:C:2003:596; Case C-212/13 *Ryneš* ECLI:EU:2014:2428; Case C-25/17 *Jehovan todistajat* ECLI:EU:C:2018:551.
[60] See section III(B)(i) below.
[61] For instance, the requirement of independence of national DPAs (Case C-518/07 *Commission v Germany* ECLI:EU:C:2010:125, para 23) and the creation of a sui generis 'right to be forgotten' applicable to search engines (C-131/12 *Google Spain and Google* ECLI:EU:2014:317, para 81).
[62] Alongside the individual's role as a protected subject, the individual may also be a responsible subject under the GDPR as a data controller, see n. 17 above.

## A. Rights-holder

The individual is confirmed as a rights-holder, who enjoys the right to the protection of their personal data, under Article 16 TFEU and Article 8 of the Charter. We have seen how this right has significance to the legislative and judicial approach to data protection. Alongside this role, the creation of a new category of rights-holder has had important legal effect, as the individual can now assert their interest outside data protection legislation. We see this in two senses, first, as the rights-holder brings their right to be weighed against other rights and interests in the application of other substantive areas of EU law, and second, as the individual can assert their right to data protection to challenge the legality of EU and national legal instruments.

The individual rights-holder's assertion of their right to data protection has had effect beyond the confines of traditional data protection cases. By way of example, in *Safe Interenvíos*, the CJEU was called upon to interpret a piece of national money laundering legislation.[63] The Court, in applying a proportionality analysis to that legislation, determined that the proportionality of the due diligence requirements in that legislation depended on the extent to which those measures intrude upon other rights and interests protected by EU law, such as the protection of personal data.[64] Thus, the status of data protection as a Charter right allows it to be a source of review or challenge in the field of money laundering legislation.

The right to data protection has had particular influence in a series of copyright infringement cases, wherein the CJEU have emphasised the need for the right to data protection to be weighed in 'fair balance' with other competing interests. In *Promusciae*, concerned with the disclosure of subscriber details in order to facilitate infringement actions, the CJEU emphasised that copyright protection 'cannot affect the requirements of the protection of personal data'.[65] Rather, the multiple Charter rights engaged (the right to property under Article 17, the right to a remedy under Article 47, and the rights to data protection and respect for private life) must be reconciled and a fair balance between them struck.[66] In this way, the breadth of the obligation to facilitate copyright infringement action was contained – the telecommunications provider was under no obligation to communicate subscriber details to copyright holders or their agents. Similar approaches were seen in *LSG*,[67] in *Scarlet Extended*,[68] *SABAM*[69] and *Bonnier Audio and Others*.[70] In this way, the

---

[63] Case C-235/14 *Safe Interenvios* ECLI:EU:C:2016:154.
[64] ibid para 109.
[65] Case C-275/06 *Promusicae v Telefónica de España* ECLI:EU:C:2008:54, para 57.
[66] ibid para 68.
[67] Case C-557/07 *LSG-Gesellschaft zur Wahrnehmung von Leistungsschutzrechten* ECLI:EU:C:2009:107, para 28.
[68] Case C-70/10 *Scarlet Extended* ECLI:EU:C:2011771.
[69] Case C-360/10 *SABAM* ECLI:EU:C:2012:85.
[70] Case C-461/10 *Bonnier Audio and Others* ECLI:EU:C:2012:219.

consideration of the impact upon the individual rights-holder has shaped the acceptable form of copyright injunction that copyright holders may obtain in accordance with EU law.

The individual's status as a rights-holder has also enabled challenges to be brought to the legality of EU legal instruments. Article 8 has become an independent tool of challenge, usually considered in conjunction with the right to respect for private life under Article 7. A body of decisions have arisen since 2010, which have seen such challenges brought and many succeed.

In *Schecke*, a section of common agricultural policy legislation was invalidated, on the basis that the disclosure rules relating to beneficiaries of the policy were incompatible with Articles 7 and 8 of the Charter.[71] The rules in question were held to fail a proportionality analysis,[72] and while acknowledging the validity of the objective of transparency underscoring the relevant rules, the Court emphasised that '[n]o automatic priority can be conferred on the objective of transparency over the right to protection of personal data ... even if important economic interests are at stake'.[73]

Article 8 has had a particular impact upon instruments which were intended to limit data protection in the name of safeguarding security, and in these cases we see the limits of the individual rights asserted, as the right to data protection is weighed against state security and defence objectives. In *Schwartz* and *Willems*, a Council Regulation concerning the use of biometrics in travel documents was challenged.[74] Each rights-holder sought to argue that they ought not to be refused a passport for a refusal to submit biometric details to the issuing authority. In *Schwartz*, the CJEU ultimately deemed that the interference with Article 8 was lawful, while emphasising that Article 8 must be interpreted in relation to its function in society, and that the objective of the Regulation – to prevent illegal entry into the European Union – was an objective of general interest recognised by the Union.[75] This determination was followed in *Willems*, and the Court said that the use of biometrics under the Regulation had already been deemed compatible.[76]

Perhaps the most striking impact of Article 8 has been a series of cases in which the individual right to data protection has been the basis (or partial basis) upon which the CJEU has judged the entirety of legislative instruments in accordance with compatibility with the protections of Articles 7 and 8. The first case, *Digital Rights Ireland*, saw the CJEU invalidate the Data Retention Directive[77] due to its

---

[71] Case C-92/09 *Volker und Markus Schecke and Eifert* ECLI:EU:C:2010:662.
[72] ibid para 76.
[73] ibid para 85.
[74] Council Regulation 2252/2004 on standards for security features and biometrics in passports and travel documents. Case C-291/12 *Schwartz* ECLI:EU:C:2013:670; Joined Cases C-446/12 to C-449/12 *Willems and Others* ECLI:EU:C:2015:238.
[75] Case C-291/12 *Schwartz* ECLI:EU:C:2013:670, paras 33, 37–38.
[76] Joined Cases C-446/12 to C-449/12 *Willems and Others* ECLI:EU:C:2015:238, para 46.
[77] 'DIRECTIVE 2006/24/EC OF THE EUROPEAN PARLIAMENT AND OF THE COUNCIL of 15 March 2006 on the Retention of Data Generated or Processed in Connection with the Provision of Publicly Available Electronic Communications Services or of Public Communications Networks and Amending Directive 2002/58/EC,' OJ L 105/54, 13/4/2006, 54–63. § (n.d.).

disproportionate impact on Articles 7 and 8.[78] The Court showed awareness of the oppressive nature of surveillance regimes, noting that the retention regime would be 'likely to generate in the minds of the persons concerned the feeling that their private lives are the subject of constant surveillance'.[79] A regime providing for generalised data retention was considered to be a wide-ranging and 'particularly serious' infringement.[80] While interferences with Article 8 can be justified under Article 52(1) of the Charter, this regime was deemed disproportionate and invalidated in its entirety. As a determination of the reach of the right to data protection, *Digital Rights Ireland* is striking in how expansively the CJEU construe the right and the determination that 'the EU legislature's discretion is reduced' due to the important role of the protection of personal data and the seriousness of the infringement.[81]

Similar approaches have subsequently been seen in a number of cases. In *Schrems*, we saw the invalidation of a Commission adequacy decision, which had legitimised certain data transfers from the EU to the US.[82] While the actual invalidation of the decision was on a somewhat formalistic basis,[83] the standards for a valid adequacy decision set out by the CJEU were deeply informed by a fundamental rights orientation.[84] In the *PNR* decision, a proposed international agreement facilitating the sharing of passenger name records between EU and Canada, was found not to comply with the Charter.[85] In *Tele2*, we see the Court assess the legality of national surveillance measures against the requirements of the Charter, and once again finding the regimes lacking.[86] Once again, in *Schrems II*, the Privacy Shield adequacy decision[87] and the Standard Contractual Clauses[88] which can legitimise data transfers out of the EEA were considered against the standards of Articles 7 and 8 of the Charter.[89] The Standard Contractual Clauses survived this scrutiny, but the Privacy Shield decision was deemed to be incompatible with the

---

[78] Joined Cases C-293/12 and C-594/12 *Digital Rights Ireland and Seitlinger and Others* ECLI:EU:C:2014:238.

[79] ibid para 37.

[80] ibid para 37.

[81] ibid para 48.

[82] Case C-362/14 *Schrems v Data Protection Commissioner* ECLI:EU:C:2015:650.

[83] The Court emphasised that the Commission had failed to formally state that the US in fact ensured an adequate level of protection, and invalidity followed from this absence of a formal determination. ibid paras 97–98.

[84] For example, the Court establishes a test for adequacy is that of protection 'that is essentially equivalent to that guaranteed within the European Union by virtue of [the Data Protection Directive] read in light of the Charter.' See para 73.

[85] Opinion 1/15 *Passenger Name Record Agreement* ECLI:EU:C:2016:656.

[86] Joined Cases C-203/15 and C-698/15 *Tele2 Sverige* ECLI:EU:C:2016:970.

[87] Commission Implementing Decision (EU) 2016/1250 of 12 July 2016 pursuant to Directive 95/46/EC of the European Parliament and of the Council on the adequacy of the protection provided by the EU-US Privacy Shield (notified under document C(2016) 4176) (OJ 2016 L 207, 1.).

[88] Commission Decision of 5 February 2010 on standard contractual clauses for the transfer of personal data to processors established in third countries under Directive 95/46/EC of the European Parliament and of the Council (OJ 2010 L 39, p. 5), as amended by Commission Implementing Decision (EU) 2016/2297 of 16 December 2016 (OJ 2016 L 344, 100).

[89] Case C-311/18 *Facebook Ireland & Schrems* ECLI:EU:C:2020:559.

protections required, due to the disproportionate interference possible with the rights to data protection and privacy under US surveillance laws.

This series of cases demonstrates the potency of the individual's Charter right to data protection, often wielded alongside the right to privacy, as a source of review for EU and national legislative measures. The individual, and their status as a protected rights-holder, is central to these determinations, as an initiator of these actions, and as the weighing of competing interests must be balanced against the impact on the individual.

## B. Data Subject

The individual also attains a new legal status within the legislative data protection scheme under the GDPR and its predecessor, the Data Protection Directive. As the protected subject of this regime – the 'data subject' – the individual is central to the logic and functioning of this legislative scheme.[90]

As I shall explain, the concept of the individual and their data is determinative of the scope of this regime, and the legality of data processing thereunder is often (though not always) judged by reference to the individual.

### i. The Scope of the GDPR is Defined in Terms of the Individual

Two related concepts are central to the scope of the GDPR and, before it, the Data Protection Directive: the data subject and personal data.

The GDPR defines its material scope by way of the concept of personal data. The GDPR applies 'to the processing of personal data wholly or partly by automated means'.[91] Processing is a very broad concept, entailing any use (including collection)[92] and therefore more attention has focussed on 'personal data' as a threshold concept. The first question in any data protection analysis thus tends to be: is the data in question 'personal data'?[93]

Personal data, in turn, is defined in terms of an individual: a living natural person.[94] In order to qualify as personal data, the data must relate to an individual – the 'data subject' – who must be identified, or identifiable.

---

[90] (For ease of reading, I refer to the GDPR throughout below. Where the GDPR reflects a change to the regime under the Data Protection Directive, this is noted.)

[91] GDPR Art 2(1).

[92] GDPR Art 4(2).

[93] We see this in a number of CJEU decisions, including determinations that the following types of data are personal data: IP addresses (Case C-360/10 *SABAM* ECLI:EU:C:2012:85); fingerprints (Case C-291/12 *Schwartz* ECLI:EU:C:2013:670); records of working time from a time clock system (Case C-342/12 *Worten* ECLI:EU:C:2013:355); evidence gathered by private detectives (Case C-473/12 *IPI* ECLI:EU:C:2013:715); video surveillance (Case C-212/13 *Ryneš* ECLI:EU:C:2014:2428); tax ID numbers (Case C-496/17 *Deutsche Post* ECLI:EU:C:2019:26).

[94] Article 4(1) provides (in part) '"personal data" means any information relating to an identified or identifiable natural person ("data subject"); an identifiable natural person is one who can be identified, directly or indirectly'.

This question of when data is sufficiently related to an individual, and whether an individual is identifiable is somewhat ambiguous on the face of the legislation.[95] Unsurprisingly, therefore, there have been a series of referrals to the CJEU on the meaning of personal data. The Court's approach has seen some change over time, with a general tendency towards a more expansive understanding of the concept.

In *YS and Others*, the CJEU was asked whether a legal analysis concerning applicants for residence permits was personal data.[96] The Court determined that while such a legal analysis might contain personal data, it was not in itself personal data.[97] The Court's interpretation was guided by the function of personal data in an access request (which the applicants had been denied).[98] The Court emphasised that the right of access was intended to enable the exercise of other procedural rights (such as rectification, or to check the accuracy of that data),[99] and that the Data Protection Directive was not intended to provide a right of access to administrative documents more generally.[100]

By contrast, the later cases of *Breyer*[101] and *Novak*[102] moved away from this instrumental approach linked to the right of access.[103] In *Breyer*, the CJEU considered whether dynamic IP addresses were personal data, in circumstances where a website operator would need to obtain data from a third party in order to identify the underlying individual.[104] The CJEU confirmed a relative vision of personal data. A controller need not hold all the information enabling the identification of the data subject, if the combination of the data rendering the individual identifiable is by way of means reasonably likely to be used.[105] The possibility for the website operator to contact the relevant third party (the internet services provider)

---

[95] See Nadezhda Purtova, 'From Knowing by Name to Targeting: The Meaning of Identification under the GDPR,' *International Data Privacy Law* (2022), ipac013, doi.org/10.1093/idpl/ipac013.
[96] Joined Cases C-141/12 and C-372/12 *YS and Others* ECLI:EU:C:2014:2081.
[97] ibid para 39.
[98] ibid para 44.
[99] ibid, par 44.
[100] ibid paras 45–46.
[101] Case C-582/14 *Breyer* ECLI:EU:C:2016:779.
[102] Case C-434/16 *Nowak* ECLI:EU:C:2017:994.
[103] *Nowak* seems at odds with the earlier *YS* decision, though the Court presents them as compatible, on the basis that the ability to obtain the examination script served the purpose of the Data Protection Directive in guaranteeing the protection of the candidate's data. The implication seems to be that the migrant applicant in *YS* on the other hand sought access to his data to review the decision-making by the public authority, rather than to safeguard his data protection. This positioning by the CJEU seems unconvincing (surely *Nowak* was interested not only in his data protection, but in improving his examination results) and conflates the rights to privacy and data protection in its reasoning. A number of scholars have commented on the unclear nature of the status of *YS*. (Benjamin Wong, 'Delimiting the Concept of Personal Data after the GDPR,' *Legal Studies* 39.3 (2019): 526, doi.org/10.1017/lst.2018.52. Orla Lynskey, 'Criminal Justice Profiling and EU Data Protection Law: Precarious Protection from Predictive Policing,' *International Journal of Law in Context* 15.2 (2019): 162–176, doi.org/10.1017/S1744552319000090. Lee A. Bygrave and Lee Tosoni, 'Article 4(1). Personal Data,' in *The EU General Data Protection Regulation (GDPR): A Commentary*, eds. Christopher Kuner et al. (Oxford: Oxford University Press, 2020), 110.).
[104] Case C-582/14 *Breyer* ECLI:EU:C:2016:779.
[105] ibid paras 43–49. See also, Data Protection Directive Recital 26.

was deemed to be means reasonably likely to be used.[106] In *Nowak*, the CJEU was called upon to determine whether an examination script was personal data, after an applicant sought access to his script after a series of failed accountancy examinations.[107] Determining that the script was personal data, the Court took a very expansive approach. The CJEU expressly determined that a broad approach to the concept of personal data was appropriate, finding that the use of the expression 'any information' in the definition of personal data 'reflects the aim of the EU legislature to assign a wide scope to that concept, which is not restricted to information that is sensitive or private, but potentially encompasses all kinds of information, not only objective but also subjective ... provided that it "relates" to the data subject'.[108] In turn, the test provided for whether information 'relates to' the data subject is also wide in scope, extending to information which 'by reason of its content, purpose or effect, is linked to the data subject'.[109] It is unsurprising, therefore, that the CJEU determined that the examination script and examiner's comments were to be regarded as personal data, attracting the full suite of data protection obligations and rights.[110]

The resulting standard of personal data is very broad, post-*Nowak*. The Court has effectively endorsed the theory that breadth in protection results in greater protection, though this has been subject to criticism.[111] Any data which touches or might touch on the individual experience comes to be subject to the GDPR, and therefore the threshold for the application of the data protection law is contingent on an analysis of the relation of that data to an individual.

### ii. *The Legality of Data Processing is Usually Judged by Reference to the Individual*

In order for data processing to be lawful under the GDPR, two general requirements must be met. First, the controller must be able to demonstrate that it has a lawful basis for that processing.[112] As I shall explain, the individual is central to the assessment of legality of each, though not the exclusive consideration. Second, the controller must comply with the data protection principles.[113] These principles take a less individually oriented approach.

---

[106] ibid para 48.
[107] Case C-434/16 *Nowak* ECLI:EU:C:2017:994.
[108] ibid para 34.
[109] ibid para 35.
[110] ibid para 47.
[111] Nadezhda Purtova, 'The Law of Everything. Broad Concept of Personal Data and Future of EU Data Protection Law,' *Law, Innovation and Technology* 10.1 (2018): 40–81, doi.org/10.1080/17579961.2018. 1452176; Lorenzo Dalla Corte, 'Scoping Personal Data: Towards a Nuanced Interpretaton of the Material Scope of EU Data Protecton Law,' *European Journal of Law and Technology* 10.1 (2019): 26.
[112] GDPR Art 6.
[113] GDPR Art 5.

As a pre-condition to data processing, the data controller must be able to justify their processing on one of six conditions. Three we might describe as individually-oriented, two have a public-orientation and the final legal basis is a hybrid, considering multiple parties.

Three legal pre-conditions explicitly invoke consideration of the individual, the data controller may adduce; the data subject's consent, necessity for the performance of a contract with the data subject, and necessity for the protection of the data subject's (or another natural person's) vital interests.[114] Consent has long been considered fundamental to data protection law,[115] and it is the sole legal pre-condition named in the fundamental right to data protection.[116] However, the GDPR has tightened the ability of controllers to rely on an individual's consent,[117] because of a concern that divergent implementations of consent across Member States were resulting in poor consent practices.[118] The Court has also recognised that the concept of consent cannot be given an overly expansive interpretation, in *Schwartz*[119] and in *Planet 49*.[120]

Two pre-conditions have a public orientation. The controller may lawfully process data where the processing of that data is necessary for compliance with a legal obligation, or where the processing is necessary for the performance of a task carried out in the public interest.[121] While we might characterise these analyses as a weighing of public concerns, in fact the impact upon the individual is still relevant to the consideration of these pre-conditions. This is because any public legislative measure which represents an interference with the right to personal data – any legislative measure which involves data processing and therefore might satisfy either the legal obligation or public interest ground – is subject to review under Article 8 of the Charter. Thus, even if processing is nominally justified under Article 6 of the GDPR under a piece of national or EU legislation, such

---

[114] GDPR Art 6(1)(a), 6(1)(b), 6(1)(d).
[115] See eg Eleni Kosta, *Consent in European Data Protection Law* (Leiden: Brill, 2013); Benjamin Bergemann, 'The Consent Paradox: Accounting for the Prominent Role of Consent in Data Protection,' in *Privacy and Identity Management. The Smart Revolution*, ed. Marit Hansen et al., vol. 526, IFIP Advances in Information and Communication Technology (Cham: Springer, 2018), 111–131, doi.org/10.1007/978-3-319-92925-5_8; Elettra Bietti, 'The Discourse of Control and Consent over Data in EU Data Protection Law and Beyond,' *Hoover Institution Aegis Paper Series* (2020), 16.
[116] Article 8(2) of the Charter provides: 'Such data must be processed fairly for specified purposes and on the basis of the consent of the person concerned or some other legitimate basis laid down by law.'
[117] See Article 7 which adds conditions to consent, and Article 8 which adds conditions to the applicability of children's consent in relation to information society services.
[118] Eleni Kosta, 'Article 7. Conditions for Consent,' in *The EU General Data Protection Regulation (GDPR): A Commentary*, ed. Christopher Kuner et al. (Oxford: Oxford University Press, 2020), 347.
[119] The CJEU recognised that an individual could not consent to the inclusion of personal data on their passport, as it was essential to own a passport. Case C-291/12 *Schwartz* ECLI:EU:C:2013:670, para 31.
[120] The Court emphasised the need for consent to be unambiguous and required active behaviour by the individual, and therefore pre-ticked boxes could not be relied upon. Case C-673/17 *Planet49* ECLI:EU:C:2019:801, para 65.
[121] GDPR Art 6(1)(c), 6(1)(e).

a measure may be subject to a second tier of legal challenge on the basis of the interference with the individual's fundamental right to data protection. We see this applied in a number of cases before the CJEU. In *Manni*, the CJEU considered that the processing of data for the purposes of the publication of a statutory companies register could be justified by a number of legal bases, including compliance with a legal obligation and public interests.[122] Nevertheless, in order to satisfy itself that this reliance on these pre-conditions was legally appropriate, the CJEU went on to analyse whether there was an interference with the fundamental rights of concerned person, ultimately determining that while there was an interference it was not disproportionate.[123] Similarly, in *Puskar*, the CJEU considered that data collection and processing in order to collect taxes and combat tax fraud would be lawful under the public interest ground, provided that the national legislation in question satisfied a proportionality analysis.[124]

Finally, a controller may justify its processing on the basis that the processing is necessary for the purposes of the legitimate interests of the controller or a third party.[125] However, this legitimate interest must not be overridden by the interests or fundamental rights and freedoms of the data subject.[126] As explained in *Rigas*, this involves a three stage analysis.[127] First, a legitimate interest pursued by the data controller or by third parties must be established. Second, it must be necessary to process the data for the purposes of that legitimate interest. Third, the fundamental rights and freedoms of the data subject must be considered, to determine if they take precedence over the legitimate interest pursued.

Therefore, while the six legal pre-conditions to processing might appear to have different orientations, nevertheless the consideration of the individual and their interests is central to each. Moreover, for certain types of individuals, particularly children and vulnerable persons, additional rules are implemented before data may be lawfully processed.[128]

By contrast, the data protection principles are less explicitly tied to the individual. Indeed, only two of the data protection principles are defined by reference to the data subject. First, the lawfulness, fairness and transparency requirement is assessed 'in relation to the data subject',[129] though the requirement of fairness in Article 8 is not so tied to the subject.[130] Second, the storage limitation principle

---

[122] Case C-398/15 *Manni* ECLI:EU:C:2017:197, para 42.
[123] ibid para 56.
[124] Case C-73/16 *Puškár* ECLI:EU:C:2017:725, paras 102–117.
[125] GDPR Art 6(1)(f).
[126] ibid.
[127] Case C-13/16 *Rīgas satiksme* ECLI:EU:C:2017:336, para 28.
[128] GDPR Arts 8, 24. See also Eva Lievens and Valerie Verdoodt, 'Looking for Needles in a Haystack: Key Issues Affecting Children's Rights in the General Data Protection Regulation,' *Computer Law & Security Review* 34.2 (2018): 269–278, doi.org/10.1016/j.clsr.2017.09.007; Gianclaudio Malgieri and Jędrzej Niklas, 'Vulnerable Data Subjects,' *Computer Law & Security Review* 37 (2020): 105415, doi.org/10.1016/j.clsr.2020.105415.
[129] GDPR Art 5(1)(a).
[130] Article 8(2) provides (in part): '*Such data must be processed fairly for specified purposes and on the basis of the consent of the person concerned or some other legitimate basis laid down by law.*'

requires that personal data is kept in a form which permits identification of data subjects for no longer than is necessary for the purpose of processing.[131] On the other hand, the purpose limitation requirement, data minimisation, data accuracy and integrity and confidentiality principles are all expressed generally, without using the data subject as a focus of the principle.[132] Accordingly, while there is a link to the individual data subject, many of the principles provide for general principles of data governance, which might be said to benefit all data subjects, rather than judging by individualised standards. These principles ensure a basic set of standards with which data controllers must abide, and in setting standards which limit a data controller's freedom to impact persons.[133]

The individual's status as this protected subject of data protection law is characteristic of the individual's centrality to the regime. It is the logic of individual protection which primarily informs the legislative provisions in their design and application. Nevertheless, these provisions are not exclusively individualistic, as other parties (controllers, other affected natural persons, the state) and interests may come to be weighed in the ultimate balance.

## C. Agent of Data Protection Law

The individual is also an agent of data protection law. Connected to the individual's status as a data subject, the legal safeguarding of the individual's actions regarding their personal data is integral to the performance of data protection law. Though the exercise of informational decision-making, the grant of procedural rights and the framing of the fundamental right to data protection, the individual is said to be empowered to enact data protection.[134] While the individual is clearly not the only agent of data protection (accountable data controllers, data protection authorities, legislative and judicial authorities all also have roles to play), given the focus of this chapter, this section focuses on the individual's role in enacting data protection. This role of the individual is seen at two phases of data protection. First, the individual is proactive – they may decide how their information is to be used. Second, the individual may act to defend their interest, in various ways.

### i. The Individual may Decide how their Information is to be Treated

Informational self-determination, or the control of one's personal data is often written about (or indeed criticised) in the context of the Data Protection Directive

---

[131] GDPR Art 5(1)(e).
[132] GDPR Arts 5(1)(b), (c), (d) and (f).
[133] Lynskey has suggested that these principles offer an opportunity to 'shift away from the individual-centric approach crystalized in other parts of the GDPR'. Lynskey (n. 1) 83.
[134] For this reason, Ausloos has linked these rights and control more broadly to the essence of the right of data protection. Ausloos (n. 36) 61.

and the GDPR.[135] After all, the principle of consent is core to the right to data protection, and one of the grounds upon which data processing is justified.

The two central ways in which the individual may be said to control their information is through two legal bases for data processing.[136] Data processing may be legal if the data subject has consented to the processing in question,[137] or where the processing is necessary for the performance which a data subject has entered into with the controller.[138] It seems, in response to concerns about the circumstances in which individuals' consent was being relied upon,[139] in the current generation of data protection legislation, reliance on individual decision making has been limited. The GDPR places conditions on consent, in an apparent attempt to ensure individuals are not coerced into providing consent. The controller is now responsible for demonstrating that the data subject has consented.[140] Consents must be separated from other matters in a written declaration, and presented 'in an intelligible and easily accessible form, using clear and plain language'.[141] Perhaps most interestingly, the GDPR introduces what Peifer and Schwartz call a prohibition on 'tying' consents.[142] By requiring that 'utmost account' must be taken of whether performance of a contract is made conditional on a consent to non-necessary processing, the GDPR suggests such circumstances in which consent is tied to the performance of a contract will mean that the consent is not freely given.[143]

Therefore, the individual may be an agent of data protection law through the exercise of decision making as to how their data will be processed, legitimated through the doctrines of consent and contractual necessity. However, the limitation of consent seen under the GDPR and the emphasis of the high threshold of 'necessity' which informs the contractual necessity ground should arguably increase our scrutiny over the extent to which decision making is truly a free exercise of agency or coerced.[144]

---

[135] See eg Antoinette Rouvroy and Yves Poullet, 'The Right to Informational Self-Determination and the Value of Self-Development: Reassessing the Importance of Privacy for Democracy', in *Reinventing Data Protection?*, ed. Serge Gutwirth et al. (Dordrecht: Springer Netherlands, 2009), 45–76, doi.org/10.1007/978-1-4020-9498-9_2; Lynskey (n. 2); Christophe Lazaro and Daniel Le Métayer, 'Control over Personal Data: True Remedy or Fairytale?', *SCRIPTed* 12.1 (2015), doi.org/10.2966/scrip.120115.3; Tobias Matzner et al., 'Do-It-Yourself Data Protection – Empowerment or Burden?', in *Data Protection on the Move*, ed. Serge Gutwirth, Ronald Leenes, and Paul De Hert, vol. 24 (Dordrecht: Springer Netherlands, 2016), 277–305, doi.org/10.1007/978-94-017-7376-8_11; Hartzog (n. 2); Bietti (n. 115); Heleen Janssen, Jennifer Cobbe and Jatinder Singh, 'Personal Information Management Systems: A User-Centric Privacy Utopia?', *Internet Policy Review* 9.4 (2020), doi.org/10.14763/2020.4.1536; Lynskey (n. 1); Ausloos (n. 36).

[136] Introduced in section III(B)(ii) above.

[137] GDPR Art 6(1)(a).

[138] GDPR Art 6(1)(b).

[139] See in particular GDPR Recitals 42 and 43. There is emphasis on the requirement that consent is freely given.

[140] GDPR Art 7(1).

[141] GDPR Art 7(2).

[142] Karl-Nikolaus Peifer and Paul M. Schwartz, 'Transatlantic Data Privacy Law', *Georgetown Law Journal* 106 (2017): 143.

[143] GDPR Art 7(4).

[144] A subject much debated in the academic literature. See n. 2 above.

## ii. The Individual is Equipped with Rights it Might Use to Safeguard their Data

The individual is also an agent of data protection law through their exercise of a suite of data rights to defend their interests. First, individuals have a series of rights which they might exercise against data controllers, in order to ensure that their data is being processed lawfully by that controller. Second, the individual has a set of procedural rights, in order to enforce their rights. Third, the individual as a rights holder may challenge state action which is contrary to the right to data protection.

Through the exercise of a number of data rights, the individual may enact data protection law by obliging the controller to treat their data in a certain fashion. One key data right is the right to access,[145] which has a special place in the fundamental right to data protection, together with the right to rectification.[146] The CJEU has observed that the right to access one's data is necessary in order to access the individual's other data rights.[147] Thus, once an individual has a copy of the data being processed in relation to them, the individual may be in a position to assess whether that processing is improper and seek to exercise other rights; to have inaccurate data rectified,[148] to have data erased,[149] to restrict processing,[150] to transmit that data to another controller[151] or to object to certain processing activities.[152] These rights thus empower the individual to hold data controllers to account for the treatment of their data.[153]

If these procedural rights are not respected, or in some other way the individual's personal data is improperly processed, the individual is then armed with procedural rights to challenge this processing. The individual has a right to lodge a complaint with their local data protection authority.[154] The data protection authority is then required to handle that complaint and investigate, to the extent appropriate.[155] The individual may also mandate a representational entity to act on their behalf.[156] Should the individual be unhappy with the outcome of the investigation (or indeed any party subject to a legally binding decision of a data

---

[145] GDPR Art 15.
[146] Article 8(2) of the Charter provides in part: 'Everyone has the right of access to data which has been collected concerning him or her, and the right to have it rectified.'
[147] Case C-553/07 *Rijkeboer* ECLI:EU:C:2009:293, para 64; Joined Cases C-141/12 and C-372/12 *YS and Others* ECLI:EU:C:2014:2081, para 44.
[148] GDPR Article 16,.
[149] GDPR Art 17.
[150] GDPR Art 18.
[151] GDPR Art 20.
[152] GDPR Art 21.
[153] See further Ausloos (n. 36).
[154] GDPR Art 77.
[155] GDPR Art 57(f).
[156] GDPR Art 80(1).

protection authority), they are entitled to an effective judicial remedy against the authority.[157] The data subject also enjoys a right to an effective judicial remedy in respect of the infringement of their rights under the GDPR,[158] made potent by the guarantee that data subjects have a right to compensation for any material or non-material damage suffered.[159]

Armed with such procedural rights, it is often the individual who brings illegal processing to the notice of data protection authorities and the courts. We can see plenty of evidence of this role in the many cases which have led to preliminary references to the CJEU which originate from individual complaints.[160] Of course, the individual is not the only agent to enforce data protection law; data protection authorities and representational entities may act without individual mandate.[161] Nevertheless, private enforcement of data protection law is an important component of the regime, particularly in light of the resourcing challenges of data protection authorities, which suggest that the capacity of data protection authorities to engage in systemic investigations beyond individual complaints is limited.[162] Thus the legal enforcement role of the individuals takes on even more practical significance.

Finally, alongside the specific procedural roles within the legislative scheme, the capacity of individuals to challenge state data processing activities in their status as a rights holder has been seen in multiple cases relating to Article 8 of the GDPR. These cases have been discussed in section III(A) above. The individual has the capacity to bring such challenges, whereas the CJEU has confirmed that an activist entity as a legal person had no standing to engage in such a challenge.[163]

Accordingly, while not the only agent of data protection law, the individual as a rights holder and data subject plays an important role in enforcing data protection law, through the exercise of data rights, procedural rights and the fundamental right to data protection.

---

[157] GDPR Art 78.
[158] GDPR Art 79.
[159] GDPR Art 82.
[160] See eg Case C-131/12 *Google Spain and Google* ECLI:EU:2014:317; Case C-212/13 *Ryneš* ECLI:EU:2014:2428; Case C-201/14 *Bara and Others* ECLI:EU:C:2015:638; Case C-362/14 *Schrems v Data Protection Commissioner* ECLI:EU:C:2015:650; Case C-582/14 *Breyer* ECLI:EU:C:2016:779; Case C-398/15 *Manni* ECLI:EU:C:2017:197; Case C-73/16 *Puškár* ECLI:EU:C:2017:725; Case C-434/16 *Nowak* ECLI:EU:C:2017:994; Case C-498/16 *Schrems v Facebook Ireland Ltd* ECLI:EU:C:2018:37.
[161] GDPR Arts 57 and 80(2).
[162] 'Data Protection in the European Union: The Role of National Data Protection Authorities' (Luxembourg: European Union Agency for Fundamental Rights, 2010), fra.europa.eu/sites/default/files/fra_uploads/815-Data-protection_en.pdf. 'First Overview on the Implementation of the GDPR and the Roles and Means of the National Supervisory Authorities' (European Data Protection Board, 26 February 2019), edpb.europa.eu/sites/edpb/files/files/file1/19_2019_edpb_written_report_to_libe_en.pdf.
[163] Case T-670/16 *Digital Rights Ireland v European Commission* ECLI:EU:T:2017:838.

## IV. Conclusion

This chapter has presented a framework for understanding the ways in which the individual is central to the framing and operation of data protection law. This centrality is seen through the examination of the multiple roles which the individual is playing, each central to various aspects of data protection law; its objectives, its scope, its interpretation, its determination of legality and its enforcement. In each of these areas of the law, the individual's interest and actions are prominent, though not entirely determinative in an absolutist individualist sense.

Individual protection serves as the objective for the operation of EU data protection law, a source of its legitimacy as well as the driving force in its interpretation and operation. The individual shapes the subject matter of regulation, as their interests shape the scope of the data protection law and are central to the assessment of legality under the GDPR. The individual is also critical to the enactment of data protection, as they challenge data controllers and protect their own interests. In this way, the individual is both acted upon, and actor. They may be seen as both object and subject of data protection law.

I suggest that a clearer understanding of how the role and place of the individual within the regime is shaping data protection law offers a contribution to the understanding of data protection law. First, it is important to recognise that the individual is playing several important parts within the regime, a matter which is often implicit rather than express in both the case law and scholarship. Moreover, once we recognise that the individual is playing such a central role to the EU data protection regime, we are in a position to question whether individually oriented approaches serve our normative goals. By offering a framework for understanding the multiple ways in which the individual is at the heart of data protection, opportunities for future research and a more precise evaluation of that role is made possible.

## References

Ausloos, Jeff. *The Right to Erasure in EU Data Protection Law: From Individual Rights to Effective Protection*. Oxford Data Protection and Privacy Law. Oxford: Oxford University Press, 2020.

Azoulai, Loïc, Etienne Pataut and Ségolène Barbou des Places. 'Being a Person in the European Union.' In *Constructing the Person in EU Law: Rights, Roles, Identities*, edited by Loïc Azoulai, Etienne Pataut and Ségolène Barbou des Places, 9. Oxford: Hart Publishing, 2016.

Bergemann, Benjamin. 'The Consent Paradox: Accounting for the Prominent Role of Consent in Data Protection.' In *Privacy and Identity Management. The Smart Revolution*, edited by Marit Hansen, Eleni Kosta, Igor Nai-Fovino and Simone Fischer-Hübner, 526: 111–131. IFIP Advances in Information and Communication Technology. Cham: Springer International Publishing, 2018. doi.org/10.1007/978-3-319-92925-5_8.

Bieker, Felix. *The Right to Data Protection: Individual and Structural Dimensions of Data Protection in EU Law*. Vol. 34. Information Technology and Law Series. The Hague: T.M.C. Asser Press, 2022. doi.org/10.1007/978-94-6265-503-4.

Bietti, Elettra. 'The Discourse of Control and Consent over Data in EU Data Protection Law and Beyond.' *Hoover Institution Aegis Paper Series*, 8 January 2020, 16.

Braun, Virginia, and Victoria Clarke. 'Using Thematic Analysis in Psychology.' *Qualitative Research in Psychology* 3 no. 2 (2006): 77–101. doi.org/10.1191/1478088706qp063oa.

Búrca, Gráinne de. 'After the EU Charter of Fundamental Rights: The Court of Justice as a Human Rights Adjudicator?' *Maastricht Journal of European and Comparative Law* 20 no. 2 (J2013): 168–184. doi.org/10.1177/1023263X1302000202.

Bygrave, Lee A. and Lee Tosoni. 'Article 4(1). Personal Data.' In *The EU General Data Protection Regulation (GDPR): A Commentary*, edited by Christopher Kuner, Lee A. Bygrave, Christopher Docksey and Laura Drechsler, 103–115. Oxford: Oxford University Press, 2020.

Chen, Jiahong, Lilian Edwards, Lachlan Urquhart and Derek McAuley. 'Who Is Responsible for Data Processing in Smart Homes? Reconsidering Joint Controllership and the Household Exemption.' *International Data Privacy Law* 10 no. 4 (2020): 279–293.

Cohen, Julie E. 'Examined Lives: Informational Privacy and the Subject as Object.' *Stanford Law Review* 52 no. 5 (2000): 1373. doi.org/10.2307/1229517.

——. 'The Biopolitical Public Domain: The Legal Construction of the Surveillance Economy.' *Philosophy & Technology* 31 no. 2 (2018): 213–233. doi.org/10.1007/s13347-017-0258-2.

Cohen, Julie E. 'Turning Privacy Inside Out.' *Theoretical Inquiries in Law* 20 (2019): 1–32.

Dalla Corte, Lorenzo. 'Scoping Personal Data: Towards a Nuanced Interpretaton of the Material Scope of EU Data Protection Law.' *European Journal of Law and Technology* 10 no. 1 (2019): 26.

'Data Protection in the European Union: The Role of National Data Protection Authorities.' Luxembourg: European Union Agency for Fundamental Rights, 2010. fra.europa.eu/sites/default/files/fra_uploads/815-Data-protection_en.pdf.

DIRECTIVE 2006/24/EC OF THE EUROPEAN PARLIAMENT AND OF THE COUNCIL of 15 March 2006 on the retention of data generated or processed in connection with the provision of publicly available electronic communications services or of public communications networks and amending Directive 2002/58/EC, OJ L 105/54, 13/4/2006, 54–63. § (n.d.).

Douzinas, Costas. *The End of Human Rights: Critical Thought at the Turn of the Century*. London: Bloomsbury Publishing, 2000.

Dupré, Catherine. *The Age of Dignity: Human Rights and Constitutionalism in Europe*. London: Bloomsbury Publishing, 2015.

Edwards, Lilian, Michèle Finck, Michael Veale and Nicolo Zingales. 'Data Subjects as Data Controllers: A Fashion(Able) Concept?' Internet Policy Review. policyreview.info/articles/news/data-subjects-data-controllers-fashionable-concept/1400.

Erdos, David. *European Data Protection Regulation, Journalism, and Traditional Publishers: Balancing on a Tightrope?* Oxford: Oxford University Press, 2019.

Fabbrini, Federico. 'The EU Charter of Fundamental Rights and the Rights to Data Privacy: The EU Court of Justice as a Human Rights Court.' In *The EU Charter of Fundamental Rights as a Binding Instrument: Five Years On*, edited by Sybe A. De Vries, Ulf Bernitz and Stephen Weatherill, 20: 261–86. Studies of the Oxford Institute of European and Comparative Law. Oxford: Hart Publishing, 2015.

Fereday, Jennifer and Eimear Muir-Cochrane. 'Demonstrating Rigor Using Thematic Analysis: A Hybrid Approach of Inductive and Deductive Coding and Theme Development.' *International Journal of Qualitative Methods* 5 no. 1 (2006): 80–92. doi.org/10.1177/160940690600500107.
Finck, Michèle. 'Cobwebs of Control: The Two Imaginations of the Data Controller in EU Law.' *International Data Privacy Law* 11 no. 4 (2021): 333–347. doi.org/10.1093/idpl/ipab017.
'First Overview on the Implementation of the GDPR and the Roles and Means of the National Supervisory Authorities.' European Data Protection Board, 26 February 2019. edpb.europa.eu/sites/edpb/files/files/file1/19_2019_edpb_written_report_to_libe_en.pdf.
Floridi, Luciano. 'Group Privacy: A Defence and an Interpretation.' In *Group Privacy: New Challenges of Data Technologies*, edited by Linnet Taylor, Luciano Floridi and Bart van der Sloot, 126: 83–100. Philosophical Studies Series. Cham: Springer, 2017.
Gellert, R. 'Data Protection: A Risk Regulation? Between the Risk Management of Everything and the Precautionary Alternative.' *International Data Privacy Law* 5 no. 1 (2015): 3–19.
Gellert, Raphaël. *The Risk-Based Approach to Data Protection*. 1st edn. Oxford: Oxford University Press, 2020.
González Fuster, Gloria. *The Emergence of Personal Data Protection as a Fundamental Right of the EU*. Vol. 16. Law, Governance and Technology Series. Cham: Springer, 2014. doi.org/10.1007/978-3-319-05023-2.
Gutwirth, Serge and Paul De Hert. 'Data Protection in the Case Law of Strasbourg and Luxemburg: Constitutionalisation in Action.' In *Reinventing Data Protection?*, edited by Serge Gutwirth, Yves Poullet, Paul De Hert, Cécile de Terwangne and Sjaak Nouwt, 3–44. The Netherlands: Springer, 2009.
Hartzog, Woodrow. 'Opinions · The Case Against Idealising Control.' *European Data Protection Law Review* 4 no. 4 (2018): 423–432.
Hustinx, Peter. 'EU Data Protection Law: The Review of Directive 95/46/EC and the General Data Protection Regulation.' In *New Technologies and EU Law*, edited by Marise Cremona. Oxford: Oxford University Press, 2017.
Janssen, Heleen, Jennifer Cobbe and Jatinder Singh. 'Personal Information Management Systems: A User-Centric Privacy Utopia?' *Internet Policy Review* 9 no. 4 (2020). doi.org/10.14763/2020.4.1536.
Koops, Bert-Jaap. 'The Trouble with European Data Protection Law.' *International Data Privacy Law* 4 no. 4 (2014): 250–261.
Kosta, Eleni. 'Article 7. Conditions for Consent.' In *The EU General Data Protection Regulation (GDPR): A Commentary*, edited by Christopher Kuner, Lee A. Bygrave, Christopher Docksey and Laura Drechsler, 345–354. Oxford: Oxford University Press, 2020.
———. *Consent in European Data Protection Law*. Leiden: Brill, 2013.
Lazaro, Christophe and Daniel Le Métayer. 'Control over Personal Data: True Remedy or Fairytale?' *SCRIPTed* 12 no. 1 (2015). doi.org/10.2966/scrip.120115.3.
Lievens, Eva and Valerie Verdoodt. 'Looking for Needles in a Haystack: Key Issues Affecting Children's Rights in the General Data Protection Regulation.' *Computer Law & Security Review* 34 no. 2 (2018): 269–78. doi.org/10.1016/j.clsr.2017.09.007.
Lindroos-Hovinheimo, Susanna. *Private Selves: Legal Personhood in European Privacy Protection*. Cambridge Studies in European Law and Policy. Cambridge: Cambridge University Press, 2021.

Lynskey, Orla. 'Criminal Justice Profiling and EU Data Protection Law: Precarious Protection from Predictive Policing.' *International Journal of Law in Context* 15 no. 2 (2019): 162–176. doi.org/10.1017/S1744552319000090.

———. 'Delivering Data Protection: The Next Chapter.' *German Law Journal* 21 no. 1 (2020): 80–84. doi.org/10.1017/glj.2019.100.

———. 'From Market-Making Tool to Fundamental Right: The Role of the Court of Justice in Data Protection's Identity Crisis.' In *European Data Protection: Coming of Age*, edited by Serge Gutwirth, Ronald Leenes, Paul De Hert and Yves Poullet, 59–84. Dordrecht: Springer Netherlands, 2013.

———. *The Foundations of EU Data Protection Law*. Oxford: Oxford University Press, 2015.

Malgieri, Gianclaudio, and Jędrzej Niklas. 'Vulnerable Data Subjects.' *Computer Law & Security Review* 37 (2020): 105415. doi.org/10.1016/j.clsr.2020.105415.

Mantelero, Alessandro. 'Personal Data for Decisional Purposes in the Age of Analytics: From an Individual to a Collective Dimension of Data Protection.' *Computer Law & Security Review* 32 no. 2 (2016): 238–255. doi.org/10.1016/j.clsr.2016.01.014.

Marx, Gary T. *Windows into the Soul: Surveillance and Society in an Age of High Technology*. Chicago: University of Chicago Press, 2016.

Matzner, Tobias, Philipp K. Masur, Carsten Ochs and Thilo von Pape. 'Do-It-Yourself Data Protection – Empowerment or Burden?' In *Data Protection on the Move*, edited by Serge Gutwirth, Ronald Leenes and Paul De Hert, 24: 277–305. Dordrecht: Springer Netherlands, 2016. doi.org/10.1007/978-94-017-7376-8_11.

Nissenbaum, Helen. *Privacy in Context: Technology, Policy and the Integrity of Social Life*. California: Stanford University Press, 2010.

Ouald Chaib, Saïla. 'Procedural Fairness as a Vehicle for Inclusion in the Freedom of Religion Jurisprudence of the Strasbourg Court.' *Human Rights Law Review* 16 no. 3 (2016): 483–510. doi.org/10.1093/hrlr/ngw020.

Pagallo, Ugo. 'The Group, the Private, and the Individual: A New Level of Data Protection?' In *Group Privacy: New Challenges of Data Technologies*, edited by Linnet Taylor, Luciano Floridi and Bart van der Sloot, 126: 159–73. Philosophical Studies Series. Cham: Springer International Publishing, 2017.

Peifer, Karl-Nikolaus and Paul M. Schwartz. 'Transatlantic Data Privacy Law.' *Georgetown Law Journal* 106 (2017): 115–179.

Poullet, Yves. 'Data Protection Legislation: What Is at Stake for Our Society and Democracy?' *Computer Law & Security Review* 25 no. 3 (2009): 211–226.

Purtova, Nadezhda. 'From Knowing by Name to Targeting: The Meaning of Identification under the GDPR.' *International Data Privacy Law*, 21 June 2022, ipac013. doi.org/10.1093/idpl/ipac013.

———. 'The Law of Everything. Broad Concept of Personal Data and Future of EU Data Protection Law.' *Law, Innovation and Technology* 10 no. 1 (2018): 40–81. doi.org/10.1080/17579961.2018.1452176.

Regan, Priscilla M. *Legislating Privacy: Technology, Social Values, and Public Policy*. US: The University of North Carolina Press, 1995.

REGULATION (EU) 2016/679 OF THE EUROPEAN PARLIAMENT AND OF THE COUNCIL of 27 April 2016 on the protection of natural persons with regard to the processing of personal data and on the free movement of such data, and repealing Directive 95/46/EC (General Data Protection Regulation), OJ L 119, 4/5/2016, 1–88 § (n.d.).

Rouvroy, Antoinette and Yves Poullet. 'The Right to Informational Self-Determination and the Value of Self-Development: Reassessing the Importance of Privacy for Democracy.' In *Reinventing Data Protection?*, edited by Serge Gutwirth, Yves Poullet, Paul De Hert, Cécile de Terwangne and Sjaak Nouwt, 45–76. Dordrecht: Springer Netherlands, 2009. doi.org/10.1007/978-1-4020-9498-9_2.

Schwartz, Paul M. 'Privacy and Democracy in Cyberspace.' *Vanderbilt Law Review; Nashville* 52 no. 6 (1999): 1609–1702.

Siedentop, Larry. *Inventing the Individual: The Origins of Western Liberalism*. Milton Keynes: Penguin Books, 2014.

Sloot, Bart van der. *Privacy as Virtue: Moving beyond the Individual in the Age of Big Data*. School of Human Rights Research Series; Volume 81. Cambridge, US: Intersentia, 2017.

Smuha, Nathalie A. 'Beyond the Individual: Governing AI's Societal Harm.' *Internet Policy Review* 10 no. 3 (2021). doi.org/10.14763/2021.3.1574.

Solove, Daniel J. 'Privacy Self-Management and the Consent Dilemma.' *Harvard Law Review* 126 no. 7 (2013): 1880–1903.

Somek, Alexander. *Individualism: An Essay on the Authority of the European Union*. Oxford: Oxford University Press, 2008.

Taylor, Linnet, Luciano Floridi, and Bart van der Sloot, eds. *Group Privacy: New Challenges of Data Technologies*. Cham: Springer International Publishing, 2017. doi.org/10.1007/978-3-319-46608-8.

Trotter, Sarah Jane. 'On Coming to Terms: How European Human Rights Law Imagines the Human Condition.' Doctor of Philosophy, The London School of Economics and Political Science, 2018. etheses.lse.ac.uk/3946/1/Trotter__On-coming-terms-European-human-rights.pdf.

Van Alsenoy, Brendan. 'The Evolving Role of the Individual under EU Data Protection Law.' *CiTiP Working Paper Series*, no 23 (2015): 36.

Viljoen, Salomé. 'A Relational Theory of Data Governance.' *The Yale Law Journal* (2021): 82.

Weiler, J.H.H. 'Van Gend En Loos: The Individual as Subject and Object and the Dilemma of European Legitimacy.' *International Journal of Constitutional Law* 12 no. 1 (2014): 94–103. doi.org/10.1093/icon/mou011.

Wong, Benjamin. 'Delimiting the Concept of Personal Data after the GDPR.' *Legal Studies* 39 no. 3 (2019): 517–532. doi.org/10.1017/lst.2018.52.

# 6

## Data Subject Rights as a Tool for Platform Worker Resistance: Lessons from the *Uber/Ola* Judgments

WENLONG LI[*] AND JILL TOH[≠]

## Abstract

Data subject rights have been increasingly used to challenge power asymmetries in different contexts, including work. This chapter looks at how platform workers have harnessed their data subject rights in the General Data Protection Regulation (GDPR) in the wider context of platform worker resistance. The strategic litigation cases against Uber and Ola, brought forth by App Drivers Workers Union (ADCU) and Worker Info Exchange (WIE) before the Amsterdam District Court (ADC), represent a prime example of data subject rights being leveraged by workers in an unconventional and potentially complicated manner. While this is not the first time that data subject rights have been interpreted before courts, these judgments have implications that merit attention from both labour protection and data protection communities. These rulings showcase how data subject rights are operationalised and envisioned as a tool of resistance, contrasting with how these rights are designed by legislators. These rulings also reveal barriers to the effective exercise of these rights in practice, which should be urgently addressed via an update on the guidelines or via more radical reform. This chapter evaluates the ADC's rulings through the lens of data protection and shows glitches, mismatches and erroneous views in need of revision in the appeal. It is argued that courts are in a distinctive and critical position vis-a-vis data protection authorities to make these rights work. While there are inherent limitations on these rights (the right of access in particular), courts play an indispensable role in removing procedural barriers and establishing avenues for balancing competing values. At the juncture where the regulatory landscape for platform work is being radically re-configured, data subject rights still, we argue, offer potential for platform workers as a tool of resistance.

---

[*] University of Birmingham, UK.
[≠] University of Amsterdam, The Netherlands.

## Keywords

GDPR, data subject rights, right of access, right to data portability, right not to be subject to automated decision-making, right to explanation, Uber, Ola, platform worker, resistance

## I. Introduction

The emergence of the platform economy has brought about many changes for workers. The assumed benefits associated with platform work include flexibility, autonomy, and the ability to decide their own working rhythm. Yet, the reality of platform workers shows otherwise. Through a combination of legal, technical and political strategies, platforms have consistently argued that platform workers are independent contractors. One key component of their strategy has been to delegate and outsource managerial functions via algorithmic systems, otherwise known as algorithmic management.[1] The platforms seek to absolve their responsibilities via opaque algorithmic systems, creating an illusion that 'your boss is an algorithm'.[2] These developments have intensified the challenges platform workers face, including pervasive surveillance and control, a lack of transparency and understanding of their working conditions, discrimination and increasing precarity, amongst other struggles.

Despite many odds stacked against platform workers, they have responded to their unjust situation with new tactics and strategies.[3] As many commentators point out, (big) data has become a new frontier in the battle for workers' rights, given the intensified level of surveillance, constant monitoring, and the precarity of workers exacerbated by algorithmic management.[4] Indeed, in parallel with the litigation cases concerning better employment protections, platform workers are now actively leveraging their data subject rights provided by the General Data Protection Regulation (GDPR). These rights, characterised in the public debate as a tool of resistance,[5] do complement the workers' existing fight for a more

---

[1] Jeremias Adams-Prassl, 'What If Your Boss Was an Algorithm? Economic Incentives, Legal Challenges, and the Rise of Artificial Intelligence at Work,' *Comparative Labor Law and Policy Journal* 41.1 (2019): 131.

[2] Antonio Aloisi and Valerio de Stefano, *Your Boss Is an Algorithm: Artificial Intelligence, Platform Work and Labour* (London: Bloomsbury Publishing, 2022), 7.

[3] Ioulia Bessa, Simon Joyce, Denis Neumann, Mark Stuart, Vera Trappmann, and Charles Umney, *A Global Analysis of Worker Protest in Digital Labour Platforms* (Geneva: International Labour Organiation, 2022).

[4] Laurie Clarke, 'Data is the Next Frontier in the Fight for Gig Workers' Rights,' *Tech Monitor*, techmonitor.ai/policy/education-and-employment/data-next-frontier-fight-for-gig-workers-rights.

[5] Karen Gregory, '"Worker Data Science" Can Teach Us How to Fix the Gig Economy,' *WIRED*, www.wired.com/story/labor-organizing-unions-worker-algorithms/.

sustainable and safe platform economy and create new forms of data-enabled opportunities.[6]

There are instances in case-law[7] or administrative measures[8] in which work-related needs are considered in the context of privacy and data protection. With a focus on the processing of personal data, however, little is said about algorithmic management. The only exception seen is the Italian DPA's imposition of fines on Foodinho (subsidiary of Glovo), a food delivery company, for having no safeguards in ensuring fairness and accuracy in the algorithms used to rate riders' performance, and for insufficient procedures to contest algorithmic decisions with a human decision-maker.[9] The four judgments delivered by the ADC in March 2021 vis-à-vis ride-hailing platforms Uber and Ola represent a timely and invaluable addition to this understated problem in the context of data protection.

This chapter evaluates the four judgments through the lens of data protection. While it is not the first-time data subject rights are considered before courts, these rulings engage a previously understated but practically important situation. While the several GDPR rights are designed to be separate in pursuit of distinct purposes, these rights are often used jointly in practice to achieve an objective not necessarily aligned with one or more purposes articulated for these rights. From the perspective of platform workers, for instance, checking the accuracy of personal data collected or lawfulness of data processing conducted is of little practical use. Data subject rights are often imagined instead as a tool to address power and information asymmetries and ultimately to address their work-related needs. The four Dutch cases vividly present the collective thinking of platform workers to pool individual datasets with a view to building a union-backed data trust. While the idea stands sound and reasonable, it runs counter to how data subject rights are perceived, expected and interpreted. It is on the basis of this tension that this chapter proceeds.

The chapter is organised as follows. After this introduction, section II contextualises the workers' exercise of their data subject rights within the platform worker resistance literature. Section III presents the details of the four Dutch judgments in a systematic and structured manner while paving the way for further analysis. Sections IV and V attend respectively to the micro and macro perspectives of data subject rights. We analyse in section IV a set of challenges that hinders the effective

---

[6] Gregory (n. 5).
[7] *Lopez Ribalda and Others v Spain* [GC] no. 1874/13. *Barbulescu v Romania* [GC] no. 61496/08. *FILCAMS CGIL, NIDIL CGIL, FILT CGIL v. Deliveroo Italia S.R.L.* no. 2949/2019.
[8] EDPB, 'Hamburg Commissioner Fines H&M 35.3 Million Euro for Data Protection Violations in Service Centre,' *EDPB*, edpb.europa.eu/news/national-news/2020/hamburg-commissioner-fines-hm-353-million-euro-data-protection-violations_en. EDPB, 'The Icelandic DPA has fined a company running ice cream parlours for processing employee's personal data via video surveillance camera installed in an employee area,' *EDPB*, edpb.europa.eu/news/national-news/2021/icelandic-dpa-has-fined-company-running-ice-cream-parlours-processing_en.
[9] EDPB, 'Riders: Italian SA Says No to Algorithms Causing Discrimination: A platform in the Glovo group fined EUR 2.6 million,' *EDPB*, edpb.europa.eu/news/national-news/2021/riders-italian-sa-says-no-algorithms-causing-discrimination-platform-glovo_en.

exercise of three data subject rights revealed by the judgments. Section V engages with broader concerns about data subject rights as a tool of resistance. These perspectives are then connected in Section VI with the ongoing legislative developments in the EU, including the proposed EU Directive on improving working conditions in platform work (hereinafter the 'proposed Platform Work Directive') and the proposed Artificial Intelligence (AI) Act. Section VII concludes.

## II. Platform Work: Challenges and New Forms of Resistance

Platform economy is an umbrella term[10] that encompasses different types of labour mediated by digital platforms. It extends across a spectrum of unpaid, micropaid and poorly paid human tasks[11] and has been part of a larger shift in work and employment, altering the ways in which work is managed and re-organised.[12] This chapter focuses on on-demand platforms, a sub-set of the platform economy that involves platform work geographically tethered and location-based (specifically in Europe) by allocating service-oriented tasks through location-based apps. Ride-hailing and courier delivery services such as Uber, Deliveroo, Bolt are prime examples of this type of platform.[13] Platform workers in this sector have been actively campaigning, organising, resisting and demanding better pay and working conditions, but also reimagining the ways in which data and technology can be utilised in service of workers, not capital.[14]

### A. The Platform Economy and its Challenges for Workers

The emergence of platform companies was initially touted as innovative and disruptive. Yet, developments in the platform economy over the past five years have

---

[10] Identifying proper terminology has been a major challenge that underlies the work and commentary in these areas and many scholars, researchers and policymakers do not explicitly agree on a definition. See Orly Lobel, 'The Law of the Platform,' *Minnesota Law Review* 137 (2016): 88. Deepa Das Acevedo, 'Regulating Employment Relationships in the Sharing Economy,' *Employee Rights and Employment Policy Journal* 20 (2016): 3.

[11] Tiziana Terranova, 'Free Labor: Producing Culture for the Digital Economy,' *Social Text* 18.2 (2000): 34. Trebor Scholz, 'Introduction: Why does Digital Labor Matter Now?,' in *Digital Labor: The Internet as a Playground and Factory*, ed. Trebor Scholz (New York: Routledge, 2012), 1.

[12] Brishen Rogers, 'The Law and Political Economy of Workplace Technological Change,' Harvard Civil Rights-Civil Liberties Law Review 55.2 (2020): 539. Antonio A. Casilli, 'Digital Labor Studies Go Global: Toward a Digital Decolonial Turn,' *International Journal of Communication* 11 (2017): 3934–3935.

[13] Jamie Woodcock and Mark Graham, *The Gig Economy: A Critical Introduction* (Cambridge: Polity Press, 2020), 55.

[14] Gregory (n. 5).

proven to be otherwise. The platform economy can largely be characterised as a continuation of long-existing trends of the casualisation of work, whereby employment protections are eroded and replaced by zero-hour contracts and workers take on the risk of the contract.[15] What is novel is its intersection with technological developments, such as algorithmic management, which exacerbates the already precarious position of workers.[16] Businesses have long used technology to build hierarchal relations with workers, including surveillance and monitoring, and the pervasiveness of modern technologies are *qualitatively* different and significant.[17] Some scholarship has documented the contractual dimension of platform work, such as the (mis)classification of employment through independent contractor statuses (or 'bogus self-employment') through narratives of flexibility and autonomy, which has impacted workers' access to basic labour rights and protections.[18] These basic employment protections provide rights to minimum wage, social protection, freedom of assembly, protection from unfair dismissals and discrimination. Other scholarship focuses on the ways in which algorithmic management re-organises labour processes and alters managerial prerogatives,[19] with implications for platform workers' income, job security, autonomy and control at work.[20] For workers, algorithmic management includes several forms of granular managerial control via systems that range from gamification strategies to GPS tracking, to task allocation, to price-setting, to ratings and to deactivation (or 'robo-firing'). Due to the mediation of work through opaque algorithmic management systems, workers are unable to understand how their wages are calculated, how performance metrics are weighted, or how they are discriminated against. Further instances of opacity include why workers are unable to login to their app and why they have been deactivated. Platform companies rely on information asymmetries and control mechanisms to manage, constrain and coerce workers.[21] These forms of control differ from traditional ones as they allow for decreased accountability

---

[15] Adams-Prassl (n. 1) 133.

[16] Mohammad Amir Anwar and Mark Graham, 'Between A Rock and A Hard Place: Freedom, Flexibility, Precarity and Vulnerability in the Gig Economy in Africa,' *Competition & Change* 25.2 (2020): 249.

[17] Phoebe Moore, Martin Upchurch and Xanthe Whittaker, 'Humans and Machines at Work: Monitoring, Surveillance and Automation in Contemporary Capitalism,' in *Humans and Machines at Work: Monitoring, Surveillance and Automation in Contemporary Capitalism*, eds. Phoebe Moore, Martin Upchurch and Xanthe Whittaker (Cham: Palgrave Macmillan, 2018), 3–4. Valerio de Stefano, '"Masters and Servers": Collective Labour Rights and Private Government in the Contemporary World of Work,' *International Journal of Comparative Labour Law and Industrial Relations* 36.4 (2020): 427.

[18] Valerio de Stefano, 'The Rise of the "Just-in-Time Workforce": On-Demand Work, Crowdwork, and Labor Protection in the "Gig-Economy",' *Comparative Labor Law and Policy Journal* 37.3 (2016): 495. Veena B. Dubal, 'Winning the Battle, Losing the War?: Assessing the Impact of Misclassification Litigation on Workers in the Gig Economy,' *Wisconsin Law Review* 4 (2017): 792.

[19] Aloisi and de Stefano (n. 2) 28. Adams-Prassl (n. 1) 131.

[20] Melissa R. Cano, Ricard Espelt and Mayo Fuster Morell, 'Flexibility and Freedom for Whom? Precarity, Freedom and Flexibility in On-demand Food Delivery,' *Work Organisation, Labour & Globalisation* 15.1 (2021): 49–52.

[21] Lutfun Nahar Lata, Jasmine Burdon and Tim Reddel, 'New Tech, Old Exploitation: Gig Economy, Algorithmic Control and Migrant Labour,' *Sociology Compass* (2022): 3–4.

via the 'outsourcing' of managerial functions to algorithmic systems.[22] Platform companies also shift a variety of risks onto workers, whether they be financial, mental, physical, occupational health, or safety risks.[23] Additionally, different forms of discrimination related to price, wage, or race have also been widely reported.[24]

While there are varied experiences amongst platform workers, the structural effects of these ongoing developments intensify the precarity and exploitation of platform workers, whose full-time workforce often belongs to racialised, marginalised, migrant communities.[25] At the core, platform workers lack legal protection on two fronts: employment protection and redress mechanisms related to transparency in algorithmic and automated decision-making systems.

## B. Platform Worker Resistance: New Tactics and Strategies

The atomised nature of on-demand platform work has posed significant challenges to collective organising. Still, platform workers have been actively campaigning for better working conditions, protection, pay and notably, insight into platform data and algorithmic systems.[26] In reaction to the changing labour context, platform worker resistance encompasses new tools and strategies to subvert, resist and challenge the current situation in the platform economy. Some authors have rightly cautioned against such optimism by questioning how these efforts can be sustained, particularly as platform companies find ways to structurally break the power of organised labour.[27] However, these efforts by platform workers persist, and new forms of resistance, protests and contestation are emerging in the platform economy. Overall, platform worker resistance is a combination of legal and non-legal strategies, including on-the-ground and online activities, which can be categorised as the following:

(a) **Online and offline coordination:** Workers coordinate demonstrations, strikes and boycotts, through formal channels such as unions, but also

---

[22] Alessandro Gandini, 'Labour Process Theory and he Gig Economy,' *Human Relations* 72.6 (2018): 1046. Lata, Burdon and Reddel (n. 21) 5.

[23] Karen Gregory, '"My Life is More Valuable Than This": Understanding Risk among On-Demand Food Couriers in Edinburgh,' *Work, Employment and Society* 35.2 (2020): 323–328.

[24] Akshat Pandey and Aylin Caliskan, 'Disparate Impact of Artificial Intelligence Bias in Ridehailing Economy's Price Discrimination Algorithms,' *AIES 2021 – Proceedings of the 2021 AAAI/ACM Conference on AI, Ethics, and Society* (2021): 827. Veena Dubal, 'The New Racial Wage Code,' *Harvard Law and Policy Review* 15.2 (2021): 526.

[25] Moritz Altenried, 'Mobile Workers, Contingent Labour: Migration, the Gig Economy and the Multiplication of Labour,' *Environment and Planning A: Economy and Space* (2021): 6.

[26] Gregory (n. 5).

[27] Niels van Doorn, 'At what Price? Labour Politics and Calculative Power Struggles in On-demand Food Delivery,' *Work Organisation, Labour & Globalisation* 14.1 (2020): 146–147. Niels van Doorn and Julie Yujie Chen, 'Odds Stacked against Workers: Datafied Gamification on Chinese and American Food Delivery Platforms,' *Socio-Economic Review* 19.4 (2021): 1362.

increasingly through informal ad-hoc worker collectives and co-operatives.[28] This involves riders organising themselves and coordinating strike action with other service sector workers, through encrypted chats and informal groups online and offline.[29]

(b) **Algorithmic activism:** Workers build and develop software or apps to 'game the system' and counteract changes in their app environment by manipulating or gaining an advantage over the platforms they work for.[30] It can also range from simple acts such as drivers resisting and rejecting performance metrics by cancelling rides,[31] to more sophisticated methods of using software to identify the location of a passenger's destination and simultaneously identifying more expensive journeys before deciding to accept a ride.[32] Increasingly, workers together with programmers, researchers, unions and activists are attempting to create data-enabled opportunities for the benefit of workers. They are building coalitions and pooling resources to build tools and apps to offer more insight into how algorithmic systems calculate wages, track working time and identify wage theft.[33] This has increasingly expanded to developing new (formalised and less formalised) ways of collectivising around data, including data trusts and data co-ops, in order to collectivise and port data, as is evident in the cases below.[34] These forms of resistance build on earlier initiatives such as worker resistance in clickwork.[35] While there remain ethical, technical and practical concerns beyond the scope of this chapter, some of these efforts have supported platform workers in gaining transparency and insight into their working conditions.

(c) **Deploying data subject rights (and other laws) to counter power asymmetries, including strategic litigation:** Workers are bringing forth legal action such as (strategic) litigation, despite challenges to accessing institutional

---

[28] Bessa et al. (n. 3) 10. Hannah Johnston and Chris Land-Kazlauskas, *Organizing On-Demand: Representation, Voice, and Collective Bargaining in the Gig Economy* (Geneva: International Labour Organisation Conditions of Work and Employment Series, no. 94) (2019): 5, 18.

[29] Callum Cant and Jamie Woodcock, 'Fast Food Shutdown: From Disorganisation to Action in the Service Sector,' *Capital & Class* 44.4 (2020): 516. Callum Cant, *Riding for Deliveroo: Resistance in the New Economy* (Cambridge: Polity, 2020), 94.

[30] Julie Yujie Chen, 'Thrown under the Bus and Outrunning It! The Logic of Didi and Taxi Drivers' Labour and Activism in the on-Demand Economy,' *New Media & Society* 20.8 (2018): 2691.

[31] Mareike Möhlmann and Lior Zalmanson, 'Hands on the Wheel: Navigating Algorithmic Management and Uber Drivers' Autonomy,' *Proceedings of the International Conference on Information Systems (ICIS) Seoul, South Korea (December 2017):* 3.

[32] *ADCU v Uber B.V.* C/13/692003/HA RK 20-302.

[33] Gregory (n. 5).

[34] 'About WIE,' Worker Info Exchange, www.workerinfoexchange.org/. 'About GigCV,' Gig CV, gigcv. org/. Ada Lovelace Institute, Exploring legal mechanisms for data stewardship (London: Ada Lovelace Institute, 2021), www.adalovelaceinstitute.org/report/legal-mechanisms-data-stewardship/.

[35] Lilly C. Irani and Michael Six Silberman, 'Turkopticon: Interrupting Worker Invisibility in Amazon Mechanical Turk,' *CHI '13: Proceedings of the SIGCHI Conference on Human Factors in Computing Systems,* (April 2013): 611.

channels of worker contestation, and the costs and resources associated with litigation. One legal tool which has emerged to challenge information and power asymmetries is data subject rights under the GDPR. In parallel with other litigation cases brought forward by platform workers related to employment status,[36] minimum wage[37] and discrimination,[38] platform workers in Europe are also asserting their data subject rights[39] to complement their existing struggles for stronger legal protection. This 'interlegality'[40] may offer different opportunities to define legal entry points for litigation, and to think more thoroughly how asserting data subject rights and strategic litigation can fit into the wider strategy of platform worker resistance.[41]

The legal ambiguity surrounding platform workers' status as independent contractors means that they are unable to claim basic worker rights associated with employment law. However, data subject rights' purpose-blind and intent agnostic nature offers some potential for platform workers in Europe to gain transparency into algorithmic systems and processes that mediate and shape their work, including understanding how their labour generates value for platform companies.[42] These rights can be invoked by any individual whose fundamental rights, freedoms or interests have been affected by the processing of personal data and automated decision-making.[43] In effect, it can overcome some of the existing complications of employment status and its associated rights. For instance, in some cases, data subject rights can act as a mechanism and first step to prove and address other forms of harms. As documented in the Managed by Bots report,[44] Uber driver Pa Edrissa Manjang was deactivated by Uber for failing his

---

[36] Valerio de Stefano and Antonio Aloisi, 'European Legal Framework for "Digital Labour Platforms"', *Publications Office of the European Union* (2018): 41.

[37] Ruth Berins Collier, Veena B. Dubal, and Christopher L. Carter, 'Disrupting Regulation, Regulating Disruption: The Politics of Uber in the United States,' *Perspectives on Politics* 16.4 (2018): 921.

[38] Chris Vallance, 'Legal action over alleged Uber facial verification bias' (*BBC*, 8 October 2021), www.bbc.com/news/technology-58831373.

[39] Hießl, Christina, 'Case law on Algorithmic Management at the Workplace: Cross-European Comparative Analysis and Tentative Conclusions,' *European Commission, Directorate DG Employment, Social Affairs and Inclusion* (September 2021): 4, papers.ssrn.com/sol3/papers.cfm?abstract_id=3982735. Cansu Safak and James Farrar, *Managed by Bots: Data-Driven Exploitation in the Gig Economy* (London: Worker Info Exchange, 2021), www.workerinfoexchange.org/wie-report-managed-by-bots.

[40] Interlegality is defined by de Sousa Santos as 'a highly dynamic process because the different legal spaces are non-synchronic and thus result in uneven and unstable mixings of legal codes'. See Boaventura de Sousa Santos, 'Law: A Map of Misreading. Toward a Postmodern Conception of Law,' *Journal of Law and Society* 14.3 (1987): 298.

[41] Yaseen Aslam and Jamie Woodcock, 'A History of Uber Organizing in the UK,' *South Atlantic Quarterly* 119. 2 (2020): 415. Bessa et al. (n. 3) 7, 8.

[42] Gregory (n. 5).

[43] Jef Ausloos, René Mahieu and Michael Veale, 'Getting Data Subject Rights Right: A Submission to the European Data Protection Board from International Data Rights Academics, to Inform Regulatory Guidance,' *Journal of Intellectual Property, Information Technology and E-Commerce Law* 10.1 (2019): 283.

[44] Safak and Farrar (n. 39) 17–21.

selfie identity verification via facial recognition software, which has been proven to have a high rate of inaccuracy on darker skinned people.[45] Pa, together with ADCU, submitted a subject access request in order to obtain the selfies he had submitted to prove that he was wrongly dismissed, as well as to bring forth a case against Uber to challenge the use of its racially discriminatory facial recognition system.

While there have been criticisms that data subject rights are individualistic in nature, a growing body of work seeks to emphasise the potential of data subject rights in protecting collective interests.[46] The sentiment of harnessing the collective potential of data subject rights is also echoed by advocates of worker and data subject rights, stressing the importance for unions (and workers) to seriously reckon with the impact that algorithmic management and other technologies have on workers. Their call is for unions to build capacity and resources to inform workers about their data subject rights, to support their process in asserting rights, as well as to negotiate for better collective (worker) protections in upcoming data and technology legislative proposals.[47] Furthermore, researchers working on digital labour have demonstrated the lack of labour perspectives and consideration of labour rights within legal discussions surrounding data and technology regulation, despite the significant implications technology will continue to have on work.[48]

The collective dimension is beginning to be addressed by other EU legal developments in reaction to algorithmic management and the datafication of the workplace, such as the proposed Platform Work Directive and the proposed AI Act. These developments may bring about some clarity for the GDPR, but also more complexities as the GDPR interacts with other legal instruments. As such, the relevance in assessing the cases brought forward by Uber and Ola drivers at the ADC has particular importance from both data protection and labour perspectives.

---

[45] Joy Buolamwini and Timnit Gebru, 'Gender Shades: Intersectional Accuracy Disparities in Commercial Gender Classification,' *Proceedings of the 1st Conference on Fairness, Accountability and Transparency*, PMLR 81 (2018): 77.

[46] René Mahieu, Hadi Asghari, and Michel van Eeten, 'Collectively Exercising the Right of Access: Individual Effort, Societal Effect,' *Internet Policy Review* 7.3 (2018): 15–17. Joanna Mazur, 'Right to Access Information as a Collective-Based Approach to the GDPR's Right to Explanation in European Law,' *Erasmus Law Review* 11 (2018): 183. René Mahieu, and Jef Ausloos, 'Harnessing the Collective Potential of GDPR Access Rights: Towards An Ecology of Transparency,' *Internet Policy Review* (2020).

[47] Christina Colclough, 'Towards Workers' Data Collectives,' *IT for Change*, projects.itforchange.net/digital-new-deal/2020/10/22/towards-workers-data-collectives/. Nakeema Stefflbauer, 'When Human rights + Digital rights = Workers' rights,' *Digital Freedom Fund*, digitalfreedomfund.org/when-human-rights-digital-rights-workers-rights/.

[48] Lina Dencik, 'Towards Data Justice Unionism? A Labour Perspective on AI Governance,' in *AI for Everyone: Critical Perspectives*, ed. Pieter Verdegem (Westminster: University of Westminster Press, 2021), 286. Niklas Jędrzej, and Lina Dencik, 'What Rights Matter? Examining the Place of Social Rights in the EU's Artificial Intelligence Policy Debate,' *Internet Policy Review* 10.3 (2021): 20–23.

## III. The *Uber/Ola* Judgments: An Overview

### A. Context

In order to contextualise these cases, it is important to understand why Uber and Ola drivers brought forward these cases against Uber and Ola. First, they wanted to prove an employment relationship by understanding the extent to which Uber and Ola exerted management control by means of algorithmic systems and automated decision-making. These cases were brought forward against the background of the six year-long employment reclassification case at the UK Supreme Court, where the court was assessing the degree in which these companies exert management control by means of algorithmic and automated decision-making systems.[49] Second, they wanted to calculate minimum wage and holiday allowances. Third, they wanted protection from discrimination, and the drivers' ratings can be severely affected if customers discriminate against them. Falling below an average rating of 4.4 (for reasons that are not wholly transparent) for drivers means that they are deactivated and 'fired'. Fourth, they wanted their data in order to understand the rationale of these systems for collective bargaining and advocacy. Lastly, they wanted to establish a data trust to be managed by Worker Info Exchange.

For these reasons, this chapter underscores the significance of these cases when considered from a broader perspective. These cases move beyond the idea that platform workers simply want to understand their minimum wage and working conditions. Rather, these drivers have longer-term goals in mind, seeking to harness their data subject rights with plans to intervene in other areas such as employment and discrimination law. Furthermore, the drivers' goal of establishing a data trust for their grassroots union demonstrates a forward-thinking initiative to rethink how information about one's data can be collectivised to the benefit of workers. In effect, these strategic litigation cases are situated within their wider strategy to fight and advocate for better workers' rights and protection, as well as to reimagine new forms of organisation.

### B. Rulings

A total of four judgments were delivered by ADC on 11 March 2021, all of which are concerned with platform drivers strategically exercising GDPR data

---

[49] These cases were brought forward between July 2020 and December 2020, where the employment reclassification case at the UKSC was still ongoing. The ruling by the Supreme Court was passed down in February 2021. See also, Jill Toh, 'UK gig drivers recognised as workers – what next?,' (*Social Europe*, 25 February 2021), socialeurope.eu/uk-gig-drivers-recognised-as-workers-what-next.

subject rights vis-à-vis ride-hailing platforms. The plaintiffs of these cases are mostly drivers based in the UK, the Netherlands and Portugal, supported by the ADCU.

In *Uber Access*,[50] ten UK-based drivers and one from Portugal filed a complaint against Uber in Amsterdam, where its European headquarter sits. Described by the media as a victory of Uber to 'fend off wide-ranging requests for data from drivers',[51] the results of this judgment were actually mixed. Indeed, the majority of access requests per Article 15 GDPR were rejected, involving the access to manual notes, 'tags', internal 'reports', to name a few. The reasons for rejection are diverse, including that the drivers' requests were not specific enough, that data access may adversely affect the rights and freedoms of others (eg, Uber customers). The court dismissed data portability requests under Article 20 on the basis that the data had already been provided to the Uber drivers in PDF format, which were deemed to be adequate and GDPR-compliant. When it came to ratings, ostensibly one of the most valuable datasets for workers to continue their work on a platform or to switch to another, the court was on the side of drivers. It was held that ratings should be provided to the drivers but in an *anonymised* form for the protection of third-party privacy.

In *Ola Access*,[52] three UK-based drivers sued the Bangalore-based ride-hailing platform Ola. Previously, Ola responded by providing a collection of documents and files, which the drivers found neither adequate nor consistent. For instance, many categories of data described in Ola's Privacy Statement or Guidance Notes were either missing or not in a requested format (ie, CSV). Moreover, the explanation for Ola's use of automated decision-making was deemed not meaningful, hence prompting the drivers to demand full access to their data. Notably, the drivers detailed the types of data and information sought as well as the legal basis on which such access is requested.[53] Three main breakthroughs are made in this case. First, the court upheld in a similar fashion a request to access ratings but only in an anonymised form. Second, it supported for the first time requests to improve the transparency of various profiles established by Ola, notably including the fraud probability score, the earning profile and the Guardian system built to 'detect irregularities'.[54] It was held that the drivers are entitled, under Article 15, to access to the personal data 'used to draw up the risk profiles as well as information about the segments into which the applicants have been classified'.[55] Note that this

---

[50] *Uber Access*, C/13/687315/HA RK 20-207.
[51] Natasha Lomas, 'Dutch Court Rejects Uber Drivers' "Robo-Firing" Charge but Tells Ola to Explain Algo-Deductions,' *TechCrunch*, techcrunch.com/2021/03/12/dutch-court-rejects-uber-drivers-robo-firing-charge-but-tells-ola-to-explain-algo-deductions/.
[52] *Ola Access*, C/13/689705/HA RK 20-258.
[53] ibid 3.1.
[54] ibid 4.48.
[55] ibid 4.36, 4.45.

profile transparency achieved was not on the basis of Article 22 but Article 15, because the explanation requests (on the basis of Article 22) were not admitted due to the burden of proof imposed on the drivers. Third, when it came to data portability, the court declared irrelevant the purpose for which such data are requested on the basis of Article 20 GDPR. In other words, the Ola drivers do not have to show 'any particular interest or state the goal that [they] want to achieve with the access'.[56] Additionally, the court dismissed all the requests on the basis of Article 22 for not meeting the legal requirements such that the decision has to be made 'solely based on automated decision' or that the decision produces a 'legal or similarly significant effect'.

The remaining two judgments are known for 'robo-firing' and concerned with Article 22 rights vis-à-vis Uber. In *Uber Deactivation I*,[57] three UK-based drivers and one from Portugal received a notification from Uber about the deactivation of their driver accounts. These drivers were punished for allegedly committing fraud and thereby violating Uber's Terms of Conditions. Related to the previous cases supported by the ADCU, the drivers' main request was not re-activation but the provision of meaningful information about the algorithmic decisions made. Again, the court delivered mixed results. On the one hand, the requests of two drivers were rejected as they had previously been given an explanation within Uber's messaging system which was deemed by the court to be sufficiently clear (without an explicit content analysis). On the other hand, two other drivers succeeded in their request for an explanation as they had not been provided with any information about why their accounts had been deactivated.

Lastly, *Uber Deactivation II* concerns five UK-based drivers and one from the Netherlands who complained that they had been wrongly accused of fraudulent activities and, as a result, dismissed by the algorithms deployed by Uber. The court held in favour of the drivers that their accounts be reinstated simply because Uber was absent during the proceedings.

It is also worth noting that drivers requested compensation and punitive measures in all the cases, but most claims were rejected as the court did not see 'reasons for damage to their humanity or good name or damage to their person in any other way'.[58] The only exception is *Uber Deactivation II*, in which the court upheld the compensation requested by the drivers, as well as an imposition of penalty for non-compliance, largely due to Uber's absence in the proceedings.

---

[56] ibid 4.6.
[57] *Uber Deactivation I*, C/13/692003/HA RK 20-302.
[58] ibid 4.31.

**Table 1** An Overview of the Four Dutch judgments vis-à-vis Uber and Ola

| Case Title | Case Reference | Plaintiffs | Request | Outcome | Penalty |
|---|---|---|---|---|---|
| *Uber Access* | C/13/687315 / HA RK 20-207 | 10 UK-based & 1 Portuguese drivers | Data access via Arts 15, 20, and 22 rights in a commonly used, structured and machine-readable format or by means of API | All requests rejected except ratings (to be provided in an anonymised form) | No |
| *Ola Access* | C/13/689705 / HA RK 20-258 | 3 UK-based drivers | Same as above | The requests upheld include ratings (4.25) and profile transparency (4.52), including the risk probability score (4.45), earning profile (4.47), the Guardian system (4.49) | No |
| *Uber Deactivation I* | C/13/692003 / HA RK 20-302 | 3 UK-based & 1 Portuguese drivers | Explanation for why the accounts were deactivated and what personal data were involved for reaching that decision | The requests of two informed drivers rejected, and those of two uninformed drivers upheld | No |
| *Uber Deactivation II* | C/13/696010 / HA ZA 21-81 | 5 UK-based & 1 Dutch drivers | Account reinstation | Upheld | Yes (a sum of € 100,474 in damages and a penalty of € for non-compliance) |

## IV. Micro-Perspectives: Making Data Subject Rights Work for Workers

In either case law or legal scholarship, each data subject right is considered in isolation and at a micro-level, often without attending to their structural and instrumental role within the larger data subject rights system. This complex web of rights, however, often causes confusion for regular data subjects who lack expertise of data protection and have little knowledge of the specific intention, scope, condition, exceptions of each right and the differences between them. Despite the original intentions, this chapter asks whether seamless, unhindered access to data can be achieved by a joint exercise of all data access rights, including the right of access, to data portability, and not to be subject to automated decision-making. The answer is far from straightforward as these rights are not designed to initiate data flows, and considerable differences are seen in these rights in terms of the scope, format and nature of personal data covered. A thorough consideration of each right is thus necessary, with particular reference to their structural and instrumental roles within the subject rights system.

### A. Right of Access

As a cornerstone of EU data protection law,[59] the right of access is intended to correct the information asymmetries between the data subject and the data controller. It hence serves an instrumental role in enabling further actions by the data subject (including the use of other data protection rights), what Ausloos et al. call the 'knock-on effect'.[60] In practice, the right of access is often relied upon to assist litigation cases by offering information that is otherwise inaccessible, but the legality of this use remains moot.

Established in the latter half of the twentieth century,[61] this right was originally devised to improve human readability, thus requiring personal data to be provided in a 'intelligible form'.[62] There should be a critical point of differentiation, as will be discussed later, between this right and the new right to data portability. The latter is characterised by the specific requirement of structured and machine-readable data, thus allowing for sharing and reuse.

For the purpose of initiating data flows towards workers, the right of access is advantageous in terms of the wide scope of data covered (theoretically concerning

---

[59] Orla Lynskey, *The Foundations of EU Data Protection Law* (Oxford: Oxford University Press, 2015), 181.
[60] Ausloos, Mahieu and Veale (n. 43) 283.
[61] Colin J. Bennett, *Regulating Privacy: Data Protection and Public Policy in Europe and the United States* (New York: Cornell University Press, 1992), 263.
[62] Data Protection Directive 1995 Art 12(a). See also GDPR Art 7(2) and Recital 42.

all the personal data undergoing processing) and of the explicit requirement for the controller to explain the logic, significance and consequences of the algorithms deployed. In this context, access might be interpreted as viewing the information via a specific medium, eg, on screen or via an app in contrast to obtaining a copy of data. This is contested, however, as the GDPR adds a new element to the right of access that explicitly allows the data subject to obtain a *copy* of personal data.

This section considers three main controversies around the enforcement of this right examined in the *Uber/Ola* judgments: (1) the accessibility of subjective data (eg, human judgements, internal notes and legal analysis), (2) the meaning of access, and (3) the practicality of full access request.

## i. Subjective Data Accessibility

An outstanding issue in relation to Article 15 concerns whether subjective data – that is, opinions rather than facts – are accessible or not via Article 15 GDPR. There is ample illustration of this type of data in the *Uber/Ola* judgments, including the drivers' profile (consisting internal notes by Uber employees), 'tags' (labels in the customer service system that are used to assess the drivers' behaviour), reports of the drivers' performance, as well as the so-called 'fraud probability score' which is automatically generated. Access to these data is of critical significance to evaluate the adverse decisions made against the drivers. It begs the question whether human judgements, internal notes and legal analysis constitute personal data and hence are accessible via Article 15 GDPR. According to *YS and Others*,[63] a CJEU ruling concerning a person exercising the right of access to contest the decision of the Dutch authority about his immigration status, legal analysis may contain some personal data, but is not accessible via Article 15 because it cannot be checked for accuracy and corrected where necessary. Originating from the Netherlands, *YS and Others* has significant ramifications for the national precedents. A general rule is developed that this right does not extend to 'internal notes that contain the personal thoughts and/or opinions of employees of the controller or third parties, exclusively intended for internal consultation and deliberation'.[64] The position held by the CJEU in *YS and Others* is contestable and may have evolved over time. Given the prominence of this precedent in the Dutch jurisprudence, later developments have not been adequately considered in the *Uber/Ola* judgments. In *Nowak*, a case concerning an Irish lawyer seeking access to the exam questions and answers, an explicit divergence from *YS and Others* is observed. The CJEU held that both objective and subjective information can constitute personal data as long as the data is, or can be linked to the data subject because of content, purpose or effect.[65]

---

[63] Joined Cases C-141/12 and C-372/12, *YS v Minister voor Immigratie, Integratie en Asiel* ECLI:EU:C:2014:2081, para 39.
[64] *Ola Access* (n. 52) 4.12. See also the three judgments from HR 29 June 2007: ECLI:NL:HR:2007: AZ4663, AZ4664 and BA3529.
[65] Case C-434/16, *Peter Nowak v Data Protection Commissioner* ECLI:EU:C:2017:994, para 34.

This chapter does not purport to engage this issue of ever-expanding definition of personal data, which remains a critical point of contention in the scholarship.[66] It suffices to say that, between *YS and Others* and *Nowak*, the determination of the scope of data access is rather context-specific. A case involving access to personal data on which an immigration decision was made with a view to revealing the logic of that decision is apparently distinct from one in which access is requested to pool all the data obtainable and build a data trust. That said, divergence manifested in *Nowak* is by itself insufficient to conclude that subjective data are generally accessible via Article 15. This is because the scope of access per Article 15 should be interpreted *teleologically*, by reference to the aims of data protection law as well as the purpose for which the personal data was collected and processed.[67] Hence, while factual data are objective and verifiable, it is contested whether subjective data as such are verifiable as well (ie, has their 'accuracy' been checked). Even if this is possible, the CJEU held in a series of case law that it is the sectoral laws (rather than data protection) that should be relied upon to contest accuracy of decisions.[68] In Wachter et al.'s words, EU data protection law grants individuals control over how their personal data are *processed*, but not how they are *evaluated*.[69] The 'accuracy' of decisions the drivers seek to check and correct was not deemed compatible with the objectives of data protection. This tradition is, however, not uncontroversial. Hallinan and Borgesius, for instance, draws on other elements of the GDPR repository, ie, the accuracy principle under Article 5 GDPR, to make a case for correcting opinions.[70] It remains to be seen how the dispute is further reflected and adapted by the court post-*Nowak*, but the teleological tradition established by the CJEU case law might have rendered the right of access not fit for purpose.

## ii. *The Meaning of Access*

Platforms often claim that they have already provided the personal data sought. Their argument is based on the idea that drivers can view them via the apps or in their Privacy Policies. Thus, access to various types of data requested – such as the start and end of a journey, customer transactions, booking history, GPS data, device data, location data – were denied mostly on that basis. It begs the question

---

[66] See for instance, Nadezhda Purtova, 'The Law of Everything: Broad Concept of Personal Data and Future of EU Data Protection Law,' *Law, Innovation and Technology* 10.1 (2018): 40–81. Benjamin Wong, 'Delimiting the Concept of Personal Data after the GDPR,' *Legal Studies* 39.3 (2019): 517–532.

[67] *Nowak* (n. 65) para 53.

[68] See Case C-28/08 P, *European Commission v Bavarian Lager* ECLI:EU:C:2010:378. YS (n. 63), paras 45–46. *Nowak* (n. 65).

[69] Sandra Wachter, and Brent Mittelstadt, 'A Right to Reasonable Inferences: Re-Thinking Data Protection Law in the Age of Big Data and AI,' *Columbia Business Law Review* 2 (2019): 443, 499.

[70] Dara Hallinan and Frederik Zuiderveen Borgesius, 'Opinions Can Be Incorrect (in Our Opinion)! On Data Protection law's Accuracy Principle,' *International Data Privacy Law* 10.1 (2020): 1–10.

as to: (1) whether app display constitutes a permissible form of compliance with Article 15, and (2) whether Article 15 allows for access to personal data in addition to what is presented in a Privacy Policy in accordance with Articles 13–14 GDPR.

Article 15 is almost silent on the form or means by which personal data should be provided, but the latest guidelines from the European Data Protection Board (EDPB) have provided some clarity. In brief, the EDPB does not explicitly and categorically exclude app display as a means of responding to a data access request. As such, oral information, inspection of files, onsite or remote access, and other 'non-permanent ways' of access without the possibility to download or copy data are all deemed sufficient. The EDPB only *encourages* the provision of a copy of data along with supplementary information as 'the main modality for providing access to the personal data'.[71] As significant leeway is given to the platforms to determine the meaning or means of access (as viewing rather than transmitting), and hence the scale and nature of data flows towards workers, it may therefore be concluded that Article 15 requests do not necessarily lead to *real* data flows.

Another related issue is whether the controller is obliged to provide more data or information that is presented in their Privacy Policies in the face of Article 15 requests. This relates to an unsettled issue about the relationship between Article 15 and Articles 13–14 under the GDPR. An abundance of commentaries seek to make distinctions between *ex ante* transparency and *ex post* transparency, between information for the general public (eg, provided in the Privacy Policies) and information specific about a particular processing activity concerning a data subject.[72] Zanfir contends that the right of access provides 'a second, deeper and more detailed layer of information' beyond the disclosure by any Privacy Policy.[73] In her view, the key difference between Article 15 and Articles 13–14 is that the right of access allows for the obtaining of 'copies of personal data' as well as '*updated* information' compared to what is provided in the Privacy Policies. Similarly, Ausloos et al. see the added value of Article 15 as providing the 'possibility for individuals to learn more about their particular situation upon request'.[74] In reality, however, Article 15 requests have been dismissed as the court considered the Privacy Policy sufficient as a source of the requested information.[75] The guidance provided by the EDPB is not clearly disproving of this view. According to the guidelines, Article 15 request should lead to 'updated and tailored information' other than what is

---

[71] EDPB, 'Guidelines 01/2022on Data Subject Rights – Right of Access', edpb.europa.eu/our-work-tools/documents/public-consultations/2022/guidelines-012022-data-subject-rights-right_en, 41-2.

[72] See for instance Jef Ausloos and Michael Veale, 'Researching with Data Rights,' *Technology and Regulation* (2021): 136–57. Lilian Edwards and Michael Veale. 'Slave to the Algorithm? Why A Right to Explanation Is Probably Not the Remedy You Are Looking For,' *Duke Law & Technology Review* 16.1 (2017): 18–84.

[73] Gabriela Zanfir-Fortuna, 'Right of Access by the Data Subject,' in The EU General Data Protection Regulation (GDPR): A Commentary, ed. Christopher Kuner, Lee A. Bygrave, Christopher Docksey, and Laura Drechesler (Oxford: Oxford University Press, 2020), 452.

[74] Ausloos, Mahieu and Veale (n. 43) 293.

[75] See, for instance, *Uber Access* (n. 50).

provided in a Privacy Policy.[76] Simply referring to the wording of a privacy policy would not be sufficient in responding to Article 15 requests.[77] Still, the guidelines indicate the circumstance to be an exception where 'tailored information is the same as the general information'.[78] The example provided by the EDPB, ie, the information about the right to complain, does imply that such a circumstance is rare.

### iii. The Practicality of Full Access Request

The last point of contention is whether it is practically possible to make a successful request for access to a full range of personal data undergoing processing. A full range request is not uncommon; it is encouraged as a means to maximise the potential of data subject rights.[79] In the Dutch rulings, the drivers strategically built their requests upon Articles 15, 20 and 22 while demanding full access to their personal data in accordance with these provisions. This strategy, however, met with various practical hurdles.

The EDPB guidelines explicitly recognise a 'right to *full* disclosure of all data relating to them'.[80] Yet, this right is subjected to a number of exceptions, thus rendering its scope of application significantly limited. These exceptions include: (1) voluntary and explicit limitations or specifications made by the data subject, (2) reasonable doubts by the controller in the case of a large volume of data, (3) manifestly unfounded or excessive access requests, (4) requests that adversely affect the rights and freedoms of others.[81]

As is evidently shown in the Dutch judgments, a full access request is far from reality as the controller is able to cling to at least one of the exceptions stated above. Chief among them is the discretion afforded to the controller to ask for specification in cases where large volumes of data are concerned. Note that this discretion is not explicitly stated in Article 15 but merely in a non-binding recital.[82] Further, the concept of 'large volume of data' is left undefined, thus making this mechanism highly elusive. In theory, this specification requirement represents a fair balance between the data subject's right of access and the burden imposed on the controller to search, identify and provide the requested data. It can, however, be easily abused or misinterpreted in practice. For instance, a range of personal data in the *Uber/ Ola* judgments, such as 'in app messages', device data and driving behaviours, are denied access on the sole ground that the drivers failed to specify their requests.[83]

---

[76] EDPB (n. 71) 41-2.
[77] ibid.
[78] ibid.
[79] See for instance, Michael Veale, 'A Better Data Access Request Template', michae.lv/access-template/.
[80] EDPB (n. 71) 35, fn 14.
[81] ibid.
[82] GDPR Recital 63.
[83] *Ola Access* (n. 52) 4.17, 4.31. *Uber Access* (n. 50) 4.35, 4.54.

In *Ola Access*, the court's view about specification was even erroneously extended to the right to data portability as it found the drivers' portability request 'too general and so not specific that it must be rejected as insufficiently determined'.[84] Misinterpretations aside, it may be concluded that a full access request is rife with uncertainties. The way in which Article 15 is formulated within the GDPR makes data flows arising out of Article 15 requests inherently intermittent and partial.

The right of access is given a new life under the GDPR, with its scope and nature refined incrementally through court interpretation. Still, numerous factors constraining the form, purpose and scope of access would prevent the right from being a working vehicle for driving data flows. As will be argued later, even when exercised in tandem with other access rights, its advantage (eg, potentially covering all personal data concerned) cannot be fully realised.

## B. The Right to Data Portability

The right to data portability is, strictly speaking, the only right newly introduced in the GDPR with no precursor in the 1995 Directive. In the early days of the GDPR's legislative process, this right was expected to be a game-changer that would fundamentally reconfigure the flow of personal data, hence exerting an impact of competition similar to number portability in the telecom sector.[85] This ambition was significantly attenuated in a later stage, with a refined objective of individual control over personal data written into the GDPR. Numerous conditions, restrictions and exceptions were added in the later phase of the GDPR's legislative process to contain its potential impact. The right is, as a result, criticised for its complexity and lack of certainty. In spite of some clarity provided by the guidelines from the Article 29 Working Party (A29WP), the predecessor of the EDPB, the applicability and effect of this right remains unclear.

Within the GDPR, the new right to data portability has a contentious status. This is partly because the right does not straightforwardly serve the purpose of data protection law, namely the protection of personal data, and partly because the right of access (strengthened by the GDPR) may arguably serve an equivalent function pursuant to Article 15(4).

By requiring the personal data to be provided in a 'commonly used, structured and machine-readable format', the right to data portability is intended to facilitate data sharing and reuse, thus making it ideal for driving personal data towards new processing systems eg, a data trust. The right's real capacity to drive data flows is, however, restricted by various factors. For instance, it allows the porting of *certain* personal data only, ie, the personal data provided by the data subject,

---

[84] *Ola Access* (n. 52) 4.60.
[85] European Commission, 'Commission Staff Working Paper GDPR Impact Assessment', SEC/2012/0072 final, 28.

actively or passively. According to the Article 29 Working Party Guidelines, this criterion includes observed data but excludes inferred or derived ones.[86] Those not provided by data subjects, as well as non-personal data (including anonymous data), fall outside the scope of this right.

It is also a missed opportunity that the GDPR does not eventually mandate interoperability but only encourages interoperable format in a recital. A right to transmit is said to be created under Article 20(2). The name of this right can be misleading as the controller is allowed not to respond on the ground of 'technical infeasibility'.[87] This means that this right literally does not exist if the participating systems do not interoperate as a matter of fact.

In the *Ola/Uber* judgments, scant attention was paid by the court to this new right, with its novelty compared to the existing ones largely ignored. This section discusses two outstanding issues in the rulings, namely: (1) whether PDF is a GDPR-compliant format, and (2) whether there is an obligation to convert data into a machine-readable format.

### i. PDF as an Interoperable Format?

In *Uber/Ola Access*, the drivers made a joint exercise of all data access rights (including Article 22) in hopes that all data and information will be provided in a commonly used, structured and machine-readable format, or by way of an application programming interface (API) that allows for continuous, seamless and real-time access. This was not fully upheld by the court for the lawful reason that machine-readability is not a mandate for all data access rights.

Among the portable data, however, the drivers found that many of the data requested under Article 20 were not provided in CSV format as initially requested, but actually in seven different ones (PDF, Docx, JEPG, PNG, MP3, WAV) which are not necessarily machine-readable.[88] The court particularly considered the PDF format, in which several types of data are provided, including 'Zendesk tickets', 'invoices', 'driver safety complaints' and 'driver documents'.

The GDPR does not provide a definition of machine-readability but refers instead to the Public Sector Reuse Directive[89] in which it is defined as

> a file format structured so that software applications can easily identify, recognise and extract specific data, including individual statements of fact, and their internal structure

Given its technical complexity, the determination of a GDPR-compliant format goes beyond legal interpretation and hence should draw on expertise of data science. Ausloos and Veale reveal that PDF is designed for printing rather than for

---

[86] Article 29 Working Party, 'Guidelines on the Right to Data Portability,' WP242, rev.01.
[87] GDPR Art 20(2).
[88] *Uber Access* (n. 50) 4.78.
[89] Directive (EU) 2019/1024 of the European Parliament and of the Council of 20 June 2019 on open data and the re-use of public sector information, PE/28/2019/REV/1, Art 2(13).

analysis.[90] According to Wong and Henderson, PDF files *may* be machine-readable if they contain text, but not so if tables, images and scans are included.[91] The A29WP Guidelines state that PDF is not compliant as data in such a format would not be sufficiently structured.[92] It is also recognised that the preservation of all metadata may ensure effective portability and reuse.[93] PDF should not be categorically deemed to be GDPR compliant or not; its lawfulness should be assessed contextually on a case-by-case basis. A more worrying issue, according to Ausloos and Veale, is the practice of intentionally transforming data into PDF files with a view to disadvantaging the data subject and foreclosing analysis opportunities.[94] Such a practice runs counter to the essence of Article 20 and should be explicitly blacklisted.

### ii. *The Obligation to Convert Data*

Article 20 of the GDPR requires personal data to be provided in a structured, commonly used and machine-readable format. However, an understated fact is that not all data are internally managed and stored in a format as such. In practice, the controller may 'return' the requested data in the exact format it was initially provided by the data subject, particularly when it comes to semi-structured or unstructured data (such as video and audio files). This was upheld by the ADC in *Uber Access* in which Uber provided data in the same format in which they have received them.[95] This raises the issue as to whether Article 20 creates an obligation to covert personal data if they are not held in a GDPR-compliant format. A textual reading of the GDPR might conclude that such a conversion is required. As the A29WP guidelines are silent on this issue, an update is urgently needed, taking into account the existence of non- or semi-structured data, as well as the costs of conversion especially when large volumes of data are concerned.

## C. The Right Not to be Subject to Automated Decision-Making

The right not to be subject to automated decision-making is ostensibly the most contested right under the GDPR. It is considerably complex and loaded with

---

[90] Ausloos and Veale (n.72) 152.
[91] Janis Wong and Tristan Henderson, 'How Portable Is Portable? Exercising the GDPR's Right to Data Portability', in UbiComp/ISWC 2018 – Adjunct Proceedings of the 2018 ACM International Joint Conference on Pervasive and Ubiquitous Computing and Proceedings of the 2018 ACM International Symposium on Wearable Computers (New York: The Association for Computing Machinery, 2018), 911–920.
[92] Article 29 Working Party, 'Right to Data Portability', 18.
[93] ibid.
[94] Ausloos and Veale (n. 72) 152.
[95] *Uber Access* (n. 50) 4.81.

conditions. For this reason, the UK Government once sought to streamline or even scrap this right as part of its post-Brexit data protection reform.[96] Conceptually, this right is the most relevant in addressing the information asymmetries caused by algorithmic management. Similar to the ill-fated right to data portability, however, the Article 22 right ended up with numerous qualifications added during the legislative process. The complex formulation of this right forces workers to take a 'detour' by pooling personal data first so as to reverse-engineer the algorithms deployed.

As it currently stands, the Article 22 right faces significant structural problems. The title of Article 22 can be misleading too as a wide range of conditions and exceptions attenuate the 'intended' effect of this right, ie, not being subjected to automated decision-making. This right may be better viewed as *two-faceted*: on the one hand, the right not to be subject to automated decision-making is conditional upon several demanding conditions, such that the decision is made *solely* on automated decision-making, that the decision exerts a legal or similarly significant effect. Serious disputes arise from the application of these conditions, and the EDPB guidelines do not necessarily and adequately address them.[97] The complexity of this 'right' has aroused a dispute in the data protection scholarship about whether Article 22 is a right or a prohibition per se.[98] On the other hand, in case such a right does not apply, Article 22 provides safeguards of more practical relevance. These safeguards include the right: (1) to obtain human intervention, (2) to express views, and (3) to contest the automated decision.[99] Other safeguards may be added by Member States by way of national legislation, according to Article 22(3).[100]

Unlike Article 15 and Article 20 rights, Article 22 is by nature not a data access right. Still, given the great difficulties in meeting the conditions for not being subject to automated decision-making, the practical value of Article 22 may lie with algorithmic transparency guaranteed jointly with Article 15(1)(h). This critical aspect has given rise to a large body of work disputing whether a 'right to explanation' (should) exist within the GDPR.[101]

---

[96] DCMS, 'Data: A New Direction,' www.gov.uk/government/consultations/data-a-new-direction.

[97] Michael Veale and Lilian Edwards, 'Clarity, Surprises, and Further Questions in the Article 29 Working Party Draft Guidance on Automated Decision-making and Profiling,' *Computer Law & Security Review* 34 (2018): 398–404.

[98] Luca Tosoni, 'The Right to Object to Automated Individual Decisions: Resolving the Ambiguity of Article 22 (1) of the General Data Protection Regulation,' *International Data Privacy Law* 11.2 (2021): 145–162. Isak Mendoza and Lee A. Bygrave, 'The Right Not to Be Subject to Automated Decisions based on Profiling,' in *EU Internet Law*, eds. Tatiana-Eleni Synodinou, Philippe Jougleux, Christiana Markou and Thalia Prastitou (Cham: Springer, 2017), 77–98. Lee A Bygrave, 'Automated Profiling: Minding the Machine: Article 15 of the EC Data Protection Directive and Automated Profiling,' *Computer Law & Security Review* 17.1 (2001): 17–24.

[99] GDPR Art 23(3).

[100] See generally Gianclaudio Malgieri, 'Automated Decision-Making in the EU Member States: The Right to Explanation and Other "Suitable Safeguards" in the National Legislations,' *Computer Law and Security Review* 35.5 (2019).

[101] Bryce Goodman and Seth Flaxman, 'European Union Regulations on Algorithmic Decision-making and a 'Right to Explanation,' *AI magazine* 38.3 (2017): 50–57. Sandra Wachter, Brent Mittelstadt

In a similar vein, this section does not intend to unpack all the controversies around Article 22 but focuses on three critical issues raised in the Dutch judgments. Many of these issues happen to be the locus of the scholarship, including: (i) the level of human judgment, (ii) the nature of 'legal or similarly significant effect', and (iii) the right to explanation.

### i. *The Level of Human Judgment*

Article 22 stipulates that the right applies only to the decision *solely* based on automated decision-making. This begs the question as to the level of human engagement that may render this condition unsatisfied. Binns and Veale reveal the complexity of decision-making that often takes multiple stages and may involve both humans and machines.[102] Wachter et al. argue that a simple arrangement of human control of a certain level may be enough to make the Article 22 right utterly impracticable.[103] This is manifested in *Uber Deactivation I*, whereby the court agreed with Uber (that there was a EMEA Operational Risk team in-charge) while imposing the burden of proof on the drivers.

The A29WP in its ADM guidelines identifies a number of factors for determining the level of human judgement or oversight, including: (1) the independent and active position of the overseer (hence rubber-stamping disallowed), (2) the authority and competence to overturn automated decisions, and (3) the description in the controller's Data Protection Impact Assessment of the level of human involvement.[104] Thus, the analysis here is inherently contextual and contingent. What is troubling about *Uber Deactivation I* is that the onus is placed on the drivers, the victims of information asymmetries, in proving that the deactivation decisions were made fully automatically. As will be shown in the next section, this procedural aspect significantly determines effective use of data subject rights and should be urgently addressed.

### ii. *Significant Effect for Workers*

The condition that the decision should exert a legal or similarly significant effect is also context-specific. In a wide range of cases involving Uber's fraud probability score, earning profile, batched matching system, as well as Ola's Guardian

---

and Luciano Floridi, 'Why a Right to Explanation of Automated Decision-Making Does Not Exist in the General Data Protection Regulation,' *International Data Privacy Law* 7.2 (2018): 76–99. Andrew D. Selbst, and Julia Powles. 'Meaningful Information and the Right to Explanation,' *International Data Privacy Law* 7.4 (2017): 233–242. Margot E. Kaminski, 'The Right to Explanation, Explained,' *Berkeley Technology Law Review* 34 (2019): 189.

[102] Reuben Binns and Michael Veale, 'Is that Your Final Decision? Multi-stage Profiling, Selective Effects, and Article 22 of the GDPR,' *International Data Privacy Law* 11.4 (2021): 319–332.

[103] Wachter and Mittelstadt (n. 69) 584.

[104] Article 29 Working Party, 'ADM', 20.

system, trip-matching system and upfront pricing system, Article 22 was deemed inapplicable because the drivers failed to prove any legal or significant effect for workers. However, this does not mean that these systems or scores do not exert legal or a similarly significant effect. The linchpin of the problem lies, again, with the burden of proof imposed on the drivers. Notably, in *Uber Deactivation I*, a distinction is made between the effect of a termination and that of temporary automated blocking. The court was of the view that the latter 'has no long-term or permanent effect, so that the automated decision has no legal consequences or significant effects on the drivers'.[105] A *strict* approach was hence taken by the ADC to interpreting the effect element of the Article 22 right, which is largely consistent with the A29WP guidelines that define the effect by reference to the exclusion of or discrimination against individuals.[106] The guidelines further consider the context of online advertising with specific criteria developed, but the lack of legal interpretation in a labour context, as has been discussed earlier, remains a gap to be filled.

### iii. Right to Explanation

The *Uber/Ola* judgment has also rekindled the gridlocked debate on the right to explanation. Some believe that this right is neither existent nor does it have any practical relevance at all.[107] Yet, one major milestone of these Dutch rulings is the declaration that the drivers have access to personal data Ola uses to 'draw up the risk profile', along with information 'about segments into which applicants have been classified'.[108] The implications of *Uber/Ola* judgments for the right to explanation are mixed. First, as the conditions for Article 22 rights are difficult to satisfy (including the burden of proof), the associated 'right to explanation' grounded in Article 15(1)(h) is inoperable. Second, a distinction is made by ADC between the concept of automated decision-making and that of profiling, which often come in pairs under the GDPR. It is on such a basis the court held that there may be profile-based processing that involves no automation at all, and that the data subject may have a right 'to access the data used as input to create a profile', in accordance with Article 15(3) GDPR.[109] Hence, a more explicit recognition on the distinction between ADM and profiling creates space for a right to profile transparency. It might still be far from an ideal form of 'meaningful explanation' but, from the

---

[105] *Uber Deactivation*, 4.25.
[106] Article 29 Working Party, 'ADM', 21-2.
[107] Raphaël Gellert, Marvin van Bekkum and Frederik Zuiderveen Borgesius, 'The Ola & Uber Judgments: For the First Time a Court Recognises a GDPR Right to an Explanation for Algorithmic Decision-Making,' EU Law Analysis, eulawanalysis.blogspot.com/2021/04/the-ola-uber-judgments-for-first-time.html.
[108] *Ola Access* (n. 52) 4.36, 4.45.
[109] *Ola Access* (n. 52) 4.35.

standpoint of building a data trust, such a recognition establishes another valid channel of data flow distinct from the previous ones.[110]

In sum, there are certainly positive developments from these judgments about each right, notably including the recognition of a right to profile transparency (based on Article 15 regardless of whether automated decision-making exists), of rating portability (in an anonymised form), and of the ability to inspect and reverse automated dismissal. Such developments are instrumental in platform worker resistance but still fall short of building a union-backed data trust for workers. The EDPB has over the years developed a good number of guidelines related to data subject rights with a view to bringing clarity and suitability. However, little or nothing is said as to how these rights are distinct from each other and, in case of joint exercise of all data subject rights, what type and scope of data can be expected. Simply interpreting the GDPR provisions word by word is not enough, and several challenges (as identified in this chapter) are not duly anticipated and presented in the text of the GDPR. Efforts should be taken to update these guidelines with a view to engaging contextual and structural problems. A more holistic and comprehensive understanding of all these rights might be provided by updating the existing guidelines or by creating a new and overarching one that covers all rights horizontally. Further, the extent to which all the data subject rights under the GDPR overlap and interplay with each other remains understated and should have been properly addressed by guidelines at EU or national levels. The ADC rulings mark the absence of *horizontal* guidance that attends not just the specifics of a data subject right but its structural and instrumental role within the data subject rights system or the overall regime. This might be fixed, it is argued, by re-adjusting the EDPB's priorities by providing holistic guidelines covering all the data subject rights as well as guidelines specifically about labour contexts. Given the presence of Article 88 expressly related, it is critical that the rights-based resistance this chapter reveals are not ignored or overshadowed for being paradigmatically different from the specific *protection* and *safeguards* for workers.

## V. Macro-perspectives: Data Subject Rights as a Tool for Platform Worker Resistance

In addition to the challenges discussed above to each data subject right under the GDPR, this section considers a deeper issue as to whether these rights, taken as a whole, can be expected as a reliable tool for platform worker resistance. The discussion is confined to the specific controversies arising out of the Dutch rulings, of which we identify three.

---

[110] Selbst and Powles (n. 101) 233. Wachter and Mittelstadt (n. 69) 494.

## A. Victims of Information Asymmetries Bearing the Burden of Proof?

The existing commentaries on data subject rights as well as related guidelines from the EDPB and national DPAs have their focus primarily on substantial matters. The issue of how procedural rules may, in reality, constitute a barrier to effective use of data subject rights remains understated. We consider the allocation of the burden of proof only in this chapter, with other procedural aspects eg, the standard of proof, omitted as they are irrelevant to the Dutch rulings.

The concept of the burden of proof, also known as the 'probative burden', 'risk of non-persuasion', or the 'persuasive burden'[111] is self-explanatory. It refers to the obligation imposed on a party by a rule of law to adduce evidence in order to prove a fact in issue.[112] As most cases involve more than one issue, the legal burden may be distributed between the parties.[113]

This issue of the burden of proof is outstanding in the four Dutch rulings in which the judges impose the burden on the data subjects in many instances. From the outset, this may be justified by reference to the maxim that 'he who asserts must prove' (*ei incumbit probatio qui dicit, non qui negat*). The realities are, however, much more complex than this. Given the significant information asymmetries the drivers (as data subjects) suffer from, the need for considering the shifting and even reversal of the burden of proof is evident.

There may be some criticism against the court's reasoning that invariably places the onus on the drivers. According to civil procedural rules,[114] this is not necessarily unjustifiable. Generally speaking, the issue of which party bears the burden of proof in relation to any given fact is determined by precedent, statutes or agreements. First, judges do not allocate the burden of proof based on any general principles. It is rather on precedents concerned with the issue of substantive law in question that the burden of proof is determined.[115] Second, the parties may expressly agree upon the incidence in some permissible cases (eg, written contracts). Beyond these cases, the burden of proof becomes the courts' construction. As Keane and McKeown contend, it is a matter of policy given the rule of substantive law in question.[116] Third, in some cases, the incidence may be

---

[111] Adrian Keane and Paul Mckeown, *The Modern Law of Evidence* (Oxford: Oxford University Press, 2016), 80.

[112] Technically speaking, there is a distinction between legal burden and evidential burden (known also as the duty of passing the judge). The latter may not amount to a burden at all as it may be discharged by evidence 'other than the evidence adduced by the defence': Keane and McKeown (ibid), 80. This chapter focuses only on the former.

[113] Keane and McKeown (n. 111) 80.

[114] Note that the allocation of the burden of proof is different in criminal and civil cases, and this chapter focuses only on civil procedural rules.

[115] Keane and McKeown (n. 111) 79–116.

[116] Keane and McKeown (n. 111) 100.

directly determined by statute. The UK's Employment Rights Act 1996 requires the employer to show the reason for any dismissal, for instance. If the employer fails to provide a reason as such, the dismissal is deemed automatically unfair.[117]

The GDPR is almost silent on the burden of proof except for on some occasions – eg, Article 21 (on the right to object) and Article 12 (on manifestly unfounded or excessive requests). Per these Articles, the onus is *explicitly* placed on the controller to demonstrate either 'compelling legitimate grounds' for processing upon the data subject's objection or 'manifestly unfounded or excessive requests'. A more tentative claim can be made that data controllers are in various circumstances – such as Article 5 (the accountability principle), Articles 13–14 (information disclosure), Article 35 (data protection impact assessment) – put in the position to prove, demonstrate or provide information about the data processing or the use of automated decision-making systems not necessarily in the context of court proceedings. Therefore, much is left for domestic civil procedure law.

From a procedural perspective, shifting the burden of proof is a rather flexible scheme that does not remove all the burden from one party to another. It allows the plaintiff suffering from information asymmetries to meet a lesser burden or a lower degree than may be required, while giving the other party the possibility to rebut. It exists in areas where 'fault or evidence is difficult to pin down but society has a large interest in protecting plaintiffs'.[118]

The exercise of data subject rights with a view to increasing transparency of data processing or algorithmic decision-making processes marks a prime case for burden shifting. Particularly in the work context, data subjects are in a disadvantaged position to solicit information and therefore deserve particular protection. A fairer procedural arrangement might be that, as a principle, the data subject seeking transparency and data access via the GDPR rights bears a limited and initial burden of proof; once discharged, it is then for the controller to disprove the fact. There may be more radical arrangements that the burden of proof is categorically reversed on to the data controller when it comes to the compliance of data subject rights. Giesen comments on some radical proposals in the European Group on Tort Law (EGTL) for the reverse of the burden of proof in case of proving fault (in the light of the gravity of the danger), enterprise liability, and damage.[119] Inspiration may be obtained, for instance, from Article 4:201 EGTL that the burden is reversed if the general principle (he who asserts must prove) would result in 'unreasonable difficulties for that plaintiff due to the technical or organisational complexity of the defendant's activities'.

It is outside the scope of this chapter to develop specific rules for placing the onus on a certain party. Yet, the case of shifting or reversing the burden of

---

[117] Employment Rights Act 1996, s 98.
[118] Legal Information Institute, 'Shifting the Burden of Proof,' www.law.cornell.edu/wex/shifting_the_burden_of_proof.
[119] Ivo Giesen, 'The Reversal of the Burden of Proof in the Principles of European Tort Law: A Comparison with Dutch Tort Law and Civil Procedure Rules,' *Utrecht Law Review* 6.1 (2010): 22–32.

proof is direly needed in cases like the *Uber/Ola* judgments with the presence of power asymmetries. It is an irony that the drivers who exercise their data subject rights precisely for the reason of getting more information are required to provide information they do not have, and which they are seeking in the first place. The 'beneficiary pays' principle, allocating the burden to the plaintiff on default, should be critically reflected in the labour context as the parties involved are not equal in power relations. Platform workers who utilise their data subject rights to address information asymmetries merit particular protection, not only substantially but also *procedurally*. Such protection is neither afforded by labour protection law nor by data protection law.

Although the allocation of the burden of proof mostly lies with the court's discretion, there might arguably also be a critical role of the EDPB. Admittedly, the board is certainly not in a position to develop procedural rules for court proceedings, but the 'spirits' of data protection about tackling information and power asymmetries should be clearly expressed in the context of procedural justice and taken seriously by judges. In fact, the emphasis of the GDPR on the controller's duty to demonstrate (the accountability principle) and to ensure transparency implies that the GDPR actually contains *unspoken* procedural rules that should be articulated in the EDPB's guidelines.

## B. Work-related Use of Data Subject Rights as Abusive?

In the *Uber/Ola* judgments, a particular claim was made by these platforms that the request for data access with a view to building a data trust instead of checking for data accuracy or processing lawfulness constitutes an abuse of right.

This term 'abuse of right' can be traced to the EU Charter of Fundamental Rights, Article 54 of which prevents activities 'aimed at the destruction of any of the rights and freedoms recognised in this Charter or at their limitation to a greater extent than is provided for herein'.[120] The abuse of right provision is presumably applicable to all the data subject rights giving expression to the fundamental right to data protection. It has been considered in the context of data protection, for instance, by AG Kokott in its opinion to *Nowak*.[121] Ausloos and Veale note that such a mechanism is 'rarely used, or at least not successfully, usually implicated in politically charged, high level issues concerning the freedom of expression or of association, often when pitted against values of the defence of democracy'.[122] In their view, the abuse of rights issue is 'resolved' by emphasising the balancing of

---

[120] Charter of the Fundamental Rights of the European Union, Article 54.
[121] Case C-434/16 *Peter Nowak v Data Protection Commissioner*, Opinion of Advocate General Kokott, delivered on 20 July 2017, paras 42–50.
[122] Lorna Woods, 'Abuse of Rights', in *The EU Charter of Fundamental Rights: a Commentary*, eds. Steve Peers, Tamara Hervey, Jeff Kenner and Angela Ward (London: Bloomsbury Publishing, 2021), 1545. Ausloos and Veale (n. 72) 151.

rights newly added to the GDPR, another issue to be discussed below. Indeed, such a defence was not successful in *Uber Access* and *Ola Access* as the ADC held that a data subject does not have to 'motivate or substantiate why he is making a request for access under the GDPR ... [or] show any particular interest or state the goal that he wants to achieve with the access'.[123]

Data access denied on the basis of purpose mismatch is not trivial (particularly in the case of the right of access), and there might be room for strategic readjustment in future events. Should this tension not be resolved via creative and future-proof reading of the GDPR provisions, it would be reasonable to conclude that GDPR rights are not a proper vehicle for platform worker resistance, and that we should look for new legislative developments beyond this framework. Before a strategic turn, however, it is important to note that many requests were rejected not necessarily because of the inherent limitations, but due to misinterpretations, confusions and inconsistencies. This may be fixed in the appeal and/or via an updated guidance from data protection authorities, with a systematic rethinking of platform workers' situation and their genuine needs. Indeed, a glimpse of hope is shown in the Dutch judgments that the court intends to detach from aged assumptions while attending to the novelty of new data subject rights.

## C. Balancing of Rights as a Potential Barrier to Initiate Data Flows towards Workers?

Both the rights of access and to data portability are subject to a balancing scheme, as per Article 15(4) and Article 20(4), which states that these rights should not adversely affect the rights and freedoms of others. According to the A29WP guidelines as well as Recital 63, these rights and freedoms include those of other data subjects (eg, customers of Uber and Ola) as well as those of the controller.[124] In contrast to what the names of these rights literally indicate (ie, access and portability), the balancing scheme may constitute a serious impediment to data flows away from data controllers.

The consideration of third-party privacy (mostly that of Uber/Ola customers) in the balancing act has rendered a variety of data inaccessible via Articles 15 and 20 GDPR, including GPS data, customer 'reports' as well as passenger details. A somewhat inconsistent finding was made, however, about ratings, arguably one of the most valuable datasets for workers. In the *Ola/Uber Access* judgments, it was held that the platform should provide ratings in an anonymous form.[125] While access to ratings is generally commendable, two main issues may arise from the Dutch rulings: first, the court fails to consider the possibility of providing access

---

[123] *Ola Access* (n. 52) 4.4–4.7. *Uber Access* (n. 50) 4.24–4.26.
[124] Article 29 Working Party, 'Right to Data Portability', 10–11.
[125] *Ola Access* (n. 52) 4.25. *Uber Access* (n. 50) 4.51–4.52.

to, or portability of, the requested data other than ratings in an anonymised form. Second, the court does not make explicit the legal basis on which such an anonymised access is granted and the potential implications of anonymisation techniques for data reusability. The fact that the ADC judgments open up a ground with reference to anonymisation techniques on which privacy and utility can be better balanced is commendable. However, without detailed and effective guidance from the court or related authorities, it leaves a range of questions unanswered, eg, what exact technique of anonymisation should be used and deemed GDPR-compliant, whether anonymised data can be re-used by the drivers in their data trust, and the extent to which privacy risks can be mitigated by the mandated anonymisation.

Moreover, the ADC also balances the drivers' data access rights with those of the platforms. In this regard, platforms claim that providing data would give the drivers insights into its anti-fraud detection systems. According to the A29WP guidelines, however, a potential business risk cannot in and of itself serve as a basis for refusing any portability request.[126] Presumably, an anti-fraud defence would not be strong enough to dismiss access or portability requests. The ADC did not perform any substantial analysis but relied again upon the burden of proof, this time imposed on the platforms. The failure to substantiate their anti-fraud claims with further information made the court rule in favour of the drivers, thereby removing another anticipated barrier to initiate data flows towards the platform workers.[127]

In sum, the general and procedural issues mentioned above have significant implications for the effective enforcement of the right to data protection but remain understated in the data protection scholarship. While authorities are committed to developing rules around the principle of accountability, little is done from the court's perspective, for instance, in establishing connection between procedural rules and the rights of data protection. Indeed, uncertainty about the GDPR provisions should not be solely clarified by judges as authorities at different levels are expected to do more heavy lifting. However, there is and should be a critical and distinctive role for the court to ensure that such general and procedural matters do not constitute undue barriers to the exercise of data subject rights.

## VI. Future Developments: Data Subject Rights vis-à-vis Other Legal Developments

The GDPR's general approach does not always adequately address power and informational asymmetries that are inherent in an employment relationship, as well as the lack of collective rights. Article 88 of the GDPR is an opening which

---

[126] Article 29 Working Party, 'Right to Data Portability', 12.
[127] *Ola Access* (n. 52) 4.46. *Uber Access* (n. 50) 4.67.

allows for Member States to provide 'more specific rules' on data protection in the workplace.[128] However, many Member States have not done so.[129] Even in cases where Article 88 was mentioned, it seems to be a marginal point.[130] A pending case at the Administrative Court of Wiesbaden and potential developments in Germany may alter this. As Abraha, Silberman and Adams-Prassl argue, the opportunity which Article 88 offers is underutilised, but the development of Article 88 laws must create more specific rules, rather than duplicate existing GDPR requirements.[131]

Other developments are more positive, specific and attentive directly to platform workers. Chapter III of the proposal for a Directive on improving working conditions in platform work, otherwise known as the Platform Work Directive Proposal (in the trialogue stage at the time of writing), for instance, provides some improvements to the GDPR in addressing algorithmic management. Most significantly, Articles 6–8 improve transparency by ensuring that workers have a right to explanation by a contact person of the platform company for any decisions taken or supported by an ADM which 'restrict, suspend or terminate the platform worker's account [...] refuse the remuneration for work performed by the platform worker, [...] affect the platform worker's contractual status or any decision with similar effects'.[132] Worker representatives will also be enabled to access information about automated systems, and overall strengthen collective consultation rights (but not collective bargaining).[133] The protection afforded by Articles 6–7 will apply to *all* platform workers, even those that fall outside of an employment relationship (Article 10). Overall, the chapter is certainly an improvement on some collective rights, better protection on personal data collection and transparency into automated monitoring and decision-making systems. However, the Directive still adopts a techno-solutionist approach to algorithmic management, assuming that these systems and practices are acceptable, simply because there is available technology to do so. Whether and the extent to which these protections will be watered down in the trialogue process is yet to be determined, and how it will interact with the proposed AI Act has become a cause of concern.[134] The proposed

---

[128] GDPR Art 88. See also Halefom H. Abraha, 'A Pragmatic Compromise? The Role of Article 88 GDPR in Upholding Privacy in the Workplace,' *International Data Privacy Law* (2022): 7, doi.org/10.1093/idpl/ipac015.

[129] Justin Nogarede, *No Digitalisation Without Representation: An Analysis of Policies to Empower Labour in the Digital Workplace* (Brussels: FEPS, 2021), feps-europe.eu/publication/826-no-digitalisation-without-representation/.

[130] In Italy: case number/name 9669974 (Municipality of Bolzano). Case number/name 9685994 (Deliveroo). Case number/name 9518890 (Gaypa s.r.l.). In Germany: Case number/name2 A 124/22 (OVG Saarlouis). Case number/name10 Sa 2130/19 (LAG Berlin-Brandenburg).

[131] Halefom H. Abraha, Michael Silberman and Jeremias Adams-Prassl, 'The Need for Employee-specific Data Protection Law: Potential Lessons from Germany for the EU,' *European Law Blog*, europeanlawblog.eu/2022/09/30/the-need-for-employee-specific-data-protection-law-potential-lessons-from-germany-for-the-eu/.

[132] Proposed EU Directive on Platform Work Art 8(1).

[133] Proposed EU Directive on Platform Work Art 6(4).

[134] Valerio de Stefano and Antonio Aloisi, 'Artificial Intelligence and Workers' Rights,' *Social Europe*, socialeurope.eu/artificial-intelligence-and-workers-rights/.

AI Act classifies some AI systems in the employment context as high-risk, which entails these high-risk systems complying with stricter requirements.[135] However, there are shortcomings which do not particularly take sufficient account of the power and informational asymmetries in a work context.[136] Essentially a model of product regulation, the AI Act regulates users and developers, but fails to provide a framework for rights and redress to empower those who are affected by AI technologies. While these new legislative proposals are crucial and necessary developments, the GDPR remains useful since its universal rights-based framework applies to a wider set of workers and work contexts beyond the platform economy.

## VII. Conclusion

The Dutch rulings are not the endgame as these cases are under appeal at the time of writing. Yet, a detailed analysis of them gives a glimpse of how these rights are tied to the logic of lawfulness or accuracy, which is far from the ideas of data utility, data flows and empowerment of data subjects. The rulings highlight a structural tension that the practical value of data subject rights is neither well envisioned nor anticipated by legislators. While not explicitly stated in the GDPR contexts, these rights are constrained by the court's teleological and restrictive reading deeply rooted in the Luxemburg jurisprudence. What the drivers explicitly and intentionally pursue, ie to drive and pool personal data into a data trust operated by the Worker Info Exchange, is rife with challenges and uncertainties.

In the digital society, courts must confront this reality of unconventional, creative use of rights and respond with certainty whether they are permissive or not, sometimes requiring a stretch of the GDPR provisions. It appears, from a global perspective, that courts tend to be more permissive, with the purpose-related constraints removed in some jurisdictions, and new rights defined without necessarily adhering to conventional interpretation. This is a welcome development, but a more thorough and systematic reflection is urgently needed. The four judgments constitute a good start but are far from initiating a valid and systematic dialogue on the configuration and facilitation of data subject rights in reality. It is of prime importance judges revisit some deeply rooted assumptions developed in the last century and ask critical fundamental questions: what is the role of intent or purpose in determining the scope and nature of data subject rights? Whether and exactly how may anonymisation techniques lawfully facilitate data flows and mitigate privacy and security concerns? Should procedural matters be developed

---

[135] Proposed AI Act Annex III 4(a), 4(b).
[136] ibid. Aude Cefaliello and Miriam Kullmann, 'Offering False Security: How the Draft Artificial Intelligence Act Undermines Fundamental Workers Rights,' *European Labour Law Journal* (2022): 2–4. doi-org.proxy.uba.uva.nl/10.1177/20319525221114474.

in line with the spirit of the fundamental right to data protection, particularly with reference to the principle of accountability and the overarching objective of addressing information and power imbalances? It is hoped that these fundamental questions will be properly addressed in the appeal, making the Dutch cases the beginning, rather than the end, of rights-based platform worker resistance.

## Acknowledgments

The authors would like to thank the organisers and participants of the Digital Ideas Lunch Series 'Law in an Algorithmic Society' 2021, Digital Legal Talks 2022 and CPDP 2022 for providing us with a platform to test our ideas, and for all the comments and input on our earlier iterations. In particular, we are very grateful to Niklas Eder, Silvia de Conca, Jef Ausloos and Joris van Hoboken for their time and extensive feedback. We are also thankful and deeply inspired by the conversations with James Farrar, Yaseen Aslam and Anton Ekker, who are fundamental to writing this chapter. This work was made possible by the Digital Transformation and Decision-Making initiative at the University of Amsterdam, as part of the Law Sector Plan in the Netherlands.

## References

Abraha, Halefom H. 'A Pragmatic Compromise? The Role of Article 88 GDPR in Upholding Privacy in the Workplace.' *International Data Privacy Law* (2022): 1–21. doi.org/10.1093/idpl/ipac015.

Abraha, Halefom H., Michael Silberman and Jeremias Adams-Prassl. 'The Need for Employee-specific Data Protection Law: Potential Lessons from Germany for the EU.' *European Law Blog*, 30 September 2022. europeanlawblog.eu/2022/09/30/the-need-for-employee-specific-data-protection-law-potential-lessons-from-germany-for-the-eu/.

Acevedo, Deepa Das. 'Regulating Employment Relationships in the Sharing Economy.' *Employee Rights and Employment Policy Journal* 20 (2016): 1–35.

Adams-Prassl, Jeremias. 'What If Your Boss Was an Algorithm? Economic Incentives, Legal Challenges, and the Rise of Artificial Intelligence at Work.' *Comparative Labor Law and Policy Journal* 41, no. 1 (2019): 123–146.

Ada Lovelace Institute. Exploring Legal Mechanisms for Data Stewardship. London: Ada Lovelace Institute, 2021. www.adalovelaceinstitute.org/report/legal-mechanisms-data-stewardship/.

Aloisi, Antonio and Valerio de Stefano. *Your Boss Is an Algorithm: Artificial Intelligence, Platform Work and Labour*. London: Bloomsbury Publishers, 2022.

Altenried, Moritz. 'Mobile Workers, Contingent Labour: Migration, the Gig Economy and the Multiplication of Labour.' *Environment and Planning A: Economy and Space* (2021): 1–16.

Anwar, Mohammad, A. and Mark Graham. 'Between a rock and a hard place: Freedom, flexibility, precarity and vulnerability in the gig economy in Africa.' *Competition & Change* 25, no. 2 (2020): 237–258.

Article 29 Working Party. 'Guidelines on the Right to Data Portability.' WP242, rev.01.
Aslam, Yaseen and Jamie Woodcock. 'A History of Uber Organizing in the UK.' *South Atlantic Quarterly* 119, no. 2 (April 2020): 412–421.
Ausloos, Jef, René Mahieu and Michael Veale. 'Getting Data Subject Rights: A submission to the European Data Protection Board from international data rights academics, to inform regulatory guidance.' *Journal of Intellectual Property, Information Technology and E-Commerce Law*, 10, no. 1. (2019): 283–309.
Ausloos, Jef and Michael Veale. 'Researching with Data Rights.' *Technology and Regulation* (2021): 136–57.
Binns, Reuben and Michael Veale. 'Is that Your Final Decision? Multi-stage Profiling, Selective Effects, and Article 22 of the GDPR.' *International Data Privacy Law* 11, no. 4 (2021): 319–332.
Buolamwini, Joy and Timnit Gebru. 'Gender Shades: Intersectional Accuracy Disparities in Commercial Gender Classification.' In *Proceedings of the 1st Conference on Fairness, Accountability and Transparency*, PMLR 81 (2018): 77–91. proceedings.mlr.press/v81/buolamwini18a.html.
Bennett, Colin J. *Regulating Privacy: Data Protection and Public Policy in Europe and the United States*. Ithaca: Cornell University Press, 1992.
Bessa, Ioulia, Simon Joyce, Denis Neumann, Mark Stuart, Vera Trappmann and Charles Umney. *A global analysis of worker protest in digital labour platforms*. Geneva: International Labour Organiation, 2022. www.ilo.org/wcmsp5/groups/public/---dgreports/---inst/documents/publication/wcms_849215.pdf.
Bygrave, Lee A. 'Automated Profiling: Minding the Machine: Article 15 of the EC Data Protection Directive and Automated Profiling.' *Computer Law & Security Review* 17, no. 1 (2001): 17–24.
Cano, Melissa R., Ricard Espelt and Mayo Fuster Morell. 'Flexibility and freedom for whom? Precarity, freedom and flexibility in on-demand food delivery.' *Work organisation, labour & globalisation* 15, no. 1 (2021): 46–68.
Cant, Callum. *Riding for Deliveroo: Resistance in the New Economy*. Cambridge: Polity, 2020.
Cant, Callum and Jamie Woodcock. 'Fast Food Shutdown: From Disorganisation to Action in the Service Sector.' *Capital & Class* 44, no. 4 (2020): 513–521. doi.org/10.1177/0309816820906357.
Casilli, Antonio A. 'Digital Labor Studies Go Global: Toward a Digital Decolonial Turn.' *International Journal of Communication* 11 (2017): 3934–3954. ijoc.org/index.php/ijoc/article/download/6349/2149.
Cefaliello, Aude and Miriam Kullmann. 'Offering False Security: How the Draft Artificial Intelligence Act Undermines Fundamental Workers Rights.' *European Labour Law Journal* (2022): 1–21. doi-org.proxy.uba.uva.nl/10.1177/20319525221114474.
Chen, Julie Yujie. 'Thrown under the Bus and Outrunning It! The Logic of Didi and Taxi Drivers' Labour and Activism in the on-Demand Economy.' *New Media & Society* 20, no. 8 (2018): 2691–2711. doi.org/10.1177/1461444817729149.
Clarke, Laurie. 'Data is the Next Frontier in the Fight for Gig Workers' Rights.' *Tech Monitor*, 24 March 2021. techmonitor.ai/policy/education-and-employment/data-next-frontier-fight-for-gig-workers-rights.
Colclough, Christina. 'Towards Workers' Data Collectives.' *IT for Change*, January 2021. projects.itforchange.net/digital-new-deal/2020/10/22/towards-workers-data-collectives/.
Collier, Ruth Berins, Veena B. Dubal and Christopher L. Carter. 'Disrupting Regulation, Regulating Disruption: The Politics of Uber in the United States.' *Perspectives on Politics* 16, no. 4 (2018): 919–937. doi.org/10.1017/S1537592718001093.

de Sousa Santos, Boaventura. 'Law: A Map of Misreading. Toward a Postmodern Conception of Law.' *Journal of Law and Society* 14, no. 3. (1987): 279–302. doi.org/10.2307/1410186.

de Stefano, Valerio. 'The Rise of the 'Just-in-Time Workforce': On-Demand Work, Crowdwork, and Labor Protection in the "Gig-Economy."' *Comparative Labor Law and Policy Journal* 37, no. 3 (2016): 471–504.

———, '"Masters and Servers": Collective Labour Rights and Private Government in the Contemporary World of Work.' *The International Journal of Comparative Labour Law and Industrial Relations* 36, no. 4 (2020): 425–443. doi.org/10.54648/ijcl2020022.

de Stefano, Valerio and Antonio Aloisi. 'European legal framework for digital labour platforms'. *Publications Office of the European Union*, (2018): 1–66. doi:10.2760/78590.

———, 'Artificial Intelligence and Workers' Rights.' *Social Europe*, 8 November 2021. socialeurope.eu/artificial-intelligence-and-workers-rights.

Dencik, Lina. 'Towards Data Justice Unionism? A Labour Perspective on AI Governance.' In *AI for Everyone: Critical Perspectives*, edited by Pieter Verdegem, 267–284. Westminster: University of Westminster Press, 2021. doi.org/10.16997/book55.o.

Dubal, Veena B. 'Winning the Battle, Losing the War?: Assessing the Impact of Misclassification Litigation on Workers in the Gig Economy.' *Wisconsin Law Review*, no. 4 (2017): 739–802.

———, 'The New Racial Wage Code.' Harvard Law and Policy Review 15, no. 2 (2021): 511–550.

EDPB. 'Hamburg Commissioner Fines H&M 35.3 Million Euro for Data Protection Violations in Service Centre.' *EDPB*, 2 October 2020. edpb.europa.eu/news/national-news/2020/hamburg-commissioner-fines-hm-353-million-euro-data-protection-violations_en.

———, 'Riders: Italian SA Says No to Algorithms Causing Discrimination: A platform in the Glovo group fined EUR 2.6 million.' *EDPB*, 5 July 2021. edpb.europa.eu/news/national-news/2021/riders-italian-sa-says-no-algorithms-causing-discrimination-platform-glovo_en.

———, 'The Icelandic DPA has fined a company running ice cream parlours for processing employee's personal data via video surveillance camera installed in an employee area.' *EDPB*, 29 June 2021. edpb.europa.eu/news/national-news/2021/icelandic-dpa-has-fined-company-running-ice-cream-parlours-processing_en.

———, 'Guidelines 01/2022on Data Subject Rights – Right of Access.'

Edwards, Lilian and Michael Veale. 'Slave to the Algorithm? Why A Right to Explanation Is Probably Not the Remedy You Are Looking For.' *Duke Law & Technology Review* 16, no. 1 (2017): 18–84.

European Commission. 'Commission Staff Working Paper GDPR Impact Assessment.' SEC/2012/0072 final.

Gandini, Alessandro. 'Labour Process Theory and the Gig Economy.' *Human relations* 72, no. 6 (2019): 1039–1056.

Gellert, Raphaël, Marvin van Bekkum and Frederik Zuiderveen Borgesius. 'The Ola & Uber Judgments: For the First Time a Court Recognises a GDPR Right to an Explanation for Algorithmic Decision-Making.' EU Law Analysis. eulawanalysis.blogspot.com/2021/04/the-ola-uber-judgments-for-first-time.html.

Gig CV. 'About GigCV.' gigcv.org/.

Giesen, Ivo. 'The Reversal of the Burden of Proof in the Principles of European Tort Law: A Comparison with Dutch Tort Law and Civil Procedure Rules.' *Utrecht Law Review* 6, no.1 (2010): 22–32.

Goodman, Bryce and Seth Flaxman. 'European Union Regulations on Algorithmic Decision-making and a 'Right to Explanation.' *AI magazine* 38, no. 3 (2017): 50–57.

Gregory, Karen. '"Worker Data Science" Can Teach Us How to Fix the Gig Economy.' *WIRED*, 7 December 2021. www.wired.com/story/labor-organizing-unions-worker-algorithms/.

———, '"My Life is More Valuable Than This": Understanding Risk among On-Demand Food Couriers in Edinburgh.' *Work, Employment and Society* 35, no. 2 (2020): 316–331.

Hallinan, Dara. Borgesius, Frederik Zuiderveen. 'Opinions Can Be Incorrect (in Our Opinion)! On Data Protection law's Accuracy Principle.' *International Data Privacy Law* 10, issue 1 (2020): 1–10.

Hießl, Christina. 'Case law on algorithmic management at the workplace: Cross-European comparative analysis and tentative conclusions.' *European Commission, Directorate DG Employment, Social Affairs and Inclusion.* (September 2021): 1–25. papers.ssrn.com/sol3/papers.cfm?abstract_id=3982735.

Irani, Lilly C. and Michael Six Silberman. 'Turkopticon: Interrupting Worker Invisibility in Amazon Mechanical Turk'. In *CHI '13: Proceedings of the SIGCHI Conference on Human Factors in Computing Systems*, (April 2013): 611–620.

Jędrzej, Niklas and Lina Dencik. 'What rights matter? Examining the place of social rights in the EU's artificial intelligence policy debate.' *Internet Policy Review* 10, no. 3 (2021): 20–23. doi.org/10.14763/2021.3.1579.

Johnston, Hannah and Chris Land-Kazlauskas. *Organizing On-Demand: Representation, Voice, and Collective Bargaining in the Gig Economy*. Geneva: International Labour Orgaisation Conditions of Work and Employment Series, no. 94. (2019): 1–41. www.ilo.org/wcmsp5/groups/public/---ed_protect/---protrav/---travail/documents/publication/wcms_624286.pdf.

Kaminski, Margot E. 'The Right to Explanation, Explained.' *Berkeley Technology Law Review* 34 (2019): 189.

Keane, Adrian and Paul Mckeown. *The Modern Law of Evidence*. Oxford: Oxford University Press, 2016.

Lata, Lutfun N., Jasmine Burdon and Tim Reddel. 'New tech, old exploitation: Gig economy, algorithmic control and migrant labour.' *Sociology Compass* (2022): 1–14.

Legal Information Institute. 'Shifting the Burden of Proof.' www.law.cornell.edu/wex/shifting_the_burden_of_proof.

Lobel, Orly. 'The Law of the Platform.' *Minnesota Law Review* 137 (2016): 87–166.

Lomas, Natasha. 'Dutch Court Rejects Uber Drivers' "Robo-Firing" Charge but Tells Ola to Explain Algo-Deductions.' *TechCrunch*. techcrunch.com/2021/03/12/dutch-court-rejects-uber-drivers-robo-firing-charge-but-tells-ola-to-explain-algo-deductions/.

Lynskey, Orla. *The Foundations of EU Data Protection Law*. Oxford: Oxford University Press, 2015.

Mahieu, René, Hadi Asghari and Michel van Eeten. 'Collectively exercising the right of access: individual effort, societal effect.' *Internet Policy Review* 7, no. 3 (2018): 1–23.

Mahieu, René and Jef Ausloos. 'Harnessing the collective potential of GDPR access rights: towards an ecology of transparency.' *Internet Policy Review*, (2020). policyreview.info/articles/news/harnessing-collective-potential-gdpr-access-rights-towards-ecology-transparency/1487.

Malgieri, Gianclaudio. 'Automated Decision-Making in the EU Member States: The Right to Explanation and Other "Suitable Safeguards" in the National Legislations.' *Computer Law and Security Review* 35, no. 5 (2019).

Mazur, Joanna. 'Right to Access Information as a Collective-Based Approach to the GDPR's Right to Explanation in European Law,' *Erasmus Law Review*, 11 (2018): 178–189.

Mendoza and Lee A. Bygrave, 'The Right Not to Be Subject to Automated Decisions based on Profiling,' in *EU Internet Law*, edited by Tatiana-Eleni Synodinou, Philippe Jougleux, Christiana Markou and Thalia Prastitou, 77–98. Cham: Springer, 2017.

Möhlmann, Mareike and Lior Zalmanson. 'Hands on the wheel: navigating algorithmic management and Uber drivers' autonomy.' In *Proceedings of the International Conference on Information Systems (ICIS) Seoul, South Korea*, (December 2017): 1–17. www.researchgate.net/publication/319965259_Hands_on_the_wheel_Navigating_algorithmic_management_and_Uber_drivers'_autonomy.

Moore, Phoebe, Martin Upchurch and Xanthe Whittaker. 'Humans and Machines at Work: Monitoring, Surveillance and Automation in Contemporary Capitalism.' In *Humans and Machines at Work: Monitoring, Surveillance and Automation in Contemporary Capitalism*, eds. Phoebe Moore, Martin Upchurch and Xanthe Whittaker, 1–16. Cham: Palgrave Macmillan, 2018.

Nogarede, Justin. *No Digitalisation Without Representation: An Analysis of Policies to Empower Labour in the Digital Workplace*. Brussels: FEPS, 2021. feps-europe.eu/publication/826-no-digitalisation-without-representation/.

Pandey, Akshat and Aylin Caliskan. 'Disparate Impact of Artificial Intelligence Bias in Ridehailing Economy's Price Discrimination Algorithms.' In *AIES 2021 - Proceedings of the 2021 AAAI/ACM Conference on AI, Ethics, and Society*, (July 2021): 822–833. doi.org/10.1145/3461702.3462561.

Purtova, Nadezhda. 'The Law of Everything: Broad Concept of Personal Data and Future of EU Data Protection Law.' *Law, Innovation and Technology* 10, no. 1 (2018): 40–81.

Popan, Cosmin. 'Algorithmic Governance in the Gig Economy: Entrepreneurialism and solidarity among food delivery workers.' In *Cycling Societies: Innovations, Inequalities and Governance*, edited by Dennis Zuev, Katerina Psarikidou and Cosmin Popan.

Rogers, Brishen. 'The Law and Political Economy of Workplace Technological Change.' *Harvard Civil Rights-Civil Liberties Law Review* 55, no. 2 (2020): 531–584.

Safak, Cansu and James Farrar. *Managed by Bots: Data-Driven Exploitation in the Gig Economy*. London: Worker Info Exchange, 2021. www.workerinfoexchange.org/wie-report-managed-by-bots.

Scholz, Trebor. 'Introduction: Why does digital labor matter now?' In *Digital Labor: The Internet as a Playground and Factory*, edited by Trebor Scholz, 1–10. New York: Routledge, 2012.

Selbst, Andrew D. and Julia Powles. 'Meaningful Information and the Right to Explanation.' *International Data Privacy Law* 7, no. 4 (2017): 233–42.

Stefflbauer, Nakeema. 'When Human rights + Digital rights = Workers' rights.' *Digital Freedom Fund*, 2 May 2022. digitalfreedomfund.org/when-human-rights-digital-rights-workers-rights/.

Tassinari, Arianna and Vincenzo Maccarrone. 'Riders on the Storm: Workplace Solidarity Among Gig Economy Couriers in Italy and the UK.' *Work, Employment and Society* 34, no. 1 (2020): 35–54. doi.org/10.1177/0950017019862954.

Terranova, Tiziana. 'Free Labor: Producing Culture for the Digital Economy.' *Social Text* 18, no. 2 (2000): 33–58. muse.jhu.edu/article/31873.

Toh, Jill. 'UK gig drivers recognised as workers – what next?' *Social Europe*, 25 February 2021. socialeurope.eu/uk-gig-drivers-recognised-as-workers-what-next.

Tosoni, Luca. 'The Right to Object to Automated Individual Decisions: Resolving the Ambiguity of Article 22 (1) of the General Data Protection Regulation.' *International Data Privacy Law* 11, no. 2, (2021): 145–162.

Vallance, Chris. 'Legal action over alleged Uber facial verification bias.' *BBC*, 8 October 2021. www.bbc.com/news/technology-58831373.

van Doorn, Niels. 'At What Price? Labour Politics and Calculative Power Struggles in on-Demand Food Delivery.' Work organisation, Labour & Globalisation 14, no. 1 (2020): 136–149. doi:10.13169/workorgalaboglob.14.1.0136.

van Doorn, Niels and Julie Yujie Chen. 'Odds stacked against workers: datafied gamification on Chinese and American food delivery platforms.' *Socio-Economic Review* 19, no. 4. (2021): 1345–1367.

Veale, Michael. 'A Better Data Access Request Template.' michae.lv/access-template/.

Veale, Michael and Lilian Edwards. 'Clarity, Surprises, and Further Questions in the Article 29 Working Party Draft Guidance on Automated Decision-making and Profiling.' *Computer Law & Security Review* 34 (2018): 398–404.

Wachter, Sandra and Brent Mittelstadt. 'A Right to Reasonable Inferences: Re-Thinking Data Protection Law in the Age of Big Data and AI.' *Columbia Business Law Review* 2 (2019): 443, 499.

Wachter, Sandra, Brent Mittelstadt and Luciano Floridi. 'Why a Right to Explanation of Automated Decision-Making Does Not Exist in the General Data Protection Regulation.' *International Data Privacy Law* 7, no. 2 (2018): 76–99.

Wong, Benjamin. 'Delimiting the Concept of Personal Data after the GDPR.' *Legal Studies* 39, no. 3 (2019): 517–532.

Woods, Lorna. 'Abuse of Rights.' In *The EU Charter of Fundamental Rights: A Commentary*, edited by Steve Peers, Tamara Hervey, Jeff Kenner and Angela Ward, 1545. London: Bloomsbury Publishing, 2021.

Woodcock, Jamie and Mark Graham. *The Gig Economy: A Critical Introduction*. Cambridge: Polity Press, 2020.

Worker Info Exchange. 'About WIE.' www.workerinfoexchange.org/.

Zanfir-Fortuna, Gabriela. 'Right of Access by the Data Subject.' In *The EU General Data Protection Regulation (GDPR): A Commentary*, edited by Christopher Kuner, Lee A. Bygrave, Christopher Docksey and Laura Drechesler, 449–468. New York: Oxford University Press, 2020.

# 7

# From the Fight against Money Laundering and Financing of Terrorism Towards the Fight for Fundamental Rights: The Role of Data Protection

MAGDALENA BREWCZYŃSKA* AND ELENI KOSTA[≠]

## Abstract

The exchange of information is a key element of the Anti-Money Laundering (AML) and Countering the Financing of Terrorism (CFT) system. The legal framework governing AML and CFT provides an outline of relevant information flows, but it does not regulate them in detail. In the European Union, this is a task of the data protection law, which in contrast to the AML/CFT regulatory regime, explicitly formulates necessary requirements for the exchanges of personal data. These requirements serve as safeguards designed with a view of protecting individuals against the power of those who process personal data. In view of this, the aim of this chapter is to provide an outline of the most common instances in the European AML/CFT framework that require sharing of personal data and to shed light on the interpretation of some core EU data protection rules in light of the objectives of the European AML/CFT framework. The analysis focuses primarily on three matters: first, on the recognition of financial information as personal data; second, on the difficulty in reconciling some of the crucial principles that underlie the data protection legal regime with the goals set out in the AML/CFT legal framework; and third on the grounds for lawful processing of personal data in the AML/CFT context.

## Keywords

Data protection, Anti-Money Laundering and Counter Financing of Terrorism (AML/CFT), data sharing, notification, access rights

* Tilburg University, the Netherlands.
[≠] Tilburg University, the Netherlands.

## I. Introduction: The Financial Crackdown on Canadian Protestors and a Universal Question of Opportunities and Risks of Data Sharing for AML/CFT Purposes

Mid-February 2022, Canada. The so-called 'Freedom Convoy' protest polarised Canadian society. The protest was a movement, which sparked in early 2022 in response to the implementation of a vaccine mandate for truckers crossing the US-Canada border and soon evolved into a massive demonstration against the continued COVID-19 restrictions and opposition to the policy of Trudeau's cabinet in times of the pandemic. In reaction to the obstructions caused by the demonstrators, who paralysed downtown Ottawa, the government had declared the existence of a public order emergency and decided to issue the Emergency Economic Measures Order.[1] Based on this Order, the government managed in essence to take away the financial resources of the 'Freedom Convoy', including the support received by the movement through the crowdfunding platforms under the Canadian's antiterrorism financing rules.

A wide range of financial service providers, most notably banks, became responsible for determining whether they are in possession or control of property that is owned, held or controlled by or on behalf of any individual or entity engaged, directly or indirectly, in the protests prohibited under the emergency laws and for suspending all transactions that involve any of such property. The Royal Canadian Mounted Police (RCMP) composed a list of around 200 account owners whose assets had to be blocked due to their engagement in the protest.[2] As a result, bank accounts holding almost eight million Canadian dollars were frozen.[3] Allegedly, the lists of people that were shared by the RCMP with relevant financial service providers did not only include information necessary for identifying the protesters (or other people indirectly engaged in the protest), but also personal details from the police database, such as whether any of them had been suspected of other crimes, had witnessed crimes or had records of other 'dealings' with the police.[4]

Soon after the financial crackdown on the protesters and a series of police interventions that eventually alleviated the crowd that had occupied Ottawa, the

---

[1] Emergency Economic Measures Order, SOR/2022-22 Canada Gazette, Part II, Volume 156, Extra Number 1. P.C. 2022-108 15 February 2022.

[2] It remains disputed whether the list of people whose assets were to be frozen concerned only the organisers and owners of trucks who had refused to leave the protest area or also persons who supported the protest financially through donations (see eg Peter Zimonjic, 'Most bank accounts frozen under the Emergencies Act are being released, committee hears,' *CBC News*, 22 February 2022, www.cbc.ca/news/politics/emergency-bank-measures-finance-committee-1.6360769).

[3] Zimonjic (n. 2).

[4] Marie Woolf, 'RCMP gave banks police info on Ottawa protesters with a list of accounts to freeze', *The Canadian Press*, 8 March 2022, www.cbc.ca/news/politics/rcmp-names-banks-freeze-1.6376955.

'Freedom Convoy' protest came to an end. On 23 February 2022 the Emergency Economic Measures Order was revoked and banks were instructed to start unlocking the accounts.[5] The protest in Canada was over, and the next day, the eyes of the world turned to the Russian invasion in Ukraine, leaving a number of fundamental questions relating to the 'Freedom Convoy' unanswered, crucial not only for Canada but all democratic constitutional states.

In this chapter, we do not wish to discuss all questions on the governmental powers and the role of banks relating to Anti-Money Laundering (AML) and Countering the Financing of Terrorism (CFT), nor do we intend to engage in the debate on the permissibility and proportionality of measures used by the Canadian government. The 'Freedom Convoy' case is used as an illustration of how powerful the engagement of the financial industry can be in tracking down persons who are on the radar of state law enforcement authorities. This is exactly what lies at the heart of AML/CFT policy.

The Canadian events can be seen as a striking example of the effectiveness of the AML/CFT measures in the restoration of public order, facilitated by a quick exchange of information between the police and financial service providers. Such quick exchanges of information, but also more complex ones, are commonplace in AML/CFT policy and occur between customers, obliged entities, Financial Intelligence Units (FIUs) and law enforcement authorities, as well as, in some cases, intelligence services. The legal framework governing AML and CFT together with the national laws on criminal procedure provide an outline of relevant information flows, but they do not regulate them in detail. In the European Union, this is a task of the data protection law, which in contrast to the AML/CFT regulatory regime, explicitly formulates necessary requirements for the exchanges of personal data. It demands, among other requirements, that any processing of personal data must be lawful – ie based on concrete legal grounds, fair, transparent, as well as adequate, relevant and limited to what is necessary in relation to the purpose for which they take place. These – in a way – procedural rather than normative safeguards have been designed with a view of protecting individuals against the power of those who may want to process their personal data. In that sense, the law of data protection can be viewed as a vital tool of transparency, which in terms of De Hert and Gutwirth, is crucial to channelling, controlling and restraining power.[6] The aim of this chapter is to provide an outline of the most common instances in the European AML/CFT framework that require the sharing of personal data and to shed light on the interpretation of some core EU data protection rules in light of the objectives of the European AML/CFT framework. In our analysis we focus on three matters that are crucial for any type of data sharing among any actors.

---

[5] Paul Vieira, 'Canada Instructs Banks to Unfreeze Freedom-Convoy Accounts' *WSJ*, 22 February 2022, www.wsj.com/articles/canada-instructs-banks-to-unfreeze-freedom-convoy-accounts-11645590500.
[6] Paul De Hert and Serge Gutwirth, 'Privacy, data protection and law enforcement. Opacity of the individual and transparency of power,' in *Privacy and the criminal law*, eds. Erik Claes, Serge Gutwirth and Antony Duff (Antwerp/Oxford: Intersentia, 2006), 61–104.

The first one concerns recognition of financial information as personal data and data that is of such a nature that allows for drawing precise conclusions about the private lives of the persons concerned, which is essential for justifying the choice of the angle of our analysis. The second point relates to the problem of reconciliation of some of the crucial principles that underlie the data protection legal regime with the goals set out in the AML/CFT legal framework. The third matter pertains to the grounds for lawful processing of personal data in the AML/CFT context. Our analysis will serve as a solid starting point for further discussion on the possibility of channelling AML/CFT powers through data protection.

This chapter begins with a brief overview of the existing EU AML/CFT legal framework and explanation of the allocation of data sharing powers (section II). After sketching out the applicable regulatory landscape, then follows the discussion on the nature of financial information (section III). Next, we take account of the most relevant of the discussed context data protection principles (section IV) and analyse the relevance of the grounds for lawful processing in the context of AML/CFT (section V). In the Conclusion (section VI), we will come back to the argument on the role of the data protection rules in safeguarding individuals against such mechanisms of power as those arising from the AML/CFT regime.

## II. Overview of the EU AML/CFT Regulatory Framework and Data Sharing Powers

### A. A Complex Regulatory Landscape

The EU interest in combating money laundering and terrorist financing is neither new, nor isolated from the worldwide initiatives. The first EU legislative endeavours in the area of AML trace back to the Council Directive of 1991 on the prevention of the use of the financial system for the purpose of money laundering (1st Anti-Money Laundering Directive or 1AMLD).[7] Over the years, the EU AML framework underwent numerous changes, ranging from the expansion of its objective to encompass also the countering of terrorism financing as a joint policy objective,[8] to the inclusion of ever more types of different market players in the catalogue of the so-called 'obliged entities', to whom the AML/CFT obligations apply.

---

[7] Council Directive 91/308/EEC of 10 June 1991 on prevention of the use of the financial system for the purpose of money laundering, OJ L 166, 28.6.1991, 77–82.

[8] Since the adoption of Directive 2005/60/EC of the European Parliament and of the Council of 26 October 2005 on the prevention of the use of the financial system for the purpose of money laundering and terrorist financing, OJ L 309, 25.11.2005, 15–36 (3rd Anti-Money Laundering Directive or 3AMLD) a single AML and CFT system was created.

After over 30 years of developments, the area of AML/CFT presents a rather complex field of EU legislation.[9] It is composed of a number of legal instruments, among which the most important in the context of data sharing are Directive 2015/849 (4th Anti-Money Laundering Directive or 4AMLD)[10] and, introducing modifications thereto, Directive 2018/843 (5th Anti-Money Laundering Directive or 5AMLD).[11] Further, the framework encompasses Directive 2019/1153,[12] which lays down measures to enhance access to and use of financial information and bank account information by competent law enforcement authorities by providing them with a direct access to information contained in national centralised registries (Directive on Access to Financial Information). This latter Directive also facilitates access of the FIUs to law enforcement information and stimulates access of investigative authorities to FIU data.[13]

In May 2020, the European Commission published a Communication on an Action Plan for a comprehensive Union policy on preventing money laundering and terrorism financing, where it expressed its intention to present new legislative proposals on AML/CFT (Action Plan).[14] In July 2021, the European Commission presented a legislative package for the reform of the European AML/CFT framework, which consisted of a Proposal for Anti-Money Laundering Regulation (AMLA Regulation),[15] a Proposal for the 6th AML Directive

---

[9] European Commission, 'Anti-money laundering and countering the financing of terrorism legislative package,' 20 July 2021, ec.europa.eu/info/publications/210720-anti-money-laundering-countering-financing-terrorism_en.

[10] Directive (EU) 2015/849 of the European Parliament and of the Council of 20 May 2015 on the prevention of the use of the financial system for the purposes of money laundering or terrorist financing, amending Regulation (EU) No 648/2012 of the European Parliament and of the Council, and repealing Directive 2005/60/EC of the European Parliament and of the Council and Commission Directive 2006/70/EC, OJ L 141, 5.6.2015, 73–117.

[11] Directive (EU) 2018/843 of the European Parliament and of the Council of 30 May 2018 amending Directive (EU) 2015/849 on the prevention of the use of the financial system for the purposes of money laundering or terrorist financing, and amending Directives 2009/138/EC and 2013/36/EU, OJ L 156, 19.6.2018, 43–74.

[12] Directive (EU) 2019/1153 of the European Parliament and of the Council laying down rules facilitating the use of financial and other information for the prevention, detection, investigation or prosecution of certain criminal offences, and repealing Council Decision 2000/642/JHA, OJ L 186, 11.7.2019, 122–137.

[13] Directive on Access to Financial Information, Article 1(1). The framework is complemented with a number of other legislative instruments, such as Directive 2014/42/EU of the European Parliament and of the Council of 3 April 2014 on the freezing and confiscation of instrumentalities and proceeds of crime in the European Union, OJ L 127, 29.4.2014, 39–50 (Directive on the freezing and confiscation of instrumentalities and proceeds of crime in the EU) and Regulation (EU) 2015/847 of the European Parliament and of the Council of 20 May 2015 on information accompanying transfers of funds and repealing Regulation (EC) No 1781/2006, OJ L 141, 5.6.2015, 1–18).

[14] European Commission, 'Communication from the Commission: on an Action Plan for a comprehensive Union policy on preventing money laundering and terrorism financing', 7 May 2020, C(2020)2800 final eur-lex.europa.eu/legal-content/EN/TXT/PDF/?uri=PI_COM:C(2020)2800&from=EN.

[15] European Commission, Proposal for a Regulation of the European Parliament and of the Council on the prevention of the use of the financial system for the purposes of money laundering or terrorist financing, COM(2021) 420 final (20.07.2021).

(6th Anti-Money Laundering Directive or 6AMLD),[16] a Proposal for the Regulation on the Anti-Money Laundering Authority (AMLA)[17] and a Proposal for the Regulation on information accompanying transfers of funds and certain crypto-assets.[18] The proposed reform aims at clarifying the existing legal situation and enhancing the EU's AML/CFT rules.[19] Several aspects of the new landscape have been debated throughout the reform process, one of them being the compliance of the sharing of information that includes personal data with data protection legislation[20] that will be affected by the new regime.

The new AML/CFT legislative package, once adopted and entered into force, is expected to have an impact on various complex relationships between multiple actors, including the AMLA, obliged entities, global organisations and governmental bodies, such as the FIUs and law enforcement authorities of the European states. However, since the legislative process is still ongoing, the present chapter focuses on the currently applicable rules.

## B. The Collection and Exchange of Information as an Essential Element of the AML/CFT Framework

### i. Obliged Entities, Customer Due Diligence and Reporting of Suspicious Activities

The AML/CFT legal framework introduces a vast array of rules incentivising the collection and exchanges of information between various entities. The 4AMLD and 5AMLD provide that obliged entities,[21] such as banks, payment service providers and life insurance companies, are assigned with the task of carrying out the so-called 'customer due diligence' (CDD) measures. CDD is a process in which obliged entities collect and evaluate information of their customers that is relevant from the perspective of risk to money laundering or terrorist financing.

---

[16] European Commission, Proposal for a Directive of the European Parliament and of the Council on the mechanisms to be put in place by the Member States for the prevention of the use of the financial system for the purposes of money laundering or terrorist financing and repealing Directive (EU) 2015/849, COM/2021/423 final (20.07.2021).

[17] European Commission, Proposal for a Regulation of the European Parliament and of the Council establishing the Authority for Anti-Money Laundering and Countering the Financing of Terrorism and amending Regulations (EU) No 1093/2010, (EU) 1094/2010, (EU) 1095/2010, COM/2021/421 final (20.07.2021).

[18] European Commission, Proposal for a Regulation of the European Parliament and of the Council on information accompanying transfers of funds and certain crypto-assets, COM(2021) 422 final (20.07.2021).

[19] European Commission, 'Beating financial crime: Commission overhauls anti-money laundering and countering the financing of terrorism rules', 20 July 2021, ec.europa.eu/commission/presscorner/detail/en/IP_21_3690.

[20] European Commission, 'Action Plan' (n. 14).

[21] Obliged entities are the actors exhaustively enumerated in 4AMLD Art 2 as amended by the 5AMLD.

Therefore, the realisation of CDD is a primary source of information in the AML/CFT system. CDD requires obliged entities to: (a) identify the customer and verify identity of the customer on the basis of documents, data or information obtained from a reliable and independent source; (b) identify the beneficial owner and take reasonable measures to verify that person's identity; (c) assess (and as appropriate) obtain information on the purpose and intended nature of the business relationship; and (d) conduct ongoing monitoring of the business relationship, including scrutiny of transactions undertaken throughout the course of that relationship to ensure that the transactions being conducted are consistent with the obliged entity's knowledge of the customer, the business and risk profile, including where necessary the source of funds and ensuring that the documents, data or information held are kept up-to-date.[22]

In cases of higher risks that are identified by Member States or by the obliged entities' own risk analysis, the 4AMLD requires obliged entities to apply, in addition to standard CDD measures, enhanced CDD measures.[23] The Directive specifies that obliged entities should be required to examine, as far as reasonably possible, the background and purpose of all complex and unusually large transactions, and all unusual patterns of transactions, which have no apparent economic or lawful purpose, and in particular, increase the degree and nature of monitoring of the business relationship, in order to determine whether those transactions or activities appear suspicious.[24]

It follows that the realisation of the CDD measures requires from the obliged entities wide collection and processing of personal data of the customers. The AML/CFT regime adopts the risk-based approach, therefore the AML/CFT rules focus on a goal, which is the detection of flows of illicit funds, rather than provide clear indicators as to the types of information that the obliged entities must collect and process. They do not set out much detail on how obliged entities should assess the risk associated with a business relationship or transaction,[25] leaving it open to the obliged entities to decide what kind of information is deemed relevant and should be sought. This opens up an entire arena for the development of various technological ways of enhancing the methods and techniques for the collection and analysis of data. Financial institutions are gradually adopting machine learning-based solutions to complement and integrate rule-based tools. The combination of rule-based and risk-based approach uses many detection techniques to simplify and at the same time to improve the detection process and implement CDD requirements to better understand who are the customers, their transactions and

---

[22] 4AMLD Art 13(1).
[23] 4AMLD Art 18(1).
[24] 4AMLD Art 18(2).
[25] Jean-Baptiste Maillart, 'European Union' in *National and International Anti-Money Laundering Law Developing the Architecture of Criminal Justice, Regulation and Data Protection*, eds. Benjamin Vogel and Jean-Baptiste Maillart (Cambridge/Antwerp/Chicago: Intersentia, 2020), 71–155, 98.

allow for more accurate identification of client risk.[26] Machine learning software are able to mine significant amounts of data to identify patterns, create profiles, cluster and categorise clients based on common features and infer additional data in respect of those inputted. Such tools can also be used by obliged entities to segment customers based on their risk category and perform pattern analysis to detect anomalies in behaviour (either personalised on a specific customer or based on customer categories). They can also perform link analysis[27] to infer relationships among customers (network), or between customers and watch-listed subjects, and to identify the beneficial owner[28] of a transaction or new account.

Regardless of the technique used for the initial collection of information, this phase does not exhaust the data processing obligations under the AML/CFT regime, but only enables information exchange. In accordance with Article 33(1)(a) 4AMLD, every obliged entity is required to inform the FIU,[29] including by filing a suspicious activity report (SAR) on their own initiative, when the obliged entity knows, suspects or has reasonable grounds to suspect that funds, regardless of the amount involved, are the proceeds of criminal activity or are related to terrorist financing. All suspicious transactions, including attempted transactions, must be reported. Furthermore, obliged entities are required to promptly respond to any requests the FIU may submit for additional information; and to provide the FIU, directly, at its request, with all necessary information, in accordance with the procedures established by the applicable law.[30]

Pursuant to Article 40 of the 4AMLD[31] obliged entities are required to keep records of transactions and information obtained through the performance of CDD measures (eg a copy of the documents and information which are necessary to comply with the CDD requirements) and the supporting evidence and records of transactions, consisting of the original documents or copies admissible in judicial proceedings under the applicable national law, which are necessary to identify transactions for a period of five years after the end of a business relationship with their customer or after the date of an occasional transaction.

---

[26] Tamer Hossam, Mohamed Zaki, Tarek S. Sobh and Khaled Mahmoud Badran, 'Design of a Monitor for Detecting Money Laundering and Terrorist Financing', *Journal of Theoretical and Applied Information Technology* 85.425, 426 (2016): 9.

[27] Link analysis is a technique used to enquire into relationships among a large number of objects of various types. When used in money laundering, the objects may comprise of people, bank accounts, businesses, wire transfers and cash deposits. Scrutinising associations between these various objects assists in indicating networks of activity, both legal and illegal. Cfr. US Congress, Office for Technology Assessment, *Information Technologies for the Control of Money Laundering* (US Government Printing Office, 1995) 56 docplayer.net/28783887-Information-technologies-for-the-control-of-money-laundering-september-ota-itc-630-gpo-stock.html.

[28] According to 4AMLD Art 3(6): '"beneficial owner" means any natural person(s) who ultimately owns or controls the customer and/or the natural person(s) on whose behalf a transaction or activity is being conducted'. The Article also provides a list of specifications and explanations in case, for instance, of trusts or other business entities.

[29] See section II(B)(ii) below.

[30] 4AMLD Art 33(1)(b) as amended by 5AMLD.

[31] As amended by 5AMLD.

## ii. Financial Intelligence Units and the Feedback Mechanism

FIUs are key players in the AML/CFT framework and have a central position between the obliged entities and the competent law enforcement authorities.[32] The FIUs should be operationally independent and autonomous, meaning that they should have the authority and capacity to carry out their functions freely, including the ability to take autonomous decisions to analyse, request and disseminate specific information.[33]

FIUs are authorities established in every Member State with the core function to receive, analyse and transmit reports of suspicions identified and filed by the private sector. The FIUs are also responsible for disseminating the results of their analyses and any additional relevant information to the competent law enforcement authorities where there are grounds to suspect money laundering, associated predicate offences or terrorist financing. This is where the exchange of information between the FIU and the competent law enforcement authorities takes place.

Article 32(4) of the 4AMLD permits competent authorities to request information from the FIUs, 'when such requests for information are motivated by concerns relating to money laundering, associated predicate offences or terrorist financing'. However, the decision on dissemination of information remains with the FIU.[34] The FIU is under no obligation to comply with the request for information.[35]

Finally, in accordance with Article 32(6) of the 4AMLD, Member States should require competent authorities to provide feedback to the FIU about the use made of the information they provided and about the outcome of the investigations or inspections performed on the basis of that information. This constitutes another information flow within the AML/CFT system. Interestingly, while the 4AMLD does not envisage the possibility of direct communication between the law enforcement authorities and obliged entities, another AML/CFT legal instrument, namely the Directive on the freezing and confiscation of instrumentalities and proceeds of crime,[36] allows law enforcement authorities to order necessary measures to enable the freezing of property with a view to possible subsequent confiscation. This implies an exchange of information relating to persons subject to the freezing or confiscation order between the competent law enforcement authority and relevant obliged entities.

Importantly, in the context of information sharing, the 5AMLD inserted a new Article 32a into the 4AMLD. This new provision requires Member States

---

[32] For the discussion on the position of FIU in the AML/CFT system and data protection implications, see Magdalena Brewczyńska, 'Financial Intelligence Units: Reflections on the Applicable Data Protection Legal Framework,' *Computer Law & Security Review* 43 (2021): 105612, doi.org/10.1016/j.clsr.2021.105612.
[33] 4AMLD Art 32(3).
[34] 4AMLD Art 32(4).
[35] 4AMLD Art 32(5).
[36] Directive 2014/42/EU of the European Parliament and of the Council of 3 April 2014 on the freezing and confiscation of instrumentalities and proceeds of crime in the European Union OJ L 127, 29.4.2014, 39–50, Art 7.

to put in place national centralised automated mechanisms (such as central registries or central electronic data retrieval systems) to allow a timely identification of any natural or legal person holding or controlling payment accounts, bank accounts and safe deposit boxes held by a credit institution established within their territory.[37] The information held in the national centralised automated mechanisms must be directly accessible in an immediate and unfiltered manner to national FIUs. FIUs must also be able to provide such information to other FIUs in a timely manner.[38] Furthermore, information held in the discussed mechanisms must be 'accessible to national competent authorities for fulfilling their [AML/CFT] obligations'.[39] The 5AMLD did not provide, however, for direct access to such information, a possibility introduced later by the Directive on Access to Financial Information.

The Directive on Access to Financial Information obliges Member States to facilitate access of the FIUs to law enforcement information.[40] Article 8 thereof provides for that '[s]ubject to national procedural safeguards and in addition to the access to information by FIUs as provided for in Article 32(4) of [4AMLD],[41] each Member State shall ensure that its designated competent authorities are required to reply in a timely manner to requests for law enforcement information made by the national FIU on a case-by-case basis, where the information is necessary for the prevention, detection and combating of money laundering, associate predicate offences and terrorist financing'. Besides the data retrieved by the FIUs from the central registries, as was explained in section II(B)(i), the primary source of FIU's information is the reporting activity of the obliged entities. However, according to the 4AMLD, the communication between the obliged entities and the FIU does not need to be restricted to one direction and the sharing of information between these two AML/CFT actors may potentially take place in both directions. Article 46(3) of the 4AMLD establishes the so-called feedback mechanism, according to which Member States shall ensure that, where practicable, timely feedback on the effectiveness of and follow-up to reports of suspected money laundering or terrorist financing is provided to obliged entities. The Directive neither specifies any details regarding the scope or frequency of feedback, nor clarifies when it is 'practicable' to provide it, but one can imagine that this mechanism can potentially be used for sharing information that concerns specific individuals between the FIU and the obliged entity.

---

[37] 4AMLD as amended by 5AMLD Art 32a(1).
[38] 4AMLD as amended by 5AMLD Art 32a(2).
[39] 4AMLD as amended by 5AMLD Art 32a(2).
[40] Directive on Access to Financial Information Art11(1).
[41] The relevant part of this provision stipulates 'Member States shall ensure that their FIUs have access, directly or indirectly, in a timely manner, to the financial, administrative and law enforcement information that they require to fulfil their tasks properly'.

## III. The Notion of Financial Information

Financial information refers to a broad spectrum of data. In the context of AML/CFT purposes, financial information has been defined in the Directive on Access to Financial Information as 'any type of information or data, such as data on financial assets, movements of funds or financial business relationships, which is already held by FIUs to prevent, detect and effectively combat money laundering and terrorist financing'.[42] The Directive on Access to Financial Information restricts the definition to data held by the FIU, which is understandable in light of the material scope of application of this legal instrument. However, when one reads this definition together with the 4AMLD, especially the provisions on CDD measures, there should be no doubt that 'information or data on financial assets, movements of funds or financial business relationships' is primarily information that originates from obliged entities. Therefore, the notion of 'financial information' in the context of the AML/CFT should not be restricted to information that has already arrived at the FIU and is processed in its databases, but it should also cover relevant information collected and processed by obliged entities. When looking at financial information, one must agree that '[t]here are few documents imaginable that are as suitable for creating such personality profiles as transaction records. They contain information on personal preferences, income, location, personal relations, and much more. Especially in a consumer age of cashless payments, bank account statements can be read as a summary of one's personal life'.[43]

In that sense, financial information bears a striking resemblance to traffic and location data and Passenger Name Records (PNR), the processing of which has been subject to the judicial scrutiny of the Court of Justice of the European Union (CJEU). The Court clarified that even if some of the data points, taken in isolation, may not appear liable to reveal important information about the private life of the persons concerned, 'taken as a whole' they can allow 'very precise conclusions to be drawn concerning the private lives of the persons [concerned]'.[44]

Undoubtedly, detailed information about financial transactions and persons involved in them has shown great investigation value and, hence, 'is quite legitimately seen as a honeypot for law enforcement authorities'.[45]

Personal data is a cornerstone concept in the European data protection framework and is defined as any information relating to an identified or identifiable

---

[42] Directive on Access to Financial Information Art 2 point 5.
[43] Lukas Martin Landerer, 'The Anti-Money-Laundering Directive and the ECJ's Jurisdiction on Data Retention: A Flawed Comparison?,' *Eucrim – the European Criminal Law Associations' Forum* 1 (2022), 67–72, 68.
[44] With respect to telecommunication data eg CJEU, Joined Cases C-293/12 and C-594/12 *Digital Rights Ireland* ECLI:EU:C:2014:238, para 27; CJEU, Joined Cases C-2013/15 and C-698/15, *Tele2 Sverige AB* ECLI:EU:C:2016:970, para 99; with respect to PNR see CJEU, Opinion 1/15, *EU-Canada PNR Agreement* ECLI:EU:C:2017:592, para 100.
[45] Landerer (n. 43) 67.

natural person ('data subject'), both in the General Data Protection Regulation (GDPR)[46] and in the Law Enforcement Directive (LED).[47] Considering the importance of identifying and verifying the identity of customers and beneficial owners, the link between financial information and the notion of personal data appears self-explanatory. The AML/CFT regime demands that information about financial assets, movements of funds or financial business relationships can be traced back to specific individuals, regardless of the business form in which they carry out their activity. This means that obliged entities should always be able to single out persons who stand behind the transactions for the relevant financial information to be considered personal data. This singling out is naturally aligned with the purposes of combatting money laundering and terrorism financing.

In view of the above, the processing of financial information should be subject to relevant safeguards, which will be discussed in the next section.

## IV. Data Protection as a Tool of Channelling Powers Arising from the AML/CFT System[48]

### A. The Impact of Data Protection Principles in the AML/CFT Context

Section II(B) presented the complex data sharing landscape arising from the AML/CFT legal system and showed the multiplicity of actors assigned powers for the processing of financial information. Such processing needs to abide by the core data protection principles. Article 5 of the GDPR lists several important principles relating to data quality. First, any processing of personal data should be carried out in a fair, lawful and transparent manner in relation to the data subjects (principle of lawfulness, fairness and transparency). Second, personal data must be collected for specified, explicit and legitimate purposes and may not be further processed in a way incompatible with those purposes (purpose limitation). The

---

[46] GDPR Art 4(1), Regulation (EU) 2016/679 of the European Parliament and of the Council of 27 April 2016 on the protection of natural persons with regard to the processing of personal data and on the free movement of such data, and repealing Directive 95/46/EC (General Data Protection Regulation), OJ L 119, 4.5.2016, 1–88.

[47] LED Art 3(1), Directive 2016/680 on the protection of natural persons with regard to the processing of personal data by competent authorities for the purposes of the prevention, investigation, detection or prosecution of criminal offences or the execution of criminal penalties, and on the free movement of such data, OJ L 119, 4.5.2016, 89–131.

[48] Some information in this section relies on the report prepared for the Council of Europe: Eleni Kosta, 'Report on the implications for data protection of mechanisms for inter-state exchanges of data for anti-money laundering/countering financing of terrorism, and tax purposes, Report for the Consultative Committee of the Convention for the protection of individuals with regard to automatic processing of personal data (Council of Europe)', July 2021, rm.coe.int/t-pd-2021-4rev-inter-state-exchanges-of-data-for-tax-purposes-and-cml-/1680a3ed30.

purpose of the processing should thus be defined at the moment of the collection and the purposes of further processing should not be incompatible with the purposes initially defined. The third data quality principle is that data should be adequate, relevant and limited to what is necessary in relation to the purposes for which they are processed (data minimisation). Data should further be accurate and, where necessary, kept up to date (accuracy). The fifth principle refers to the duration of storage of data and sets out that data may not be kept in a form permitting identification of data subjects for longer than is necessary for the purposes for which the data were collected or for which they are further processed (storage limitation). The final principle requires data to be processed in a manner that ensures appropriate security of the personal data (integrity and confidentiality). The data protection principles can be found in essence in the same form in the LED, with the exception of the principle of transparency, which due to the nature of law enforcement does not exist in the LED.

The following sections will analyse some of the core data protection principles, ie fairness and transparency (section B), purpose limitation (including proportionality) (section C) and data minimisation and storage limitation (section D), which present interpretation and application challenges in the AML/CFT context. The lawfulness principle will be analysed under the prism of the legitimate grounds for data processing in section V.

## B. The Principle of Fairness and Transparency in the Processing of Personal Data for the AML/CFT Purposes and the Question of Notification of Persons Concerned

Article 5(1)(a) GDPR and Article 4(1)(a) LED repeat after Article 8(2) of the Charter of Fundamental Rights of the European Union (CFR), that personal data must be processed 'fairly'. The principle of fairness is described by many, including the European Data Protection Supervisor (EDPS), as a 'core' principle of data protection[49] The principle of fairness is in proximity to both lawfulness and transparency, which is apparent throughout the GDPR. The principles of fairness and transparency can be manifested in the provision of a data subject with the right of access, which in turn is a key enabler for other rights such as, depending on the circumstances, the rectification or erasure of data or objection to the processing of personal data by the data controller.[50]

In the context of the AML/CFT the possibility of an effective exercise of those rights poses a great challenge. The obstacles arise from the general secrecy surrounding the AML/CFT policies and prohibition of disclosure established

---

[49] European Data Protection Supervisor, 'Opinion 8/2016 on Coherent Enforcement of Fundamental Rights in the Age of Big Data', 23 September 2016, para 8.
[50] CJEU, Case C-434/16 *Nowak* ECLI:EU:C:2017:994, para 57.

under Article 39 of the 4AMLD. Article 39(1) of the 4AMLD provides for a prohibition of disclosure to the customer concerned or to other third persons of the fact that information is being, will be or has been transmitted to the FIU or that a money laundering or terrorist financing analysis is being, or may be, carried out. Given that the Directive does not introduce any temporal limits regarding non-disclosure obligations, it can be concluded that such obligation continues regardless of the results of the processing of the SAR, including the assessment by the FIU.

Yet, from the perspective of the permissibility of restricting the principles and rights attributed to data subjects under the GDPR, such restriction must meet the requirements provided for in Article 23 GDPR. This provision grants the possibility to limit the rights attributed to data subjects and the application of all basic principles of the processing of personal data, ie the rights established in 'Articles 12 to 22 and Article 34, as well as Article 5 in so far as its provisions correspond to the rights and obligations provided for in Articles 12 to 22',[51] to the extent that these principles relate to the aforementioned rights and obligations. Given that the fundamental right to data protection cannot be ensured without respecting a data subject's rights and adhering to the principles of processing by data controllers, it is crucial to emphasise that restrictions under Article 23 must be considered exceptions. These exceptions from the general rules should therefore be applied narrowly and only under specifically prescribed circumstances.[52]

When personal data are exchanged for AML/CFT, the rights of the data subject may be restricted in three main cases, according to Article 23 GDPR: (a) in the name of prevention, investigation, detection and prosecution of crime, (b) in the name of national security, or (c) in the name of other important objectives of general public interest.

### i. Restrictions in the Name of Prevention, Investigation, Detection and Prosecution of Criminal Offences

Article 23 of the GDPR allows restrictions in the name of prevention, investigation, detection or prosecution of criminal offences. The European Data Protection Board (EDPB), in its guidelines on the interpretation of Article 23 GDPR, recognised that in some cases, such as for instance in the AML/CFT framework, the provision of information to the data subjects that are under investigation may jeopardise the investigation itself.[53] However, the data subjects shall be notified when the notification will not jeopardise the investigation anymore.

The notification of concerned persons is probably the most prominent right of the affected data subjects that is often at odds with the goals of AML/CFT.

---

[51] GDPR Art 23.
[52] European Data Protection Board, 'Guidelines 10/2020 on Restrictions under Article 23 GDPR', 15 December 2020, para. 3.
[53] European Data Protection Board, 'Guidelines 10/2020', para 24.

The AML/CFT framework does not provide for a possibility to inform persons whose transactions were under scrutiny for AML/CFT purposes or were shared with the FIUs or law enforcement authorities, not even when there is no risk of jeopardising any of the ongoing operations. Conversely, there is a prohibition to notify such persons that may further extend to a non-disclosure within court proceedings. However, the notification of the data subjects when personal data are exchanged is a right of the relevant data subjects, which can only be restricted, as described above under specific circumstances and offering concrete safeguards to the data subjects. The European Court of Human Rights (ECtHR) and the CJEU have provided some guidance on the issue of notification.

It has been established case law of the ECtHR in the context of the interception of communications that the notification of concerned individuals is 'inextricably linked to the effectiveness of remedies before the courts'[54] and that the persons concerned should be informed '[a]s soon as notification can be carried out without jeopardising the purpose of the restriction after the termination of the surveillance measure'.[55] This was also repeated in later case law on secret surveillance: 'after the surveillance has been terminated, the question of subsequent notification of surveillance measures is inextricably linked to the effectiveness of remedies before the courts and hence to the existence of effective safeguards against the abuse of monitoring powers'.[56]

The issue of notification of the affected individuals was crucial in the *Tele2/Watson* decision, where the CJEU stated that 'the competent national authorities to whom access to the retained data has been granted must notify the persons affected, under the applicable national procedures, as soon as that notification is no longer liable to jeopardise the investigations being undertaken by those authorities. That notification is, in fact, necessary to enable the persons affected to exercise, inter alia, their right to a legal remedy'.[57] This position was repeated in the CJEU Opinion 1/15 on the EU-Canada PNR agreement.[58]

Although the right of data subjects to be notified when their personal data are processed can be restricted in the framework of combating money laundering and financing of terrorism, this shall not be done in a blanket way. Based on the case law of the CJEU and the ECtHR, the relevant authorities may refrain from informing the data subjects about their processing of their personal data. However, these authorities must notify the persons affected, under the applicable national procedures, as soon as that notification is no longer liable to jeopardise the investigations.

---

[54] See among others, ECtHR, *Roman Zakharov v Russia*, App no 47143/06 (4 December 2015), para 234.
[55] ECtHR, *Roman Zakharov v Russia*, para 287, with reference to ECtHR, *Klass and Others v Germany*, App no 5029/71 (6 September 1978), para 58 and ECtHR, *Weber and Saravia v Germany*, App no 54934/00 (29 June 2006), para 135. Similar reflections were made by the Court in ECtHR, *Szabó and Vissy v Hungary*, App no 37138/14 (12 January 2016), para 86.
[56] ECtHR, *Roman Zakharov v Russia*, paras 233–234.
[57] CJEU, Joined Cases C-2013/15 and C-698/15 *Tele2 Sverige AB* ECLI:EU:C:2016:970, para 121.
[58] CJEU, Opinion 1/15 *EU-Canada PNR Agreement* ECLI:EU:C:2017:592, paras 222 and 224.

Supervisory authorities shall have the power to examine whether the notification of the data subjects is actually realised.

In *La Quadrature du Net (LQDN)* – a case about French authorities that collected traffic and location data – the CJEU established a general obligation for the national competent authorities to publish information of a general nature relating to the automated analysis of the data, without having to notify the persons concerned individually.[59] However, the CJEU established a much stricter obligation when the data matches the parameters specified in the measure authorising automated analysis and that authority identifies the person concerned in order to analyse in greater depth the data concerning these persons. In these cases, the CJEU finds it necessary to notify that person individually. In line with its established case law, the CJEU concluded that notification must occur only to the extent that and as soon as it is no longer liable to jeopardise the tasks for which those authorities are responsible.

This position of the CJEU is of great importance when automated analysis of data takes place in the context of the AML/CFT framework. It is unclear, however, whether the CJEU aimed at imposing such an obligation to notify individually the persons concerned when these persons have been singled out based on automated analysis only to national authorities or whether such an obligation should be expanded to private entities as well. This latter concern would have great impact on obliged entities in the AML/CFT framework, which are already making use of AI in order to carry out data mining and profiling operations.

## ii. Restrictions in the Name of National Security

In its recent case law, the CJEU has offered some clarifications on the limitations and restrictions established for national security. In *Privacy International*, the CJEU examined national legislation enabling a state authority to require providers of electronic communications services to forward traffic data and location data to the security and intelligence agencies for the purpose of safeguarding national security. The CJEU concluded that 'although it is for the Member States to define their essential security interests and to adopt appropriate measures to ensure their internal and external security, the mere fact that a national measure has been taken for the purpose of protecting national security cannot render EU law inapplicable and exempt the Member States from their obligation to comply with that law'.[60] In simple words, the CJEU clearly found that national measures taken for the purpose of protecting national security cannot render EU law inapplicable as such and exempt the Member States from their obligation to comply with that law.[61]

---

[59] CJEU, Joined Cases C-511/18, C-512/18 and C-520/18 La *Quadrature du Net and others* ECLI:EU:C:2020:791, para 190.
[60] CJEU, Case C-623/17 *Privacy International* ECLI:EU:C:2020:790, para 44.
[61] ibid.

A similar conclusion was reached in the *LQDN* judgment where the CJEU concluded that 'national legislation which requires providers of electronic communications services to retain traffic and location data for the purposes of protecting national security and combating crime (…) falls within the scope of [European Union legislation; in this case] Directive 2002/58'.[62] Following the reasoning of the CJEU, private entities involved in the exchanges of personal data either for tax purposes or – even maybe more prominently – for AML/CFT remain under the scope of the GDPR, even when the exchange has been requested by a competent authority (which could also be an FIU in case of AML/CFT). As such, careful examination of the regime under which the exchange of data is realised (especially when private entities are involved) is essential, in order to restrict rights of the data subjects.

### iii. Other Important Objectives of General Public Interest

The GDPR allows restrictions for other important objectives of general public interest, mentioning as examples 'an important economic or financial interest of the Union or of a Member State, including monetary, budgetary and taxation matters …'.[63]

It is questionable which would be the most appropriate ground to justify the restrictions to the rights of the data subjects. The primary aim of the AML/CFT framework is to detect financial transactions that may involve illicit assets or contribute to financing terrorism, but not to protect against those per se. Therefore, perhaps it would be more suitable to justify an interference with a view of pursuing other important objectives of general public interest of the Union or of a Member State, which in this case, as follows from many recitals to the AML Directive, would be the protection of the financial system. Such reasoning can be supported with the wording of Recitals 1 and 2 to the 4AMLD, which point at such interests as integrity, stability and reputation of the financial sector, international development, or confidence in the financial system.

This is in line with the fact that the 4AMLD was adopted on the basis of Article 114 of the Treaty on the Functioning of the European Union (TFEU), ie on the internal market legal basis. It must be noted, however, that as we explained in section II(A), the AML/CFT regulatory landscape is composed of a number of legal instruments, not all adopted as internal market basis. For instance the Directive on Access to Financial Information was adopted on the basis of Article 87(2) TFEU and the Directive on the freezing and confiscation of instrumentalities and proceeds of crime in the EU was adopted on the basis of Article 82(2) and Article 83(1) TFEU, both adopted as instruments in the Area of Freedom, Security and Justice (AFSJ).

---

[62] CJEU, Joined Cases C-511/18, C-512/18 and C-520/18 *La Quadrature du Net and others* ECLI:EU:C:2020:791, para 102.
[63] GDPR Art 23(1)(e).

## C. The Principle of Purpose Limitation

Article 5(1)(b) GDPR and Article 4(1)(b) LED provide for the principle of purpose limitation. The principle calls for establishing the purpose clearly. The availability of a specific and explicit purpose is the first requirement of the purpose limitation principle, followed by ensuring the legitimacy of that purpose. The principle further stipulates that further processing can only take place on condition that it is not 'incompatible' with the initial purpose.

The 4AMLD contains a clear provision on purpose limitation in Article 41(2): 'Personal data shall be processed by obliged entities on the basis of this Directive only for the purposes of the prevention of money laundering and terrorist financing as referred to in Article 1 and shall not be further processed in a way that is incompatible with those purposes. The processing of personal data on the basis of this Directive for any other purposes, such as commercial purposes, shall be prohibited'.[64]

The EDPS has identified a danger for the purpose limitation principle that can potentially arise in relation to Public-Private Partnerships (PPPs) in the AML/CFT context that are created for the sharing of operational information or intelligence. The EDPS is concerned that '[i]n particular, obliged entities participating in PPPs might be tempted to integrate the information shared by law enforcement authorities through this platform in their global databases, so as to re-use it later, as part of their customer profiles. This could lead to discrimination against certain clients, for instance, those offering low profitability for the bank and presenting a significant level of risk, conceivably resulting in the financial exclusion of vulnerable individuals and communities (the so-called 'de-risking' of financial entities whereby relationships with clients that may pose risks are terminated or restricted)'.[65]

## D. The Principle of Data Minimisation and Storage Limitation

Article 5(1)(c) of the GDPR formulates the principle of data minimisation. According to that principle personal data that is processed should be 'adequate, relevant and limited to what is necessary in relation to the purposes for which they are processed'. Article 4(1)(c) LED uses a different formulation and compels Member States to provide for personal data to be 'adequate, relevant and not excessive in relation to the purposes for which they are processed'. This subtle difference in the wording is non-accidental. In case of the LED it reflects the need for the reconciliation of the ever-expanding demands of the competent authorities for as vast as possible arrays of data with the rights of the individuals, whose behaviour

---

[64] 4AMLD Art 41(2).
[65] European Data Protection Supervisor, 'Opinion 5/2020 on the European Commission's action plan for a comprehensive Union policy on preventing money laundering and terrorism financing', 23 July 2020, para 46.

does not justify the processing of their data in the law enforcement context. Since the character of the law enforcement tasks requires a good understanding of criminal activities and detecting links between different criminal offences and persons who could be involved, in some cases, the collection of large sets of data can be inherent. Corresponding recitals to Article 5(1)(c) GDPR and Article 4(1)(c) LED suggest that '[p]ersonal data should be processed only if the purpose of the processing could not reasonably be fulfilled by other means'.[66] The entities sending the data must be able to justify, in each case of sharing of personal data, why the specific data were needed for the specific purpose. The legislation, wherever possible, shall be as concrete as possible regarding the data that can be collected by an entity and the data that can be shared for specific purposes.

An attempt to introduce the principle of data minimisation to the AML/CFT legal framework can be seen in the Directive on Access to Financial Information, which clarifies that '[g]iven the sensitivity of financial data that should be analysed by FIUs and the necessary data protection safeguards, this Directive should specifically set out the type and scope of information that can be exchanged between FIUs, between FIUs and designated competent authorities and between designated competent authorities of different Member States'.[67]

Closely related to the principle of data minimisation is the principle of storage limitation. It requires that data shall also be 'kept in a form which permits identification of data subjects for no longer than is necessary for the purposes for which the personal data are processed [...]'.[68] The storage limitation principle requires relevant legislation to clearly mention the retention periods during which data shall be retained after their exchange. The determination of the retention period shall respect the proportionality principle. The EDPB criticised for instance that the retention periods proposed in 4AMLD are too long: 'The retention period is the business relationship plus five years (article 40 of Directive (EU) 2015/849). Where the business relationship only covers a single transaction, the retention period is five years. Where there is a long-term business relationship, such as a bank has with its customers, the retention period will often extend over several decades. Retention periods can be extended by Member States with an additional five years'.[69]

## E. The Proportionality Test for Limiting Data Protection Principles

The data protection principles, and in particular the purpose limitation, the data minimisation and the storage limitation principles, shall be interpreted in light

---

[66] GDPR Recital 39 and LED Recital 27.
[67] Directive on Access to Financial Information Recital 19.
[68] GDPR Art 5(1)(e).
[69] European Data Protection Board, 'Statement on the protection of personal data processed in relation with the prevention of money laundering and terrorist financing', 15 December 2020.

of the principle of proportionality. The proportionality principle established in Article 52(1) CFR is 'at the very core of the modern understanding of human rights'[70] and can be found throughout the GDPR.

The CJEU applied the proportionality test to the Data Retention Directive[71] in the famous *Digital Rights Ireland* case.[72] The Data Retention Directive obliged Internet Service Providers (ISP) to retain for a maximum of two years all traffic data of every user in order to share them with the authorities in the context of possible investigations. The Data Retention Directive did not pass the proportionality test. According to the Court, the kind of surveillance carried out by ISPs was particularly intrusive. Despite that, the Data Retention Directive did not provide any safeguards for the protection of the individuals surveilled, who were unaware and uninformed of the collection of their traffic data, and of their uses. It also failed to limit the number of people that could have access to said data. Furthermore, the Data Retention Directive was deemed not specific enough in its formulation, due to a lack of connection of the surveillance activities with one or more specific crimes and any lack of evidence of the actual effectiveness of the measure.

In the light of the above, it is reasonable to raise doubts concerning the use of data-driven technologies for AML/CFT.[73] The *Digital Rights Ireland* case presents several similarities with the kind of activities carried out in the context of AML/CFT. Data-driven technologies used for AML/CFT imply a significant intrusion into the fundamental rights of individuals (due to the indiscriminate surveillance and data collection and retention of all bank customers[74]), they also include a risk-assessment and they do not provide for certain safeguards (individuals are not aware of being flagged by the system and being investigated, there is a lack of procedures to object to the treatment or its results).

The following points, in particular, appear problematic from the point of view of non-discrimination, based on the principle of proportionality and how it has been applied by the CJEU.[75] While AML/CFT screening activities are supported by 4AMLD (as amended by 5AMLD), it is debatable whether this latter is specific enough; the freedom of manoeuvre left to obliged entities, together with the lack

---

[70] Lorenzo Dalla Corte, 'On Proportionality in the Data Protection Jurisprudence of the CJEU,' *International Data Privacy Law*, 21 July 2022, ipac014, doi.org/10.1093/idpl/ipac014.

[71] Directive 2006/24/EC of the European Parliament and of the Council of 15 March 2006 on the retention of data generated or processed in connection with the provision of publicly available electronic communications services or of public communications networks and amending Directive 2002/58/EC, (Data Retention Directive), OJ L 105, 13.4.2006, 54–63.

[72] CJEU, Joined Cases C-293/12 and C-594/12 *Digital Rights Ireland* ECLI:EU:C:2014:238. See also: CJEU, Joined Cases C-2013/15 and C-698/15 *Tele2 Sverige AB*.

[73] Astrid Bertrand, Winston Maxwell and Xavier Vamparys, 'Are AI-Based Anti-Money Laundering Systems Compatible with Fundamental Rights?' (2020) papers.ssrn.com/sol3/papers.cfm?abstract_id=3647420.

[74] Recital 44 of the 4AMLD establishes, to avoid a ripple effect of the *Digital Rights Ireland* decision, that the retention should be longer than five years, and that appropriate safeguards need to be in place. It is not clear whether this formulation is specific enough.

[75] Gloria González Fuster, Serge Gutwirth and Erika Ellyne, 'Profiling in the European Union: A high-risk practice' (2010) INEX Policy Brief no. 10.

of specific safeguards, might hint in the direction of the law not being specific enough.[76] Recital 43 4AMLD, affirming that the 4AMLD complies with the CFR, and Recitals 65 and 66 4AMLD, establishing that Member States must ensure the respect of the right to non-discrimination, appear challenging to apply in practice. Moreover, the lack of transparency, together with the lack of information given to the individuals who are flagged by a software, and the lack of a procedure within obliged entities to object to the procedure/result represent important issues in terms of lack of safeguards for the fundamental rights of individuals. The black box effect can be aggravated by the circumstance that the software programs used for AML/CFT purposes are usually proprietary technologies and their use within an organisation can be protected by trade secrets. Intellectual Property laws might hinder the disclosure of important information about the logic and training of algorithms.

## V. Legitimate Ground for Data Processing in AML/CFT

The principle of lawfulness is the first principle mentioned both in the GDPR and the LED and requires that the processing of personal data relies on at least one of the appropriate legal grounds. While the GDPR offers a catalogue of six legal grounds for data processing, the processing to which the LED applies is lawful 'only if and to the extent that processing is necessary for the performance of a task carried out by a competent authority for the [law enforcement] purposes (…) and that it is based on Union or Member State law'.[77]

The identification of the applicable legal framework and the legal basis for the exchange of data is complicated in the field of AML/CFT, where various actors are involved. As regards the processing by the obliged entities in the pursuit of the CDD measures, as regulated in the 4AMLD, one can agree that the GDPR should apply. This is because the GDPR as a general regime applies to any processing operation, unless the conditions for any of the exceptions set out in Article 2(2) and (3) GDPR are met.[78] Considering that the obliged entity is not a competent authority in the meaning of the LED and does not process personal data for law enforcement purposes, or at least not directly, as well as that no other exceptions are relevant, the GDPR must be the applicable regime. Nevertheless, the selection of the correct legal basis for the processing of personal data by obliged entities remains a challenging exercise, as this could be a legal obligation, legitimate interest or even the

---

[76] Astrid Bertrand et al. (n.73) 17.
[77] LED Art 8(1).
[78] GDPR Art 2(2) excludes application of the GDPR for the processing of personal data: (a) in the course of an activity which falls outside the scope of Union law; (b) by the Member States when carrying out activities which fall within the scope of Chapter 2 of Title V of the TEU; (c) by a natural person in the course of a purely personal or household activity; (d) by competent authorities for the purposes of the prevention, investigation, detection or prosecution of criminal offences or the execution of

performance of a task carried out in the public interest. Especially with regard to the processing of personal data that relate to CDD obligations, one can argue that obliged entities can rely on compliance with a legal obligation, which however, due to the vagueness of their formulation may not meet the rule of law requirements. It remains thus questionable whether this should be considered as the correct legal basis for the processing. When it comes to the exchange of personal data within a group (with branches and subsidiaries in third countries), this can be realised mainly on the basis of Article 6(1)(c) GDPR, when the processing is necessary for compliance with a legal obligation, when data are exchanged for compliance with CDD obligations for instance. However, Article 43 4AMLD may be interpreted as allowing obliged entities to process more data than those absolutely necessary for compliance with CDD obligations. In these cases, obliged entities could potentially rely on the legitimate interest, either of the obliged entity or of a third party. Obliged entities could process personal data arguing that these are necessary for the performance of a task carried out in the public interest, although this would be accepted in exceptional circumstances. However, the EDPS has argued that 'the relevant legitimate ground for the processing of personal data should more appropriately be the necessity to comply with a legal obligation by the obliged entities, competent authorities and FIUs (i.e. Article 7(c) [now 6(1)c) 4AMLD]'.[79]

The situation may be different with regard to FIUs. The 4AMLD lays down basic rules for the functioning and tasks of the FIUs. Recital 42 4AMLD states that '[t]he fight against money laundering and terrorist financing is recognised as an important public interest ground by all Member States',[80] a statement further elaborated on in Article 43 4AMLD, which stipulates that 'the processing of personal data on the basis of this Directive for the purposes of the prevention of money laundering and terrorist financing as referred to in Article 1 shall be considered to be a matter of public interest under [the GDPR]'.[81] Considering the role of the FIUs in the AML/CFT legal system and character of the FIUs, and particularly those of the law enforcement type, one can argue that not the GDPR, but the LED should be the applicable legal framework.[82] Therefore, it should be concluded that despite the wording of Article 43 of the 4AMLD, the GDPR does not necessarily apply to all data processing operations for the purposes of the prevention of money

---

criminal penalties, including the safeguarding against and the prevention of threats to public security. GDPR Art 2(3) provides for an exception to the processing of personal data by the Union institutions, bodies, offices and agencies.

[79] See European Data Protection Supervisor, 'Opinion on a Proposal for a Directive of the European Parliament and of the Council on the Prevention of the Use of the Financial System for the Purpose of Money Laundering and Terrorist Financing, and a Proposal for a Regulation of the European Parliament and of the Council on Information on the Payer Accompanying Transfers of Funds', 4 July 2013, para 33.

[80] 4AMLD Recital 42.

[81] 4AMLD Art 43.

[82] Teresa Quintel, 'Follow the Money, If You Can – Possible Solutions for Enhanced FIU Cooperation Under Improved Data Protection Rules' (2019) University of Luxembourg Law Working Paper No. 001-2019.

*From the Fight against Money Laundering and Financing of Terrorism* 179

laundering and terrorist financing that are foreseen in the 4AMLD. When it comes to processing of data carried out by the FIUs, the lawful basis can be Article 6(1)(c) GDPR, ie that the data processing is necessary for compliance with a legal obligation of the FIUs. Alternatively, FIUs can process personal data on the basis on Article 6(1)(e) GDPR, ie the processing is necessary for the performance of a task carried out in the exercise of official authority vested in the controller, the FIUs in this case.

The choice of a legitimate ground is a complicated exercise and needs to be carried out with great care as it is the first step to legitimate data processing. Traditionally AML/CFT actors were not really detailed on the legal basis on which they relied for their data sharing. Gradually more awareness is raised on this issue, along with the pressure for compliance with the data protection rules that comes from the heavy fines foreseen in the GDPR. Therefore, careful analysis of the data processing operations shall take place and the data sharing shall rely on the appropriate legal basis.

## VI. Conclusion

This chapter embarked on a critical discussion on the interpretation of core EU data protection rules that are relevant for data sharing in the AML/CFT context. It aimed at highlighting the need for reconciliation of the rules of the European AML/CFT framework with the ones of European data protection, especially in cases of data sharing. It was not the aim of this chapter to provide a complete overview of the data processing operations that entail processing of financial information, nor to provide an exhaustive mapping of all rules and obligations that apply in such cases. This chapter focused on three issues, which are the starting points for any data protection analysis in the context of AML/CFT.

First, this chapter provided a brief overview of the instances in the European AML/CFT framework that require sharing of data and embarked on offering an understanding of the relationship between financial information and personal data. Recognising financial information as personal data, in principle, triggers the application of the EU legal framework on data protection. This chapter focused mainly on the provisions of the GDPR which are as a rule applicable to obliged entities.

Secondly the chapter discussed some core data protection principles. As regards the principles of fairness and transparency, the restrictions that can be imposed based on Article 23 GDPR were discussed and the grounds that are relevant for the context of AML/CFT were analysed. Although one could intuitively argue that such restrictions may be imposed in the name of prevention, investigation and prosecution of criminal offences, it seems more plausible to actually rely on a general monetary public interest. Another crucial issue relating to fairness and transparency was that of notification of persons concerned. The goals of the AML/CFT framework are based on the assumption of secrecy of any data-sharing operation from the persons concerned. The recent case law of the ECtHR and the CJEU, however, placed the notification of the concerned persons in a prominent position rendering notification a cornerstone right of the individuals concerned. Such notification, even if it takes place after the end of an AML/CFT operation, may raise important risks for the functioning of the AML/CFT framework and is in essence contrary to its actual goals. If the European legislator wishes to restrict the notification right, this shall be done by law and in line with the principle of proportionality and the established case law of the ECtHR and CJEU. The chapter further discussed the importance of the proportionality principle which shall be used as a yardstick for the interpretation of the data protection principles in the context of AML/CFT, in line with relevant CJEU jurisprudence in similar fields.

The last point of the analysis was dedicated to the choice of legitimate grounds for data processing. This is a difficult exercise in itself and the complexities of the AML/CFT context, combined with the lack of precise legislative provisions ordering data sharing, intensify the problem. Depending on the actors involved, the GDPR or the LED may apply, which has an impact on the legal basis for the processing of personal data. Obliged entities may process or share data based on a legal obligation, while in other instances they may rely on their legitimate interest or even process data for the performance of a task carried out in the public interest. Especially with regard to the processing of personal data that relates to CDD obligations, one can argue that obliged entities can rely on legal obligation, which however may not meet the rule of law requirements. It remains thus questionable whether this should be considered as the correct legal basis for the processing. Similar considerations were discussed in relation to the FIUs.

There is undoubtedly tension between the aims and goals of the two frameworks. However, given the wealth of personal data processed and shared in the context of AML/CFT, there is an urgent need for the reconciliation of the European framework on data protection on the one hand and on AML/CFT on the other. Our chapter illustrated some core areas of conflict between the two fields and attempted to provide guidance on concrete issues, while it also highlighted the importance for final resolution of open ones. Our chapter aimed at highlighting the central role of data protection in safeguarding individuals against mechanisms of power such as those which the AML/CFT regime may pose. It showed that the secondary European legislation that governs the processing of personal data introduces several universal democratic principles and meta-concepts, such as lawfulness, fairness or transparency, which however translate into rather pragmatic rights and obligations, such as access rights or notification mechanisms. In view of the assumption that in democratic constitutional states power shall be 'by definition limited',[83] data protection law introduces 'default' limitations to its exercise. It sets out the boundaries of the permissible use of personal data and equips

---

[83] De Hert and Gutwirth (n. 6) 63.

individuals with tools for verification if those boundaries are respected. In this way, it shields individuals from possible interferences both from the state and the industry. These interferences, as shown in the example of the 'Freedom Convoy' in Canada, may have significant implications for the realisation of other constitutional guarantees.

# References

Legislation and policy documents:

Council Directive 91/308/EEC of 10 June 1991 on prevention of the use of the financial system for the purpose of money laundering, OJ L 166, 28.6.1991, 77–82.

Directive (EU) 2015/849 of the European Parliament and of the Council of 20 May 2015 on the prevention of the use of the financial system for the purposes of money laundering or terrorist financing, amending Regulation (EU) No 648/2012 of the European Parliament and of the Council, and repealing Directive 2005/60/EC of the European Parliament and of the Council and Commission Directive 2006/70/EC, OJ L 141, 5.6.2015, 73–117.

Directive (EU) 2018/843 of the European Parliament and of the Council of 30 May 2018 amending Directive (EU) 2015/849 on the prevention of the use of the financial system for the purposes of money laundering or terrorist financing, and amending Directives 2009/138/EC and 2013/36/EU, OJ L 156, 19.6.2018, 43–74.

Directive (EU) 2019/1153 of the European Parliament and of the Council laying down rules facilitating the use of financial and other information for the prevention, detection, investigation or prosecution of certain criminal offences, and repealing Council Decision 2000/642/JHA, OJ L 186, 11.7.2019, 122–137.

Directive 2005/60/EC of the European Parliament and of the Council of 26 October 2005 on the prevention of the use of the financial system for the purpose of money laundering and terrorist financing, OJ L 309, 25.11.2005, 15–36.

Directive 2006/24/EC of the European Parliament and of the Council of 15 March 2006 on the retention of data generated or processed in connection with the provision of publicly available electronic communications services or of public communications networks and amending Directive 2002/58/EC, (Data Retention Directive), OJ L 105, 13.4.2006, 54–63.

Directive 2014/42/EU of the European Parliament and of the Council of 3 April 2014 on the freezing and confiscation of instrumentalities and proceeds of crime in the European Union OJ L 127, 29.4.2014, 39–50.

Emergency Economic Measures Order, SOR/2022-22 Canada Gazette, Part II, Volume 156, Extra Number 1. P.C. 2022-108 15, February 2022.

European Commission, 'Anti-money laundering and countering the financing of terrorism legislative package', 20 July 2021, ec.europa.eu/info/publications/210720-anti-money-laundering-countering-financing-terrorism_en.

European Commission, 'Beating financial crime: Commission overhauls anti-money laundering and countering the financing of terrorism rules', 20 July 2021, ec.europa.eu/commission/presscorner/detail/en/IP_21_3690.

European Commission, 'Communication from the Commission: on an Action Plan for a comprehensive Union policy on preventing money laundering and terrorism financing', 7 May 2020, C(2020)2800 final, eur-lex.europa.eu/legal-content/EN/TXT/PDF/?uri=PI_COM:C(2020)2800&from=EN.

European Commission, Proposal for a Directive of the European Parliament and of the Council on the mechanisms to be put in place by the Member States for the prevention of the use of the financial system for the purposes of money laundering or terrorist financing and repealing Directive (EU) 2015/849, COM/2021/423 final (20.07.2021).

European Commission, Proposal for a Regulation of the European Parliament and of the Council on the prevention of the use of the financial system for the purposes of money laundering or terrorist financing, COM(2021) 420 final (20.07.2021).

European Commission, Proposal for a Regulation of the European Parliament and of the Council establishing the Authority for Anti-Money Laundering and Countering the Financing of Terrorism and amending Regulations (EU) No 1093/2010, (EU) 1094/2010, (EU) 1095/2010, COM/2021/421 final (20.07.2021).

European Commission, Proposal for a Regulation of the European Parliament and of the Council on information accompanying transfers of funds and certain crypto-assets, COM(2021) 422 final (20.07.2021).

European Data Protection Board, 'Guidelines 10/2020 on Restrictions under Article 23 GDPR', 15 December 2020.

European Data Protection Board, 'Statement on the protection of personal data processed in relation with the prevention of money laundering and terrorist financing', 15 December 2020.

European Data Protection Supervisor, 'Opinion 5/2020 on the European Commission's Action Plan for a comprehensive Union policy on preventing money laundering and terrorism financing', 23 July 2020.

European Data Protection Supervisor, 'Opinion 8/2016 on Coherent Enforcement of Fundamental Rights in the Age of Big Data', 23 September 2016.

European Data Protection Supervisor, 'Opinion on a Proposal for a Directive of the European Parliament and of the Council on the Prevention of the Use of the Financial System for the Purpose of Money Laundering and Terrorist Financing, and a Proposal for a Regulation of the European Parliament and of the Council on Information on the Payer Accompanying Transfers of Funds', 4 July 2013.

Regulation (EU) 2015/847 of the European Parliament and of the Council of 20 May 2015 on information accompanying transfers of funds and repealing Regulation (EC) No 1781/2006, OJ L 141, 5.6.2015, 1–18.

US Congress, Office for Technology Assessment, Information Technologies for the Control of Money Laundering (US Government Printing Office 1995) 56 docplayer.net/28783887-Information-technologies-for-the-control-of-money-laundering-september-ota-itc-630-gpo-stock.html.

Literature:

Bertrand, Astrid, Winston Maxwell and Xavier Vamparys. 'Are AI-Based Anti-Money Laundering Systems Compatible with Fundamental Rights?' (2020) papers.ssrn.com/sol3/papers.cfm?abstract_id=3647420.

Brewczyńska Magdalena. 'Financial Intelligence Units: Reflections on the Applicable Data Protection Legal Framework,' *Computer Law & Security Review* 43 (2021): 105612, doi.org/10.1016/j.clsr.2021.105612.

Dalla Corte Lorenzo. 'On Proportionality in the Data Protection Jurisprudence of the CJEU,' *International Data Privacy Law*, 21 July 2022, ipac014, doi.org/10.1093/idpl/ipac014.

De Hert, Paul and Serge Gutwirth. 'Privacy, data protection and law enforcement. Opacity of the individual and transparency of power.' In *Privacy and the criminal law*, edited by Erik Claes, Serge Gutwirth and Antony Duff, 61–104. Antwerp/Oxford: Intersentia, 2006.

Fuster, Gloria González, Serge Gutwirth and Erika Ellyne. 'Profiling in the European Union: A high-risk practice' (2010) INEX Policy Brief no. 10.

Hossam, Tamer, Mohamed Zaki, Tarek S. Sobh and Khaled Mahmoud Badran, 'Design of a Monitor for Detecting Money Laundering and Terrorist Financing', *Journal of Theoretical and Applied Information Technology* 85, no. 425, 426 (2016).

Kosta Eleni, 'Report on the implications for data protection of mechanisms for inter-state exchanges of data for anti-money laundering/countering financing of terrorism, and tax purposes, Report for the Consultative Committee of the Convention for the protection of individuals with regard to automatic processing of personal data (Council of Europe)', July 2021, rm.coe.int/t-pd-2021-4rev-inter-state-exchanges-of-data-for-tax-purposes-and-cml-/1680a3ed30.

Landerer, Lukas Martin. 'The Anti-Money-Laundering Directive and the ECJ's Jurisdiction on Data Retention: A Flawed Comparison?,' *Eucrim – the European Criminal Law Associations' Forum* 01 (2022), 67–72.

Maillart, Jean-Baptiste. 'European Union.' In *National and International Anti-Money Laundering Law Developing the Architecture of Criminal Justice, Regulation and Data Protection*, edited by Benjamin Vogel and Jean-Baptiste Maillart, 71–155. Cambridge/Antwerp/Chicago: Intersentia, 2020.

Quintel Teresa, 'Follow the Money, If You Can – Possible Solutions for Enhanced FIU Cooperation Under Improved Data Protection Rules' (2019) *University of Luxembourg Law Working Paper* No. 001-2019.

Vieira, Paul. 'Canada Instructs Banks to Unfreeze Freedom-Convoy Accounts' *WSJ*, 22 February 2022, www.wsj.com/articles/canada-instructs-banks-to-unfreeze-freedom-convoy-accounts-1164559050.

Woolf, Marie. 'RCMP gave banks police info on Ottawa protesters with a list of accounts to freeze', *The Canadian Press*, 8 March 2022, www.cbc.ca/news/politics/rcmp-names-banks-freeze-1.6376955.

Zimonjic, Peter. 'Most bank accounts frozen under the Emergencies Act are being released, committee hears,' *CBC News*, 22 February 2022, www.cbc.ca/news/politics/emergency-bank-measures-finance-committee-1.6360769.

# 8

## Cybercrime Convention-based Access to Personal Data Held by Big Tech

### *Decades of Council of Europe's Greenlighting Codified in a New Protocol*

PAUL DE HERT[*] AND ANGELA AGUINALDO[≠]

> **Article 39, §3 Cybercrime Convention interpreted by the Council of Europe in the past decennia**
>
> (text made up by the authors)
>
> 'Nothing in this Convention shall affect other rights, restrictions, obligations and responsibilities of a Party, hence there is no problem with unilateral state actions outside the realm of the Convention'

## Abstract

On 17 November 2021 the Second Additional Protocol to the Convention on enhanced cooperation and disclosure of electronic evidence was adopted by the Council of Europe. Through this Protocol it is hoped to strengthen judicial cooperation mechanisms including direct cooperation with service providers and joint investigation teams. Considering this development, this chapter mainly focuses on how the Council of Europe and its Member States primarily used soft law as an effective tool to influence policy as regards transborder access to online evidence in criminal matters. Starting with the 2001 Cybercrime Convention that does not explicitly provide for unilateral transborder access to data, this chapter encourages the reader to witness an intentional evolution from its original provisions to the adoption of soft law instruments such as different recommendations, and more importantly, guidance notes, which have eventually led to the momentum

---

[*] Vrije Universiteit Brussel, Belgium.
[≠] Ateneo de Manila University, Philippines.

of adopting a Protocol. The chapter reflects on the agenda being pushed through these soft law instruments: to eventually expand on the interpretation of 'domestic reach' vis-à-vis electronic evidence in criminal matters. While laudable in terms of promoting efficiency, the law enforcement-centric greenlighting has its obvious pitfalls, one of which is the want of contribution to the promotion of better standards and protections for data protection and other relevant rights.

## Keywords

Cybercrime Convention, Budapest Convention, Second Additional Protocol, Guidance Notes, Council of Europe, European Union, transborder access to online evidence, policy laundering, greenlighting

## I. International Criminal Cooperation without Laws and the Council of Europe: Presentation of the Chapter

On 17 November 2021, the Committee of Ministers of the Council of Europe (CoE) in celebration of the 20th Anniversary of the Cybercrime Convention adopted the Second Additional Protocol to the Convention on enhanced cooperation and disclosure of electronic evidence. This new protocol is meant to clarify matters on transnational access to electronic evidence and is supposed 'to set out, among other things, a clearer framework and stronger safeguards for existing practices of transborder access to data and safeguards, including data protection requirements'.[1] The Second Additional Protocol relaunches the 'applicative sphere of the basic Convention, confirming its centrality in the procedures of international cooperation vis-a-vis crimes committed in cyberspace',[2] and includes 'provisions for an efficient and effective mutual legal assistance, direct transborder cooperation with providers, framework and safeguards for practices of transborder access to data',[3] where stronger judicial cooperation mechanisms are strongly emphasised, including direct cooperation with service providers as well as joint investigations between states.[4]

---

[1] Sofie Depauw, 'Electronic evidence in criminal matters: How about e-evidence instruments 2.0?,' *EuCLR European Criminal Law Review* 8.1 (2018): 62, 66; Luca Tosoni, 'Rethinking Privacy in the Council of Europe's Convention on Cybercrime,' *Computer Law & Security Review* 34.6 (2018): 1214.

[2] Filippo Spiezia, 'International cooperation and protection of victims in cyberspace: welcoming Protocol II to the Budapest Convention on Cybercrime' (paper presented at the ERA Forum, 2022), 4.

[3] Council of Europe, 'Legal Opinion on Budapest Cybercrime Convention'; Paul De Hert, Cihan Parlar, and Juraj Sajfert, 'The Cybercrime Convention Committee's 2017 Guidance Note on Production Orders: Unilateralist transborder access to electronic evidence promoted via soft law,' *Computer law & security review* 34. 2 (2018); Alexander Seger, 'e-Evidence and Access to Data in the Cloud Results of the Cloud Evidence Group of the Cybercrime Convention Committee,' in *Handling and Exchanging Electronic Evidence Across Europe* (Cham: Springer, 2018), 40.

[4] Spiezia (n. 2) 4.

Our contribution is no deep dive into the various features of this new Second Additional Protocol,[5] but delves into its historical and functional development mainly through soft law guidance produced by the Council of Europe experts. As such it highlights a process of apparent policy laundering,[6] in the sense of implementing a quasi-legal policy at the international level without treaty basis approved by Member State legislators. A familiar concept is *greenlighting*, using the Council of Europe expert recommendations to optimise and go beyond all the investigative options created in the 2001 Cybercrime Convention to facilitate swift law enforcement access to personal data and electronic evidence in criminal matters without having to respect rules of 'cumbersome' mutual legal assistance.

Mostly as a response to the growing effect of globalisation in a digital and digitised society and how it affects criminal matters, this chapter mainly focuses on how the Council of Europe and its Member States primarily used soft law as an effective tool to influence policy. We do this by first providing an overview of the Council of Europe as the progenitor of the 2001 Cybercrime Convention (CC), the leading and most complete instrument tackling cybercrime and its expert body, the Cybercrime Convention Committee responsible for much soft law guidance to the Convention. We discuss the Convention provisions on international cooperation in criminal matters (section II). Contracting parties (including not only European, but also non-European states) are enjoined to give each other the widest possible form of assistance in criminal matters. Mutual legal assistance (as opposed to unilateral state action) is provided by the Convention as the default route for cross-border exchange and transborder access to online evidence. Interestingly, the original text does not provide explicit powers on (unilateral) transborder access due to a lack of agreement among the parties but does not exclude the possibility of transborder access to publicly available data and transborder access to data based on consent (Article 32 CC).

So far, the Council of Europe has undertaken five interpretative steps to facilitate transborder access to online evidence. First, in the Explanatory Report to the Convention maximum use is proposed of the exceptional unilateral transborder powers in Article 32 CC – read together with Article 39 CC – to open the Convention door for further developments (section III).

Second, in a 2014 soft law document, Guidance Note 3, the Council of Europe experts pushed for a broad understanding of consent, mentioned in Article 32 CC as a basis for transnational access to data without need for traditional mutual legal assistance (section IV).

Two more bending steps were taken with regard production orders in Article 18 CC. This provision allows law enforcement authorities to use production orders to obtain data from persons and providers within their country.

---

[5] See Stanisław Tosza, 'Internet service providers as law enforcers and adjudicators. A public role of private actors,' *Computer Law & Security Review* 43 (2021).

[6] On policy laundering, see Gus Hosein, 'Policy Laundering, and Other Policy Dynamics,' *Cyberwar, netwar and the revolution in military affairs* (2006): 228–241.

Guidance Note 10 (2017) expands the meaning of Article 18 CC by turning this treaty basis for domestic powers into a treaty basis for transnational powers (sections V and VI). Fifth, these soft law experiments were codified in the 2021 Second Additional Protocol to the Convention (section VII).

After a short caveat about parallelism in policymaking between the Council of Europe and the European Union (section VIII), we reflect on the use of soft law instruments like the Guidance Notes in the wider context of global criminal law policy-making and informal international law-making (section IX). We speculate about the agenda of the Council of Europe experts with their guidance notes filled with doubtful legal interpretations. This guidance embodies a radical change of perspective not only as regards the irrelevance of 'transnational reach' of domestic production orders but also with regard to consent-based mechanisms with foreign service providers being a contested practice. Why is the Council of Europe taking this road and what is it hoping to realise by trying to bend the text of a twentieth century Convention unfit to respond to calls for unilateral powers? Clearly there is an agenda to impact international law reasoning on territoriality.

In the final section we summarise all sections of this contribution on developments occurring within the Council of Europe regarding transborder access to online evidence (section X).

## II. The 2001 Cybercrime Convention and its Expert Committee (T-CY)

The Council of Europe is a traditional and intergovernmental regional organisation in the whole of Europe (now 47 Member States).[7] Unlike the European Union (EU), it does not have a constitutional and fundamental framework,[8] or an overarching authority that dictates policies and decisions to its Member States nor does it have a heavy-weight compliance mechanism that would hold Member States liable in case of non-compliance. It is a popular choice for international agreements equally among European states and non-European states.[9]

---

[7] Katitza Rodriguez, Danny O' Brian and Maryant Fernandez, 'Behind the Octopus: The Hidden Race to Dismantle Global Law Enforcement Privacy Protections,' (2018). www.eff.org/deeplinks/2018/08/behind-octopus-hidden-race-dismantle-global-law-enforcement-privacy-protections. The Council of Europe was inspired Winston Churchill's idea of having a 'United States of Europe' after World War II.

[8] Michaela Hailbronner, 'Beyond Legitimacy: Europe's Crisis of Constitutional Democracy,' in *Constitutional Democracy in Crisis?*, eds. Mark Graber, Sanford Levinson and Mark Tushnet (Oxford: Oxford University Press, 2018).

[9] Florence Benoît-Rohmer and Heinrich Klebes, *Council of Europe Law: Towards a Pan-European Legal Area* (Council of Europe, 2005), 13; Rodriguez, O'Brian and Fernandez (n. 7) 2. See for further elaboration on the 'two Europes' and their respective similarities and differences, as well as an explanation on why and how is the Council of Europe the more favoured international/regional forum nowadays as regards policymaking, Angela Aguinaldo and Paul de Hert, 'European Law Enforcement and US Data Companies: A Decade of Cooperation Free from Law,' (2020), 99–106.

As European Union-policy making on criminal matters and cooperation in the twentieth century was either slow or avoided, the Council of Europe remained the more favoured forum for multilateral agreements at the international level on cross-border cooperation. The 1957 European Convention on Extradition and the 1959 European Convention on Mutual Legal Assistance in Criminal Matters are just of the sample core agreements in Europe that were made possible through the Council of Europe.[10]

This leading role became more significant in addressing problems arising from computer crimes. Due to increasing cybercrimes and the lack of domestic legislation addressing them, the CoE's Committee of Ministers adopted in 1989 recommendation R89(9) on computer-related crime. This recommendation required Member States to consider computer crimes in the review of their respective laws and equally advocated improved international cooperation.[11] A 1995 recommendation R95(13) on the harmonisation of criminal procedural laws relating to information technology clarified the application of recommendation R89(9).[12] These recommendations notwithstanding, domestic investigations continued to be admittedly slow and challenging and many countries remained bereft of the necessary domestic legal infrastructure to combat these crimes.[13]

With obvious support from the US government, the Council of Europe then formed a Committee of Experts on Crime in Cyberspace in 1997.[14] The Cybercrime Convention (or Budapest Convention), finalised on 8 November 2001 and opened for signature on 23 November 2001, resulted from these efforts.[15] The Convention, that was drafted together with a protocol, harmonises substantive law and aligns procedural laws applicable to criminal investigations with a digital component; and implements a system of international law enforcement anti-cybercrime cooperation.[16] The First Additional Protocol tackles the criminalisation of acts of a racist or xenophobic nature committed through computer systems as well as the inclusion of hate speech and child pornography to 'content' cybercrime.[17]

---

[10] Steve Peers, 'Mutual Recognition and Criminal Law in the European Union: Has the Council Got It Wrong,' *Common Market L. Rev.* 41 (2004): 5, 6.

[11] Shannon L. Hopkins, 'Cybercrime Convention: A Positive Beginning to a Long Road Ahead,' *J. High Tech. L.* 2 (2003); Anna-Maria Osula, 'Remote search and seizure in domestic criminal procedure: Estonian case study,' *International Journal of Law and Information Technology* 24 (2016); Amalie M. Weber, 'The Council of Europe's Convention on Cybercrime,' *Berkeley Technology Law Journal* 18 (2003): 425, 428.

[12] Hopkins (n. 11); Weber (n. 11) 429.

[13] ibid.

[14] ibid.

[15] ibid.

[16] Roderic Broadhurst, 'Developments in the global law enforcement of cyber-crime,' *Policing: An International Journal of Police Strategies & Management* (2006); Tosoni (n. 1) 2. Presently having 56 contracting states, accession to the agreement was not restricted to the European Member States but it likewise allowed non-Member States such as Canada, Japan, South Africa and the US, among others to accede. See Hopkins (n. 11) 106.

[17] The 'First Additional Protocol to the Cybercrime Convention' entered into force on 1 March 2006 and presently has been ratified by 32 states. Council of Europe Treaties Office, 'Details of Treaty

It is often overlooked, but the Cybercrime Convention builds on the work of the G8 group of Nations.[18] Having the US as one of its members, the G8 has an influential clout over matters involving the governance of cyberspace and high-tech crimes, including cybersecurity and cyberwarfare issues especially after the 11 September 2001 terrorist attacks in the USA.[19] The G8 heads of state during the Halifax Summit (1995) established the Lyon Group, a cross-disciplinary group of senior government experts, to address methods of combating transnational crime.[20] This expert group came up with a series of recommendations in 1996 regarding increasing efficiency and capacity to tackle high-tech crime and building more effective regimes for cross-border cooperation.[21] The Lyon Group then developed into a permanent, multidisciplinary body helping to provide information for meetings of the G8 justice and interior ministers.[22] Among the developments initiated was the establishment of a high-tech crime subgroup that led to the expansion of the 24/7 computer security network, which now includes countries outside the G8 countries.[23] The existence of this 24/7 computer security network eventually found its way into the Cybercrime Convention provisions. The G8 was also instrumental in establishing the 1999 Principles on Transborder Access to Stored Computer Data,[24] that would equally influence the drafters of the Cybercrime Convention (see below).[25]

Alongside the Convention, the Cybercrime Convention Committee was established (otherwise referred to as the T-CY) with representation of the State Parties to the Convention. Based on Article 46 CC, consultations within the T-CY aim to facilitate the effective use and implementation of the Convention, the exchange of information and consideration of any future amendments.

The T-CY, during the 8th Plenary (December 2013), decided to issue guidance notes that would facilitate the effective implementation of the Convention

---

No. 189: Additional Protocol to the Convention on Cybercrime, concerning the criminalisation of acts of a racist and xenophobic nature committed through computer systems' 2019) www.coe.int/en/web/conventions/full-list/-/conventions/treaty/189. See also Broadhurst (n. 16) 10.

[18] In the Explanatory Report several references to this work are made. When clarifying CC Art 35 on a 24/7 Network channel of collaboration, it is for instance said that this channel is 'based upon the experience gained from an already functioning network created under the auspices of the G8 group of nations.' (Explanatory Report to the Convention on Cybercrime, Budapest, 23 November 2001, (60 pages), §298 via rm.coe.int/16800cce5b).

[19] Jeffrey A. Hart, 'The G8 and the Governance of Cyberspace,' in *New Perspectives on Global Governance* (London: Routledge, 2017), 146; Ian Walden, 'Crime and security in cyberspace,' *Cambridge Review of International Affairs* 18 (2005): 51.

[20] Hart (n. 19) 146; David Wall, *Crime and deviance in cyberspace* (London: Routledge, 2017), 530.
[21] Wall (n. 20) 530.
[22] Hart (n. 19) 146.
[23] Wall (n. 20) 530.
[24] Wall (n. 20) 530.
[25] Note also that after the activation of this convention by the CoE, a joint communique of the G8 Home Affairs Ministers was made at their Washington meeting (10 May 2004) that called for action 'to encourage the adoption of the legal standard on a broad basis' and 'all countries must continue to improve laws that criminalize misuses of computer networks and that allow for faster cooperation on inter-related investigations'. See Wall (n. 20) 530.

provisions especially in light of legal, policy and technological developments.[26] Thus far, the T-CY has issued ten guidance notes, two of which are relevant to the present discussion. Prior to the discussion of these guidance notes, it is imperative however to put focus first on the provisions of the Convention relevant for the issue of organise transborder access to evidence.

## III. 'Notoriously Complex' Mutual Legal Assistance as a Rule (Article 25 CC) *Unless* Article 32 *juncto* 39 CC Applies (Step 1)

The introduction of the Cybercrime Convention is momentous, significant and complete in terms of regulating cybercrime and providing the needed international standards to date.[27] Its provisions cover questions on jurisdiction, harmonise national substantive and procedural criminal law and provide international cooperation mechanisms in the field of computer crime and digital evidence.[28] Through Article 18 CC the Convention provides a framework for production orders allowing law enforcement authorities to obtain data from persons and providers *within* their territory. Article 19 CC allows an extended network search through by extending an existing search and seizure procedure in a house, building, dwelling, or any other location to 'computers lawfully accessible to the computer on the search location'.[29] This extended search should however remain within the national borders.[30] The extended search should thus be conducted *only* on computers and servers within the state's territory.[31]

The default rule in the Convention in terms of online evidence and information is to fall back on mutual legal assistance to obtain data stored abroad. Mutual legal assistance shall be provided to the 'widest extent possible for the purpose of investigations or proceedings concerning criminal offenses related to computer systems and data, or for the collection of evidence in electronic form of a criminal offense'

---

[26] See Guidance Note No. 3 on Transborder Access (Cybercrime Convention Art 32).
[27] De Hert, Parlar and Sajfert (n. 3); Hopkins (n. 11) 111; Ian Walden, 'Accessing Data in the Cloud: The Long Arm of the Law Enforcement Agent,' in *Privacy and Security for Cloud Computing*, ed. Siani Pearson and George Yee (Cham: Springer, 2013), 45–71.
[28] Broadhurst (n. 16); Ben Hayes et al., 'The law enforcement challenges of cybercrime: are we playing catch up?,' (Brussels: European Parliament's Policy Department for Citizens' Rights and Constitutional Affairs). www.europarl.europa.eu/thinktank/en/document.html?reference=IPOL_STU(2015)536471; Ulrich Sieber and Carl-Wendelin Neubert, 'Transnational Criminal Investigations in Cyberspace: Challenges to National Sovereignty,' in *Max Planck Yearbook of United Nations Law Online* 20 (2017); Walden (n. 27); Weber (n. 11) 45.
[29] Hayes et al. (n. 28); Walden (n. 27) 51.
[30] Bert-Jaap Koops and Morag Goodwin, 'Cyberspace, the Cloud, and Cross-Border Criminal Investigation: The Limits and Possibilities of International Law,' (2014); Juan Carlos Ortiz Pradillo, 'Fighting against cybercrime in Europe: the admissibility of remote searches in Spain,' *Eur. J. Crime Crim. L. & Crim. Just.* 19 (2011); Walden (n. 27) 52.
[31] Koops and Goodwin (n. 30); Pradillo, (n. 30) 375.

(Article 25, §1 CC). Parties must adopt legislative and other measures necessary to carry out obligations vis-à-vis mutual legal assistance (Article 25, §2 CC). Mutual legal assistance could then be subject to the conditions provided under the respective domestic laws of the respective contracting states, including grounds to refuse assistance, except as may be otherwise provided for in the relevant provisions of the Convention (Article 25, §5).[32]

Mutual legal assistance is historically believed thought to be 'notoriously complex, slow and bureaucratic, which is particularly unsuitable for cloud-based' or even cyberspace-related investigations.[33] Often voiced in law enforcement circles, this view had arguably a lasting impact on the drafting of the Convention. It explains the exempting circumstances under Article 32 CC that allow unilateral judicial action (without the requirement of international cooperation mechanisms) in two cases with a transnational element:

**Figure 1** Article 32 CC: Transborder access to stored computer data with consent or where publicly available

---

*Article 32 CC — Transborder access to stored computer data with consent or where publicly available*
A Party may, without the authorisation of another Party:
a) access publicly available (open source) stored computer data, regardless of where the data is located geographically; or
b) access or receive, through a computer system in its territory, stored computer data located in another Party, if the Party obtains the lawful and voluntary consent of the person who has the lawful authority to disclose the data to the Party through that computer system.

---

Two scenarios are dealt with in Article 32 CC. First (under a), with respect to publicly available data, authorisation of another party is not required, regardless of where this data is located geographically.[34] In the second scenario (under b) non-public data available in another state can be accessed through a computer system if the party 'obtains the lawful and voluntary consent of the person who has the lawful authority to disclose the data'.[35]

These two exceptional unilateral transnational criminal investigative powers are limited in scope and do not extend the domestic powers established in Articles 18 or 19 CC. These exempting circumstances do not allow broader unilateral extraterritorial searches. As the drafters explained in the Explanatory Report to the Convention 'it was not yet possible to prepare a comprehensive, legally binding regime regulating the area'.[36] This failure was attributed to the Committee's admitted lack of experience with such situations and the 'notions that the permissibility of unilateral assertions of power would turn on 'the precise circumstances of

---

[32] One such relevant provision is CC Art 27 stating that absence of any agreement or treaty in place between the parties allowing for mutual legal assistance, its provisions shall apply (CC Art 27).
[33] Walden (n. 27) 55. See also Paul De Hert, Cihan Parlar and Johannes Thumfart, 'Legal Arguments Used in Courts Regarding Territoriality and Cross-Border Production Orders: From Yahoo Belgium to Microsoft Ireland,' *New Journal of European Criminal Law* 9 (2018): 328.
[34] Sieber and Neubert (n. 28); Weber (n. 11) 433.
[35] CC Art 32(b); Sieber and Neubert (n. 28) 274.
[36] Explanatory Report to the Convention on Cybercrime, Budapest, 23 November 2001, §293.

the individual case, thereby making it difficult to formulate general rules'.[37] This is without prejudice though to any future developments:

> Ultimately, the drafters decided to only set forth in Article 32 of the Convention situations in which all agreed that unilateral action is permissible. They agreed not to regulate other situations until such time as further experience has been gathered and further discussions may be held in light thereof. In this regard, Article 39, §3 provides that other situations are neither authorised, nor precluded.[38]

So, the law enforcement view that mutual legal assistance (or MLA) is 'notoriously complex' not only led to two MLA-exceptions in Article 32 CC, but also to an open, enabling final provision in the Convention, that more unilateral powers are not inconceivable. Interestingly, the said Article 39, §3 CC does not say this explicitly: it does not say that 'other situations are neither authorised, nor precluded' as suggested in the quote, but rather, and more cryptically that: 'Nothing in this Convention shall affect other rights, restrictions, obligations and responsibilities of a Party.'

The usage of this provision as the legal basis to lay down the predicate that unilateral state actions outside the realm of Article 32 'are not precluded' is an obvious sly attempt by the Explanatory Report to grant Member States discretion in their choice of action. A legalistic reading of the text of the Convention, and this contrary to the Explanatory Report, is that the Convention does *not* allow transnational evidence gathering other than the two cases identified in Article 32 CC. ('*Expressio unius est exclusio alterius*'). This view is reinforced by the Council of Europe 2008 Guidelines for the Cooperation between Law Enforcement and Internet Service Providers against Cybercrime, stating that law enforcement authorities 'should be encouraged not to direct requests directly to non-domestic internet service providers', but should make use of interstate procedures contained in international cooperation treaties.[39]

## IV. Guidance Note 3 and Easy Transborder Access to Data Based on Consent (Step 2)

Despite these 2008 Guidelines for the Cooperation, evidence came to light around that time that transborder access has been occurring without a formal inter-state

---

[37] Explanatory Report to the Convention on Cybercrime, Budapest, 23 November 2001, §293.
[38] Explanatory Report to the Convention on Cybercrime, Budapest, 23 November 2001, §293.
[39] Guidelines for the Cooperation between Law Enforcement and Internet Service Providers against Cybercrime, adopted by the global Conference Cooperation against Cybercrime, 1–2 April 2008 Guideline 36; Didier Bigo et al., 'Fighting cybercrime and protecting privacy in the cloud,' (Brussels: European Parliament's Policy Department for Citizens' Rights and Constitutional Affairs), 32. www.europarl.europa.eu/RegData/etudes/etudes/join/2012/462509/IPOL-LIBE_ET%282012%29462509_EN.pdf; Koops and Goodwin (n. 30) 58; Walden (n. 27) 51; Ian Walden, 'Law enforcement access to data in clouds,' in *Cloud Computing Law*, ed. Christopher Millard (Oxford: Oxford University Press, 2013), 301.

process such as mutual legal assistance. It became a standard procedure by law enforcement agents in many countries to routinely turn to foreign service providers (often based in the US) to request and be provided with data from these providers, with the latter having readily available mechanisms to grant these requests because online evidence is normally in the custody of these private sources.[40]

These developments lead to discussions amongst the members of the Cybercrime Convention Expert Committee (T-CY) about complementing the Convention to regulate the issue of transborder access to data either with an amendment, a protocol, or a recommendation (6th Plenary Session of 23–24 November 2011). An ad-hoc sub-group on jurisdiction and transborder access to data and data flows composed of law enforcement experts was then created to study the matter.[41] In December 2012, the T-CY adopted the report of this expert group and gave it an additional mandate to prepare a first draft text of a possible protocol to the Convention.[42]

However, much time and bureaucracy are needed to amend a treaty and negotiate the necessary ratifications. Agreeing on soft law instruments requires less time and could do the job as well.[43] This prompted the T-CY to change its strategy and to favour a soft law approach. The limits for this approach were clear for all: as clarified by the preamble of the Convention, unilateral transborder access is 'an exception to the principle of territoriality' and Article 32 of the Convention (only) permits unilateral transborder access without the need for mutual assistance under two limited circumstances.[44]

The T-CY issued in December 2014 a Guidance Note on transborder access to data stored abroad when based on consent 'of the person who has the lawful authority to disclose the data to the Party through that computer system', as stated in Article 32(b) CC.[45]

Guidance Note No. 3 posits that there are divergencies in domestic practices concerning Article 32 CC and corresponding concerns about defence rights, privacy and sovereignty. This causes confusion among those who are on the receiving end of law enforcement authorities' request for cooperation, namely service providers which may have different applicable suits in different locations. There are

---

[40] See more in detail, Spiezia (n. 2) 4.
[41] Cybercrime Convention Committee (T-CY) Ad-Hoc Subgroup on Transborder Access and Jurisdiction, *Transborder access to data and jurisdiction: Options for further action by the T-CY* (Council of Europe, 2012), 3; Cybercrime Convention Committee (T-CY) Ad-Hoc Subgroup on Transborder Access and Jurisdiction, *Report of the Transborder Group for 2013* (Council of Europe, 2013), 3; Koops and Goodwin (n. 30) 57; Micheál O'Floinn, 'It wasn't all white light before Prism: Law enforcement practices in gathering data abroad, and proposals for further transnational access at the Council of Europe,' *Computer Law & Security Review* 29 (2013): 511.
[42] Koops and Goodwin (n. 30) 57. Subsequently, interested stakeholders (such as Google, Paypal, etc) and experts were invited to discuss the report in a 3 June 2013 hearing in the Council of Europe. See O'Floinn (n. 41) 511.
[43] Koops and Goodwin (n. 30) 10.
[44] Guidance Note 3 on Transborder Access (Article 32 Cybercrime Convention), 3.
[45] Guidance Note No. 3 on Transborder Access (Article 32 Cybercrime Convention), (8p), issued 3 December 2014, via rm.coe.int/16802e726a.

questions, for example, on what constitutes consent, lawfulness of consent, who could give it and how data protection obligations could be reconciled with one another.[46] In response, the Guidance Note wishes 'to correct misunderstandings regarding transborder access under this treaty and to reassure third parties'. Considering these, Guidance Note No. 3 offers no less than five clarifications.

First, Guidance Note No. 3 renders extended searches more flexible in an international context.

The Guidance Note starts with two 'typical situations' that illustrate the scope of Article 32(b). We learn that when suspects consent to it, Article 32(b) CC makes possible extended searches with a transborder dimension and Article 19 CC (limited to domestic extended searches) can be disregarded.[47]

Even more flexibility for extended transborder searches is offered in the Guidance Note when it asserts that Article 32(b) does not cover 'situations where the data are not stored in another Party or where it is uncertain where the data are located'. In these cases, we find ourselves in one of these grey area situations that are 'neither authorised, nor precluded' by the Convention as allegedly based on Article 39(3) CC. Because this provision, in the view of the Guidance Note, provides unbridled discretion to Member States to determine domestic application, there is this risk for them to revel in such a grey area, albeit they will have to assess the legitimacy of these unilateral situations in light of relevant domestic and international law and practices.[48] No further explanation is provided thereafter.

Second, Guidance Note No. 3 does not impose *a posteriori*-notifications. This has been a constant sticky subject considering that notification to concerned citizens is at the crux of data protection and human rights case law on surveillance,[49] and notification to concerned states is an element of good behaviour between states. The Guidance Note arguably attempts to sand off the sharp edges of unilateral measures by being careful not to create additional duties for domestic law enforcement authorities when investigating data abroad, such as by obliging them to notify other states when they accessed data abroad.[50]

---

[46] Koops and Goodwin (n. 30); O'Floinn (n. 41); Sieber and Neubert (n. 28) 275.

[47] We will come back to the Guidance Note's understanding of the relationship between CC Art 32(b) and the powers in CC Art 18 (domestic production orders) and CC Art 19 (extended searches to the domestic context) at the end of this section.

[48] Guidance Note 3, §3.2.

[49] Franziska Boehm and Paul De Hert, 'Notification, an important safeguard against the improper use of surveillance–finally recognized in case law and EU law,' *European Journal of Law and Technology* 3.3 (2012).

[50] The note further rationalises with claims that all Member States can be trusted in terms of human rights, so the obligation of notification of relevant authorities may be nice to have but not necessarily be an obligation. cf. Guidance Note 3, §3.1 and 3.3: 'As pointed out above, it is presumed that the Parties to the Convention form a community of trust and that rule of law and human rights principles are respected in line with art. 15 Budapest Convention. The rights of individuals and the interests of third parties are to be taken into account when applying the measure. Therefore, a searching Party may consider notifying relevant authorities of the searched Party (...) Article 32b does not require mutual assistance, and the Budapest Convention does not require a notification of the other Party. At the same time, the Budapest Convention does not exclude notification. Parties may notify the other Party if they deem it appropriate'.

If we revert to the text of Article 32(b) CC, we indeed see no notification requirement,[51] although one could legally presume that there should have been one if one considers the rudiments of data protection and international law *in pari materia*. The silence in the Convention on notification and the interpretation given in Guidance Note No. 3 is inconsistent with the principles the G8 adopted in 1999 on transborder access, which served as a precursor for Article 32(b) CC.[52] Therefore, while notification is not mandatory, unless the state presumably has interest in the information, it would have been a valuable addition (in hindsight) to Article 32(b)CC and to this Guidance Note.[53]

Third, Guidance Note No. 3 defines what constitutes *consent*. Consent, the note states, must be lawful and voluntary, which means 'the person providing access or agreeing to disclose may not be forced or deceived'.[54] The Guidance Note does not provide that explicit consent is required but observes that most countries require this.[55] In most countries a general agreement by a person to terms and conditions of an online service might not suffice as consent even if the general agreement includes disclosure to law enforcement authorities.[56] Without an express prohibition of said measure, it is not in contravention if a jurisdiction considers that a general agreement to terms of service would suffice for allowing such potential disclosures.[57]

Fourth, Guidance Note No. 3 clarifies *who* may give the required consent. The document answers with 'it depends': the answer is dependent on the circumstances, laws, and regulations applicable, and could be either a natural or legal person.[58] As to the legal capacity of service providers to provide the consent on behalf of the individual consumers, the Guidance Note provides that service providers are 'unlikely to be able to consent validly and voluntarily to disclosure of users' data under art. 32' – further stating that normally 'service providers will only be holders of such data; they will not control or own the data, and they will, therefore, not be in a position validly to consent'. It further notes that in criminal investigations express consent is often necessitated (Guidance Note 3, §3.6).[59] Law enforcement

---

[51] Koops and Goodwin (n. 30) 55.

[52] See G8, 'Principles on Transborder Access to Stored Computer Data'; Koops & Goodwin (n. 30) 55.

[53] As Koops and Goodwin quoted Gercke, 'with slight modifications, such a provision could ensure that affected states are aware of investigations taking place in their own territory. It would not prevent conflict with international law, but at least guarantee a certain degree of transparency', see Koops and Goodwin (n. 30) 55.

[54] Guidance Note 3, §3.4. Further, subject to domestic legislation, 'a minor may not be able to give consent, or persons because of mental or other conditions may also not be able to consent' (Guidance Note 3, §3.4).

[55] Guidance Note 3, §3.4.

[56] Guidance Note 3, §3.4.

[57] Sieber and Neubert (n. 28) 276. It follows then that while there is good reason to interpret Art 32(b) vis-à-vis consent narrowly and to require an informed, individual decision to disclose data, problems may still arise by virtue of this Guidance Note as to its domestic application.

[58] Guidance Note 3, §3.6.

[59] Guidance Note 3, §3.6.

agencies 'may be able to procure data transnationally by other methods, such as mutual legal assistance or procedures for emergency situations'. Nonetheless, there is no express prohibition or proscription of the practice. Thus, it gives enough space for contracting parties to act as they see fit and define at their own terms their domestic policies.[60]

Fifth, Guidance Note 3 tackles *where* the person providing consent should be. The Guidance Note provides that generally the person providing access is physically located in the territory of the requesting party.[61] However, Member States are left with the discretion to consider different scenarios that could arise and provide their own parameters. It is thus completely permissible that the person was not actually present in the territory on either or both instances of acceding to disclose and actually providing access.[62]

Guidance Note 3's broad understanding of consent basically frees the way for unilateral cross border access to computer data by assuming that *suspects* can legitimately consent (see the first clarification), and that *data subjects or their service providers* can consent (see the fourth clarification). Its interpretation of the unilateral powers defined in Article 32(b)CC bypasses the territorial limitations attached to the powers in Article 18 CC (domestic production orders), and Article 19 CC (extended searches to the domestic context). Based on the Note's provisions, requirements under Articles 18 and 19 CC can be dispensed with nor is mutual legal assistance necessary for computer data found in another party if a suspect or data subject consents to it and the data's location is known. Otherwise, either of Articles 18 or 19 CC apply. Practically speaking, law enforcement authorities are enabled to simply go directly to the service providers for access to this online evidence if circumstances warrant.[63]

To sum up, the 2014 Guidance Note No. 3 offers the broadest and most law enforcement friendly interpretation possible regarding transborder access to data based on consent.[64] The Note succeeds in its objective spelled out in its preamble to 'help Parties to take full advantage of the potential of the treaty with respect to transborder access to data'. However, it apparently does little to 'reassure third parties' because as it stands there is too much unbridled discretion for Member States to define the course. Needless to state, Guidance Note 3 on the interpretation of Article 32(b) of the Convention leaves many questions or concerns

---

[60] The Guidance Note is not directly saying that a service provider is *not* allowed to consent and disclose on behalf of the data subject and does not explicitly delve into data protection obligations on service providers. It is also not addressing the possibility for contracting parties to use a service provider's terms of service as a form of consent. That way, there remains an opportunity for contracting parties to provide otherwise in their respective domestic laws.

[61] Guidance Note 3, §3.8.

[62] Guidance Note 3, §3.8.

[63] Guidance Note 3, §3.7. To illustrate, see De Hert, Parlar and Thumfart (n. 33) 328–340.

[64] See Cybercrime Convention Committee (T-CY), *T-CY Assessment Report: The Mutual Legal Assistance Provisions of the Budapest Convention on Cybercrime* (Council of Europe, 2014), 123; De Hert, Parlar and Thumfart (n. 33) 328.

unanswered.[65] For the sake of clarity, we integrated all its 'clarifications' in the following rewriting of the text:

**Figure 2** Unofficial version of Article 32 as interpreted by the Council of Europe in 2014

> *Unofficial version Article 32 (on Transborder access) as interpreted by the Council of Europe in 2014 (made up by the authors)*
> A Party, without the authorisation of another Party:
> a) (...)
> b) may access or receive or carry out extended transborder searches, through a computer system in its territory, stored computer data located in another Party, if the Party obtains the lawful and voluntary consent of the person who has the lawful authority to disclose the data to the Party through that computer system. Each party can provide their own domestic guidelines and standards wherein consent in the purview of Article 32(b) <u>can mean the general agreement by a person to terms and conditions of an online service and there is no explicit prohibition for Parties to obtain the consent from a provider only and to ignore data protection aspects</u>"
>
> Provided, that no notification is required <u>to the other Party or the data subject</u> in cases where the consent is not obtained directly from him or her. Provided further, that the transborder access contemplated in this paragraph is not covered by art. 18 on domestic production orders, art. 19 on extended searches, and the relevant provisions of the Convention on international cooperation.
>
> Provided however, Article 32(b) does not cover situations where the data are not stored in another Party or where it is uncertain where the data are located, and in these cases Parties are not prohibited to carry out unilateral state actions outside the realm of the Convention.

## V. Guidance Note 10 and Use of Domestic Orders for Providers *not* in the Country (Step 3)

In 2017 the T-CY concentrated its interpretative work on Article 18 CC (on domestic production orders) in a tenth Guidance Note.[66] We recall that Article 18 CC is prima facie about domestic production orders issued for online evidence within the territory. The provision delineates and differentiates in a first paragraph to whom a production order within a territory can be issued (either persons or providers) and what can be asked: *computer data production orders* can be issued to *persons* and *subscriber data production orders* can be issued to *service providers*. The second paragraph of the provision defines what constitutes *subscriber information*, which is distinct from and less intrusive compared to other categories of data like traffic and content data.

According to the text of Article 18 CC, computer data production orders can only be sent to persons *within the territory* of the issuing party whilst subscriber data production orders can only be sent to service providers offering their services *in the territory of said issuing party*. The text does not seem to offer a broader basis for direct access or contacts by law enforcement officers to or with service providers abroad although, as mentioned above, there is a nascent

---

[65] See Marco Gercke, 'Understanding Cybercrime: a Guide for Developing Countries,' *International Telecommunication Union (Draft)* 89 (2011); Koops and Goodwin (n. 30) 58.

[66] Cybercrime Convention Committee (T-CY), Guidance Note10 Production orders for subscriber information (CC Art 18), adopted by the T-CY following the 16th Plenary by written procedure (28 February 2017), (13p.), via rm.coe.int/16806f943e, §1.

**Figure 3** Article 18 CC – Production Order

> **Article 18 CC – Production order**
> 1 Each Party shall adopt such legislative and other measures as may be necessary to empower its competent authorities to order:
> a) a person in its territory to submit specified computer data in that personas possession or control, which is stored in a computer system or a computer-data storage medium; and
> b) a service provider offering its services in the territory of the Party to submit subscriber information relating to such services in that service provider's possession or control.
> 2 The powers and procedures referred to in this article shall be subject to Articles 14 and 15.
> 3 For the purpose of this article, the term 'subscriber information' means any information contained in the form of computer data or any other form that is held by a service provider, relating to subscribers of its services other than traffic or content data and by which can be established:
> a) the type of communication service used, the technical provisions taken thereto and the period of service;
> b) the subscriber's identity, postal or geographic address, telephone and other access number, billing and payment information, available on the basis of the service agreement or arrangement;
> c) any other information on the site of the installation of communication equipment, available on the basis of the service agreement or arrangement.

practice of these authorities to approach service providers abroad directly to obtain information.[67]

We first discuss the Guidance Note 10's clarifications vis-à-vis subscriber data production orders organised in Article 18(1b) CC and defined in Article 18(3) CC. The Guidance Note first discusses the definitions of *subscriber* information and of *service*. By reading between the lines, however, one can discern an attempt to expand the notion of subscriber information defined in Article 18(3) VV.[68] Upon the suggestion from the final report of the T-CY Cloud Evidence Group (on which the Guidance Note was grounded), the Guidance Note gives subscriber information an interpretation that no longer limits it to static information that identifies a user, but extends it to all IP-addresses regardless of being static or dynamic.[69]

Also, who can be considered a 'service provider' in the sense of Article 18(1b) CC is equally given a serious interpretative extension. The Guidance Note states that domestic orders apply with respect to any service provider offering its services in the territory of the Party, *even if the provider is not present in the country*.[70] As long as said service providers have possession and/or control of the subscriber information

---

[67] We recall in this context that the Council of Europe itself in April 2008 discouraged the practice of direct contacts in its guidelines for the cooperation between law enforcement authorities and service providers and insisted on using the traditional framework of cooperation (on the Guidelines for the Cooperation between LEAs and Service Providers. See Koops and Goodwin (n. 30); Walden (n. 27) 59.

[68] CC Art 18 originally intended 'subscriber information' to mean 'information contained in the form of computer data or any other form that is held by a service provider, relating to subscribers of its services other than traffic or content data,' and by which can establish the following: (a) the type of communication service used, the technical provisions taken thereto and the period of service; (b) the subscriber's identity, postal or geographic address, telephone and other access number, billing and payment information, available on the basis of the service agreement or arrangement; and (c) any other information on the site of the installation of communication equipment, available on the basis of the service agreement or arrangement (CC Art 18.3). In other words, subscriber information is static information independent of any communication process or activity the user engages in.

[69] See Guidance Note 10, §3.2. cf. De Hert, Parlar and Sajfert (n. 3) 328. This stretches arguably what constitutes 'subscriber information' because dynamic IP addresses should already be considered 'traffic data' due to their dynamic nature and being already intrinsically produced and entangled in the communication itself.

[70] Guidance Note 10, §§3.2, 3.6.

being requested and they offer their services to the specified territory,[71] the Note does not deem this scenario as being 'extraterritorial' in nature but instead it is still considered a domestic order that could be issued by local authorities.[72]

Based on the foregoing, while the abovementioned seemingly innocuously pertains only to subscriber information, there is a creeping effect to expand applicability to non-static information and to providers who neither are legally nor physically present in the issuing party's territory.

**Figure 4** Unofficial version Article 18, §1b and 3 (on production orders) as interpreted in 2017

---

*Unofficial version Article 18, §1b and 3 (on production orders) as interpreted by the Council of Europe in 2017 (made up by the authors)*
1. Each Party shall adopt such legislative and other measures as may be necessary to empower its competent authorities to order: (…)
b. Any service provider offering its services in the territory of the Party, <u>even if the provider is neither physically or legally present in the country</u>, to submit subscriber information relating to such services in that service provider's possession or control.
2. (…)
3. subscriber information includes both static *and* <u>dynamic information, the latter of which are all the IP addresses associated with a user or data subject</u>

<u>Provided, that domestic subscriber information production orders shall suffice and mutual legal assistance or any other tool of international cooperation does not apply.</u>

---

## VI. Guidance Note 10: Providers Present in the Country Need to Give *all* Data (Step 4)

The same Guidance Note equally attempts to broaden the applicability and understanding on the issuance of computer data (domestic) production orders organised in Article 18(1a) CC. Here the Note's authors advance a simplistic argument: 'a provider' is 'a person'. Hence, next to sending subscriber data production orders to these service providers which provide services in the issuing Party's territory (Article 18(1b) CC), this interpretation opens also a possibility to confront the same providers with the more powerful computer data production orders in the sense of Article 18(1a) CC on the sole condition that this service provider is a person in the territory.

Such interpretative proposition is quite awkward considering Article 18 CC explicitly separating the provisions on persons and service providers into two separate paragraphs, which indicates as per rules of statutory construction, different treatments of the same. But based on the Note, service providers may now also be issued a production order for data other than subscriber information.[73]

---

[71] 'Persons are enabled to subscribe to the service providers' services without being blocked and there is a real and substantial connection to the subscribing persons, e.g. use of data in the conduct of the provider's activities, etc.' (Guidance Note No. 10, §3.2.
[72] Guidance Note 10, §3.3.
[73] The Cybercrime Convention Committee interprets 'specified computer data' in Art 18(1)(a) to be not limited to subscriber information alone but instead, may involve other forms of data such as traffic and even content data (Guidance Note 10, §3.1).

As a result, a production order within the territory could be issued despite the person not having possession of the 'specified computer data' within the specified territory, if said person could control such data from within the territory in question.[74] From that perspective, it becomes irrelevant where the data is located. Any loss of location would no longer pose any hurdle. The operative term would be 'control' because a production order can be issued for any data to any person if that person can still control the data from the specified territory of the relevant authorities. Said production order is still deemed a domestic order and no mutual legal assistance is necessary.[75]

We spell out these interpretations in a convention-like way. It suffices to compare with the official text version of Article 18 CC (see section V) to note the expansive dimensions:

**Figure 5** Unofficial version Article 18 (on production orders addressed to service providers) as interpreted by the Council of Europe in 2017

---

*Unofficial version Article 18 (on production orders addressed to service providers) as interpreted by the Council of Europe in 2017 (made up by the authors)*
1. Each Party shall adopt such legislative and other measures as may be necessary to empower its competent authorities to order:
a. persons and service providers in its territory to submit specified computer data in that providers possession or control, (…) and
b. service provider offering its services in the territory of the Party, even if the provider is not present in the country, to submit subscriber information relating to such services in that service provider's possession or control. Provided that "possession and control" refers to physical possession in the issuing Party's territory and/or situations in which data is produced outside of the person's physical possession but the person can nonetheless freely control production of the date from within the ordering Party's territory.
2. (…)
3. Subscriber information includes static *and* dynamic IP addresses

---

# VII. Second Additional Protocol: Building the Momentum from the Guidance Notes (Step 5)

In our introduction we mentioned that mid November 2021, the Council of Europe adopted the Second Additional Protocol to the Cybercrime Convention on enhanced cooperation and disclosure of electronic evidence. We will not expound on the features of the Protocol here but limit ourselves to some selective observations that are relevant in view of the preceding sections.

The Protocol consists of a preamble, four chapters including 25 articles. It builds up on the momentum brought by the earlier issued Guidance Notes and provides for direct cooperation with service providers and registrars, effective means to obtain subscriber information and traffic data, immediate co-operation in emergencies or joint investigations and subject to a system of human rights and rule of law guarantees, including data protection safeguards.

---

[74] Guidance Note 10, §3.1.
[75] Guidance Note, §3.4 provides a 'production order' under Art 18 is a domestic measure and is to be provided for under domestic criminal law. A 'production order' is constrained by the adjudicative and enforcement jurisdiction of the Party in which the order is granted.

The Second Additional Protocol's central idea is to establish a procedure that allows for direct cooperation between law enforcement authorities and service providers in another party's territory to obtain domain name registration and subscriber information, which coincidentally expands the original scope and coverage of Article 18 CC and validates the expansive interpretation offered by Guidance Notes 3 and 10. This is done in at least three ways.

First, the contentious issue tackled in Guidance Note 3 is the concept of consent vis-à-vis Article 32 CC – on who can give it and where it should be given – so such access to any evidence would not be under the penumbra of 'extraterritorial searches' that necessitate mutual legal assistance or any international cooperation mechanism. While Guidance Note 3 encouraged Member States to interpret consent in various expansive law enforcement-friendly ways, the Second Additional Protocol ultimately did not see fit to discuss it. Instead, it provided a straightforward directive for contracting parties to provide in their respective domestic legal systems mechanisms that allow law enforcement authorities to approach service providers directly for domain name registration and subscriber information. Contracting parties are also encouraged to minimise bureaucracies in their domestic procedures that may subject service providers to different liabilities in case of good faith compliance to production orders issued to them, such as exclusions of data protection obligations vis-à-vis notification of the data subject itself. In fact, the data subject is admittedly an afterthought. Although Article 14 of the Protocol may provide that data protection standards must apply, including transparency, notice and remedies to the data subject from both requesting and transferring parties, these safeguards remain subject to contracting parties' discretion and may be limited under unilaterally determined and defined circumstances. Any consent of the data subject is technically non-existent, and any remedy is limited to documentation and rectification of data.

Second, the Second Additional Protocol evolved further the delineation and differentiation between computer data production orders and subscriber information production orders under Guidance Note 10. At the outset, the Protocol does not completely disregard mutual legal assistance because direct cooperation is supposedly limited to types of data that are believed to be less intrusive. Therefore, there is a glaring direct proportional relationship between the type of data involved and the strictness of the enforcement mechanism to access it. In terms of domain registration and subscriber information that are believed to be the less intrusive yet important in criminal proceedings, the Protocol expands Article 18 CC in the same manner as Guidance Note 10 because law enforcement authorities can simply issue domestic production orders vis-à-vis this aforementioned information despite the service provider being located on another's territory (Articles 6 and 7). This is regardless of where the data is located. What matters is the possession and control of the service provider involved. And should direct cooperation fail for any reason, the requested party can 'give effect' to these orders if the service provider is in its territory regardless of where the data is located (Article 8). The requested party could also do the same for traffic data. These mechanisms seem innocuous but there is an obvious clincher. Like Guidance Notes 3 and 10, location of data is inconsequential in all these provisions although it has territoriality and jurisdiction repercussions. Moreover, like Guidance Note 10, the Protocol expands the scope of new competences by widening the coverage of what constitutes 'subscriber information', which includes data traditionally considered traffic data. Although contracting parties are free to give reservations, unbridled discretion is served on a silver platter to enable wider definitions of these 'less intrusive' data that pose a potential risk and lack of effective guarantees vis-à-vis data protection.

Third, notification of the contracting party on whose territory the service provider or data is located has never been provided in the Guidance Notes. In other words, direct cooperation does not need its participation. The Protocol seemingly provides something positive in this direction because there is now the option for a contracting party to receive notification simultaneously if an order is sent to a service provider found in its territory. There is even the option for the provider to consult the receiving party on certain circumstances. However, this remains discretionary and problematic for two reasons. First, the requesting party can opt to instruct the service provider not to disclose and the Protocol also provides that any notification requirement should not be counterproductive to the efficiency of the procedure. Second, the notification requirement never applies to the contracting party on whose territory the data is found or stored. In other words, location of data is irrelevant.

## VIII. Council of Europe and European Union as Sounding Boards

Considering the abovementioned circumstances on how the Council of Europe successfully transitioned changes in policy from soft law to treaty, it is interesting to look also at the European Union for a better perspective. Within the Union it is the European Commission that drives and initiates the law-making process. Between the period covering the drafting plenaries of the Council of Europe for the Second Additional Protocol, the European Commission published its own e-evidence proposals (in April 2018) including *a proposed regulation for European Production and Preservation Orders* as well as *a proposed directive* supplementary thereto, which creates within the Union the same central idea of direct cooperation with service providers, including the establishment of legal representatives of service providers within the EU which could be served with orders.[76]

The co-existence of both trajectories is not mere coincidence. The T-CY Secretariat emphasised that these EU proposals were inspired by its work,[77] and

---

[76] Council of Europe, 'Legal Opinion on Budapest Cybercrime Convention:', 1–2. See also Depauw (n. 1) 64.

[77] Council of Europe, 'Legal Opinion on Budapest Cybercrime Convention', 2.

vice versa. As a result, the EU proposals also minimise the required bureaucratic process by omitting the need to go through the traditional process of mutual legal assistance.[78] There would be no multiple exchanges between many hands but coordination and access shall be directly between the legal representatives to the authority requesting the data.[79] The main idea is that certificates of judicial orders will be transmitted directly to the legal representatives of online service providers. These will be obliged to respond within ten days or, in urgent cases, within six hours.

In terms of their respective work on cross-border access to online evidence, these regional organisations are one another's sounding boards.[80] Needless to state, the two organisations have a unique relationship wherein they influence each other on their respective policies.[81]

Elsewhere we have characterised their relationship in terms of policy entrepreneurship, rent seeking behaviour and rational choice institutionalism.[82] For the purposes of the present chapter however, it is apparent that how these two organisations move forward hinges on what the other may do. There are similarities in their decisions and policymaking, likewise mirroring concepts and ideas the other one creates. We see many examples. First, there is the e-evidence proposal from the EU referring to the European Production and Preservation Orders which came directly after formal work has been started in the Council of Europe and T-CY to have Guidance Notes and the Second Additional Protocol in respect of cross-border exchange and transborder access to online evidence in criminal matters. Second, we can point to the provisions of the Second Additional Protocol, which does not only involve expansion of certain concepts, such as subscriber information, with respect to direct cooperation between law enforcement authorities and service providers, which is more in tune with the scope of the European Preservation and Production Orders, but also terminologies and characteristics that are commonly found in Union language (ie European Investigation Order) are made apparent in the preliminarily agreed provisions on 'giving effect' to orders through the introduction of time limits, 'orders', horizontal cooperation, etc in the Second Additional Protocol.

After the Lisbon Treaty setting up the final (constitutional) architecture of the Union, there was the expectation that the formulation of a European criminal law policy agenda would be dominated by Brussels (European Union) and no longer

---

[78] See Proposed Regulation on the European Preservation and Production Orders Arts 2, 4–7.

[79] See Proposed Regulation on the European Preservation and Production Orders Arts 4–7. This also covers direct access through a seized device without needing to go through the service provider itself.

[80] The T-CY explicitly provides that it shall take note of the developments within the European Union as stated above.

[81] In fact, when the Council of Europe came up with 2008 Guidelines as stated above, the European Union's Justice and Home Affairs Council recommended in November 2008 that the European Commission work on the basis of the said guidelines adopted by the Council of Europe whilst taking note of eight specific recommendations. See Bigo et al. (n. 39) 32.

[82] Paul De Hert and Angela Aguinaldo, 'A leading role for the EU in drafting criminal law powers? Use of the Council of Europe for policy laundering,' (London: SAGE Publications, 2019), 99–106.

by Strasbourg (Council of Europe). For many reasons this scenario did not realise itself. The Council of Europe with its lack of resources and binding law instruments, but with the opaque policy structures of all international organisations and the participation of key players like the US with the Cybercrime Convention, seems to suit certain agendas better than the European Union. With a simple cost-benefit analysis, too much constitutionalising and checks and balances on decision procedures might not be so rationally effective. Thus, the rational choice institutionalism was undeniable in this scenario. While the Council of Europe began the discussion in forwarding direct cooperation vis-à-vis transborder access to digital evidence, all the EU needed to do first is take a back seat and watch how the process of green lighting prevailed whilst observing the various oppositions and roadblocks the CoE encountered from different stakeholders. And when the time was right, the EU then came out with its own policies that integrate its constitutional framework and protections that further gave the impetus to choose the CoE as the favoured forum for concretised policies such as the Second Additional Protocol.

## IX. Looking Back at the Role of the Guidance Notes and their Impact on International Law

Altogether the interpretative work of the Council of Europe in the past decade has introduced more unilateralism in the interpretation of the 2001 Cybercrime Convention based on cooperation. The Guidance Notes have provided a radical change in perspective vis-à-vis cross-border access to online evidence by redefining domestic production orders and providing direct cooperation with service providers, as well as legitimising unilateralism.

The Guidance Notes were quite transparent about their attempt to push the envelope and to contribute to an obvious paradigm shift vis-à-vis production orders and transborder access to data from what was believed previously to be 'a contested practice'. Given that it purports to embody 'the common understanding as to the contracting parties' use of Article 18 CC for example, it signals 'a strong official statement of the parties' policies and should lead to improved cross-border cooperation between criminal justice authorities and service providers'. The Guidance Notes, one author observes, were a kind of proclamation from the contracting parties produced to constitute *opinio juris* and thus create customary law.[83]

---

[83] While this is expedient from the perspective of criminal justice, it also means that the Parties to the Convention will limit their exclusive right to exercise jurisdiction. The T-CY hastens to add that '[a]greement to this Guidance Note does not entail consent to the extraterritorial service or enforcement of a domestic production order issued by another State nor creates new obligations or relationships between the Parties'. Tomáš Minárik, 'Cybercrime Convention Committee Adopts Guidance Note on Production Orders for Subscriber Information,' in *The NATO Cooperative Cyber Defence Centre of Excellence*, 1.

This last observation is a point well taken. International instruments on transborder access to online data could be further developed based on either treaty law or customary law.[84] As discussed, the 2001 Cybercrime Convention provided almost no explicit treaty basis for permissible transnational access to data. The Guidance Notes tried to fuel this other motor of international law, namely customary international law. This branch of international law could indeed be used to justify transborder access if the existence of a general practice and corresponding *opinio juris* could be shown.[85] These two elements could reinforce each other to prove that customary law as regards transborder access exists. Guidance Notes come into play at this precise point, and they perform a double function: they reinforce a certain understanding of both general practice and *opinio juris* and they simultaneously contribute to the formation of general practice and *opinio juris*.[86] Thereafter, through the Second Additional Protocol the Council of Europe was able to cover all the bases by legal justification through treaty.

To push this analysis a bit further it is useful to contrast two, not converging, understandings of the Cybercrime Convention. Most commentators would agree with the following elements of interpretation of the Convention: it is silent on transnational powers; it only envisages cooperation with private partners at the national level, not at the international level; it is based on the territoriality principle and on the idea that data can be located in space; and it does not offer 'light' MLA procedure for requests like obtaining subscriber data; and the text of this convention is bereft of any provision that would permit law enforcement authorities to directly contact foreign service providers in pursuit of cross-border access and exchange of online evidence in criminal matters.

Most commentators would also agree with the view that the Cybercrime Convention is, as most treaties were in the twentieth century, poor on defence rights as well as on privacy and data protection.[87] Authors like Tosoni[88] and

---

[84] Sieber and Neubert (n. 28) 265.

[85] Sieber and Neubert (n. 28) 265.

[86] With respect to general practice, initial studies and/or surveys of the Council of Europe and the UNODC prior to the issuance of Guidance Note on Production Orders would show that while most respondent parties admit to exercising cross-border investigations vis-à-vis online data, there is no consistency as to the conditions and extent of the practice (Sieber and Neubert (n. 28) 265.). Based on the responses given to the survey of the T-CY between 2009 to 2010, for example, there are different conditions and practices exercised by law enforcement authorities vis-à-vis transborder searches, which in many cases, have evolved ever since (*Transborder access to data and jurisdiction: Options for further action by the T-CY*, 29). Thus, there is the lack of generality necessary for the formation of custom. However, the Guidance Notes could prove themselves to be the much needed game changer. Provided with a general interpretation that could harmonise practice among the contracting parties, one could later gain a generality in practice sufficient to form custom.

With regard to the element of *opinio juris*, the Guidance Notes can serve as building blocks to prove a unified front as regards transborder access to data. Should the Cybercrime Convention Committee be able to show a widespread acceptance of the Guidance Notes by the contracting parties, especially those regarding transborder access and production orders, then the existence of *opinio juris* necessary to customary international law shall be proven.

[87] Jonathan Clough, 'A world of difference: the Budapest convention of cybercrime and the challenges of harmonisation,' *Monash UL Rev.* 40 (2014): 698, 710.

[88] Tosoni (n. 1) 1197–1214.

Van De Heyning[89] try to move against the current and point at the small references in the text of the original 2001 Convention to the need to respect principles of human rights law and data protection law, but both authors have great difficulty in showing the efficiency of the Convention in getting these subtle messages across and are faced with contradicting practices by the law enforcement community.[90]

We tend to follow Jonathan Clough, for whom the Cybercrime Convention drafted more than two decades ago is hardly any better than its contemporaries on issues like data protection, defence rights and human rights. The references to human rights and due process that *are* incorporated in the Convention are no more than aspirational statements that set no specific or hard standards. For Clough this is not a lone curiosity but illustrative of a mechanism of flexible harmonisation, a process of saying less rather than more and of facilitating instrumentalist law enforcement goals, but omitting necessary detail for due process and other fundamental rights.[91]

Guidance Notes perfectly fit this mechanism of flexible harmonisation. Rather than filling in the detail and harmonising understandings on human rights respect, they have used the interpretative void to harmonise in the opposite direction and create even more flexibility for governments and their law enforcement authorities. Informality and invisibility of 'government networks' like the T-CY, 'marrying hard and soft power and using information, persuasion and socialization'[92] are key in understanding contemporary global law agendas, Mitsilegas observes.[93] This scholar gives a detailed account of the role and work of the Financial Action Task Force (FATF), an ad hoc body, established by the G7 in 1989 under the auspices of the OECD. He highlights the productive soft law output of this FATF, taking the form of Recommendations, that cover a wide range of aspects of the fight against money laundering. The success of these recommendations puts a different light on the 'soft law'. How 'soft' should we call these recommendations when their influence on the development of EU anti- money laundering law is more than considerable? Informal law-making in selective network-settings as a precondition for traditional law-making[94] seems to be the rule in global law settings.

---

[89] Catherine Van De Heyning, 'The Boundaries of Jurisdiction in Cybercrime and Constitutional Protection: The European Perspective,' in *The Internet and Constitutional Law: The Protection of Fundamental Rights and Constitutional Adjudication in Europe*, ed. Oresto Pollicino and Graziella Romeo (London: Routledge, 2018), 26–47.

[90] Especially memorable are Luca Tosoni's criticisms on Guidance Note 10, and his appeal to the principle of effectiveness in the interpretation of treaties; Tosoni (n. 1) 1212.

[91] Clough (n. 87) 709.

[92] Valsamis Mitsilegas and Niovi Vavoula, 'The evolving EU anti-money laundering regime: challenges for fundamental rights and the rule of law,' *Maastricht journal of European and comparative law* 23.2 (2016): 264.

[93] Valsamis Mitsilegas, Peter Alldridge, and Leonidas Cheliotis, *Globalisation, criminal law and criminal justice: theoretical, comparative and transnational perspectives* (London: Bloomsbury Publishing, 2015), 153–198; Mitsilegas and Vavoula (n. 92) 263–264.

[94] 'Informal law-making is defined as dispensing with certain formalities traditionally linked to international law having to do with output, process, or the actors involved'. Mitsilegas and Vavoula (n. 92) 264.

Delerue offers a complementary analysis, this time from the perspective of international law with regard to cyberspace. State practice on the regulation of cyber operations shows that states are more inclined to discuss non-binding norms than those of a legally binding nature. This is true at discussions at UN level, and in other international organisations and other fora, such as the Organization for Security and Co-operation in Europe (OSCE), the G20 and the Shanghai Cooperation Organisation (SCO).[95] Striking is Delerue's observation that this soft law production of non-legally binding norms is only in some cases a reflection of binding norms, providing an expression on how they should be interpreted. 'However, most norms are completely new and disconnected from existing binding norms, and thus are disconnected from the question of the application of norms of international law to cyber-space and cyber operations.'[96]

The remarks of these two authors echo recent historical analysis of Western international criminal cooperation at the end of the nineteenth century by authors such as Wouter Klem and Beatrice de Graaf.[97] Political inspired attacks either by anarchist or others (nationalist, nihilist, ...) forced police forces to act. Growing mobility of suspects (or rather, rumours about their international mobility and networking) forced countries to look beyond borders. Spain stood out as a country that approached 'the international question' most open-mindedly. Its proposals to collaborate more closely and to harmonise rules based on a treaty were, however, no success. They were met with distrust by 'liberal' states such as the UK and France that feared abuse of political crimes-oriented regulation by less liberal states such as Turkey, Russia and the Austrian state. The outcome was policy rather than law or treaty-making: informal support for police efforts to improve data exchange and collaborations, but hardly any formal parliamentary supported changes to law. Only when these green lit practices were more firmly established, when trust in the expertise of the police 'to handle the transnational' grew, were steps taken towards some international codification.

In his *The Will to Knowledge* Michel Foucault famously writes about the desire of power to work invisibly to be acceptable.[98] Global law making has well understood the message.[99] New cooperation methods and needs are tested out 'in the grey', propelled or sanctioned by political and expert opinions before they are

---

[95] François Delerue, 'Reinterpretation or contestation of international law in cyberspace?,' *Israel Law Review* 52.3 (2019): 315–316.

[96] Delerue (n. 95) 315–316.

[97] Wouter Klem, *De antiterroristen: De Europese strijd tegen het anarchisme 1890-1914* (New York: Prometheus, 2022); Beatrice de Graaf and Wouter Klem, 'Joining the international war against anarchism: The Dutch police and its push towards transnational cooperation, 1880–1914,' in *Shaping the International Relations of the Netherlands, 1815-2000*, eds. Ruud Van Dijk et al. (London: Routledge, 2018).

[98] Michel Foucault, 'Histoire de la sexualité. 1. La volonté de savoir. Paris (Gallimard) 1976,' (1976).

[99] Compare with a more naive vision of global law, Paul De Hert, 'Globalisation, crime and governance. Transparency, accountability and participation as principles for global criminal law,' in *Transitional Justice and its public spheres: engagement, legitimacy and contestation*, eds. Chrisje Brants and Susanna Karstedt (Oxford: Hart Publishing, 2017), 91–124.

deemed fit for more traditional law-making processes. The presence of a multitude of international and regional actors created in the second half of the twentieth century has only accelerated and simplified this process. Simply stated, there is today more grey than ever before in the slipstream of the multilevel governance-mechanism that has been developed.

## X. Conclusion: A Going Concern for Policy Laundering

This chapter discusses the distinct developments within the Council of Europe as regards the cross-border exchange and transborder access to online evidence in criminal matters which evinces the important role the Council of Europe plays in terms of policy laundering. We discussed the leading role of the Council of Europe as regards international cooperation in criminal matters as well as matters involving cyberspace and cybercrime. We noted that the often overlooked role and influence of the G8 on how the Cybercrime Convention evolved, particularly through the leadership and normative power the US exercises in such forum.

The chapter then turned to the 2001 Cybercrime Convention (CC) and its expert committee, the T-CY. Mutual legal assistance is provided by the Cybercrime Convention as the traditional route for cross-border exchange and transborder access to online evidence. The Convention and its Explanatory Report were explicit in mentioning that the Convention does not contemplate transborder access in general because there has been no agreement therein yet among the parties and no experience thus far. At most, the exception would be Article 32 CC which concerns two scenarios. Therefore, there is a small opening in the original Cybercrime Convention to unilateralism, inflated by the Explanatory Report to the Convention that refused to prohibit unilateral state actions not foreseen in the Convention.

After the turn of the century a not so hidden practice developed of law enforcement authorities engaging in direct cooperation with foreign service providers or granting transborder access in one way or another. The Cybercrime Convention did not seem to be playing any relevant role here. In discussions, these authorities were quick to point out the ineffectiveness and delays encountered through traditional mutual legal assistance procedures. At the level of policymaking within the CoE there was a consensus to come up with either an amendment, revision or protocol to the Cybercrime Convention to address these concerns. However, because amendments would take time and the needed agreement of the contracting parties, the T-CY gave priority to working with soft law instruments.

Important to the discussion were Guidance Notes Nos. 3 and 10 on transborder access (Article 32 CC) and domestic production orders (Article 18 CC) respectively. These Guidance Notes admittedly offer paradigm shifts and loose interpretations of existing provisions of the Cybercrime Convention that are law enforcement friendly but risky in terms of data protection, defence rights and even state considerations.

In 2021 the Second Additional Protocol was adopted. It built on the momentum made by the Guidance Notes to push changes in policy even further. Through treaty, different expanded interpretations found in the Guidance Notes were validated. The central idea of direct cooperation was concretised, the expansion of subscriber information was allowed, contracting parties are authorised to work together to operationalise orders to compel service providers to issue the data needed, while minimising important concepts such as consent, the rights of the data subject, the importance of state participation and location of data.

Considering these developments, how then should one make sense of these Guidance Notes? We connect insights from literature about informal international law making, network governance and global criminal law agendas. Analysing the two regional organisations alongside each other, it would be erroneous to consider that their respective efforts occur independently of one another, or that the Council of Europe can compete with the European Union in terms of criminal law regulation. In this specific area, the Council of Europe was skillfully used as and has offered to function as a regulatory sandbox, or testing environment, for global criminal law making in areas where the European Union was not feeling confident enough.

While there already is the Second Additional Protocol, the Guidance Notes were a gamechanger in the manner in which they are described to embody the mutual understanding (being careful not to explicitly say 'practice') by state parties. Thus, they may be utilised later for the purpose of establishing custom. If so, together with the Second Additional Protocol, what we have based in 'custom' is now based in treaty to proceed with unilateral cross-border exchange and transborder access to online evidence in criminal matters.

Nonetheless, there are still issues and concerns that the Council of Europe need to iron out. The Protocol so far has not and shall not make up for 20 years of unregulated law enforcement initiatives towards foreign service providers and the lack of any data protection oversight on behalf of concerned nations and individuals. The Council of Europe, through the T-CY, has pushed the envelope on what is allowed. While it has been at the forefront of tackling international cooperation in criminal matters, discussing important issues and solutions to handling cyberspace and cybercrime in general, the Council of Europe has now been the enabling forum for law enforcement authorities to get what they supposedly need to counter crimes involving online evidence. However, we do not live in a Machiavellian society. There should be an assurance that their ends do not justify the questionable means they have been pursuing so far. Indeed, we are all in favour of changing the rules of the game if necessary but without losing sight of non-negotiables such as the needed protection and promotion of data protection and fundamental human rights. Further, it does not suffice that commitments to these are mentioned. Motherhood statements at the end of the day are just motherhood statements. What is more important is that these non-negotiables are operationalised and followed. Additionally, loose ends ought to be tied as regards long running issues on sovereignty, jurisdiction, etc. which shall serve as the foundations and rudiments to cross-border access to online evidence. These issues should not be swept under the rug in the name of convenience and efficiency. Thus, we continue to enjoin policymakers to keep these consequences in contemplation whilst they carry on in changing the rules on transnational access to online evidence. We do not reserve this for the Council of Europe alone. As mentioned earlier, forums bounce off each other in their policies, eg the Council of Europe and European Union keeping tab of each other's policies, the G8 being influential in their guidelines, etc. Hence, these forums should make conscientious decisions that do not solely push efficacy and efficiency forward in criminal prosecutions and investigations, but likewise find balance with competing values, rudiments and norms.

# References

Aguinaldo, Angela and Paul de Hert. 'European Law Enforcement and Us Data Companies: A Decade of Cooperation Free from Law.' 1–16, 2020.

Benoît-Rohmer, Florence and Heinrich Klebes. *Council of Europe Law: Towards a Pan-European Legal Area*. Council of Europe, 2005.

Bigo, Didier, Gertjan Boulet, Caspar Bowden, Sergio Carrera, Julien Jeandesboz and Amandine Scherrer. 'Fighting Cybercrime and Protecting Privacy in the Cloud.' Brussels: European Parliament's Policy Department for Citizens' Rights and Constitutional Affairs. www.europarl.europa.eu/RegData/etudes/etudes/join/2012/462509/IPOL-LIBE_ET%282012%29462509_EN.pdf.

Boehm, Franziska and Paul De Hert. 'Notification, an Important Safeguard against the Improper Use of Surveillance – Finally Recognized in Case Law and Eu Law.' *European Journal of Law and Technology* 3 no. 3 (2012).

Broadhurst, Roderic. 'Developments in the Global Law Enforcement of Cyber-Crime.' *Policing: An International Journal of Police Strategies & Management* (2006).

Clough, Jonathan. 'A World of Difference: The Budapest Convention of Cybercrime and the Challenges of Harmonisation.' *Monash UL Rev.* 40 (2014): 698.

de Graaf, Beatrice and Wouter Klem. 'Joining the International War against Anarchism: The Dutch Police and Its Push Towards Transnational Cooperation, 1880–1914.' In *Shaping the International Relations of the Netherlands, 1815–2000*, edited by Ruud Van Dijk, Samuël Kruizinga, Vincent Kuitenbrouwer and Rimko Van der Maar, 56–79. London: Routledge, 2018.

De Hert, Paul. 'Globalisation, Crime and Governance. Transparency, Accountability and Participation as Principles for Global Criminal Law.' In *Transitional Justice and Its Public Spheres: Engagement, Legitimacy and Contestation*, edited by Chrisje Brants and Susanna Karstedt, 91–123. Oxford: Hart Publishing, 2017.

De Hert, Paul and Angela Aguinaldo. 'A Leading Role for the Eu in Drafting Criminal Law Powers? Use of the Council of Europe for Policy Laundering.' London: SAGE Publications, 2019.

De Hert, Paul, Cihan Parlar and Juraj Sajfert. 'The Cybercrime Convention Committee's 2017 Guidance Note on Production Orders: Unilateralist Transborder Access to Electronic Evidence Promoted Via Soft Law.' *Computer law & security review* 34 no. 2 (2018): 327–336.

De Hert, Paul, Cihan Parlar and Johannes Thumfart. 'Legal Arguments Used in Courts Regarding Territoriality and Cross-Border Production Orders: From Yahoo Belgium to Microsoft Ireland.' *New Journal of European Criminal Law* 9 (2018): 326–352.

Delerue, François. 'Reinterpretation or Contestation of International Law in Cyberspace?'. *Israel Law Review* 52 no. 3 (2019): 295–326.

Depauw, Sofie. 'Electronic Evidence in Criminal Matters: How About E-Evidence Instruments 2.0?'. *EuCLR European Criminal Law Review* 8 no. 1 (2018): 62–82.

Foucault, Michel. 'Histoire De La Sexualité. 1. La Volonté De Savoir. Paris (Gallimard) 1976.' (1976).

Gercke, Marco. 'Understanding Cybercrime: A Guide for Developing Countries.' *International Telecommunication Union (Draft)* 89 (2011): 93.

Hailbronner, Michaela. 'Beyond Legitimacy: Europe's Crisis of Constitutional Democracy.' In *Constitutional Democracy in Crisis?*, edited by Mark Graber, Sanford Levinson and Mark Tushnet. Oxford: Oxford University Press, 2018.

Hart, Jeffrey A. 'The G8 and the Governance of Cyberspace.' In *New Perspectives on Global Governance*, edited by John Kirton, Michele Fratianni and Paolo Savona, 137–151. London: Routledge, 2017.

Hayes, Ben, Julien Jeandesboz, Francesco Ragazzi, Stephanie Simon and Valsamis Mitsilegas. 'The Law Enforcement Challenges of Cybercrime: Are We Playing Catch Up?'. Brussels: European Parliament's Policy Department for Citizens' Rights and Constitutional Affairs. www.europarl.europa.eu/thinktank/en/document.html?reference=IPOL_STU (2015)536471.

Hopkins, Shannon L. 'Cybercrime Convention: A Positive Beginning to a Long Road Ahead.' *J. High Tech. L.* 2 (2003): 101.

Hosein, Gus. 'Policy Laundering, and Other Policy Dynamics.' *Cyberwar, netwar and the revolution in military affairs* (2006): 228–241.

Klem, Wouter. *De Antiterroristen: De Europese Strijd Tegen Het Anarchisme 1890–1914*. New York: Prometheus, 2022.

Koops, Bert-Jaap and Morag Goodwin. 'Cyberspace, the Cloud, and Cross-Border Criminal Investigation: The Limits and Possibilities of International Law.' (2014).

Minárik, Tomáš. 'Cybercrime Convention Committee Adopts Guidance Note on Production Orders for Subscriber Information.' In *The NATO Cooperative Cyber Defence Centre of Excellence*.

Mitsilegas, Valsamis, Peter Alldridge and Leonidas Cheliotis. *Globalisation, Criminal Law and Criminal Justice: Theoretical, Comparative and Transnational Perspectives*. London: Bloomsbury Publishing, 2015.

Mitsilegas, Valsamis and Niovi Vavoula. 'The Evolving Eu Anti-Money Laundering Regime: Challenges for Fundamental Rights and the Rule of Law.' *Maastricht journal of European and comparative law* 23 no. 2 (2016): 261–293.

O'Floinn, Micheál. 'It Wasn't All White Light before Prism: Law Enforcement Practices in Gathering Data Abroad, and Proposals for Further Transnational Access at the Council of Europe.' *Computer Law & Security Review* 29 (2013): 610–615.

Osula, Anna-Maria. 'Remote Search and Seizure in Domestic Criminal Procedure: Estonian Case Study.' *International Journal of Law and Information Technology* 24 (2016): 343–373.

Peers, Steve. 'Mutual Recognition and Criminal Law in the European Union: Has the Council Got It Wrong.' *Common Market L. Rev.* 41 (2004): 5.
Pradillo, Juan Carlos Ortiz. 'Fighting against Cybercrime in Europe: The Admissibility of Remote Searches in Spain.' *Eur. J. Crime Crim. L. & Crim. Just.* 19 (2011): 363.
Rodriguez, Katitza, Danny O'Brian, and Maryant Fernandez. 'Behind the Octopus: The Hidden Race to Dismantle Global Law Enforcement Privacy Protections.' 2018. www.eff.org/deeplinks/2018/08/behind-octopus-hidden-race-dismantle-global-law-enforcement-privacy-protections.
Seger, Alexander. 'E-Evidence and Access to Data in the Cloud Results of the Cloud Evidence Group of the Cybercrime Convention Committee.' In *Handling and Exchanging Electronic Evidence across Europe*, 35–41. Cham: Springer, 2018.
Sieber, Ulrich and Carl-Wendelin Neubert. 'Transnational Criminal Investigations in Cyberspace: Challenges to National Sovereignty.' *Max Planck Yearbook of United Nations Law Online* 20 (2017): 239–321.
Spiezia, Filippo. 'International Cooperation and Protection of Victims in Cyberspace: Welcoming Protocol Ii to the Budapest Convention on Cybercrime.' Paper presented at the ERA Forum, 2022.
Tosoni, Luca. 'Rethinking Privacy in the Council of Europe's Convention on Cybercrime.' *Computer Law & Security Review* 34 no. 6 (2018): 1197–214.
Tosza, Stanisław. 'Internet Service Providers as Law Enforcers and Adjudicators. A Public Role of Private Actors.' *Computer Law & Security Review* 43 (2021): 105614.
Van De Heyning, Catherine. 'The Boundaries of Jurisdiction in Cybercrime and Constitutional Protection: The European Perspective.' In *The Internet and Constitutional Law: The Protection of Fundamental Rights and Constitutional Adjudication in Europe*, edited by Oresto Pollicino and Graziella Romeo. London: Routledge, 2018.
Walden, Ian. 'Accessing Data in the Cloud: The Long Arm of the Law Enforcement Agent.' In *Privacy and Security for Cloud Computing*, edited by Siani Pearson and George Yee, 45–71. Cham: Springer, 2013.
———. 'Crime and Security in Cyberspace.' *Cambridge Review of International Affairs* 18 (2005): 51–68.
———. 'Law Enforcement Access to Data in Clouds.' In *Cloud Computing Law*, edited by Christopher Millard, 285–310. Oxford: Oxford University Press, 2013.
Wall, David. *Crime and Deviance in Cyberspace*. London: Routledge, 2017.
Weber, Amalie M. 'The Council of Europe's Convention on Cybercrime.' *Berkeley Technology Law Journal* 18 (2003): 425–446.

# 9

## 'Privacy in the Resilient State of the Human Condition'

### *Closing Remarks at the Computers, Privacy and Data Protection Conference*

WOJCIECH WIEWIÓROWSKI*

Dear esteemed friends, colleagues, dear participants from near and afar,

I greet you online today, for I cannot be with you in person.

It is funny how quickly times change. A year ago, it was normal to be participating online. At the time, little else was possible. Today, times are changing again, and online participation is going back to being the exception, rather than the rule.

While it is magnificent to be able to interact and share moments with people in person again, a part of me is struck by how quickly our norms and etiquettes in our daily lives can actually change. It makes me realise how much our reality and paradigms are in fact transitory.

This truth for me is perfectly reflected in this year's theme of the CPDP conference: 'Data Protection and Privacy in Transitional Times'.

The last two years have brought with them many transitions. So many of our environments have been reimagined and redefined, and together with them our approaches to data protection and privacy.

Life, as we know it, has changed. It has transitioned; it is transitional.

Yet, throughout the course of the pandemic, and, also throughout the course of the ongoing war in Ukraine, there has been one large constant.

This constant has been, and still is, the resilient state of the human condition.

In our papers and conferences, we talk a lot about enforcement; about the powers of data protection authorities; about the impact of data transfers on current business models; about the use of algorithms in innovation. But, sometimes we get

* European Data Protection Supervisor, Belgium.

caught up in this noise. Sometimes we lose sight of what we are fundamentally protecting at the end of the day: the rights of people.

In many ways, this recognition of the individual is thankfully embedded in the structure of the current data protection framework. But, sometimes we forget that as people we are not static. Instead, we are dynamic. We can be vulnerable, we can be weak, but we can also be resilient; strong; united.

But, what recent times have shown us is that people can also be influenced, or deprived of choices and opportunities.

Insights from behavioural economics and behavioural science have shown us that just as easily as nudge theory or subconscious bias can be used to promote good; they can also be used to promote alternative interests.

One must think of the growing use of dark patterns on the internet; the cunning design of certain cookie banners that subconsciously influence users to act in one way or another.

Or, one can think of the effects of targeted advertising, and how the use of pervasive profiling can lead to an asymmetry of power between the data subject and the data controller, who can infer things about the data subject that the data subject may not even be able to infer about themselves.

One thing that life has reminded us of over the last few years is that the human condition is vulnerable in so many ways.

But, for me, vulnerability can often simply mean a lack of choice. Whether this concerns people who have to flee war and civil unrest, or women who are striving for education in oppressive regimes, it is often the lack of choice that turns vulnerability into something that is paralysing.

Which brings me to the realisation that in fast-changing times, where we have competing priorities and exponential levels of technological development; there is an even greater need to address the vulnerability of people.

To address vulnerability means to give people real choices, real opportunities and sincere opinions. Because this in itself builds the resilience of people.

At the same time, I believe the ability to adapt and reflect in such changing conditions is what makes the human mind unique.

Some have said that the human mind is nothing but a form of computation; an information processing system that can be replicated by a machine. Indeed, such was the reasoning of Alan Turing, who argued that any symbolic algorithm executed by a human can be replicated by what is called a 'Turing machine'. Wiener's 'Cybernetics' also attempts to explain a systematic functioning of the brain.

But, I believe that the cognition and consciousness that humans have is unique. Many philosophers actually make great cases for why computers will never achieve such consciousness and cognition.

Of course, there might come a day where we are confronted with 'super-intelligent AI', whose intellect exceeds our ability to cognitively perform in all domains. And then, we might philosophically analyse whether such AI would have the same vulnerability or resilience that humans have, or whether such AI would be 'moral' at all.

But, I think these days are yet to come. Amidst all of the technological innovations, humankind is still unique. It contains in it something not replicable in machines or AI – a consciousness otherwise unfound.

It is this consciousness that I draw your focus to today. Because when we speak about data protection, we speak about protecting the data of people, whose vulnerabilities, their ebbs and flows, are in so many ways non-replicable.

I think we have a duty to ensure that people are provided with choices during moments of vulnerability, and that our societies are structured in a way that protect the most vulnerable in times when they cannot protect themselves.

Privacy in the resilient state of the human condition means providing people with choices and opportunities about their own information. I believe it is our moral duty during such transitional times to maintain sight of the human-centric approach to fundamental rights. This also means the ways in which we give effect to their enforcement.

I am saying these words to you on the fourth anniversary of the GDPR, a landmark piece of legislation, which was crafted with one main objective: to ensure real, consistent, and effective implementation of the fundamental rights to data protection and privacy.

This task has not been completed yet. The choices that data protection is meant to give to people are still too often made elsewhere. We owe it to each other to have these choices. Data protection authorities, in particular, have a critical role to play in this.

Because through choice we can turn vulnerability into resilience. And we need the resilience in ourselves in order to build the resilience in our communities.

Thank you very much. I am happy to be with you at this conference, and I am happy to present to you the position of the EDPS. But, this conference has only been possible because of the incredible work of all of the people who organise CPDP, despite the problems that we had in January, and made it such a great conference now in May. Thank you very much.

# INDEX

**Abraha, Halefom H** 149
**abusive use of data subject rights** 146–7
**accelerated digitalisation** 1, 4, 6, 18–20, 22
**access, right of**
   access, definition of 133, 134–6
   Access to Financial Information Directive 161, 166–7, 173, 175
   fairness, lawfulness and transparency 169
   full access requests, practicality of 133, 136–7
   individual in EU data protection law, role of 105–6
   platform workers, data subject rights for 119, 132–7, 147
   subjective data accessibility 133–4
**accountability** 12, 15, 45, 123–4, 145–6, 148, 151
**accuracy of data** 121, 134, 146, 150, 169
**Adams-Prassl, Jeremias** 149
**adequacy of data** 129
**Advanced Data Protection Control (ADPC)** 79, 85
**agents** 93, 105–6, 109–12
**ad-tech companies** 76–8, 84
**algorithms**
   activism 125
   intellectual property rights (IPRs) 177
   management 120–1, 123–4, 127–30, 133, 140, 149
   platform workers, data subject rights for 120–1, 123–4, 127–30, 133, 140, 149
**AML/CFT regulatory regime** 157–83
   Access to Financial Information Directive 161, 166–7
   Action Plan 161–2
   Charter of Fundamental Rights of the EU 169, 176–7
   CJEU, case law of 171–3, 176, 180
   customer due diligence (CDD) 162–4, 167, 178, 180
   data protection principles 157, 168–79
   discrimination 174–7
   ECtHR 171, 180

   exchange of information 157, 159, 162–6
   fairness, lawfulness and transparency 168, 169–73, 179–80
   feedback mechanism 165–6
   Fifth Anti-Money Laundering Directive (5AMLD) 161, 162, 165–6, 176
   financial information 157, 160, 166–8, 179
   Financial Intelligence Units (FIUs) 159, 161–2, 165–7, 170–1, 173, 175, 178–9, 180
   First Anti-Money Laundering Directive (1AMLD) 160
   Fourth Anti-Money Laundering Directive (4AMLD) 161, 162–7, 170, 174–9
   General Data Protection Regulation (GDPR) 168–71, 173–4, 177–80
   law enforcement 161–2, 165, 168–9, 174, 177–8, 180
   legitimate ground for processing 177–9, 180
   minimisation, principle of data 169, 174–6, 180
   national security 170, 172–3
   notification of concerned persons 170–2, 180
   obliged entities 160, 162–4, 165–6, 174, 178–9
   powers from AML/CFT system, data protection as a tool of channelling 168–77
   prevention, investigation, detection and prosecution of crime 170–2, 179
   proportionality test 175–7, 180
   public interest 170, 173, 178–80
   Public-Private Partnerships (PPPs), obliged entities participating in 174
   purpose limitation 168–9, 174, 175–6
   quality of data 168–9
   recognition of financial information as personal data 157, 160, 179
   reform package 160–2
   risks of data sharing 158–60
   rule-based approach 163–4

Sixth Anti-Money Laundering Directive
(6AMLD)  161
soft law  207
storage limitation  169, 175–6
suspicious activity reports (SAR)  164, 165
Transfer of Funds Regulation, proposal for  162
transparency  159, 168, 169–73, 177, 179–80
**anonymisation**  30, 129, 147–8
**anti-money laundering** *see* **AML/CFT regulatory regime**
**Application Programming Interfaces (APIs)**  7, 8, 10, 80–1, 138
**apps**
Covid-19  23
deep machine learning  28–9, 32–3, 37–8
payment processing  10
retail banks and risk  8–10, 23
**Article 29 Working Party (A29WP)**  137–9, 141–2, 147–8
**artificial intelligence (AI)**
AI Act, proposal for  127, 149–50
Data Protection Impact Assessment (DPIA)  16
deep machine learning  27, 28–9, 40
responsible AI  40
retail banks and risk  6, 16
super-intelligent AI  217
**augmentation of data**  30–2, 33–4, 36
**Ausloos, Jeff**  132, 135, 138–9, 146
**automated decision-making (ADM), right not to be subject to**
algorithmic management  140
burden of proof  145
explanation, right to  141, 142–3, 149
legal or similarly significant effect for workers, nature of  141–2
platform workers, data subject rights for  124, 126, 128–9, 132, 139–43, 145, 149
two-faceted, right as  140
**Azoulai, Loïc**  92

**balancing of rights**  146–8
**banks and financial institutions** *see also* **European retail banks and risk**
behaviour  5, 7
data sharing  158–9
Open Banking  6, 8, 10, 20
trust in banks  20

**Barings Bank, collapse of**  5
**Basel Committee on Banking Supervision (BCBS)**  12, 13, 15, 22
**Beacon API**  80–1
**Beck, Ulrich**  2
**Binns, Reuben**  141
**Black, Julia**  3, 5–7, 9
**blocking**  75, 77, 79–82, 85
**Borgesius, Frederik Zuiderveen**  134
**browsers**  76, 78–85

**Canada**
Freedom Convoy, financial crackdown on  158–60, 181
EU/Canada PNR Agreement  97–8
**Charter of Fundamental Rights of the EU**
AML/CFT regulatory regime  169, 176–7
individual in EU data protection law, role of  89, 91–2, 94–7, 101–4, 107–8
platform workers, data subject rights for  146
proportionality test  176
**Chief Data Officers (CDOs)**  12, 15–16, 18
**Chief Risk Officers (CROs)**  2–3
**children**  4, 63, 108, 189
**China**  43–73
blacklists of overseas entities  53
censorship protocols  48
Central Cyberspace Affairs Commission  50
central government institutions  43, 45–7, 50, 58–9, 67, 70
children online, rights of  63
China Judgments Online  59
Civil Code  45–7, 50–62, 70
civil public interest litigation  58–9, 62–3, 67, 69–70
consent  51, 55–6, 60
Constitution  51
Consumer Protection Law  59, 62
courts, role of  43, 46, 50, 57–70
complementary, role as  67–70
insignificant, role as  67–70
privacy litigation  58–70
Cybersecurity Law  29, 45, 49–50
cyber-sovereignty concept  53
Cyberspace Administration of China (CAC)  60, 67
Data Security Law  45, 50

# Index

data subject rights 43–5, 50
  Civil Code 50, 52, 56–8, 70
  list of rights 52
  Personal Information Protection Law
    (PIPL) 50, 52, 56–8, 70
enforcement 44, 49–50, 56–70
facial recognition technology, litigation
  on 58, 61–2
fifth-generation (5G) low latency
  networks 44
Five Year Plan (14th) 44
General Data Protection Regulation
  (GDPR) 45, 51–3, 70
Golden Shield Project 48
governance structure 43, 44–50, 57–9, 67–9
Informatization Office 49
international supply chains, dependency
  on 45
Internet 48–9, 56, 63
key instances of violation of privacy 52, 56
large-scale platforms/market
  participants 44, 46–7, 56, 58–9,
  62–3, 67, 69–70
legal framework for data protection 43–53
litigation on privacy 43, 58–70
  civil public interest litigation 58–9,
    62–3, 67, 69–70
  list of cases 64–6
  trends and data 58–70
mediation 59, 68
national security 45, 52–3
offensive and defensive cyber capabilities,
  operationalizing 48
personal data protection 43–58
personal information, definition of 51, 56
Personal Information Protection Law
  (PIPL) 45–7, 49–53, 55–9, 67, 70
personality rights 44, 54–5, 68
power 44–6, 68–9
privacy, definition of 56
private sector 51, 54, 60, 62, 67–70
private-to-private or private-to-government
  relationships 69
public bodies 45–6, 61
public interest litigation 58–9, 62–3, 67,
  69–70
publicity 56
regulation 43–50, 56–9, 63–70
risk assessment 52
sector-specific standards and laws 45, 49,
  55
security 45, 47–53, 57, 63, 70

settlement 59, 68
standards 45, 47, 49–50, 53, 67–8
surveillance 58
transfer of data abroad 52–3
transition to a market-based economy
  47–8, 54–5, 68
**Clough, Jonathan** 207
**Cohen, Julie E** 92
**collective organising** 123–7, 128, 149
**Competition Markets Authority (CMA)** 7
**computer data production orders** 198–9,
  200, 202–3
**Computers, Privacy and Data Protection
  Conference (CPDP)** 11, 217
**confidence crimes** 10
**confidentiality** 3, 169
**Confiscation Directive** 165
consent
  China 55–6, 60
  cookies 79
  Cybercrime Convention 2001 187, 192–8,
    201–2, 209–10
  definition 195–6
  dialog measurement pipeline 79–80
  explicit consent 196–7
  General Data Protection Regulation
    (GDPR) 107, 110
  'I Accept' 77, 85, 88
  individual in EU data protection law, role
    of 107, 110
  opt-ins 78, 85–6
  opt-outs 78, 84
  privacy preference signals 79, 84–6
  reputational risk 15
  third-party providers (TPPs), consent to
    sharing data with 6–7, 8
  transborder access to data 187, 193–8,
    202, 209–10
  Transparency & Consent Framework
    (TCF) 76–86
**consciousness and cognition** 216–17
**contactless payments** 19
**cookies** 4, 75, 78–81, 83, 88, 216
**copyright infringement** 101–2
**Council of Europe (CoE)** *see also* **Cybercrime
  Convention's Expert Committee
  (T-CY), Guidance Notes of;
  Cybercrime Convention 2001;
  Second Additional Protocol to
  Cybercrime Convention 2001**
  European Convention on Extradition
    1957 189

European Convention on Mutual Legal
    Assistance in Criminal Matters
    1959   189
European Production and Preservation
    Orders   203–4
European Union   203–5
    direct cooperation with service
        providers   203, 205
    European Commission, evidence
        proposals of   203
    European Production and Preservation
        Orders, proposed regulation and
        directive on   203–4
    legal representatives of service providers,
        transmission of judicial orders
        to   204
    greenlighting   205
    international agreements on cross-border
        cooperation   188–9
    recommendations by Committee of
        Ministers   189
    soft law   203
**counter-terrorism** *see* **AML/CFT regulatory**
    **regime**
**Covid-19**
    accelerated digitalisation   1, 4, 7, 18–20,
        22
    contactless payments   19
    digital assistants   19
    identity fraud and phishing   20, 23
    lockdowns   19, 23
    online payments   19
    perceptions of risk   18–20, 23
    reputational risk   20
    research   11
    retail banks and risk   1, 4–7, 10–11, 18–23
    social distancing   19, 23
    telecom providers, partnerships with
        19–20
    transitional period   1, 18–20, 215
    vaccine mandate   158–60
**credit rating agencies**   5
**crime** *see also* **AML/CFT regulatory regime;**
    **Cybercrime Convention 2001;**
    **fraud**
    confidence crimes   10
    convictions and offences, processing of
        data concerning   3
    money laundering   101
**customary international law**   205–6
**customer due diligence (CDD)**   162–4, 167,
    178, 180

**cyber-attacks**   28
**Cybercrime Convention 2001** *see also*
    **Cybercrime Convention's Expert**
    **Committee (T-CY), Guidance**
    **Notes of; Second Additional**
    **Protocol to Cybercrime**
    **Convention 2001**
    Committee of Experts on Crime in
        Cyberspace   189
    content crime   189
    Cybercrime Convention Committee   187
    defence rights   206–7, 210
    domestic production orders   198
    electronic evidence, transborder access
        to   187–8, 191–2
    First Additional Protocol   189
    G8, work of   190, 196, 209, 211
        14/7 computer security network   190
        Lyon Group   180
        Principles on Transborder Access to
            Stored Computer Data 1999   190,
            196
    hate speech   189
    human rights   207
    international cooperation in criminal
        matters   187
    interpretation   206
    mutual legal assistance (MLA)   187,
        191–3, 194, 206, 209
    notification of other states   196
    policy laundering   209
    production orders   187–8, 191
    racist and xenophobic nature, acts of a
        189
    searches   191–3
    soft law guidance   187–8, 207–9
    State practice   208
    territoriality principle   194, 206
    transborder access to data based on
        consent   187
    unilateral transborder access   187–8,
        192–5, 197, 209–10
**Cybercrime Convention's Expert**
    **Committee (T-CY), Guidance**
    **Notes of**   188–91
    access to personal data   187
    all data, Guidance Note 10 on providers
        in country giving   200–1,
        209–10
    computer data production orders issued
        to persons   198–9, 200
    Cloud Evidence Group   199

## Index

consent, Guidance Note 3 on transborder access to data based on 187–8, 193–8, 202, 209–10
   definition of consent 195–6
   emergencies 197
   explicit consent 196–7
   location of person providing consent 197, 202
   mutual legal assistance 194, 197, 202
   terms and conditions, general agreement to 196
   who may give consent 196–7, 202
customary international law 205–6
defence rights 194
electronic evidence 187–93, 198–202, 205–9
emergencies 197
establishment of T-CY 190
European Union 203–4
Explanatory Report 187, 192–3, 209
flexible harmonisation 207
impact on international law 205–9
implementation, facilitating 190–1
interpretation 188, 207, 209–10
location of data 201
mutual legal assistance 194, 197, 202
notification of other states 195–6
*opinio juris* 205–6
policy laundering 209
presence in territory 197
production orders, Guidance Note 10 on use of domestic 188, 198–200, 209–10
   computer data production orders issued to persons 198–9
   subscriber data production orders issued to service providers 198–200
   subscriber information 198–200
role of T-CY 190
searches 195
Second Additional Protocol, draft text to 194
soft law 185–8, 194, 209
subscriber data production orders issued to service providers 198–200
subscriber information 198–200
**cybernetics** 216

**data minimisation, principle of** 169, 174–6
**data portability, right to**
   Application Programming Interfaces (APIs) 138

convert data, obligation to 139
   interoperability 138–9
   machine-readibility 138–9
   PDF as an interoperability format 138–9
   platform workers, data subject rights for 129, 132, 137–9, 143, 147–8
**Data Protection Directive** 89, 91–2, 94–6, 98–100, 104–5, 109–10
**Data Protection Impact Assessment (DPIA)** 2, 14–17, 24
   analytics and artificial intelligence 16
   ISO standards, following 2
   privacy and data protection teams 13–17, 23
   software 15–16
**Data Protection Officers (DPOs)** 13–18, 23
**data protection principles**
   accountability 45, 145–6, 148, 151
   accuracy of data 121, 134, 146, 150, 169
   AML/CFT regulatory regime 157, 168–79
   data minimisation 169, 174–6
   individual in EU data protection law, role of 106, 108–9
   integrity and confidentiality 109, 169
   purpose limitation 168–9, 174, 175–6
   storage limitation principle 108–9, 169, 175–6
**Data Retention Directive** 102–3, 176
**data subject rights** *see also* **access, right of; platform workers, data subject rights for**
   agents 109
   China 43–5, 50, 52, 56–8, 70
   Data Protection Directive 100, 104–5
   Data Protection Impact Assessment (DPIA) 2
   General Data Protection Regulation (GDPR) 3, 100, 104–6
   individual in EU data protection law, role of 89–94, 104–9
   legality of data processing is judged by reference to the individual 106–9
   retail banks and risk 3, 17
   risk assessment 1, 2, 3
   vulnerable persons 22
**data trusts** 121, 125, 128, 134, 137, 143, 146, 148, 150
**de Graaf, Beatrice** 208
**De Hert, Paul** 159

## 224  Index

decision-making *see* **automated decision-making (ADM), right not to be subject to**
**deep machine learning**  27–42
  anonymisation  30
  apps  28–9, 32–3, 37–8
  artificial intelligence  27, 28–9, 40
  augmentation of data  30–2, 33–4, 36
  bias, fairness and inclusion metrics  33, 39
  case studies  27–42
  design ML pipelines  29
  diversity coverage  31–2, 40
  encoder-decode paradigm  32
  encryption mechanisms into ML pipelines, integration of  30
  federated learning  30, 33
  gender bias  33–4, 39
  General Data Protection Regulation (GDPR)  29
  generative adversarial networks (GANs)  38–9
  generative modelling  36, 38–9
  handwriting recognition problem, case study on  30, 35–6, 40
    styles of writing  35–6
    unconstrained handwriting recognition  35–6
  language modelling  34
  leakage risk  28
  limitations  27, 30
  mitigation  27, 30, 32
  models  27, 31–2, 34, 36, 38–9
  privacy by design  30–1
  privacy, preservation of  27–42
  regulation  29
  responsible AI  40
  robustness of models  31–2
  statistical language modelling, case study on  30, 32–4, 39
  style transfer  30, 38–9
  swiping keyboard input, case study on  30, 37–9, 40
  synthetic data generation  27–43
  training models  27, 30, 33–4, 39–40
**Delerue, François**  208
**design, privacy by**  30–1
**Dieter, Michael**  8–9
**digital assistants**  19
**digital ethnography**  11
**discrimination**
  AML/CFT regulatory regime  174–7
  gender bias  33–4, 39
  indirect  2, 23
  platform workers, data subject rights for  120, 123–4, 127–8
  risk assessment  3
**disruptive technologies**  4, 122–3
**Do Not Sell signals**  78–9, 85
**Do Not Track (DNT) mechanism**  75–80, 83–5
**domain name registration**  202

**effective remedy, right to an**  97, 112, 171
**electronic evidence** *see also* **Second Additional Protocol to Cybercrime Convention 2001**
  Cybercrime Convention 2001  187–8, 191–2
    Guidance Notes on  187–93, 198–202, 205–9
    production orders  187–8, 191
  European Union  203–5
  production orders  187–8, 191
**emergencies**  158–9, 201
**employees** *see* **platform workers, data subject rights for**
**encryption**  30
**enforcement**
  AML/CFT regulatory regime  161–2, 165, 168–9, 174, 177–8, 180
  China  44, 49–50, 56–70
  individual in EU data protection law, role of  90–4, 100
  law enforcement  161–2, 165, 168–9, 174, 177–8, 180
  platform workers, data subject rights for  148
  privacy preference signals  75
**EU data protection law, role of the individual in**  89–117
  access, right of  105–6
  agents of data protection law  93, 109–13
  centrality of the individual  89–91
  Charter of Fundamental Rights of the EU  89, 91–2, 94–7, 101–4, 107–8
  children and vulnerable persons  108
  CJEU, case law of  89, 91, 94–5, 97–108, 112
  competence for data protection  94, 96
  conceptual framework  89
  consent  107, 110
  criticism of place of individual  89–90
  data controllers  92, 95, 98–100, 107–13
  Data Protection Directive  89, 91–2, 94–5, 98–100, 104–5
  data protection principles  106, 108–9
  data subjects  89–94, 104–9

decision-making 89–90, 93, 110
enforcement 90–4, 100
fairness 108–9
free movement of personal data 94, 95, 98–9
functions of the individual 89–90
fundamental rights 93–6, 98–9, 107–8, 111–12
General Data Protection Regulation (GDPR) 89, 91–2, 95, 97–100, 104–8, 110, 112–13
group perspective 90
harmonisation of standards 94, 96
individualistic, criticism of data protection law as 89–91, 98
informational self-determination 109–10
interpretation 93, 94, 98–100, 107
legal bases for processing 110
legitimate interests 108
Lisbon Treaty 94, 96
market harmonisation of privacy standards 94–6
material application 99–100
multi-dimensional role of individuals 89–93, 113
natural persons 91
normative basis for EU data protection law 94–6
object of data protection law, individual as the 91–100
pre-conditions to processing 107–8
primary law basis for EU data protection law 96–8
private and family life, right to respect for 94–5, 98, 101–2
procedural rights 93, 111–12
public interest 107–8
purposive interpretation 93, 94, 98–100
rights-holders, individuals as 94–8, 101–4, 111–12
security 102
social perspective 90
standards 94, 96
storage limitation principle 108–9
subject of data protection law, individual as a 91–3, 100–12
supervision 97
territorial application 99
TFEU 96–8, 101
transparency 102–3, 108–9
**European Convention on Extradition 1957** 189

**European Convention on Human Rights (ECHR)** 171, 180
**European Convention on Mutual Legal Assistance in Criminal Matters 1959** 189
**European Production and Preservation Orders (EPPOs)** 203–4
**European retail banks and risk** 1–26
accelerated digitalisation 1, 4, 6, 18–20, 22
accountability 12, 15
analytical framework 5–10
Application Programming Interfaces (APIs) 7, 8, 10
apps 8–10, 23
Basel Committee on Banking Supervision (BCBS) 12, 13, 15, 22
behaviour
  banks 5, 7
  individuals 6, 9, 21
  organisations 6, 21
Chief Data Officer (CDO) 12, 15–16, 18
contextual factors 10–11
Covid-19, effect of 1, 4–7, 10–11, 18–23
Data Protection Impact Assessment (DPIA) 2, 14–17, 23–4
Data Protection Officers (DPOs) 13–18, 23
data subjects' deprivation of rights and freedoms 3, 17
digital environment 11
disclosure, severity of risk of 16
document analysis 11
experts 11, 18, 22
findings 5, 12–20
fraud 22
General Data Protection Regulation (GDPR) 1–2, 7, 10, 13–17, 22–4
globally systemically important banks (G-SIB) 11–13, 16
goals and values 6, 21
governance 12–17, 21–2
identity fraud and phishing 10, 20, 23
infrastructure 6, 7–9
interviews 11–12
knowledge and understanding of risk 6, 10, 16, 21–3
large banks 12–15
methodology 5, 10–12, 23
mitigation 1, 16
New Activities Committee 15, 18
new types of risk 1
Open Banking 6–8, 10, 20

# 226  Index

operational risk   2, 5, 18
organisation of personal data protection in practice   5
oversight   17–18
payment data, sharing   6–7
payment-processing apps   10
perception of risks   5, 18–20, 22–3
personal data protection, empirical study on   1–26
platformisation   6, 8, 10, 22
political dissent, investigations of   10
pseudonymisation, unauthorised reversal of   3, 4, 17, 22
Register of Processing Activities   13–14
regulation   5–6, 12–13, 18, 21–3
reputational risk   15, 17–18, 20–1, 23–4
research   11–12
risk assessment   1, 2, 21–4
risk categories   3–4, 10, 16–17
rule-makers   5–6
sensitive data   7, 22
supervisory authorities   5, 12, 18
third-party providers (TPPs), consent to sharing data with   6–7, 8
transitional period   1, 18–20
trust and legitimacy   6, 20–1
updating procedures   16
vulnerable persons   22

**European Union** *see also* **AML/CFT regulatory regime; Charter of Fundamental Rights of the EU; EU data protection law, role of the individual in; European retail banks and risk; General Data Protection Regulation (GDPR)**
Canadian/EU PNR Agreement   97–8
Confiscation Directive   165
Council of Europe   203–5
Cybercrime Convention, Second Additional Protocol to   203–5
Data Retention Directive   176
direct cooperation with service providers   203, 205
electronic evidence   203–5
Law Enforcement Directive   168–9, 174, 177–8, 180
Lisbon Treaty   94, 96, 204–5
mutual legal assistance (MLA)   204
Payment Services Directive (PSD2)   6
Platform Work Directive, proposal for   127, 149
Public Sector Reuse Directive   138–9

evidence *see* **electronic evidence**
experts   11, 18, 22 *see also* **Cybercrime Convention's Expert Committee (T-CY), Guidance Notes of explanation, right to**   141, 142–3, 149
extradition   189

facial recognition technology   58, 61–2
fairness, lawfulness and transparency   169–73
access, right of   169
AML/CFT regulatory regime   168, 169–73, 179–80
Charter of Fundamental Rights of the EU   169
FIUs   170–1, 173
General Data Protection Regulation (GDPR)   169–71, 173, 179
individual in EU data protection law, role of   108–9
national security   170, 172–3
prevention, investigation, detection and prosecution of crime   170–2, 179
public interest, objectives of general   170, 173, 179–80
**Financial Action Task Force (FATF)**   207
financial information
Access to Financial Information Directive   161, 166–7, 173, 175
AML/CFT regulatory regime   166–8, 179
definition   166–8, 179
recognition of financial information as personal data   157, 160, 179
**Financial Intelligence Units (FIUs)**
Access to Financial Information Directive   166, 167
AML/CFT regulatory regime   159, 161–2, 165–7, 170–1, 173, 175, 178–9, 180
Confiscation Directive   165
exchange of information   159, 164–5
independence and autonomy   165
investigative authorities to FIU data, access of   161
law enforcement information, access to   161
suspicious activity reports (SAR)   165
**financing terrorism** *see* **AML/CFT regulatory regime**

## Index

**Foucault, Michel** 208
**fraud**
   anti-fraud detection systems 148
   identity fraud and phishing 3, 10, 20, 23
   platformisation 22, 129–30, 133, 141–2, 148
   probability score 129, 133, 141–2
**free movement of personal data** 94, 95, 98–9
**Freedom Convoy in Canada** 158–60, 181
**freedom of speech** 2, 23
**fundamental rights** *see* **human rights/ fundamental rights**

**G8 (Group of 8)** 190, 196, 209, 211
**gender bias** 33–4, 39
**General Data Protection Regulation (GDPR)**
   access, right of 133–5, 137
   AML/CFT regulatory regime 168–71, 173–4, 177–80
   anonymised data 148
   automated decision-making, right not to be subject to 139–43, 149
   balancing of rights 146–7
   categories of risk 3–4
   China 45, 51–3, 70
   consent 15, 77, 107, 110
   Data Protection Impact Assessment (DPIA) 2, 13, 24
   data subjects 3, 22, 100, 104–6
   fines 17, 24
   human rights 3, 95–6, 107–8
   individual in EU data protection law, role of 89, 91–2, 95, 97–100, 104–7, 110, 112–13
   objectives 99–100
   one-stop-shop 97
   personal data, definition of 104–6, 168–9
   platform workers, data subject rights for 119–21, 126–9, 133–43, 146–50
   privacy preference signals 76–7, 80, 83, 85
   pseudonymisation, unauthorised reversal of 17, 22
   public interest 173
   purpose limitation 174
   quality of data 168–9
   regulation 29
   reputational damage 17
   retail banks and risk 7, 13–17, 22–4
   right to data protection and privacy 217
   risk assessment 3–4

   risk-based approach 1–2
   risk categories 19, 17–18
   sensitive data 22
   tying consents, prohibition on 110
   vulnerable data subjects 22
**Giesen, Ivo** 145
**global financial crisis 2008** 5, 12
**Global Privacy Control (GPC)** 75–84, 86
**globalisation** 187
**globally systemically important banks (G-SIB)** 11–13, 16
**GPT-3** 33
**greenlighting** 187, 205
**guidance notes** *see* **Cybercrime Convention's Expert Committee (T-CY), Guidance Notes of**
**Gutwirth, Serge** 159

**Hallinan, Dara** 134
**handwriting recognition problem, case study on** 30, 35–6, 40
**harmonisation** 94–6
**hate speech** 189
**Henderson, Tristan** 139
**human rights/fundamental rights** *see also* **access, right of; Charter of Fundamental Rights of the EU; data subject rights**
   automated decision-making (ADM), right not to be subject to 124, 126
   children online 63
   Cybercrime Convention 2001 201, 207, 210
   ECtHR 171, 180
   General Data Protection Regulation (GDPR) 3, 95–6, 107–8
   freedom of speech 2, 23
   individual in EU data protection law, role of 93–6, 98–9, 107–8, 111–12
   private and family life, right to respect for 94–5, 98, 101–2
   right to data protection and privacy 217
   risk assessments 3
**Hustinx, Peter** 97

**identity fraud, phishing and other scams** 3, 10, 20, 23
**impact assessments** *see* **Data Protection Impact Assessment (DPIA)**
**independent contractor status** 120, 123, 126
**individuals** *see* **EU data protection law, role of the individual in**

# Index

information asymmetries  123, 132, 140–1, 144–6, 148, 151
intellectual property rights (IPRs)  101–2, 177
international law  205–6
Internet *see also* Cybercrime Convention 2001
   blocking  75, 77, 79–82, 85
   browsers  76, 78–85
   censorship  48
   children, rights of  63
   China  44, 48–9, 56, 63
   cookies  4, 75, 78–81, 83, 88, 216
   individual in EU data protection law, role of  100
   payments  19
   privacy preference signals  76–9, 81, 84–5
interpretation
   AML/CFT regulatory regime  160, 179
   consent  107
   Cybercrime Convention 2001  187–8, 206–7, 209–10
   Data Protection Directive  98
   electronic evidence  187
   General Data Protection Regulation (GDPR)  98
   individual in EU data protection law, role of  93, 94, 98–100
   platform workers, data subject rights for  142, 150
   privacy preference signals  75–7
   purposive interpretation  93, 94, 98–100
   soft law  208
   teleological  134, 150

judiciary  93, 101, 185–6

Keane, Adrian  144
keyboard input, case study on swiping  30, 37–9, 40
Klem, Wouter  208

labour protection  119–56
large platforms/market participants  12–15, 46–7, 56, 58–9, 62–3, 67, 69–70
law enforcement
   AML/CFT regulatory regime  161–2, 165, 168–9, 174, 177–8, 180
   Law Enforcement Directive  168–9, 174, 177–8, 180
legitimate ground for processing  177–9, 180
Lupton, Deborah  22
Lynskey, Orla  95

machine-learning  163–4
machine-readability  138–9
McKeown, Paul  144–5
Marx, Karl  92
minimisation, principle of data  169, 174–6
Mitsilegas, Valsamis  207
mobile devices  35, 37–9
money laundering  101 *see also* AML/CFT regulatory regime
Murray, Andrew  6–7, 9
mutual legal assistance (MLA)
   Cybercrime Convention 2001  187, 191–3, 194, 197, 202, 206, 209
   European Convention on Mutual Legal Assistance in Criminal Matters 1959  189
   European Union  204
   refusal of assistance, grounds for  192
   searches  191–3

national security  45, 52–3, 170, 172–3
Netherlands  119–56

on-demand platforms *see* platform workers, data subject rights for
OneTrust  78
Open Banking  6, 8, 10, 20
operational risk  2, 5, 18
*opinio juris*  205–6
OptMeowt add-on  79

PaLM  33
Passenger Name Records (PNR)  97–8, 167
payments
   apps for processing  10
   authenticity of payments  10
   contactless  19
   Payment Services Directive (PSD2)  6
   sharing data  6–7, 10
Peifer, Karl-Nikolaus  110
personal data, definition of  104–6, 134, 167–9
personality rights  45, 54–5, 68
phishing  10, 20, 23
platform workers, data subject rights for  119–56
   abusive, work-related use of data subject rights as  146–7
   access, right of  119, 132–9, 147
   accountability  123–4, 146, 148, 151
   accuracy of personal data  121, 134, 146, 150

# Index

algorithmic activism 125
algorithmic management 120–1, 123–4, 127–30, 133, 140, 149
anonymisation 129, 147–8
App Drivers Workers Union (ADCU) 119, 127, 130
Application Programming Interfaces (APIs) 138
Article 29 Working Party (A29WP) 137–9, 141–2, 147–8
automated decision-making (ADM), right not to be subject to 126, 128–9, 132, 139–43
  burden of proof 145
  explanation, right to 141, 142–3, 149
  legal or similarly significant effect for workers, nature of 141–2
  transparency 124
  two-faceted, right as 140
balancing of rights 146–8
barriers to exercise of rights 119
benefits of platform work 120
burden of proof 142, 144–6, 148
casualisation of work 123
challenges 122–7
  new tactics and strategies 124–7
  workers, for 122–4
collective organising 123–7, 128, 149
context 128, 134, 141
data controllers 132–3, 135–7, 147
data portability, right to 129, 132, 137–9, 143, 147–8
data trusts 121, 125, 128, 134, 137, 143, 146, 148, 150
discrimination 120, 123–4, 127–8
enforcement 148
fraud 129–30, 133, 141–2, 148
full access requests, practicality of 133, 136–7
future developments 148–50
General Data Protection Regulation (GDPR) 119–21, 126–9, 145–50
  access, right of 133–5, 137
  automated decision-making, right not to be subject to 139–43, 149
  full access requests, practicality of 137
holiday allowances 128
independent contractor status 120, 123, 126
individualistic, data subject rights as 127
information asymmetries 123, 132, 140–1, 144–6, 148, 151

intelligible form, personal data to be provided in an 132
instrumental role of rights 132, 143
labour protection 119–56
macro-perspectives 143–8
micro-perspectives 132–43
migrant communities 124
minimum wage 128
Netherlands 119–56
new forms of resistance 122–7
online and offline coordination 124–5
overview of judgments 131
personal data, definition of 134
Platform Work Directive, proposal for 127, 149
power asymmetries 119, 125–7, 148, 151
precarity 120, 123–4
Privacy Policies 134–6
ratings 123, 128–9
  access 129, 147–8
  anonymisation 129, 147–8
  portability of data 143, 148
requests for data, rejection of 129
resistance, data subjects rights as tool for 119–27, 143–8, 151
  abusive, work-related use of data subject rights as 146–7
  balancing of rights as barrier to initiating data flows to workers 147–8
  information asymmetries and burden of proof 144–6
risks onto workers, shift of 123–4
robo-firing 123, 130
rulings 128–31
strategic litigation 119, 125–9
structural role of rights 132, 140, 143
surveillance and control 120, 123
tactics and strategies 124–7
third-party privacy 147–8
trade unions 119, 121, 124–5
transparency 120, 124–5, 130, 135, 143, 145–6, 149
*Uber/Ola* judgments 119–56
union-backed data trust, building a 121
Worker Info Exchange (WIE) 119, 128, 150
worker representatives 149
working conditions 120, 125, 128
zero-hour contracts 123
**platformisation** 6, 8, 10, 20, 22 *see also* **platform workers, data subject rights for**

# 230　Index

**policy entrepreneurship**　204
**policy laundering**　187, 209–11
**political dissent, investigations of**　10
**politically inspired attacks**　208
**portability of data** *see* **data portability, right to**
**power**
  asymmetries of power　119, 125–7, 148, 151, 216
  China　44–6, 68–9
  retail banks and risk　5, 6
  sources of power　6
**Power, Michael**　2, 5
**preference signals** *see* **privacy preference signals**
**prevention, investigation, detection and prosecution of crime**　170–2, 179
**privacy, definition of**　56
**Privacy Policies**　134–6
**privacy preference signals**　75–88
  ad-tech companies　76–8, 84
  Advanced Data Protection Control (ADPC)　79, 85
  ambiguity　75, 77–8, 82, 85–6
  Application Programming Interfaces (APIs)　80–1
  background　77–9
  blocking　75, 77, 79–82, 85
  browsers　76, 78–85
  Californian Consumer Privacy Act (CCPA)　76–8, 84
  collecting preferences　83–4
  Colorado, privacy law in　84
  conflicting signals　77, 85
  consent　77–80, 84–6, 88
  cookies　75, 78–81, 83
  data collection　80–1
  Do Not Sell signals　78–9, 85
  Do Not Track (DNT) mechanism　75–80, 83–5
  enforcement　75
  General Data Protection Regulation (GDPR)　76–7, 80, 83, 85
  Global Privacy Control (GPC)　75–84, 86
  interpretation　75–7
  method　79–81
  multiple signals, transmission of　75–8, 82, 85
  niche and emerging signals　78–9
  opt-ins　78, 85–6
  opt-outs　78, 84, 86
  QuantCast　78–81, 88

  research ethics　81
  results　82–3
  robustness　82–3
  semantics　78–9, 85
  study participants　79–80
  Transparency & Consent Framework (TCF)　76–86
  *US Privacy String* format　78–9
  validity　85
  websites　76–9, 81, 84–5
**private and family life, right to respect for**　94–5, 98, 101–2
**production orders**
  computer data production orders issued to persons　198–9, 200, 202
  Cybercrime Convention 2001　187–8, 191, 198–200, 202–3
  good faith compliance　202
  subscriber data production orders issued to service providers　198–200, 202–3
**professional secrecy**　3
**proportionality analysis**　101–4, 108
  AML/CFT regulatory regime　175–7, 180
  Charter of Fundamental Rights of the EU　176
  CJEU, case law of　176, 180
  data minimisation, principle of　175–6
  data protection principles　175–7
  purpose limitation　175–6
  storage limitation　175–6
**pseudonymisation, unauthorised reversal of**　3, 4, 17, 22
**public interest**
  AML/CFT regulatory regime　170, 173, 178–80
  China, litigation in　58–9, 62–3, 67, 69–70
  individual in EU data protection law, role of　107–8
**Public-Private Partnerships (PPPs)**　174
**purpose limitation**　168–9, 174, 175–6
**Public Sector Reuse Directive**　138–9

**quality of data**　168–9
**QuantCast**　78–81, 88

**rational choice institutionalism**　204–5
**Register of Processing Activities**　13–14
**regulation** *see also* **AML/CFT regulatory regime**
  China　48–9, 56
  deep machine learning　29
  global financial crisis 2008　5

Open Banking   6
platform workers, data subject rights
        for   119
polycentrism   6
retail banks and risk   5–6, 12–13, 18, 21–3
risk management   6
**rent seeking behaviour**   204
**reputational risk**   3, 15, 17–18, 20–1, 23–4
**resistance, data subjects rights as tool
        for**   119–27, 143–8, 151
**retail banks** *see* **European retail banks and
        risk**
**right of access** *see* **access, right of**
**right to data portability** *see* **data portability,
        right to**
**rights of data subjects** *see* **data subject rights**
**risk** *see also* **European retail banks and risk**
    assessments   1–4, 21–4
        classical risk assessment
            methodologies   23
        organisational risk assessments   3
    categories   3–4, 10, 17–18
    check-the-box mindset   4
    Chief Risk Officers (CROs)   2–3
    Data Protection Impact Assessment
        (DPIA)   2, 14–16, 23, 24
    data sharing   158–60
    management   3
    operational risk   2–3, 5, 18
    procedural approach,   1, 4
    reputational risk   3, 15, 17–18, 20–1, 23–4
    retail banks   1–26
    risk-based approach   1–2, 163
    risk society   2
    social and cultural norms, concepts and
        habits   22
    vulnerable groups   4, 22
    workers, shift of risks onto   123–4
**robo-firing**   123, 130
**rule-based approach**   163–4
**rule-makers**   5–6

Schwartz, Paul M   110
**Second Additional Protocol to Cybercrime
        Convention 2001**
    consent   202–3
    contents   201
    custom   210
    direct cooperation between law
            enforcement authorities and service
            providers   201–3, 204, 210
    draft text   194

emergencies   201
European Union   203–5
extraterritorial searches   202
globalisation   187
Guidance Notes   185–6, 188, 201–3, 206,
        210
    consent, easy transborder access to
        data based on   202–3
    impact on international law   205–9
    production orders, transnational reach
        of   188
historical and functional development
    187
human rights   201, 210
international criminal cooperation without
        laws   186–8
judicial cooperation   185–6
mutual legal assistance   202
policy laundering   187, 209–11
production orders, Guidance Note 10 on
        use of domestic   202–3
searches   202
soft law   185–8
subscriber information   201–3, 204
traffic data   201, 202–3
**security**
    China   45, 47–53, 57, 63, 70
    individual in EU data protection law, role
        of   102
    national security   45, 52–3, 170, 172–3
    risk categories   17
    security measures, data processing
        concerning   3
**semantics**   78–9, 85
**sensitive data**   7, 22
**signals** *see* **privacy preference signals**
Silberman, Michael   149
**soft law** *see also* **Cybercrime Convention's
        Expert Committee (T-CY),
        Guidance Notes of**
    AML/CFT regulatory regime   207
    binding norms   208
    Council of Europe   203
    Cybercrime Convention 2001   187–8,
        207–9
        recommendations   185–6
        Second Additional Protocol   185–8
    interpretation   208
    police, trust in the   208
    politically inspired attacks   208
    State practice   208
    territoriality   188

## 232  Index

**sovereignty**  53, 194
**Soviet Union Civil Code**  54
**standards**
   China  45, 47, 49–50, 53, 67–8
   Data Protection Impact Assessment (DPIA)  2, 14
   harmonisation  94–6
   market harmonisation of privacy standards  94–6
   setters  5
**statistical language modelling, case study on**  30, 32–4, 39
**storage limitation, principle of**  108–9, 169, 175–6
**strategic litigation**  119, 125–9
**subscriber data production orders**  198–200, 202–3
**subscriber information**  198–204
**supervision**  5, 12, 17–18, 97
**surveillance**  58, 103–4, 120, 123, 171, 176, 195
**suspicious activity reports (SAR)**  164, 165
**swiping keyboard input, case study on**  30, 37–9, 40
**synthetic data generation**  27–43

**T-CY** *see* **Cybercrime Convention's Expert Committee (T-CY), Guidance Notes of targeted advertising**  216
**territoriality principle**  99, 188, 194, 206
**terrorism** *see* **AML/CFT regulatory regime**
**third parties**
   platform workers, data subject rights for  147–8
   third-party providers (TPPs), consent to sharing data with  6–7, 8
**Tkacz, Nathaniel**  8–9
**Tosoni, Luca**  206–7
**trade unions**  119, 121, 124–5
**traffic location data**  167, 201, 202–3
**training**  17, 27, 30, 33–4, 39–40
**transborder data**
   Cybercrime Convention 2001  187, 191, 193–8, 202–3, 209–10
   international agreements on cooperation  188–9

   Principles on Transborder Access to Stored Computer Data 1999 (G8)  190, 196
   unilateral access  187–8, 192–5, 197, 209–10
**transfer of funds and certain crypto-assets proposal for the Regulation on information accompanying**  162
**transparency**
   AML/CFT regulatory regime  159, 168, 169–73, 177, 179–80
   automated decision-making (ADM), right not to be subject to  124
   fairness, lawfulness and transparency  168, 169–73, 179–80
   individual in EU data protection law, role of  102–3, 108–9
   platform workers, data subject rights for  120, 124–5, 130, 135, 143, 145–6, 149
   Transparency & Consent Framework (TCF)  76–86
**Trudeau, Justin**  158
**Turing machine**  216

**United States**
   California Consumer Privacy Act (CCPA)  29, 76–8, 84
   Colorado, privacy law in  84
   Cybercrime Convention 2001  205
   G8  190, 209
   Health Insurance Portability and Accountability Act (HIPPA)  29
   September 11 terrorist attacks  190
   *US Privacy String* format  78–9

**Van De Heyning, Catherine**  206–7
**Veale, Michael**  138–9, 141, 146
**vulnerable persons**  4, 22, 108, 216

**Wachter, Sandra**  134, 141
**websites and privacy preference signals**  76–9, 81, 84–5
**Weiler, Joseph**  92
**Wiener, Norbert**  216
**Wong, Janis**  139
**workers** *see* **platform workers, data subject rights for**

**Zanfir-Fortuna, Gabriela**  135
**zero-hour contracts**  123

Printed in the USA
CPSIA information can be obtained
at www.ICGtesting.com
LVHW022131081223
765719LV00005B/244